ALIENS IN THE EAST

A New History of
Japan's Foreign Intercourse

By

HARRY EMERSON WILDES

Philadelphia
UNIVERSITY OF PENNSYLVANIA PRESS
London: Humphrey Milford: Oxford University Press

1937

Copyright 1937

UNIVERSITY OF PENNSYLVANIA PRESS

Manufactured in the United States of America

FOREWORD

MOST Americans are thoroughly convinced that Japan was introduced to Western culture by Matthew Calbraith Perry's visit of 1853. They believe that the Mikado's secluded Empire was stunned by the Commodore's display of modern guns, machinery, and scientific wonders. They assume that once the Japanese recovered from their shocked surprise, the amazed Orientals immediately accepted western ways with wild enthusiasm, that the nation emerged, almost in a summer's afternoon, from medieval superstition into the full light of Western civilization, and that for all these benefactions the Japanese are gratefully appreciative.

Almost none of these beliefs—accepted even by many professional historians—is true. Europe and America were no mysteries to Japan. For four full centuries prior to Perry the Japanese had been consorting with foreign merchants, missionaries, and military men. Before the Great Armada sailed to conquer Britain, Japanese envoys were officially entertained at Madrid, Lisbon, and in France; certain rebel leaders were bowing in both spiritual and political submission at the Vatican; commercial and military spies were seeking to discover the secrets of Europe's power. Foreign achievements, especially in the fields of medicine and armaments, were early known to Japanese authorities.

Little of this information has been available. Log books of sea captains, narratives of globe-trotters, letters from castaways have hinted at the arrival of adventurers in strange provinces of Japan, but official records have seldom been presented for corroboration of the tales. Only recently, with the opening of the files of the Hudson's Bay Company, the Dutch and English East India Companies, and with the publication of port records from such out-of-the-way harbors as Napa in the Luchus, has it been possible for the historian to gather and collate authentic material. Hitherto secret documents of the *Bakufu,* the Foreign Office of the Tokugawa Shogunate, and diplomatic correspondence of the early days of Japan's foreign intercourse, have made it possible to verify what have, in past years, been merely disconnected rumors.

The writer has enjoyed the advantage of extremely valuable assistance from the librarians and research experts of the United States Navy, the Coast Guard, the United States Marine Corps, and the British Admiralty in the tracking down of ships and individuals active in Japan's trade of a century or more ago. Extraordinary assistance has been rendered by the staffs of libraries in the United States, particularly in New York, Philadelphia, and Washington, and of learned societies in this country and Japan. The extraordinary collection of *Transactions* of the Asiatic Society of Japan has been prolific of suggestions, as have the historical publications of the Essex Institute of Salem. The kind permission of the *New York Times* in allowing the use of an article, contributed by this writer to its magazine, must also be gratefully acknowledged.

Among the many individuals who have offered invaluable suggestions for the writer's guidance in completing this first account of Japan's foreign intercourse, the most grateful thanks are due to Edward W. Mumford, secretary of the University of Pennsylvania, John Malcolm Bulloch of London, Edward Shenton, editor and ruthless critic, and Katharine E. Dealy of Philadelphia, who prepared the index and supervised the preparation of the manuscript. Nor should any writer overlook the quiet, unobtrusive, but extremely constructive helpfulness of those who must endure an author's temperament while a book is in course of preparation. This writer has been particularly fortunate in such comradeship. The book could not otherwise have been complete.

HARRY EMERSON WILDES

Valley Forge
August, 1937

CONTENTS

CONTENTS

I

THE PORTUGUESE PIONEERS
1543–1585

JAPAN was discovered, if one may trust the records, by three Portuguese pirates wrecked upon a rocky island. Credit for the discovery, made just fifty-one years after Columbus found America, was stolen by a picturesque, but wholly unreliable, adventurer.

To nationalistic Japanese the combination of mutiny, flight from justice, piratical raiding and ill wind, all sadly misrepresented by a charlatan, seems singularly appropriate to explain the advent of the Westerners. Japan's strong stress on its "pure spirit," so evident today, stems from the belief that Occidentals, ever since the first arrival of the pirates, have brought little but ill luck to the Empire.

For years prior to 1543, when the Portuguese arrived, Japan's name had been a synonym for mystery and magic. Europe had thrilled to rumors of a fabulously rich, secluded realm, peopled by a race entirely different from all other nationalities. Marco Polo's brief account of Zipangu, written from hearsay two centuries before the actual discovery, promised an abundance of pure gold and myriads of jewels to those who might gain access to that land of wizards. Scholars, to be sure, placed little credence in his tales, but adventurers were tempted to seek the inexhaustible treasures. To them the lure of the unknown, especially when baited by promise of Golconda profits, was irresistible. For gold, for glory, for adventure, and for propagation of the faith, explorers dashed forth to search for islands where treasures were abundant and where the heathen panted for salvation.

Luck, which plays so large a rôle in Europe's early relations with the East, gave the prize to unsuspecting and, indeed, unwilling sailors. The first white men to see the islands of Japan were terror-stricken fugitives.

1

Antonio de Moto, Diego Francesco Zeimoto, and Antonio Pei-xotto, seamen on a trading ship in Siamese waters, were mutineers. To escape punishment they hurriedly embarked upon a small Chinese junk. Whether they were aware that they were taking refuge on a pirate craft is perhaps beside the point, but as it happened they were soon made part of the pirate crew. Then the junk, caught in a storm somewhere near Formosa, lost its rudder and drifted helplessly in the Kuroshiwo, the great Black Stream of the Pacific that takes a course like that of the Atlantic's Gulf Stream. In October 1543 the broken craft was cast up on the island of Tanegashima, off the southern tip of the main islands of Japan.

None of the three Portuguese was sufficiently well educated to write down his experiences, nor, in all probability, were any of them anxious for publicity. The record of the arrival of these first white men to set foot within the Empire of Japan is drawn wholly from Japan's own annals. The report reveals an oriental opinion of the strangers, for their Chinese associates, anxious perhaps to disclaim too great intimacy with the Westerners, reported them as "strange people, wholly ignorant of etiquette, knowing nothing of the proper use of wine cups or of chopsticks, and in fact little better than the beasts of the field." Neither Chinese nor Portuguese protested the immediate deportation to China which was decreed by the local Japanese governor.

The Japanese annals, while lamentably incomplete, clarify a problem which, for more than three centuries, baffled the historians. For many years it was believed, on the sole strength of his own claim, that Fernando Mendez Pinto, a Portuguese adventurer, had been the first European to travel in Japan. It was, however, impossible to reconcile the known date of discovery with the actual facts of Pinto's chequered career. The chroniclers were aware that a foreign ship, presumably Portuguese, had come to Tanegashima in 1543 but Pinto, the supposed discoverer, was certainly in jail at Peking at that moment. Since none of his contemporaries disputed Pinto's claim of discovery, historians have tended to believe that the date was incorrect and that Pinto was indeed the pioneer European to set foot on Japan's soil.

The port records, lately made available, show that the Tanegashima ship was Chinese and not Portuguese, that Pinto's name does not appear upon the roster of passengers and crew, and that, indeed, he did not arrive in Japan until two years after the first ship came to Tanegashima.

Pinto, an imaginative genius, was not at all averse to appropriating the acts of others as his own. His narration of many shipwrecks and of travels into exotic lands, his tales of how he had been seventeen times sold into slavery, his accounts of raids upon the tombs of Chinese kings and of exile into Chinese frontier towns are exciting stories, but whether the events occurred to him or to others from whom he borrowed the details is open to debate.

The truth appears to be, as nearly as may now be reconstructed, that Pinto, following his release from Peking's prison, wandered southward to Macao where he fell in with Diego Francesco Zeimoto, one of the three original discoverers. Zeimoto stirred memories of the ancient legends telling of the mysterious rich Empire of Zipangu. Pinto, ever anxious for loot and for adventure, joined with Zeimoto in a second expedition. In relating the story at a later time, Pinto deliberately confused the facts so that his own coming in 1545, at Usuki, in Bungo province at the south end of the Inland Sea, might seem to have been the original Tanegashima discovery. Zeimoto, probably fearful of prosecution for mutiny, did not dispute the Pinto claim if, indeed, Zeimoto ever knew of Pinto's filching of the credit.

Pinto's report is undoubtedly far more colorful than truthful. Published in 1614, long after his death, his story echoes many of the more amazing incidents undergone by Spanish and Portuguese explorers in other unknown lands. Much of the detail was dictated, as he confessed, "less by strict regard for the truth than by desire to satisfy the desire for wonders and to magnify the king and country of Portugal."

Stripped of its embroidery the report appears to show that the Bungo ruler paid the Portuguese adventurers a thousand taels of silver in return for their setting up a musket factory. Sixty guns were fashioned in a year, though Pinto insists that ten times that number were built in half the time. Within seven years, according to Pinto's wholly unreliable estimate, Japan possessed more than three hundred thousand firearms.

The guns almost proved fatal to Pinto himself. A seventeen-year-old prince, whom Pinto calls Arichaudono, clamored for permission to play with Pinto's musket. Pinto agreed to teach the boy to shoot. The lad, too eager to wait, stole the weapon while Pinto was asleep, greatly overloaded it and was severely wounded when the weapon burst.

Pinto, hearing the explosion, rushed out to find the lad "bleeding and insensible upon the ground, deserted by his comrades." He bound up the wounds, and restored Arichaudono to consciousness, but was at once arrested on a charge of attempted murder. Only his success in healing the boy when the local medical men dared not attempt a cure, saved Pinto from execution, according to Pinto's own account.

Whether these adventures actually befell Pinto in person or whether he is appropriating the experiences of the 1543 discoverers is a matter for speculation, but there is no possible doubt but that the events actually occurred. Japanese records verify the gift of guns, though they intimate that the weapons first came through the governor of Tanegashima. Soon afterward the Portuguese returned to China, after a stay of about six months in Japan.

Ningpo, the Portuguese entrepôt in northern China, decreed Te Deums when Pinto and Zeimoto returned. The news of Japan's amazing wealth, surely not minimized by the spectacular Pinto, stirred the envy of the merchants. Traders stampeded to the ships to profit by the Japan trade. Nine junks hurriedly put to sea, but none was carefully prepared and few were manned by careful sailors. When a typhoon burst suddenly, eight ships sank, drowning more than seven hundred men and sinking cargoes valued at a third of a million dollars.

Pinto's vessel, on which the adventurer was returning to Bungo, was blown far out of its course and struck upon the Luchus. Pinto, only survivor of the ship, according to his own inaccurate report, swam ashore through mountainous waves. Enlisting the aid of a native girl he joined the crew of a junk, planning to return to China. For some reason which he does not state the vessel turned southward to Malacca. There he persuaded certain Portuguese traders to outfit an expedition of their own with himself as commander.

Pinto's second arrival in Japan, if one is to credit his own story, occurred at Tanegashima, and later at Bungo, probably in 1547. The reception was again most friendly. Pinto's cargo contained strange goods hitherto unknown in Japan. Before trading could be begun, however, civil wars broke out. The friendly Bungo ruler was killed, his family was exiled or murdered, the chief city was destroyed. It was the first of a series of coincidences which, to the minds of the superstitious, proved that the arrival of aliens inevitably brought catastrophe upon Japan.

Trade was out of the question, particularly as the Pinto ship was not carrying any vast amount of guns, and hence Pinto sailed southward to find new markets. Bungo, he had now learned, was but a minor provincial region whose trade, even in normal times, was insignificant in comparison with the larger and richer province of Satsuma on the south coast of the island. Pinto therefore proceeded to Kagoshima, the Satsuma capital. Others, it appears, had preceded him here during the interval between his leaving Ningpo and his second coming to Japan. The market was overstocked with Chinese goods but Pinto was lucky. Two thousand vessels belonging to his rivals—the figures are indicative of Pinto's trustworthiness—were destroyed by a gale; Pinto's ship alone rode out the storm. Pinto regretted the calamity but was convinced that this miracle was an intervention on the part of the Most High for his particular advantage. "So we got ready to depart, well pleased to see ourselves so rich but sad at having made the gains at the cost of so many lives."

As he was weighing anchor, however, three men rode hastily to the shore waving a great cloth as signal to the ship. Pinto was implored to receive them aboard his vessel and, though fourteen pursuers threatened him with death if he gave the riders shelter, he took the fugitives aboard. The horsemen proved to be Anjiro, an accidental murderer, with his two servants. Pinto took the men to Malacca, where Anjiro, moved to remorse for his deed, was converted to Christianity and was baptized as Paulo de Santa Fé. The two servants were newly christened John and Antonio. These three, and particularly Anjiro, were to provide the inspiration for the arrival in Japan of one of the greatest of modern Europeans, St. Francis Xavier.

Luckily, indeed, the Japanese were now to learn of Western ways not from greedy Ningpo merchants nor adventurous Portuguese, anxious to strip the land of all its wealth, but from one of the most devoted of European idealists. Xavier, an original clerk of the Society of Jesus, took for his life's work the evangelization of foreign fields. After he had preached in Ceylon and India, and had pioneered in the Spice Islands, he was drawn to service in newly opened Japan. Fired by the living example of Anjiro he burned to bring an empire to the service of his Lord.

The decision to visit Japan was furthered by the receipt of a letter stating that the lord of Satsuma desired that missioners he sent immediately. This daimyo, or territorial baron, knew something of the Christian doctrine, but a strange occurrence made him anxious to know more.

Portuguese merchants at Kagoshima, the Satsuma capital, were, it appears, lodged in a supposedly haunted house. The reputation was evidently not ill grounded, for the luckless merchants suffered torments. All night long the house resounded to horrible rumblings. The Portuguese were pulled out of bed by unseen hands, and were beaten severely by ghostly torturers. The native servants, all trustworthy men, reported seeing frightful apparitions "such as painters draw for a picture of the Devil." But, so soon as the Portuguese set up crosses in each room, the agonies abruptly ended.

News that the haunted house had quieted came to the daimyo's ears. Wondering at the efficacy of the symbols, he caused similar crosses to be erected at all crossroads in his dominions. Then, desiring to know why the demons feared the cross, and hesitating to receive his information from the lips of traders, he sent to India for authentic explanation.

Xavier at once responded to the invitation. Hastily he embarked upon a Chinese junk, evidently without sufficiently inquiring into the nature of his transport. The ship was surely ill adapted for a missionary. Its pirate crew, captained by Necoda the Robber, burned offerings to "a demon's image" and sent up constant prayers to heathen gods. Xavier and his five comrades, including Anjiro, labored to convert the sailors, but the pirates were far too fond of dalliance with wine and women to be interested in the austerities of Christian doctrine.

Arriving at Kagoshima, in August 1549, Xavier found himself an honored guest. Daimyo Shimadzu was anxious to divert the coveted Portuguese trade toward his own Satsuma ports. For purely economic motives he was willing to be tolerant. Xavier, given almost complete freedom for missionary work, hoped to win sufficient of the people, and especially of the influential leaders, to provide a firm foundation for the faith.

Xavier's own writing shed little light upon the more dramatic incidents of his campaign. The depositions of his associates, made by direction of John III of Portugal soon after the saint's death, credit him with marvelous achievements. The missionary knew but little Japanese but he acquired enough in forty days to translate the Lord's Prayer and a few Gospel passages. Hundreds of questions were propounded, varying from queries concerning the motions of the heavens, the eclipses of the sun, and the colors of the rainbow, to inquiries about sin and grace, hell and heaven, and the immortality of the soul. He received the gift of tongues and so was miraculously enabled to reply to all in a few words. "These words, being multiplied in their ears by a virtue all divine, gave them to understand what they

desired to know as if he had answered each of them in particular."
This, we are assured, was "no extraordinary thing with him but a
common practice."

Not even miracles could, however, guarantee a permanent stay at
Kagoshima. Shimadzu, angered when the Portuguese preferred to
trade at the deeper water of Hirado Harbor, withdrew his patronage
from both traders and missionaries. In July 1550, less than a year after
Xavier's arrival, Shimadzu issued an edict forbidding all his subjects, under penalty of death, from renouncing their ancestral gods.
It was evident that he endured aliens only for their goods.

Xavier, with a hundred converts to his credit, set off for Hirado.
Takanobu Matsuura, daimyo of this new trading center, received
him eagerly, mindful of the profits that the foreigners could furnish.
Xavier was now obsessed by a more grandiose ambition than either
trade or the conversion of a minor principality. Nothing less than
the Christianization of the Empire was his goal.

The Portuguese had now been trading with Japan for less than
seven years, but they were already realizing that the local daimyos
were comparatively unimportant figures in the Japanese economy.
Over the sixty-six provinces—which the Portuguese once thought to
be kingdoms—there was a superior official to whom all the daimyos
were nominally subject. This chief official, commanding the great
cities of Miako (now called Kyoto), Osaka, and Yedo, bore the title
of Shogun, though the Portuguese more often used the term Kubo-
sama, Lord-General, the name employed by commoners.

To unravel Japanese internal politics would be a complicated task.
Here it is enough to point out that the Ashikaga family of Shoguns,
in power since 1336, was beset on all sides by rebellion. The feudal
underlings were in a state of turmoil and unrest, each seeking to
protect himself and to annex his weaker neighbors. Under such
circumstances, it is evident, the ability to import an unlimited stock
of European firearms was of matchless advantage. The hope of
foreign guns was in itself sufficient to inspire a daimyo toward toleration of an alien creed.

Xavier's plan, therefore, of carrying the Gospel direct to the overlord of all Japan seemed likely to succeed, but Xavier unluckily knew
too little about Japan's traditions. His scheme of action, though based
on eminent Western precedent, was scarcely one to commend itself to
Japanese. With three attendants he proceeded, meanly clad, barefoot,
and in poverty, to travel overland to meet the Kubo-sama at Miako.

Japan, accustomed to pomp and ceremonial, saw nothing in the pilgrimage save a beggar's wandering. The people were unmoved by Xavier's promises of glories in the world to come. At Yamaguchi, capital of the southernmost province of Japan's main island, he was stoned from the city. On the road to Miako the missioners were pressed into servile tasks and were forced, according to the chroniclers, to run on foot while the masters galloped ahead on horseback. Xavier found Miako in civil strife. Wars and fire had made the city almost uninhabitable. Nor would the Kubo-sama grant an audience to such poverty-stricken pilgrims.

One great lesson was learned from these discouragements, that the most effective way to win attention from the mighty of the land was to appear in gorgeous raiment, loaded down with gifts. Xavier was no man to make a second error. Returning to Hirado, he gathered an impressive escort, carried letters of recommendation from the viceroy of the Indies and, foreswearing the rôle of suppliant, descended upon Yamaguchi to demand an audience with Yoshitaka Ouchi, daimyo of the province. The new plan was to win Yamaguchi first, then, converting Japan a province at a time, to come before the Kubo-sama as victors rather than petitioners.

Yamaguchi, under the Ouchi daimyos, ranked among the topmost cities of the realm. For almost a century it had been a refuge for scholars fleeing from the chaos of Miako. By winning the right to preach within its walls, Xavier pressed a wedge into the very heart of Japanese conservatism. Only at Miako itself would success have been more spectacular.

Unluckily, however, Xavier's victories came late. The Ouchis had been dominant for generations but the family was degenerating. A young, ambitious underling, Motonari Mori, was about to overthrow his master and to set up a new dynasty which was to become one of five leading houses of the Empire. This Mori family, welded into the Choshu clan, was violently anti-Christian.

Little of this future was apparent in 1551 to Xavier and his men. Success came quickly to their efforts, though the depth of understanding by the converts could not have been great. None of Xavier's followers, save Anjiro who had been forced to flee to China, was well equipped to translate the tenets of a mystic religion into the vague phrases of a Japanese philosophy. The very words of the Latin Mass itself conveyed a false impression to the listeners, for the word *deus* seemed close in sound to a native word for "falsehood" and the adjective *sancte,* applied to all the saints, was translated in an obscene sense.

More than one convert was convinced that the Portuguese were preaching merely some new variant of Buddhism. The rituals were not dissimilar, nor were the holy personages much unlike. Japan was well acquainted with the goddess Kwannon, whose quality of mercy was akin to that of the Virgin; the Buddhist saints seemed parallel to those of Christianity; the statues of the Buddha needed little alteration to pass as those of Christ. The Christian golden rule matched closely the injunctions of the Buddhist teachers. Once Xavier had learned the danger of insisting that all the unbaptized dead would suffer an eternal torture—a doctrine abhorrent to ancestor worshipers—he could gain adherents by stressing the commandment of parental reverence.

Such similarities favored Xavier's band, but one serious stumbling block remained. Japan was culturally dependent upon the Chinese classics. Traditionalism, especially strong in Yamaguchi and Miako, prevented the acceptance of new thoughts, however similar in type to old ideas. Xavier realized that custom, rather than conviction, was his enemy. Once China was converted, Japan, he thought, would readily follow her cultural mentor. China, he became convinced, must first be Christianized before Japan could be completely won.

In September 1551, therefore, St. Francis Xavier bade farewell to Yamaguchi. Scarcely had he left the city before rebellions flared. Civil wars laid Yamaguchi waste; the streets "overflowed with blood for eight days"; the daimyo was driven to suicide. Motonari Mori's mobs raged through the province searching for the foreigners who, by attacking the Japanese gods, had brought calamity upon the helpless citizenry. Though Portuguese merchants, safely distant at Hirado, were tolerated for the wares and weapons they could bring, the missionary movement suffered serious setbacks. Only in the southern island of Kyushu, semi-independent of the Kubo-sama's sway, was Christianity tolerated. Not until 1928 was a monument in memory of Xavier, whom the Japanese called "Zaburio," set up in Japan. It stands near the ancient well of Yamaguchi, where he baptized many of his converts, but the inscription tells nothing of the persecutions nor of the hardships suffered by the man it celebrates.

The Kyushu tolerance was due to political rather than theological conditions. For more than a century feudal lords throughout Japan had been engaged in civil war. The old controls had long since broken, leaving no strong central government whose decrees could be enforced beyond a lance-throw from the castle walls. The nominal Emperor, or Dairi, derived a theoretic power from his divine ancestry but was less powerful, in actuality, than his own Lord-General, the Kubo-sama. More than two hundred and fifty daimyos, as uncontrolled as Europe's medieval barons, were battling for supremacy.

To gain a redivision of their fiefs, if not for total independence, these daimyos sought every possible alliance. Some enlisted the aid of various religious sects, thus precipitating a succession of fanatical uprisings which, for bigotry and cruelty, vie with the contemporary religious wars of Europe. Others allied themselves with discontented peasants in their rivals' realms, and thus, to weaken the strength of neighbor lords, caused social upheavals like those of John Ball and the Jacquerie. Some, who feared central power less than they dreaded their equals, called in the Kubo-sama's help against powerful opponents.

Under such circumstances it was no wonder that the little lords of Kyushu, realizing that tremendous gains might come by friendship with Europeans having guns and ammunition, should have desired Portuguese assistance. These Kyushu daimyos feared for their safety. Motonari Mori, chief of the Choshu clan, had become the master of ten provinces just across the straits of Shimonoseki from Kyushu island. The powerful Shimadzus, leaders of Satsuma, were marching north from Kagoshima to make all Kyushu a tributary territory.

Caught between the Mori and the Shimadzu armies, the independent Kyushu daimyos turned to the Portuguese for aid. The presence of a militant-minded religious order, trained to think in warlike terms and drilled in soldierly discipline, intensified the eagerness of Kyushu men to win assistance.

Shimadzu tried to checkmate this appeal. Withdrawing his edict of intolerance, he allowed three priests to land at Kagoshima in August 1552, and permitted them to enroll some hundreds of new converts. Whether the explanation for this change of policy lies in the persuasive abilities of the missionaries or, as the anti-Christians now allege, in the Shimadzu strategy of having trusted retainers profess conversion in order to have access to Western military knowledge, is beside the point. The new missionaries were too clever to be deluded by any childish scheming.

Realizing the official friendliness was evanescent, they set themselves to win so strong a popular support that their position would be safe. To show to sceptics that their religion was beyond reproach the three newcomers adopted a rule of rigid asceticism with austerities and self-denials far exceeding the requirements of their discipline. Hospitals, asylums, schools, and other social services were made as freely available to the unconverted as to the proselytes. For more than a quarter of a century these missioners and their assistants made rapid progress. When, in 1577, Father Alexander Valignani, visitor-general of Jesuit establishments in the East, arrived to inspect the mission, he was amazed at the advance. Japan, he discovered, was eligible for promotion to a missionary bishopric.

To Valignani is due, in all probability, the credit for a spectacular coup. He realized that the building of seminaries and monasteries was essential, but he planned for the conversion of leading officials as a means for adding distinction to his cause. And, because he knew that Yoshishige, daimyo of Bungo, had been a friend of Xavier in the past, Valignani tried to win Yoshishige to the cause. If once a daimyo could be converted, Valignani thought, the people would be more easily persuaded.

What inducements were held forth to persuade Yoshishige are not now known. The Church maintained that Yoshishige saw the error of his carnal ways; sceptics say that a young Christian girl was used as lure to have the daimyo renounce a false religion. Whatever may be the explanation, the facts remain that Yoshishige of Bungo accepted baptism under the new name of Daimyo Francis. Two other daimyos, newly christened Protais of Arima and Bartolemi of Omura, followed Francis into the Catholic fold. With these three converted the rest was easy. Subjects were commanded, by orders highly reminiscent of the mass conversions in the age of Clovis, to accept the Christian faith. Kyushu suddenly turned Catholic, one missionary baptizing no less than seventy thousand converts within two months. More than two hundred thousand converts—some figures run into the millions—were readily enrolled.

Then, to clinch the conversions and to advertise to the world the triumphs of the missioners, the three proselytes were persuaded to dispatch to Rome a special mission whose purpose was to pay homage to the Holy Father as their spiritual and temporal lord.

A letter carried to the Pope by two sixteen-year-old envoys, Mancio Ito, Yoshishige's nephew, and Michael de Cingiva, heir to Arima, is almost groveling in its submissiveness. Presented to the Pope early in 1585, it purported to place at the Vatican's disposal all the lands

and subjects under the sway of the three Christian daimyos. Just
how far the letter represents the true feelings of the Japanese and
just how much abject humility was injected into the Latin version
through the pious zeal of the missionary interpreters is now difficult
to judge. The Japanese original is no longer available and the translation is, of course, sharply challenged by patriotic Japanese. The
phrases of subjection may or may not represent the customary Japanese self-derogation which is never to be accepted at face value. It is
likely that the content of the message was not fully comprehended
by the youths who comprised the embassy. Perhaps the etiquette required at Papal audiences was not fairly presented to the Japanese.
Nationalistic-minded Japanese historians are unanimous in rejecting
the mission as in any measure typical of true native sentiment.

That none of the daimyos had the legal right to place his realm
under papal suzerainty is evident. By all rights of law the title to the
land remained in imperial possession even though the exercise of any
rights of ownership by the Emperor was grown shadowy. The
Kyushu fiefs were in revolt but their independence had not yet been
recognized. Until such time as freedom had been won the lords had
no right to alienate their sovereignty even had they had so remarkable an intention.

In any case the situation in Japan had changed. Scarcely had the
sixteen-year-old lads left with their letter to the Pope before Shimadzu roared down upon the three Christian principalities. Yoshishige, the Daimyo Francis, was overwhelmed, losing almost all his
lands except the fields immediately adjacent to his own castle. In
June 1582, long before Ito and de Cingiva had reached Lisbon on
their mission to Rome, a new master had arisen in Japan. Hideyoshi,
a monkey-faced former groom, reduced the more important sections
of Japan's main island and made himself the Kubo-sama. Satsuma
alone disputed Hideyoshi's complete sway.

The political purpose of the Ito-de Cingiva mission was thus
rendered wholly futile. Portugal and the Pope might conceivably
have been willing to aid one feudal lord against another, with a view
toward keeping the Empire in a state of continued confusion, but to
aid a small group of feeble daimyos against a Japanese Napoleon was
quite a different story. Bungo, Arima, and Omura joined the vic-
torious Kubo-sama, abandoning their own envoys to their fate.

The mission, now returned from Rome as far as Macao, was left
orphaned. It waited to discover how the military campaigns would

end and whether it would be safe to come home to Japan. Quite un-derstandably the boys were reluctant to place themselves within the power of a conqueror who might exact vengeance for their abject submission to the Pope. For Ito and de Cingiva, by eagerness in ask-ing alien aid, had shown themselves anxious to enroll foreigners against Hideyoshi's might. In the Kubo-sama's eyes the young en-voys were traitorous rebels from whom a death penalty might readily be exacted. By waiting at Macao until the victor's wrath had cooled, the envoys hoped that they might return in safety to their homes.

Europe remained in complete ignorance of this sad outcome of the Japanese "submission." For years thereafter, pious Christians were confident that Japan was wholly Christian at heart, and that the day was near at hand when the great mysterious empire of the East would join with the Church to create a vast international society for the brotherhood of man.

II

ADAMS AIDS THE KUBO-SAMA

1586–1609

HIDEYOSHI'S ascendency was indisputable. Only Shimadzu of Satsuma stood in the Kubo-sama's path, but Shimadzu's opposition, despite boasts that a quarter million men could be arrayed against the conqueror, proved feeble. By guile and threat of force the monkey-faced Hideyoshi drew Shimadzu's allies into his own ranks. The Kubo-sama was supreme.

Much of his success, no doubt, is traceable to superstition. Almost at the moment when he began his move to unify Japan a fearful earthquake shook the land "for forty days successively." So severe were the shocks, according to contemporaries, that "a strong castle, built at the top of a high hill, sank down and disappeared. The earth gaped, a lake quickly filling the place where the foundations had been. Some of the openings in the earth were so wide and deep that, guns being fired into them, the balls could not be heard to reach the other end. Such a stench and smoke issued out of them that the people would not venture to travel that way."

Irrespective of the literal accuracy of such descriptions, it is evident that many Japanese believed that nature itself was favoring the Kubo-sama. To scientifically minded folk there is no necessary connection between the actions of mundane monarchs and a subsequent natural phenomenon, but Japan was not then permeated by the truths of modern science. Europe was itself in no more scientific mood. In any contemporary nation the populace would have been convinced that disasters could be traced to some divine discontent.

This 1586 earthquake had serious bearing upon Japan's relations with the outer world. Gossip had been rife for almost a year concerning the actions of a certain ruddy-skinned foreigner who had been making mysterious measurements along the coast. His blue eyes, fair complexion, and blond hair checked almost exactly with the descriptions of "foreign devils" as laid down in classic writings. His strange instruments and his curious notations smacked of magic. His activities worried Japan.

There was, to be sure, no magic in the work of this Dirk Gerritszoon. Coming to Japan in 1585 as gunner on a Portuguese ship, he had remained for half a year to survey the coastline. His sole intention was to scout trade possibilities. On his return to his home town of Enkhuizen in Holland he was to win the nickname "China" Gerritszoon for his incessant conversation about his travels in the East. Gerritszoon was wholly ignorant of the legends that were woven around his memory.

Scarcely had Gerritszoon departed from Japan before the earthquake devastated the provinces where he had stayed. Both local lords and Kubo-sama were convinced that this giant "Red Hair" was leagued with evil spirits. It was an understandable conclusion, and one that would have been drawn in Europe had a Japanese been seen in any area just before disaster struck. And, by curious coincidence, the first linking of foreigners with wizardry was followed by many more "indisputable proofs" that aliens brought calamity. Seismic disturbances and social upheavals seemed inseparable from the landing of Europeans. To make the impression more convincing, the Japanese soon came to think that no great troubles came at times when aliens were absent from Japan.

Hideyoshi had long believed that the freedom of foreigners required curbing, but hitherto the presence of civil war had restrained him from effective action. Now that his political enemies were reduced the Kubo-sama could safely turn against the aliens. The Portuguese constituted, he believed, a dangerous secret clique within the realm. Any group of militantly minded men, openly professing an allegiance to a foreign king would, in any land, be looked upon as menaces to continued peace.

Missionaries in particular were his special hatreds. They insisted that they obeyed a ruler greater than any earthly monarch, and they had persuaded three daimyos to renounce the Kubo-sama in favor of a spiritual sovereign. They were, moreover, financed by foreign subsidy. The thousand ducats annually paid by the Portuguese crown for the upkeep of the missionaries seemed ample proof that the Christians were in foreign pay and that part of their service was to act as spies.

Buddhist hostility toward practices permitted under Christian rule encouraged Hideyoshi in his desire to weaken the foreigners. The Buddhists, loath to take life, counseled the sparing of animals which might contain the souls of past generations expiating their sins. The missionaries denying the truth of transmigration, allowed their proselytes to kill and eat both beef and pork. To pious Buddhists the eating of such meat was an unpardonable crime. They were angry, moreover, because Xavier's followers violently assailed the native priests as "devils in human form" who lived by hypocrisy, greed, and corruption.

Early in 1587, therefore, Hideyoshi dispatched a message in which he demanded that the missionaries explain their action in "sowing discontent." He demanded, too, that they cease what he called their complicity in allowing pirates at Hirado and Nagasaki to sell Japanese coolies into slavery. In the event that the Christian answer should be unsatisfactory, he warned, permission to reside in Japan would be withdrawn.

Father Gaspard Cuello, chief of the missionaries, knew that no defense would convince a biased despot, but tried to soften the Kubo-sama's wrath. He apologized profusely for beef-eating, stating that the offense had been committed in ignorance of Japanese custom and that it would not be repeated. He disclaimed all connection with the slave trade and promised coöperation in its suppression. As to the Christian policy toward the native priests, Father Cuello pointed out, the missioners could not be fairly held responsible for the excesses of their enthusiastic converts. No Buddhist, he said, had been unfairly maligned and none had been ridiculed "except for their absurdities." The disclaimer fell far short of convincingness.

The response, as might have been expected, failed to persuade the Kubo-sama. On June 25, 1587, the dreaded expulsion order was proclaimed. Trade was permitted to the Portuguese, but all missionaries were to be deported and no more were to be sent to Japan.

Hideyoshi's motives in issuing the edict were not difficult for the Christians to fathom. Disregarding all explanations that no ruler desires an *imperium in imperio,* the missionaries commented simply on the character of Hideyoshi. All men knew, they said, that Kyushu was celebrated for its pretty girls. The region was becoming Christian. Monkey Face could recruit no members for his harem from this most desirable section of his realm. Hence Hideyoshi hated the Christians.

A second explanation, equally naïve, was that Hideyoshi was insulted. A Portuguese sea captain refused to sail a new ship into a port of central Japan where Hideyoshi might inspect it. Angered at the insult, so the story ran, Hideyoshi ordered the expulsion of the missionaries. The chief flaw in the explanation is that by Hideyoshi's order the merchant captains, against whom he was indignant, might continue to visit his ports while the blameless missionaries suffered punishment.

The Kubo-sama refrained from putting the edict into effect. The deportation, originally scheduled to take place within three weeks, was postponed for half a year and was then tacitly ignored. For this delay the missionaries had an even more naïve explanation. Hideyoshi, they declared, desired to conquer Korea. Kyushu was to supply two hundred thousand warriors for the expedition. All these, said the missionaries, would be Christian and thus, by killing off the converts, the religious problem would be solved.

Such were the conditions when Father Valignani and his orphaned embassy returned from Rome, in June 1590, after eight years' absence. They had left Japan violently racked by civil war; they came home to find that Japan was, for the first time in decades, completely peaceful under a strong dictator. In 1582 Japan had been surrendering to Christianity; when Valignani and his young princes arrived in Nagasaki eight years later, Christianity was officially discredited.

Valignani hoped, by appealing to the Kubo-sama's vanity, to win back favor. Packing a vast array of presents and appealing humbly to the Shogun as "the greatest monarch who has reigned in Japan for ages," Valignani pleaded for permission to continue preaching. Hideyoshi refused. Japan desired to continue trade, he replied, but "this new preaching can only serve to introduce into Japan a diversity of worship very prejudicial to the State."

There is no reason for questioning Hideyoshi's sincerity. He desired national unity and domestic peace, both of which he thought were threatened by religious dissent. His grandiose plans for conquest in Korea, China, and the Philippines could not be carried out if Japan were to be embroiled in civil or spiritual strife. On these matters the Kubo-sama's answers to Valignani were definite and specific.

Hideyoshi's spy service brought information strengthening the master's determination. Manila, since its establishment in 1565, had been clamoring for a share in the rich Japan trade. Its merchants demanded that the old monopolies granted to Macao be repealed, and that Manila be admitted to Japan on equal terms. Hideyoshi, hearing of the dispute, sent letters to Manila offering trade but demanding homage as his price.

Manila, aghast at the suggestion, seized the opportunity to send an embassy to Japan to investigate trade possibilities. Negotiations dragged out slowly, chiefly because the Kubo-sama faced domestic complications. A new-born son, Hideyori, required protection. To assure the succession to the throne for the baby, Hideyoshi demanded that the former heir-apparent, Hideyoshi's nephew, commit hara-kiri. Then, to remove all possibility that the unfortunate nephew might himself leave heirs to claim the rule, the Kubo-sama commanded a public execution of the nephew's thirty-one widows and of all his children. Hideyoshi took no chances on dynastic wars.

By 1596 the time again seemed propitious to Manila for opening trade relations. But again ill luck betrayed the Europeans. The *San Felipe,* the great annual galleon which bore Philippine goods to Acapulco in New Spain, was wrecked by typhoon. She drifted close to Shikoku, the island north of Kyushu. There the captain was induced, partly by persuasion and partly by force, to seek repairs at Urato, a harbor of Tosa. Once within the harbor the *San Felipe* was confiscated on the ground that she was bringing missionaries to Japan.

The accusation was decidedly unfair, for the ship had not been intended for Japan, but the *San Felipe's* rich cargo was too precious for Hideyoshi to surrender. Greed alone might have proved itself a decisive argument for confiscation, but certain gossip passed on from Tosa made the action certain.

There is at this late date no guarantee that the incident responsible for the gossip ever actually occurred but, according to rumor, the Spanish pilot, in trying to impress the Tosa men, boasted too loudly of his monarch's might. Showing a globe, he pointed out the wide Spanish domains and threatened Japan with vengeance if the Spaniards were detained. The Tosa guardsmen, unimpressed by the threat, asked curiously how Spain had won such vast dominion. The pilot carelessly replied that the method was simple. "First," said he, "we send out missionaries to convert the people; then traders follow. When trade is flourishing we send our armies who, with the native turncoats, annex the nation."

Unquestionably the flippant answer contained much more than a modicum of truth, though in Japan at least the sequence of missioner, trader, and soldier was not consciously planned. To Japanese, however, the remarks seemed wholly accurate. Tosa reported the conversation to Hideyoshi and the latter flew into a violent rage. He swore that the galleon would not now be surrendered, accused the Spaniards of piracy, and decreed death for all clerics in Japan.

No Japanese official dared risk decapitation by refusing to enforce the edict. By December 1596 a list of all foreign missionaries and of all native converts was compiled. The numbers were necessarily large, for the total proselytes were now reckoned at more than a quarter million. Many of the priests were safely smuggled out of danger, but six Spanish monks and three native priests were arrested, together with seventeen lay followers.

These twenty-six were treated barbarously, perhaps, as it is now explained, to save their fellows. By scrupulous enforcement of the edict, it was hoped, the Kubo-sama's ire might be satisfied without too large a flow of blood. The completion of the law, after an initial token had been displayed, could be allowed to wait "until a more convenient moment." In this way the Kubo-sama might be mollified without the need for wholesale butchery.

The prisoners were mutilated and then were paraded for public derision in Miako and in every town between the capital and Nagasaki. This city, the new port for foreign trade, was chosen as the place for execution because it was the center of the foreign faith. Crosses were erected on the hills overlooking the harbor and, on February 5, 1597, the twenty-six martyrs were crucified. Lances were thrust upward through the bodies in such fashion that they crossed near the heart and emerged through the shoulders. The corpses were left to hang upon the crosses until the following summer.

Hoping to prevent continuance of the terror, the Portuguese applied to Yodogimi, Hideyoshi's favorite concubine and the mother of the infant Hideyori. By rich presents she was won to the belief that the Kubo-sama's wrath applied only to Spaniards. Through her intercession with the Kubo-sama, the Portuguese were enabled to remain in peace, particularly as Hideyoshi had no real desire to isolate his Empire from the desirable foreign goods. Temporarily Portugal retained a monopoly of both trade and missionary work.

Japan, it is evident, was ready for commercial intercourse, perhaps even for close political relationship with Western lands, provided only that religious complications and imperialistic aggression could be avoided. Neither Portugal nor Spain was wholly trusted, for each had been suspected of intrigue and each was believed guilty of stirring civil discontent, but Portugal seemed the less evil at the moment.

Luckily for Japan's purposes, other European nations were evidencing interest in the East. Britain and Holland, admitted to the oceans by the collapse of Philip II's Armada, were embarking on overseas adventure. The motives were extraordinarily mixed. Religious fervor, a strong nationalistic sentiment, a passion for adventure into unknown seas, desire for revenge upon Spaniards and Portuguese who long controlled the oriental seaways, greed for enormous profits, all contributed to the craze for Eastern trade.

"China" Gerritszoon was chiefly responsible for the new adventure. On his way home to Enkhuizen, he told his shipmates of the profits to be won by trade with the Kubo-sama's realm. Among his listeners was a fellow townsman, Jan Huyghen van Linschoten, who had spent five years in India for the Portuguese. Van Linschoten, knowing the comparative ease of the Good Hope voyage, and acquainted at first hand with the weakness of the Portuguese defenses, published in 1595 a *Discourse of Voyages*. This volume, promising huge profits for Hollanders who traded in the East, received corroboration by the testimony of two other distinguished navigators. Cornelius Houtman, a ship captain who had served on Portuguese vessels and who had been embittered against his employers as the result of a sentence in a Lisbon jail, approved the Van Linschoten promises. William Adams, a rollicking Englishman who had traded for eleven years with the Barbary coast, confirmed the comments of both Gerritszoon and Van Linschoten.

Eight ships sailed from Amsterdam in 1595 for India, China, and Japan. Four vessels, commanded by Van Linschoten, sought a Northeast Passage, but were compelled by storms and ice to turn back at the Kara Sea. Four others, under Houtman, went by the Good Hope route. The latter expedition skirmished with the natives and with Portuguese, lost a ship by fire, and suffered from disease, but the survivors came home in 1598, triumphantly carrying a trade treaty signed by the Sultan of Bantam in Java. Before the year was over, no less than four separate expeditions left Amsterdam for the East. One was wholly lost; two others circumnavigated the world, returning with cargoes that fetched a handsome profit. The fourth, piloted by the Kentishman Will Adams, failed of immediate success, but led to vast political and trade advantages.

The fever spread to Britain. Even before the Armada, Englishmen were searching seaways to the East. One curious report, preserved at Nagasaki, insists that two Britishers, John Tintam and William Fabian, were prepared to sail for Guinea and "the East" as early as 1481. The report adds that the trip was called off by Edward IV at the personal request of King John of Portugal. More probably, England first heard of Japan through the black-letter volume, *History of Travayle,* compiled in 1577 by Richard Eden and Richard Willis from the Jesuit *Relations.* This was far from authentic in its information concerning Japan, since it dismissed the land as unimportant. "The country is barren, not so much by fault of nature as through the slothfulness of the inhabiters. . . . Gentlemen, for the most part, do pass the night in banqueting, music, and other vain discourses; they sleep the daytime."

Discouraging news did not prevent the English from exploring. Daring pioneers like Sir Hugh Willoughby and Charles Jackson plunged into the Arctic, seeking a Northwest Passage. Certain none-too-authentic Japanese annals assert that British ships actually penetrated to Japan as early as 1564, though it is more probable that the real truth is that one or two expatriated English sailors arrived at Japan on Portuguese trading ships.

Barely three years after the wrecking of the Armada, Sir James Lancaster ventured on England's first rounding of Good Hope. On his return in 1594, after a profitless trip to Ceylon, a second effort was essayed, but this too failed. Then came news of Holland's excitement over the Van Linschoten *Discourse,* and with it a renewed British interest. London merchants petitioned the Privy Council in 1599 for a charter establishing Indian trade. The Privy Council, fearing the effect of its permission on the peace negotiations then in progress with Spain, postponed its answer for a year. On the last day of the century, the semi-sovereign English East India Company received a charter. Lancaster again sailed with five ships in 1601, and came home from Java with a profit of approximately ninety-five percent on his investment. England was convinced that riches were now close at hand, but the impression was destroyed when Sir Edward Michelbourne's party, in 1604, met disaster. Michelbourne, with John Davis of Arctic fame as navigator, planned to open trade with the Far

East, but after reaching Singapore was killed in "attempting to seize a Japanese junk." Michelbourne turned back with remnants of his expedition. England hesitated for three years before dispatching another party.

Meanwhile conditions in Japan were changing for the worse so far as foreigners were concerned. The Kubo-sama, Hideyoshi, was desperately ill. His concern for foreign trade gave place to a more intense preoccupation for securing divine honors to himself. Believing himself the embodiment of Hachiman, the god of war, Hideyoshi was insisting, with all the feeble strength he still possessed, that Japan be studded with temples in his honor.

Hideyoshi was anxious also to secure the succession to the Shogunate for his four-year-old son Hideyori. This desire implied a certain measure of hostility toward foreigners since many of them, the religious groups in particular, had shown partiality toward the surviving relatives of that nephew whom Hideyoshi had compelled to harakiri. Hideyoshi, fearing a possible rebellion of the daimyos after he himself should die, tried to protect the rights of his young heir. In order to guarantee his arrangements he set up a regency, headed by Iyeyasu Tokugawa, daimyo of the Yedo region, to rule in Hideyori's name. In September 1598, at just about the time the twenty-two Dutch ships were sailing from the Texel for the East, the great Hideyoshi, Japan's mightiest of warriors, died.

Iyeyasu immediately proved faithless. Instead of executing the orders of his dead master, the Regent seized the chief power for himself. Mori, Shimadzu, and Uyesugi of Echigo province, his three strongest rivals, proclaimed rebellion, ostensibly in the interest of young Hideyori, but in reality to recover their former feudal freedom. The civil wars that had racked Japan for a century prior to Hideyoshi were again returning.

Such was the situation when Will Adams, after a two years' ordeal of shipwreck, starvation, war, mutiny, piracy, and disease, steered his 160-ton *Liefde* into Beppu Bay on the north shore of Kyushu Island. After one of the most epic voyages in history he had succeeded in bringing the first North European vessel to Japan, but of the original crew of 110 men only twenty-four were still alive. All but five of these were too sick to stand. His fellow captain, "China" Gerritszoon, who had left Amsterdam with Adams, had been driven off his course by storm, and had been compelled for want of food to surrender to the Spaniards at Valparaiso.

Luckily for Adams he landed, on April 11, 1600, at a port which had been recaptured by Iyeyasu's forces. The *Liefde* was promptly pillaged of everything movable. The helpless Hollanders were imprisoned, but the governor, Sorin Otomo, safeguarded their lives. None of the new arrivals could speak a word of Japanese nor could Otomo's officers understand either Dutch or English. "Within two or three daies after our arrivall," Adams wrote, "ther cam a Iesuit from a place called Langasacke, which, with other Iaponers that were Christians, were our interpreters, which was not to our good, our mortal enemies being our Truchmen." The "truchmen" (then a common word for interpreters), finding that the *Liefde* men were enemies of Portugal, declared that the sailors were pirates. Two of the Hollanders, hoping perhaps to save their own lives, agreed with the Portuguese and denounced their shipmates as rogues.

Iyeyasu was not impressed. Believing that the Mori-Shimadzu-Uyesugi coalition planned to use Christian converts as the nucleus for new armies for setting up its independence, he suspected that the hasty Portuguese denunciations might not be wholly true. He sent ships to Beppu Bay to bring the survivors before him for questioning. To his delight, the Shogun learned that the Hollanders were well acquainted with gunnery and cannon casting. Enkhuizen, the home of most of the *Liefde* survivors, was at this time the chief arsenal of the United Provinces, holding a place in Dutch industry similar to that of Bethlehem or Pittsburgh in present-day United States. Had Iyeyasu combed all Europe for immigrants, he could have discovered no more suitable men than these *Liefde* sailors who combined a knowledge of cannon casting with that of shipbuilding and of navigation.

Adams met Iyeyasu at precisely the best moment. Resistance to Spain and Portugal, and to the ideas for which they stood, was a patriotic duty to all Englishmen and Hollanders. Adams had no hesitancy, therefore, in making counter charges. Slanders against both Portuguese and Spaniards for their supposed designs upon Japan, reports of their cruelty against conquered peoples, charges that they were subsidized to betray the Japanese could be made freely and without undue strain upon the conscience of a loyal Britisher. Iyeyasu listened intently to Adams' counter charges against the Nagasaki interpreters and then, after forty days of questioning and deliberation, freed Adams and the *Liefde* men.

The friendliness was fortunate. Soon after the *Liefde's* arrival the

great battle of Sekigahara, in October 1600, gave victory to the white
hilts of the Tokugawa armies against the red scabbards of the Satsuma allies. Adams was thus allied with the conquering Shogun
Iyeyasu rather than with the defeated Mori-Shimadzu-Uyesugi faction. He was entrenched at Yedo, from which city the hereditary
Kubo-samas were to rule Japan for almost three centuries. A powerless Son of Heaven, the Imperial Dairi, would continue to reside at
Miako, but the real government would be wielded by a *de facto*
dictator ruling in the Dairi's name.

Trained sailors such as the Dutchmen were no novelty to Japan,
but experts in the field of gunnery, in naval architecture, and in shipbuilding, had been rare. Adams was regarded as a master in these
matters. Iyeyasu therefore refused to allow any of the *Liefde* men to
leave Japan. He ordered them indemnified for their losses, granted
each a daily dole of two pounds of rice, and gave them an annuity
of $24, with Adams receiving $140 yearly. Indeed, when Adams
proved restive, Iyeyasu increased the pension. The expatriate was
given "a living like unto a lordship in England, with 80 or 90 hus-
bandmen as servants and slaves." The revenues of an entire village
were assigned him for his use and he was encouraged to invite as
many of his countrymen as he desired to come to bear him company.
His letters home to England were probably influential factors in the
determination of the newly established English East India Company
to set up a factory in Japan.

Adams, thus become Iyeyasu's most important adviser on foreign
relations, was excellently situated as a European commercial agent.
Iyeyasu was passing through precisely the same cycles of thought
that Hideyoshi had experienced. Now that domestic tranquillity was
restored, as a result of the victory at Sekigahara, Iyeyasu feared little
rivalry at home. Christianity, especially of the Portuguese variety,
was however looked upon as dangerous. The intense loyalty of its
converts to a superhuman king whose power was regarded as supreme above all earthly monarchs, the earnest protestations that
temporal affairs were subject to a spiritual leader, the focusing of
faithfulness upon a sovereign living far beyond the reach of any
Shogun, stirred the suspicions of the Japanese administrators. The
religious passions that ran high in seventeenth-century Europe were
potent influences in far-away Japan.

Adams was a loyal Briton in such matters, even though he was
now serving Holland's commercial interests. When, in 1603, he

learned that Manila contemplated a campaign to conquer the Malaccas he relayed the news to Iyeyasu as new proof of the untrustworthiness of both Portuguese and Spaniards. Iyeyasu, always ready to suspect the worst, decreed new laws to control the foreign merchants and the missionaries who remained in violation of the 1587 edict. All clerics were again ordered into exile, a command which, like the 1587 law, was not rigidly enforced. Another ukase established spies, *metsuke,* in each district to denounce any Japanese who might befriend the alien missionaries.

With Spaniards and Portuguese under an official ban, Adams urged that both Holland and Britain be granted trade privileges. Neither, he assured the Shogun, would be guilty of either political or religious aggression. Each had all the goods that Spain and Portugal could supply and each would sell more cheaply. Adams was of course exceeding his duties as a Dutch employe in thus asking for the admission of the British into territory that the Dutch desired exclusively, but he justified his action on the plea that he himself was British born. Not for some years thereafter, however, did the Dutch discover that their agent had been active in other interests. The immediate result of his pleadings benefited only Holland. Iyeyasu, moved by Adams' arguments, granted Holland, in September 1608, the right to trade at any Japanese port. Britain was not included because of the report that the Michelbourne expedition had been guilty of unprovoked attack against a Japanese vessel.

Unforeseen incidents plunged Portugal into deeper disgrace. A trading junk, sent by the daimyo of Arima to buy aloes wood in Annam, was driven into Macao harbor by bad weather. There the sailors fought with Portuguese. Fifty men were killed, among them twenty-eight Japanese. The ship, together with its cargo, was confiscated by Pessoa, the Macao governor.

News of the brawl came to Nagasaki in the Portuguese trading ship of 1609, commanded, as it happened, by Pessoa himself. Aboard the vessel was a Japanese who reported the affair to the Nagasaki port authorities. The Arima daimyo was about to burn the ship, but warning was given to the Portuguese by friendly converts. Pessoa fled, but his ship was cornered in a cove by Arima's forces. Fire boats were allowed to drift against the Portuguese vessel, the craft was burned, and, on December 18, 1609, Pessoa was beheaded. Iyeyasu issued angry orders to expel all Portuguese merchants and to kill all Portuguese missionaries. This was the third anti-clerical edict.

Both Spain and Holland leaped to use the Portuguese disgrace for their selfish gain. Don Rodrigo de Vivero, governor of Manila who chanced to be shipwrecked in Japan, contended with Will Adams in professing loyalty to the Shogun.

Adams, after an eight years' residence, was an excellent judge of Japanese political conditions. Knowing that Captain Krombeck had but recently arrived at Hirado harbor with two ships, *Roode Leeaw* (Red Lion), and *Griffioen* (Griffon), he sent urgent calls to Krombeck to hasten to Iyeyasu's court. Before Don Rodrigo was wholly aware of what was happening, Krombeck and Adams, through lavish gifts and exceptional diplomacy, gained from the Shogun a letter to be carried back to Holland offering trade and friendship. This document, granted in 1609, is the first formal missive sent by a ruler of all Japan to the chief of any European nation. It merits particular attention since the spirit of the document is widely variant from the ideas later to be expressed by Iyeyasu and his successors.

Under a charter of such broad privileges, it would seem, no future difficulties could be anticipated. Not only were rights more extensive than even a "most-favored-nation" clause extended to the Dutchmen, but all the rights and privileges attached to merchants in Japan were seemingly extended to the Hollanders.

There were, however, several drawbacks of which the Dutch were evidently unaware. The charter bore neither signature nor date and hence could easily be repudiated by the Kubo-sama if he so desired. Though it came ostensibly from Iyeyasu and was in fact presented to the Dutchmen at an official audience at which Iyeyasu was present, it could be construed as a forgery or as a fraud if ever the occasion might arise. Nor were the Dutchmen aware of the comparatively low social status in which native Japanese commercial men were wont to move. In the eight great classes of contemporary society, merchants ranked sixth, far below the court nobility, the daimyos, samurai, landed proprietors and artisans. Only the actors and the tanners were of lower social rank. Iyeyasu's charter, seemingly so generous, admitted Dutchmen to the class of underprivileged subjects. It is noteworthy, too, that in all the long list of privileges awarded not a word is said about land ownership, or even of leases of land. Houses might indeed be built, but Japanese were under no compulsion to provide the sites.

None of these drawbacks were to be overlooked in Japan's subsequent dealings with the Dutchmen. Much of the scurvy treatment of which complaints were later to be made sprang directly from the strict interpretation of Iyeyasu's superficially generous charter of privileges.

Europe was to learn, in later years, that documents bearing upon Japan's international relationships required extremely careful scrutiny. Over and over again, later envoys were to find, the Japanese officials offered concessions which seemed superficially complete but which, because of the absence of proper seals or signatures, were not binding on Japan. The Japanese, it became evident, took full advantage of the cryptic nature of their language to veil their true intentions. If, in consequence of clever diplomatic maneuverings, the aliens allowed themselves to be deceived, Japan assumed no real responsibility. The Iyeyasu concession was an excellent example of what Japan's statesmen regarded as clever diplomacy.

III

INSULTS AND MASSACRES
1611–1638

HOLLAND, having won the opening advantage, prepared to maintain her privileges. No ordinary rules of commercial fair play, no considerations of abstract justice, no moral compunctions were to be respected. Holland had outwitted her rivals, including two of her bitterest enemies, and she intended to enjoy her rights.

The Dutch began their trading, however, with a misconception of their privileges. Troubles befell them at the outset of their trade. Upon the arrival of the *Brach,* their first ship, at Hirado in July 1611, port officials demanded a copy of the manifest. This the Dutch refused to give, partly because the Portuguese were subject to no such requirement and Holland understood that she had "most-favored-nation" rights. A more potent reason for refusal lay in the fact that the *Brach,* hastily loaded, carried so slight a cargo of silks, woolens, pepper, ivory, and lead—the commodities Japan particularly desired—that the Dutch were unwilling to advertise the unimportance of their wares. Too much had been promised Iyeyasu concerning the riches to be imported to Japan.

Shigenobu Matsuura, daimyo of Hirado, was reluctant to take sides. He suggested that the Hollanders send a special commission to call upon the Shogun to settle the dispute. Jacob Specx, chief of the Hirado agency, set out therefore with a small escort to meet Iyeyasu and en route to call upon Hideyori, son of the late Hideyoshi. Specx was anxious to make friends with all possible factions of the government.

The Hollanders were facing handicaps, largely of their own making. The visit to Hideyori, however innocent in motive, was completely misconstrued by the Shogunate. Specx was obliged to disclaim all thought of political interest and to reiterate his complete loyalty to the Iyeyasu cause. The drabness of the tiny Dutch commission, so sharply in contrast to the lavish rich liveries of the missions once sent by Spain and Portugal, seemed a studied insult to the Japanese who judged so often by outward appearances. The very cargo of the *Brach,* composed as it was of excellent Dutch cheese and butter, was repugnant to the fastidious Orientals. It would have been difficult to discover commodities less desired by Japanese.

Probably only the stupidity of the Spanish saved the Holland cause. Don Rodrigo de Vivero, the Manila governor who had been outwitted by Will Adams some months earlier, worked unwittingly in Holland's interest. After two years of wholesale flattery, lavish gifts, and skilful diplomacy, Don Rodrigo was winning permission for his people to return. Spanish shipbuilders and silver miners were granted the right of residence. A treaty, it was understood, was ready to be signed awarding to Spain all the trading privileges once owned by Portugal.

But the Spaniard went too far. On the arrival of Specx at the capital, Don Rodrigo flew into a temper. Denouncing the Dutch as rebellious subjects of the Spanish king, Don Rodrigo demanded that all Hollanders be expelled from Japan. Iyeyasu refused the demand, saying, "Were the Dutch devils they shall be well treated so long as they obey the law."

Specx was prompt to point out to the Shogun that Don Rodrigo was really asking for power to interfere in Japan's domestic politics. Then came news, through the Shogun's spies, that the Spaniards were inviting the daimyo of Mutsu, in the northern end of the main island, to sign a separate trade treaty without the Shogun's knowledge, and that Spaniards were charting Japan's harbors. It was not difficult to explain that such activities indicated Spain's hostility to Iyeyasu's rule. Don Rodrigo was thus easily discredited and Holland was restored to favor.

Holland, having defeated two important trading rivals, was now about to meet a third. News of the Dutch charter excited the English East India Company's interest in Oriental trade. The knowledge that an Englishman was residing at the Shogun's court seemed sufficient inducement to send a trading venture to Japan. That Will Adams was employed by Holland for Dutch interests was evidently a minor matter; London evidently believed that his nationalistic spirit would be strong enough to cause him to transfer his efforts to the English cause. Certainly his letters of invitation seemed sufficiently encouraging.

In April 1611, therefore, John Saris, veteran in Bantam commerce, headed toward the East with three ships, bearing a letter from James I to the "Emperor" of Japan. Progressing slowly, pausing frequently to trade, to fight, and to rest, Saris reached Bantam after the passage of eighteen months. There he delayed three months more before starting off with one ship, the *Clove,* for Hirado. In June 1613 Saris came to Hirado harbor.

Daimyo Shigenobu Matsuura greeted the arrivals warmly. A cautious diplomat, he reasoned that since these foreigners were compatriots of Adams and since Adams was a prime favorite at the Shogun's court, it would be well to win their friendship. Thus, though the Dutchmen almost always outnumbered Britons by a hundred to one at Hirado, Matsuura showed the Englishmen a favoritism which the Netherlanders bitterly resented. He was particularly intrigued by the five Negro sailors on the *Clove.* They were, he said, the first of their race whom Japan had ever seen.

Seventeen days after the *Clove's* arrival, Will Adams came from Yedo. The British reliance that national pride would win him over to service in the English Company was well justified. Adams joined forces with Saris and, at Matsuura's suggestion, took Saris to Yedo to visit Iyeyasu and to secure a trading charter similar to, or better than, the Dutch concession.

Though the journey began in Matsuura's state barge the travelers were badly treated. At Hakata, two days distant from Hirado, the two men were stoned as "false-hearted foreigners." The authorities, Saris complains, made no effort to prevent the violence. Saris was shocked, too, at the summary executions in the street. After criminals were killed, he writes, "every passerby was allowed to try his sword upon the dead bodies until they were chopped into small pieces and left for the birds of prey to devour."

Iyeyasu, probably out of friendship for Will Adams, gave unqualified acceptance to all the British requests (except the right to sell in Japan goods taken by British privateers in China), and in fact gave to England more freedom than either Portugal or Holland enjoyed. By strict construction of the charter British merchants were free not only of customs duties but also of the annoying port formalities which plagued the Dutch. Until the time of Perry's treaties incoming merchant ships were usually obliged to lie at anchor until word of arrival could be sent to Yedo and permission be received for unloading. No such delays were required of the British by Iyeyasu's charter. The result was to quicken the British turnover, provided the monsoons were favorable, and to allow the British to sell at somewhat cheaper rates.

The advantage was supposedly accentuated by allowing England to set up branches in the chief cities of the Empire. Holland traded wholesale, selling entire shiploads to a few favored Nagasaki merchants; England was to open retail stores in nine large cities. The scheme, however, proved unworkable because the cargoes which brought the largest profits were those which could best be sold to a limited number of large customers. Iyeyasu, for example, commandeered for his own use the five large cannon and all the gunpowder carried on the *Clove*. They were of great advantage to him at the siege of Osaka in 1615.

Probably it was an error for the British to refuse an offer for establishing the chief East India Company factory at Yedo. Adams, who best knew Japanese political conditions, urged that the offer of free building sites in Yedo be accepted; Saris, thinking only of the friendliness of Matsuura, overruled the suggestion. Had the factory been established at the metropolis, under the Shogun's close care, it would have enjoyed official prestige and would have been free from annoyance from rival traders. By spurning the offer England lost a splendid opportunity for winning the friendship of the real rulers of Japan.

More important than even the trading privileges was the grant of extra-territorial rights accorded to the English factory. The Cape merchant, or chief trader, was to adjudicate and punish all offenses, evidently of whatever nature, either against British or native law, committed by his subordinates.

The charter was favorable, with conditions more liberal than Britain was prepared to enjoy, but the profits made during its operation were disappointing. The *Clove,* for example, lingered at Hirado for six months, waiting for the monsoon to shift, but even with the long delay the Englishmen could neither sell their wares nor collect a full cargo for the voyage home. The vessel cleared in ballast, carrying only a few curios as gifts for King James. The *Clove's* experience was typical of the brief, stormy, and unprofitable course of British trade under the Iyeyasu charter.

The explanation is traceable partly to the death of the seventy-year-old Matsuura and to the accession of an heir who was less staunchly pro-British, but is even more due to sudden sweeps of anti-foreign hysteria. Iyeyasu believed that aliens were plotting to dismember his Empire.

Christians were alleged to be the advance agents of foreign conquest. A hundred missionaries, arrested at Nagasaki almost simultaneously with the *Clove's* arrival at Hirado, were tortured into admissions that they were instigators of sedition. A nation-wide pogrom began, directed by a newly established official agency, the Christian Inquiry. Rewards for the arrest of missionaries and their converts were published in every populous center. Special inducements invited parents to inform against their children and husbands to denounce their wives. "Revelations" that Governor Okubo, of Sado, an island in the Japan Sea, planned to lead a Christian insurrection led Iyeyasu to approve extreme measures of repression. Christians were hanged, crucified, strangled, or drowned. Ingenious refinements of torture were devised. Suspected apostates were hurled from the heights of precipices; others were buried alive or were torn asunder. Some captive Christians were tied into rice bags which were then set afire. Converts were caged and left to starve with food in plenty set before their eyes, but beyond their reach.

Under the circumstances it was perhaps fortunate for the British that no English ship arrived for nearly two years after the departure of Saris, in December 1613. Adams, during the interval, tried to rid himself of the unsalable goods by chartering a Japanese junk for a trading adventure to Siam. One expedition failed when several of his men were killed by outraged Siamese who mistakenly attacked the Englishmen thinking they were Dutch pirates; another, in 1615, collapsed when fifty-eight of his Japanese sailors mutinied near the Luchus. The English made no profit by the Siamese attempt, but, because of absence from Japan, escaped probable persecution from the Christian Inquiry which conducted anti-foreign pogroms during Adams' absence.

Three British ships arrived in the monsoon season between September 1615 and the following July but, with the mismanagement that characterized so much of the early trade relations with the East, the ships brought the wrong type of imports. Ordnance, woolen cloth and cottons came, and these had ready sale, but a large portion of the cargo consisted of goods which are difficult to explain. A gross of glass bottles, two gross of knives, eighteen huge mirrors, and twenty-three dozen pairs of spectacles are typical of the trade goods offered to the Japanese.

Other difficulties appeared when the sailors released their pent-up energies ashore. England was embroiled in almost constant quarrels. In the very first days of the *Clove's* visit, seven members of the crew ran off to Nagasaki for a spree. There, as might have been anticipated, they battled with the Portuguese, partly because of the difference in language, faith, and customs, partly because the Portuguese resented the arrival of trade competitors. The British killed several of their rivals—a matter which the Japanese might have overlooked—but made themselves further obnoxious by their drunken clamoring for women and by their loud complaints that they were being cheated by unscrupulous tavern keepers. The British declared that they were being treated more like dogs than men. Japan, in turn, appealed to the English authorities to keep better discipline over the crew.

The Hirado Britishers complied by issuing rules which could not possibly be enforced. Sailors were forbidden to possess any liquor under penalty of being thrice ducked from the yard and being flogged with ropes' ends. "If a man stays all night on shore, he shall be clapped in irons for three days, thrice dropped from the yard, and get twenty strokes with the rope's end with nothing on but his drawers." A curious clause forbade English sailors from "running about the streets naked. . . . And, in case anyone goes so far—which God forfend— as to steal from or cheat Japanese, or on board ship, he shall be three times drawn through the water under the ship and be rope's ended" —a terrible penalty in view of the barnacled conditions of the keels, and of the British practice of following sixty lashes with a bath in salt brine, and then with forty lashes more.

The rules, however, were ineffective, partly because the Japanese invited the sailors to debauchery. "As som of our men goe along the streetes, the Japons kindly call them in and give them wine and whores till they be drunk, and then stripp them of all they have (some of them stark naked) and soe turn them out of dores. And som they keepe presoners, forging debtes upon them, which som of our men sweare they owe not; yet it is noe beleeving of all, for som of our men are bad enough."

Japan, on one occasion, punished the roisterers by cutting off the heads of two drunken sailors who had drawn knives and "gave a skram or two to some Japons, yet killed noe man." The heads were sent to the ships' captains and, when the Europeans refused to receive them, were thrown into the fields to be eaten by the dogs.

The British reputation was not improved by the reports that were received from twelve Japanese sailors who had shipped with Saris. These men, returning from their voyage to London, alleged that Saris had refused to pay the rate of wages that had been agreed upon. Knowing that Adams was the official intermediary between English-men and Japanese they sought him out, seized him by the throat and threatened to kill him unless he interceded in their behalf. Adams luckily was rescued but, when he lodged complaints with the daimyo, he received no satisfaction. Instead the English factory was picketed by Japanese guards. The assailants were unpunished.

Much of the difficulty is perhaps traceable to the change that had occurred in Japan's government. The Shogunate was no longer faced by possible insurrection for, by the successful siege of Osaka in 1615, all opposition had been quelled. Again, as in Hideyoshi's time, the central government could set itself to reduce the likelihood of foreign interference. Renewed assaults against the liberty of foreigners had followed the end of civil war in 1587 and in 1600; anti-alienism was, therefore, to be expected now that the rebellious daimyos had been overwhelmed.

In May 1616, moreover, the Shogun Iyeyasu died. The new Shogun Hidetada refused to renew the liberal charter which, according to the Japanese, gave foreigners more freedom than natives might enjoy. By the new grant of trading privileges Great Britain was reduced to the same level as Portugal and Holland. No alien might hereafter live or trade in any locality except Nagasaki or Hirado.

The right to cancel Iyeyasu's original charter was, of course, questionable since no time limit had been placed upon the grant and since, presumably, the charter was perpetual, but British protests were unheeded. Had England been prepared to exert force to compel Japan to respect the agreement the cancellation might have led to grave consequences, but in 1616 Britain was in no position to wage war single-handedly in the Far East. Hidetada's limitations could not be successfully resisted.

Further humiliations followed fast. In August 1617 a letter arrived from London expressing King James's happiness at the establishment of trade relationships and assuring Japan of England's friendliness. To Japanese, however, the message proved exceedingly unwelcome for, upon presentation of the document, the addressee was seen to be Iyeyasu who had died a year before. The letter was accordingly re-fused as "an ominous portent," a refusal which the British not un-naturally misconstrued as a sign of Japan's boorishness.

Even Adams was discovering that Englishmen were unwelcome. He was assailed a second time upon the streets but, because he was well aware that under the strict Japanese law the culprits would be cut to pieces, he refused to press a charge. His seeming willingness to endure insult strengthened the belief that Britishers might be attacked with complete impunity.

English prestige declined still more when, in August 1618, the Dutch brought into Hirado harbor as a prize of war the British ship *Attendance*. The Englishmen protested but Hidetada refused to intervene. Any act of aggression outside the waters of Japan, he intimated, was none of his concern. The victor might bring his prize to sell in Japan's harbors. Hidetada, in short, granted to the Dutch the very boon which Iyeyasu, five years before, had refused to give to Adams. Holland took advantage of her freedom by taking two other British ships and displaying them proudly at Hirado. Eng-land, it was evident to Japanese, was weak and helpless in comparison to the mighty Netherlands.

Indeed, when three English sailors escaped from the captured ships the Dutchmen, aided by a mob of Japanese, dared to storm the gates of the Hirado factory. The Hirado daimyo, hearing that Holland had proclaimed war against the British "both by sea and land with fire and sword," professed neutrality. To save his own people from chance shots he forbade the natives to walk near the English houses but he took no steps to prevent the Hollanders from sailing to and fro before the English wharves brandishing their swords and shouting threats. Not until Adams fired upon the Dutch ships was any stop put to this warfare and then only, the English complained, because a cannon ball killed a Japanese.

In July 1620 the ship *James Royall*, commanded by Martin Pring, discoverer of Penobscot Bay, brought the welcome news that Britain and Holland were again at peace. His rollicking mariners, however, brought no peace for the Hirado Englishmen. They were, in Pring's own words, "an incorrigible scum of rascals, sea-gulls, and sea-apes whom the land hath rejected for their wicked lives and ungodly behavior." The sole British consolation seemed to be that, in their view, the Dutch were worse. "They goe stagring drunk up and downe the streetes, slashing and cutting ofe each other with knyves lyke mad men."

By riots in the taverns, the sailors, Dutch and British alike, constantly disturbed the peace. Innkeepers, too often bilked, were resorting to the practice of keeping the roisterers captive until the bills were paid in full; the sailors, relying on their superior size, fought their way to freedom. Japanese were injured in the skirmishes.

How long this might have continued, it is impossible to say, but England's need for her Hirado factory was drawing to a close. The trading had been insignificant and now that Holland was an ally, no further necessity remained for England's holding Hirado as a base for naval operations. The further hope that Hirado might prove valuable as a center from which to open trade with China was found baseless. Convinced that there was no longer either peace or profit to be won by further commerce with Japan, the British closed their headquarters. In 1623, the grounds and buildings were returned to the local daimyo, the trading license was surrendered, and English ships ceased to arrive.

The subsequent remembrance of these episodes by Japanese is somewhat curious. For years, Japan ignored the one-time presence of the British, then suddenly, when modern English merchants began to delve into past history, the Japanese professed warm interest. In 1927, a tablet was erected to mark the site of the former English House at Hirado, but without mention of the hardships that the English had to overcome and without comment on the character of the sailors who had reveled in the town.

Will Adams, too, was virtually forgotten after his death in 1620. For years his burial place was unknown, though a Tokyo street was named in his honor. Then, in 1872, a Yokohama Englishman, after long research into the records, located the site of a supposed tomb, and arranged for a memorial, neatly palisaded. A sum of money was set aside by him for upkeep. By 1901, however, the site was again a dilapidated ruin, "encrusted with mud and overgrown with lichens." Again the British community arranged for a fitting memorial at Yokosuka, yet again, by 1909, the site was sadly neglected, the railings being stolen and the monument broken. At irregular intervals since that time, Buddhist memorial services have been held in his honor.

With British competition removed, Holland bent every effort toward discrediting her remaining rival, Portugal. Misrepresentation of Portugal's intention, intrigue at the Shogun's court, price undercutting, and, according to Holland's enemies, deliberate forgery, were instruments relied upon to win a complete trade monopoly for the Netherlands.

Indeed the British were not clear of Hirado before the Dutch opened their campaign. In December 1620 a Dutch man-of-war escorted into port a small Portuguese frigate which, the Hollanders declared, carried two disguised missionaries. Further investigation disclosed a small packet of letters seemingly sent from foreign nations to native Christians in Japan. The letters promised help to Japanese converts to overthrow the Shogun.

Few people would today place full trust in the authenticity of the documents so conveniently discovered, but Japanese officialdom received the letters at face value. Again an anti-foreign feeling, cunningly fanned by Holland, raged within the Empire. The captured letters seemed to corroborate the whispered rumors of another northern plot.

Masamune Date, daimyo of Sendai, across the island from the disaffected Sado, gave occasion for the new fears of insurrection. Date, one of the rebels who had opposed Hideyoshi but who, because he had turned pro-Shogun after the battle of Odawara in 1590, had been confirmed in his fief, dispatched a private mission to Europe. Three months after the arrival of the *Clove,* this secret embassy, headed by the Christian-trained Rokuyemon Hasekura, slipped away from Sendai. Avoiding the usual track of traders, Hasekura crossed the Pacific with his ten companions, arrived at Acapulco in Mexico and, in January 1615, had an audience with Philip III of Spain. After an eight months' stay in Spain, a delay which the Shogun interpreted as a period of intrigue against the established Japanese administration, Hasekura passed on to Rome where he won the favor of Pope Paul V. Upon receipt of a letter, signed by Date, submitting "our crown and all our vassals to Holy Church," and adding, "I desire that my subjects shall actually make themselves Christian," the Pope made Hasekura a Roman citizen and a senator of the papal state. Date's postscript that he himself "would embrace the Christian teachings if certain matters did not hinder me and if invincible motives did not stand in my way" was interpreted as implying merely a postponement of the daimyo's eventual conversion. Rich gifts were prepared by the Vatican for the delight of Hasekura's daimyo.

Holland's diplomatic agents flashed the news of this mysterious mission to Amsterdam and, eventually, to Hirado, adding embellishments which would be certain to convict the southern Europeans of activities treasonable in Japanese eyes. The captured letters amply proved the guilt of Hasekura and seriously implicated Masamune Date. The latter, perhaps to save his own province, disowned the presumed duplicity of his agent, reaffirmed loyalty to the Shogun, and condemned Hasekura to death upon the envoy's eventual return.

Even to this day the true motives prompting this Hasekura mission are in doubt. Probably the expedition was wholly religious and commercial in character, but there is strong evidence to indicate that Date had in mind a remarkable ulterior purpose. Certain ancient documents presented to Emperor Meiji on the occasion of a state visit to Sendai in 1876, and since carefully concealed in the secret vaults of the Foreign Office suggest that Date actually considered a military attack upon Europe. "Date planned, if the detested Christian creed again obtained a foothold in Japan, to raise an army, sail for Europe, and attack Christianity in its very heart at Rome." The plan was abandoned when Hasekura reported that the distance was too great for any expedition to be sent.

Japanese Christians did not escape the consequences of this new plot. In August 1622, after protracted torturings to compel confession, to learn the complicity of confederates and to secure every possible detail of the supposed conspiracy, the disguised missionaries, together with the officers and crew of the captured frigate, were burned to death.

Other massacres followed. During 1622, 118 suspected Christians were put to death, after long imprisonments in which men, women, and children were confined in narrow cells where they could neither walk a single step nor stand erect. Three grown people were alloted to a space eighty-four inches long by thirty-two inches in width.

The crimes for which the prisoners were taken sometimes were trivial. Seven-year-old children were beheaded and burned for gathering relics from the place of execution; an eighty-five-year-old man was thrown into the sea with two big stones, "each heavier than four men could carry," tied to his feet as a penalty for unwittingly harboring a fugitive. Old women were beheaded on suspicion of praying.

The usual punishment was decapitation, but forty-six of the prisoners were slowly roasted to death. Carefully the executioners placed the convicts at some distance from the flames in order to prolong the torture and, with the same intent, the fires were deliberately subdued whenever the flames mounted. Thus the roastings were timed to last between an hour and a half and two hours for each victim.

Englishmen were reluctant witnesses to both the conviction and the execution of these unfortunates. Thirteen Dutch and British ships were in harbor during most of the anti-foreign fury but, as Richard Cocks wrote to his superiors at London, "yf we had not absolutely proved the Portingalls to be padres, that themperour ment to have put Captain Leonard Camps and me to death and to have sezed on all we had in the cuntrey. . . . God send us well out of Japon, for I doubt it wilbe every day worse than other."

England had no hope of gain, seeking only, as Cocks intimated, to be well out of the land, but Holland expected to be rewarded by the gift of complete commercial monopoly. Probably she would have received her wish but, by the usual ill luck that followed early European activities in the East, the Dutchmen were detected in what the Japanese termed sharp practice of another sort.

A special Netherlandish commission, headed by Peter Nuyts, came up from Batavia to arrange for an exclusive trade concession. In order to magnify his status in Japan, Nuyts announced himself as "ambassador from the King of Holland." The Shogun, ever anxious to observe punctilious etiquette, ordered that Nuyts be appropriately received. But when the credentials were examined the signatures on the Nuyts papers were discovered to be those of the Java Council. The Shogun, considering the Java Council no higher in rank than members of his own provincial groups, believed himself insulted. Nuyts was dismissed in disgrace. Holland failed to receive the longed-for trade monopoly.

Soon thereafter Nuyts was appointed Dutch governor of Formosa. Angered by his treatment in Yedo, he exacted a childish vengeance. When two small junks, sailing from Japan to Foochow for silk, touched at one of the harbors under his control, Nuyts refused clearance papers to the ships. He seized their sails and rudders—a practice later copied by Japan—and delayed the junks until the monsoon had changed.

Word was smuggled to Japan that the crews were in captivity. Yahei Hamada of Nagasaki, a frequent trader to Formosa, gathered five hundred adventurers to free the prisoners. When near the island, in April 1628, they disguised themselves in the huge hats and heavy straw raincoats of peasant colonists and asked admission. Some days later, after the "immigrants" had supposedly scattered to the fields, the warriors assembled, attacked the governor's mansion, seized Nuyts and insisted on indemnity for all the losses of the junks. Hamada demanded that Nuyts load, in addition, one Dutch ship and two Japanese junks with tribute and that Nuyts send his twelve-year-old son as a hostage to Japan.

Nuyts was forced to agree to these conditions and to swear that no gun was ever to be fired at any future time from Fort Zeelandia, the Dutch stronghold on Formosa. As further penalty the Shogun seized nine Dutch ships then in Japanese harbors and ordered the suspension of all Dutch trade over a three-year period. Nuyts was himself eventually compelled to go to Yedo to seek forgiveness. On his arrival he was jailed.

The series of events sadly lowered the Netherlandish prestige. That Holland had been crushed in war and that Japanese arms were amply sufficient to overwhelm the Europeans became widely accepted beliefs. The arrival of at least two embassies to solicit Japan's pardon intensified the feeling of superiority to the fair-haired foreigners. Insults, it was believed, could freely be offered to people of such low estate.

Instead of winning a monopoly, therefore, the unhappy Dutchmen found themselves in danger of exclusion from the Empire. A special mission, led by Hendrik Haganaar, was sent out from Batavia, in September 1635, to restore Holland to favor. With him, as assistant and interpreter, went François Caron, a clever diplomat and an excellent observer of social and political conditions. Caron, Dutch-born of French parentage, had first visited Japan as cook upon a freighter. Leaving the ship at Hirado he joined the Dutch factory, married a Japanese and made himself a thorough master of the language. Caron and Haganaar, arriving in Yedo, were refused an audience by the Shogun. For more than a year they waited, while Nuyts remained in prison, until the Shogun "had time to study their request." They used the interval to prepare what is undoubtedly the most complete account of Japan that had ever been compiled.

Caron and Haganaar found Japan obsessed by anti-alien hysteria. A new Shogun, Iyemitsu, was compelling every foreigner to trample yearly on a picture of Jesus. This practice, the so-called *fumiye,* effectively separated the more intense Christians from their less stubborn brethren and thus, as the Shogun believed, disclosed those aliens who were plotting sedition. The device could also be employed against Japanese suspected of being Christian converts. The same practice was used as late as 1935 to detect adherents of a banned religious sect.

For those who refused the *fumiye,* a second means of detection was called into activity. This was the "torment of the fosse." A deep hole was dug and over it a gallows was erected. The victim, tightly bound, was then hung head downward into the hole. Closely fitted boards were fastened over the opening around the suspect's waist so that all light and air were excluded from the pit. One hand of the victim was fastened to his side; the other was left free to enable him, if he desired, to make a sign of recantation. Those who abjured their faith were freed; others slowly suffocated.

There were, of course, other modes of torture. On arriving at Hirado, Haganaar saw thirty-seven Christians beheaded and then cut into small pieces. Converts who refused to rejoin their ancestral faiths were wrapped in straw sacks and burned to death. Some had their backs slit open, others were thrown into hot springs to boil to death.

Haganaar was in Japan when Iyemitsu, seeking to enforce his anti-Christian edict of 1635, fifth in a series of similar ordinances, ordered that all Portuguese be confined to the tiny island of Deshima in Nagasaki Harbor. Guardhouses were erected on all the land approaches to the city. No traveler was henceforth to be allowed to enter or leave Nagasaki without a permit from the Shogun.

Short-sightedly the Dutchmen gloated when these restrictions were imposed. The measures seemed preliminary to an impending exclusion of the Portuguese merchants. Willingly they swore oaths that they were not Christians but Hollanders, a distinction that seemed at the time to satisfy Iyemitsu's desires. Haganaar and his associates were sure that all the trade would now be a Dutch monopoly, since Portugal could not conduct much commerce from Deshima.

Portugal's permission to reside even at the Deshima prison was short-lived. Both merchants and missionaries were soon to be deported for complicity in an agrarian rebellion.

Opinions differ as to the cause that compelled the farmers of Shimabara, a lovely port town near Nagasaki, to rise against their daimyo, Nobutsuna Matsudaira. By one explanation, five Christian warriors desired to restore the missionaries to their former influence. The plan, according to anti-alien Japanese, was to capture Nagasaki, to open all Japan to foreign trade, and then to invite foreign troops to help overturn Iyemitsu's rule. The leader of the insurrection, Shiro Masuda, was allegedly in Portuguese pay.

A second, and probably more trustworthy, explanation accused Matsudaira of imposing impossible taxation upon the peasantry. The farmers, it is said, aided by the five former soldiers who had been reduced from military prominence to a sort of serfdom, rebelled. They were especially incensed by the practice of *mino-odori,* a fire dance required of all who could not pay their taxes. Those in arrears were compelled to don straw raincoats which were set on fire while the daimyo and his men lay bets on which of the victims would live longest. The torment of the fosse was required of wives of debtors, the women being suspended naked by the legs for an hour at a time.

The revolt began in October 1637, when Masuda gathered nine thousand followers, among whom were a thousand women. Mystical elements, perhaps a propaganda campaign, helped swell the ranks. Masuda, a samurai youth of only seventeen, was, it was believed, a sort of Japanese Messiah. Prophecies made a quarter of a century before predicted that "a remarkable youth will appear. He, without study, will acquire all knowledge." As a portent of his coming, it was said, "a wistaria flower will blossom on a dead tree." Masuda was believed to be the youth thus anticipated. "He excelled all men in knowledge and skill, especially in literature and the arts of war." He was so gentle that he could call down a flying bird and cause it to light on his hand, and "he could run over the white waves." Moreover, as one of the deposed warriors testified, a red wistaria had suddenly appeared on a dead cherry tree at Shimabara.

The mutineers seized the daimyo's stores of rice. Then, shutting themselves within the walls of a supposedly impregnable castle, they demanded Matsudaira's resignation. Disaffection spread rapidly. Two neighboring provinces joined the revolt. By December the number of rebels increased to over forty thousand.

Iyemitsu, fearing foreign intervention, ordered five nearby daimyos to unite their armies and to suppress the insurrection. He demanded Masuda's instant submission. The boy leader replied that he would willingly agree to die if Iyemitsu should command it, but that the rebels would not yield to any other officer. Iyemitsu refused the offer, and sent seventy thousand troops to besiege the castle.

Foreigners were soon embroiled. The rebels, having no noble leader to whom to swear allegiance, accepted the Christian insignia.

The war cry adopted by the insurrectionists was "San Diego," their badge a linen coat upon which the crucifix had been embroidered. To what extent these symbols represent the influence of deeply held religious conviction has long been a matter for heated argument, though, except for the five leaders, few convinced Christians were included in the rising. Iyemitsu, however, fearing the influence of the missionaries, held the Portuguese largely responsible for fomenting the disorder.

Holland came to the Shogun's aid. Nicolaes Koeckebacker, *opperhoofd,* or chief, of the Dutch East India Company factory at Hirado, offered assistance in defeating the rebellious peasants. He had, as he admitted, two motives for the offer. The first was economic, for one of the daimyos under attack owed the Hollanders a debt of two thousand florins which would not be collectible if the rebels should succeed. There was a second factor in that, with Portugal seemingly mixed up with the insurrectionists, Holland could win political advantage by aiding the Shogun.

In January 1638, Koeckebacker sent six barrels of powder, all he then possessed, to the forces besieging the rebels. A month later, when a Dutch ship came into Hirado, he forwarded five of its largest guns to bombard the rebel stronghold.

His offer was at first refused, either, as the Japanese asserted, because it was beneath native dignity to use foreign weapons to quell domestic discord, or because the loyal troops were so arrayed that bombardment would peril their safety. The latter reason is probably more trustworthy because, after fifteen more Dutch guns had been procured and after the loyal troops were moved, more than four hundred cannon balls were shot into the rebel ranks. In April 1638 the peasants surrendered, after a siege of more than a hundred days.

The vengeance exacted was terrible. Forty thousand rebels were massacred. Seventeen thousand heads, including that of the young Masuda, were displayed on poles as a warning to all conspirators. Nagasaki Bay was full of floating corpses. One man alone was spared of all the rebel forces, an aged idol maker who was allowed to go to Yedo to apologize to Iyemitsu, in the name of all his murdered fellows.

Iyemitsu was unquestionably worried over the possibility of foreign intervention. Portuguese complicity in the Shimabara uprising seemed to indicate that alien influence might again be exerted to his detriment. Not content, therefore, with restricting the arrival of foreigners in Japan, and dissatisfied with the limitations already placed upon their freedom, Iyemitsu enforced still other regulations to prevent too close contact between Japanese and Westerners.

A series of edicts forbade Japanese subjects from traveling abroad. Any native of Japan who might ever leave the country, either by accident or by design, was forbidden to return under penalty of death. To reduce the possibility that Japanese might go abroad, drastic laws were passed to control native shipping. All ships of foreign design were ordered to be destroyed. Only clumsy junks, built with open sterns and large square rudders unfit for the open sea, could henceforth be employed in coastal shipping. Because the mountainous nature of the country made sea travel indispensable Iyemitsu could not forbid all shipping, as he might no doubt have preferred, but he could prevent seaworthy ships from becoming available to his people.

These laws, as subsequent events were to show, caused the death of thousands of Japanese fishermen and traders. Once the junks were forced off the coast by stress of storm the crude rudders would be washed away by heavy seas, the vessels would fall into the troughs of waves and the single masts would be rolled out. The junks would then be helpless and the men would drift at the mercy of the ocean currents. No sailor, unluckily carried off to sea, could legally return alive.

Japan was thus isolated by edict of the Shogun, but additional controls upon the foreigners were deemed advisable. As a first step toward Japan's future safety Iyemitsu planned to rid the Empire of the Portuguese.

IV

CURBING THE DUTCHMEN
1638–1686

EVERY Portuguese was now deported. Not even a half-caste child was permitted to remain. Stringent orders decreed that if Japanese mothers sought to adopt Eurasian children into their own families every relative was to suffer punishment. All Spanish and Portuguese ships arriving in Japan were to be burned and their crews were to be executed.

Final steps were taken to suppress the hated Christian faith. The torment of the fosse was used increasingly to induce recantations. Clerics who abjured their faith were compelled to be identified with executed criminals, taking the names, swords, properties, and even the wives of the dead men. Those unwilling to comply were put to death.

Portugal still hoped, however, that Japan might change her mind. Not even the execution of sixty-one survivors of a galleon wrecked off Kyushu in 1640 weakened the Portuguese hopes. If only Japan knew, the Portuguese believed, that the hatred against Portugal was due to unfair propaganda by unscrupulous trade rivals, the exclusion laws might be repealed.

Two ships, therefore, were sent from Macao in 1644 to reopen trade. The embassy was particularly charged not to stress the religious note but to reassure Japan of Portugal's willingness to comply with Japan's domestic laws. Portugal, in all probability, was moved chiefly by the hope of securing some of the excellent Japanese copper for use in the casting of bronze cannon at Macao.

The reception was distinctly hostile. Japan, anticipating a punitive expedition, gathered huge armies. Women and children were taken inland for safety. Plots were matured to take the Portuguese by surprise. These plots were, however, foiled when the Portuguese leaders refused to allow more than three Japanese at a time to visit the ships. Cleverly the Portuguese refused to surrender their dignity when they declined to carry on negotiations with any Japanese other than the Shogun himself. Nagasaki officials kept the foreigners in a sort of internment until Yedo could be consulted. Upwards of six hundred junks were drawn in solid line across the harbor to prevent escape.

The great armament, the largest ever gathered to defend Japan against invasion, was not intended for display alone. As soon as the line of boats was stretched across the harbor, a pontoon bridge was built. Over this an armed horseman rode brandishing a spear and threatening to lead his cavalry against the ship if any hostile move were made. For a month the Portuguese embassy was held under close observation. Then orders were received from Yedo to release the prisoners with instructions that they must never come again.

"So long as the sun shall warm the earth let no Christian come to Japan," the Portuguese were warned. "Even the Christian's God, if he violate this prohibition, shall pay for it with his head."

Holland had achieved her purpose of banishing her commercial rivals, but Holland was itself to suffer an attack upon its privileges. Within two years after the Shimabara rising the Dutch were transferred from Hirado to the Deshima quarters vacated by the Portuguese. The annual fleet of Dutch ships allowed to trade was reduced in numbers and, when the Dutch commercial chief went up to Yedo for his annual visit of homage, the Shogun required him to wait three months for an audience.

For continued trade privileges Holland suffered serious abasement. Her merchants were called upon each year to swear not to hold any communication with the Christian sect, not to bring ministers into the Empire, and to act as spies for the Shogun. Each year the Hollanders were compelled to report all news of foreign activities which "it may be desirous for the Shogun to hear." These regulations, thus clapped upon the Netherlanders as a result of the grim religious conflicts of the seventeenth century, were largely responsible for the failure of subsequent European efforts to reopen the Japanese markets. Holland, to ensure its trade monopoly, reported every proposed expedition of her trade rivals in the East as a renewed missionary enterprise. She discredited her rivals as either imperialists bent on taking Japan's territory or as religious fanatics seeking to destroy Japan's cherished faith.

Though the Dutch privileges were reduced, Holland still hoped for a wider range. Haganaar had brought back to Batavia reports that the Spaniards were drawing rich treasure from the so-called "Gold and Silver Islands," located, it was rumored, some four hundred miles eastward of Japan. Gold was also believed plentiful on a northern island called Yeso.

After Matthys Kwast had failed to find either of these areas, Anthony van Diemen, governor of Batavia, ordered a second scouting voyage. Two ships, the *Kastrikoom,* under Marten Gerritzen de Vries, and the *Breskens,* under Hendrik Cornelys Schaep, were assigned in 1643 to check up on the rumors.

"You are to behave in a friendly and obliging manner to the inhabitants you shall meet," the instructions read, "and are to make inquiry of them of the condition of the country. You are to see if the inhabitants have gold and silver, and, if so, in what estimation they are held, who is the sovereign of the land and what commodities are prized. You are to take leave in all friendship."

The two ships left Batavia in February 1643 but three months later were separated by a storm. The *Kastrikoom* ventured as far as Yeso or the Hokkaido, finding tall pines suitable for masts—a most welcome discovery for Dutchmen whose homeland provided no such naval stores. Yetorup and Urop in the Kuriles were also sighted but beyond them the *Kastrikoom* came to "the wide wild north sea." De Vries preferred to turn back toward Batavia. En route he put in at Nambu, a northern Japanese port, where several of his men were arrested and were sent off to Yedo. De Vries did not delay to learn their fate, but put to sea again.

The *Breskens* was meanwhile following in the *Kastrikoom's* wake. No land was discovered that would correspond to the mythical "Gold and Silver Islands," though Schaep reports sighting what he thought to be the American continent in latitude 47 degrees, longitude 173 degrees. Charts of the Pacific show no land whatever in this vicinity.

On his way home to Batavia, Schaep also called at Nambu, the port in Mutsu province where the *Kastrikoom's* men had been arrested. Schaep was well aware that events had been occurring during the past five years that might make Japan unsafe for exploration parties but he allowed himself to be "deceived from his guard by the quiet and civil manners of the Japanese." Trade was brisk and the inhabitants seemed "pleasant people of good understanding," but suddenly, when Schaep and his chief officers were at a garden party, the Dutchmen were arrested. The ostensible charge was that the ship had fired a gun off the Japanese coast, contrary to Japan's law; the real accusation, it later appeared, was that the Hollanders were Christians.

Eleven of the Hollanders were manacled, were tightly corded, and were jailed. Schaep, after much entreaty, was permitted to send a letter to his ship informing the remainder of his men that he was arrested and suggesting that they wait four months before undertaking any relief mission. Then the prisoners were led across Japan. For twenty days they were conducted, still manacled and corded, through northern Japan until they came to Yedo.

Severe cross-examinations, "conducted in a most embarrassing and captious manner," then ensued. The Hollanders, afraid to admit that they had been sent to seek the Gold and Silver Islands, excited suspicion by their evasive answers. Apostate priests were called in to advise the Japanese inquisitors concerning the religion of the captives. These apostates "who looked exceedingly pitiful; their eyes and cheeks strangely fallen in, their hands black and blue, and their whole bodies sadly misused and macerated by torture," terrified the *Breskens* captives. Similar suffering, Schaep was sure, would be their lot.

Word came, fortunately, from the chief director, or *opperhoofd,* of the Deshima establishment vouching for the honesty of the Dutch prisoners. After a four months' confinement, Schaep and his men were released, but only after signing a bond that, should it ever be discovered that either the *Kastrikoom* or the *Breskens* had landed missionaries, the captives would be produced "from any part of the world" to stand trial. The lives and property of the entire Dutch establishment at Deshima were pledged to this condition.

Dutch prestige was not improved by the Schaep incident. Holland's willingness to endure insult seemed almost boundless. To maintain exclusive privileges which, at the time of the *Breskens* affair, produced net yearly profits of approximately four million dollars, or about ten percent on the investments made in the Dutch East India Company, the Netherlanders suffered discourtesies which, in almost any other region of the world, would certainly have led to war. Far from issuing strong protests at the treatment of the *Breskens* men, the Dutch sent a formal embassy to crave Japan's forgiveness for Schaep's violation of the law.

Holland had, however, an additional motive in the matter. Her diplomats at Amsterdam had recently concluded a treaty to aid Portugal against the Spaniards and had followed the treaty, in 1645, with a formal alliance. It was essential that the news of such a change in Dutch policy should be broken to Japan in the most conciliatory manner possible. Dr. Peter Blockhuys, rector of a Latin school, was selected to represent Holland, at the munificent salary of thirty dollars monthly.

En route to Batavia, Blockhuys fell seriously ill. The Java officials, realizing the psychologic value of having a European, especially sent from Holland, conduct negotiations in Japan, insisted that he complete his mission. There was to be no repetition of the Nuyts affair! But as the physicians were well aware that Blockhuys might succumb to his illness en route, special instructions were secretly supplied his secretary, Andries Frisius. If Blockhuys were to die before reaching Nagasaki, Frisius was ordered to embalm the body, to enclose it in a coffin of fine wood, smuggled aboard the ship for this express purpose, and to carry the corpse to Nagasaki as proof that an envoy had actually been sent. Blockhuys did die before his ship came to Japan; the body was embalmed and was exhibited to the Nagasaki officials. An elaborate funeral was held at Deshima after the mission's arrival.

Frisius assumed command of the embassy. He was under explicit instructions to conceal the truth about Holland's being a republic, for republics were not approved by Japan's rulers. He bore instructions purporting to be signed by the "King of the Netherlands." Frisius was told to memorize his answers to such questions as might be anticipated so that when the questions were asked a second time his replies could be identical. In the event that he was asked unexpected questions, he was to plead his low estate as an excuse for not answering. The peace between Holland and Portugal was to be passed off as part of a pan-European scheme to ally all Europe against the wicked Turks. Frisius was particularly cautioned to thank the Japanese seven times for every courtesy and, above all, "to take special heed that no one indulges in strong drink or lechery. Punish all such ill-doers severely. See to it that the members of your suite keep their nails trimmed short, their hair well combed, that they wear clean clothes, and that they wash often."

Probably the instructions were drafted by François Caron, who had been on the Haganaar mission of 1635 and who was rightfully regarded as the foreigner best informed on Japanese customs. But even Caron's careful instructions failed to guarantee Frisius a warm welcome. Whether the arrival of a dead ambassador seemed an evil omen to Japan, or whether the Shogun was genuinely angry at the *Bres-*

kens affair, the mission was rejected. After waiting in Yedo for four months, Frisius received his answer. The Shogun was superficially friendly, granting small presents to the members of the Dutch suite, but he refused to restore the Dutch to favor.

Holland accepted the rebuff. Probably the hope of continuing the annual ten percent net profits was too alluring for the Netherlanders to insist too stiffly on their dignity. Knowing little of oriental psychologies, the Dutch assumed that tolerance of insult and concessions to native pride would be the surest means for regaining friendship. The Hollanders did not realize that acceptance of discourtesies without exaction of proper reparation proved that the Dutch were folk of exceedingly low caste.

The Netherlands were protected also, in a sense, because the knowledge of the abasement could not spread to Europe. Only a narrow circle of Dutch merchants knew how cavalierly the traders were treated. By their complete censorship over outgoing Japanese news the Hollanders could keep the reports of their humiliation from their European rivals, and even from the great majority of their own countrymen.

A further effort was resolved upon to regain favor. Zacharias Waggenaar assumed the task of begging Japan's pardon for Schaep's misadventures and of putting the Portuguese alliance in the "proper light." The project now seems a comparatively simple matter but, through misfortune and mismanagement, years elapsed before complete trust was restored. Waggenaar tried brilliantly with bribery and flattery, but to no avail. Japan accepted what she construed as Holland's homage, but held herself aloof. Even the offering of a cassowary, a strange ostrich-like bird found only in Molucca, failed to soften Japan's attitude. The port officials, baffled by the problem of transporting the huge bird from Nagasaki to the capital, refused to allow the monster to be landed. Waggenaar was ordered to take the present back to Batavia. Worried over the cost of feeding the huge bird, he sought to rid himself of the burden. On the return voyage to Java, the cassowary conveniently fell overboard.

Still another effort at conciliation collapsed because of an ill-timed arrival. Waggenaar landed at Deshima soon after a series of disasters which were regarded by the superstitious as results of divine anger due to Japan's departure from the ancient ways. Land tenancy disputes, complicated by religious fanaticism, were causing riots in the provinces. A great fire in 1657 destroyed two-thirds of Yedo. Kiuchi Sogoro, a peasant leader, ventured to petition the Shogun in protest against misrule and, although both Sogoro and his wife were crucified for their temerity, after watching the beheading of their children, the Shogun was still indignant at their breach of etiquette.

For much of these calamities the foreigners were blamed. Statesmen were certain that the gods were angry because too great concessions had been made to strangers. The violation of Japan's sacred soil, the native religious leaders explained, merited punishment. Japan could regain favor only by strict repression of the alien ideas that were polluting the Empire.

New religious persecutions started. Beginning with the discovery that a seventy-five-year-old woman was keeping a picture of "the evil religion" in a cave at Kori, in Kyushu, the pogrom spread throughout the southern island. As in the Shimabara uprising of twenty years before, there was a mystical content to the new excitements. Predictions were made that on December 15, 1657, a world catastrophe would occur and that a thirteen-year-old boy, grandson of the aged Christian woman, would "play the rôle of Savior of the World." The boy was, it was believed, "more marvelous than Shiro Masuda," the Shimabara prodigy.

More than six hundred victims suffered in this so-called "Kori Debacle." Four hundred and eleven of the suspects were executed and ninety-eight died in jail. Women and very young children were victims of the persecution. A five-year-old boy was kept captive until his death half a century later. Among the martyrs were 103 persons under fifteen years of age, and ninety-six women.

Such was the domestic situation of Japan when Waggenaar arrived to plead for Holland's restoration to favor. Under the most favorable circumstances his task would have been difficult but, as it happened, he was himself an unprepossessing envoy. Word had arrived from China, by the annual trading junks, that Waggenaar had been expelled from Canton for his niggardliness in not giving proper presents. Although Waggenaar explained that Chinese officials had demanded bribes heavier than trade prospects warranted, his loss of face by his expulsion, his consequent low-caste status in the eyes of Japanese, and his evident parsimony all limited his efficiency. Holland was fortunate to keep any commercial rights whatever under such conditions. For a brief time, indeed, it seemed as though Netherlandish trade would end. Disasters to Dutch arms in Formosa when, in 1661, 1,500 Hollanders were beaten by the pirate chief Koxinga, ended Japan's fear of Holland's military might. A wave of nationalistic sentiment engulfed Japan, for although Koxinga was born of a Chinese father, his mother was a Japanese of the proud Tagawa family. Koxinga's victory was regarded as the second Japanese conquest of the Dutch.

France and Britain were taking steps to enter into competition with the harassed Hollanders. François Caron, the cook who had risen to become head of the Dutch trading center and who had helped Hagenaar, had gone to Paris. There he persuaded Jean Baptiste Colbert, the great mercantilist, that the Orient afforded opportunity for profit. Through his suggestions two expeditions were dispatched to open trade routes to the East. La Salle visited Canada to discover an overland passage to the Orient; Caron sailed toward Japan with a letter to the Shogun asking trade privileges. Neither expedition was successful. La Salle was diverted into making other explorations, while Caron was drowned by shipwreck off the coast of Portugal.

England had much better luck. In 1665 the Dutch ship *Slot Hooningan* was driven by tempest into the very midst of a British fleet. Aboard the vessel was a mass of correspondence giving the secrets of the Dutch East India Company trade. These letters, turned over to the English Company, reawakened interest in oriental commerce. Though internal jealousies and the loss at sea of two ships postponed the British attack on Japan's trade, the 340-ton *Return* was finally dispatched from Bantam for Japan.

The Dutch were dismayed at the possibility that the British might resume their competition, but dared offer no open resistance. Pretending to be favorable to the British scheme, they asked the *Return* to call at Formosa to pick up certain Dutch passengers and then, assured that the Britishers would be delayed in transit, wrote warning letters to Deshima. Replies were received in October 1672, that the Shogun was grateful for the advance notice of Britain's arrival and that Holland could be assured that the British would be forbidden any privileges.

Wholly unaware of this double dealing, the English trade commissioners, Simon Delboe, Hammond Gibben, and William Ramsden, sailed for Japan. In order to avoid any possible connection with the Portuguese or with the proscribed religious beliefs, they made changes in the British flag. The usual Cross of St. George was not displayed. The *Return* sailed into Nagasaki Harbor, July 9, 1673, under a flag striped red and white.

Evidently the precautions were well taken. The *Return* was treated as an enemy. Port officials searched her carefully for contraband. Every scrap of paper was closely inspected and the contents of the documents were noted in the officials' memorandum books. Sails, rudder, and arms were taken from the ship. Orders prevented anyone from leaving the vessel until Yedo should give permission for the ship to unload. Five guard boats and two armed junks were anchored nearby to keep watch over the intruder.

Meanwhile the Englishmen were plied with questions. Why, the Japanese inquired, had so many years elapsed since the last arrival of a British ship? Who was the English King, to whom was he married, and what children did he have? This evidently was an important question, for it was asked over and over again without change of wording to each member of the crew. The identical question was repeated many times for three successive days. The cross-examination was tedious, since the questions were asked in Portuguese, translated into Dutch, while the replies came back in Spanish, via a Dutch interpreter.

No information whatever was supplied to the Britishers' queries. The letter sent by Charles II to His Imperial Japanese Majesty (by whom the Shogun, not the Dairi, was intended) was refused because no official seal was attached. Fish, fruit, vegetables, eggs, and bread were supplied but "at an extraordinarily dear price."

A month passed, and then the reason for the constant insistence on Charles II's family relationships became clear. Yedo refused to trade because the English King was married to a Portuguese. The *Return,* it was announced, must sail at once. "We lived in the port of Nangasacque," writes Ramsden, "under continual fear." The *Return* sailed September 6, the last day of grace permitted, "though a small gale was blowing." Forty towboats pulled the vessel from the harbor, while five hundred guard boats lay nearby, filled with soldiers and munitions, "to prevent any tricks."

England was disappointed in the effort to renew her friendship with Japan, but there were brash individuals in the East India Company who hoped to win by trickery the trade forbidden them. Knowing that a limited intercourse was permitted to the Chinese, certain directors suggested that a colony of Chinese merchants be moved to Madras. These decoys, it was proposed, should load a ship with

British goods, and send a ship, manned by a Lascar crew, to Naga-saki. The plan proved impossible, however, since the Chinese straw men insisted on too large a share of the expected profits.

Failing in the attempt at deception, the Honorable East India Company then threw open trading privileges in Japan to any of its Madras employes. Little use was made of the privilege, but in 1683 an English ship touched at a port which the author, Christopher Fryke, calls "Nagato" (an old name for Shimonoseki), but which, from his description, seems more likely Nagasaki. By Fryke's account, three or four other British and some French vessels were also in the harbor at the time, though he cites no names and gives no particulars. No other corroboration seems available for the presence of such ships.

When we had begun to unlade, a parcel of Japaneses came to us to offer us some women, and asked us if we would not have some of them while we stayed there. But nobody hearkened to their proposal but the Master, and the Book-keeper.

While we lay there, I was invited on Board an English merchantman, and there had proffers made me if I would have gone along with them. But I would by no means hearken to their proposal, because it was as much as my life was worth, and what was yet more, I should have been Perjured if I had accepted it and forsook the Company.

In this Port dyed three of our men, and a Carpenter's Boy. Some Japanese carried them out of the Harbour in a small boat, into open sea, where they threw them over, for they are so far from suffering any foreigner to be Buried among them that they will not permit them to be thrown so much as in the water that is near them.

Fryke's ship foundered on the passage home, and thereafter British efforts lapsed. Portugal tried in 1686 to open trade by the scheme of restoring twelve Japanese sailors cast away near Macao. The Portuguese ship, after lying interned in harbor for a month, awaiting word from Yedo, was ordered to leave Japan. The castaways were, however, received, though no information is available as to their future fate. The laws of 1636 decreed death for sailors who attempted to return after touching foreign shores.

Holland now had her trade monopoly but the price demanded was exorbitant. Rival nations were convinced that the Dutch merchants were piling up enormous profits; the truth is that Holland would have made a greater gain by sending ships in ballast to Japan. Sugar, cloves, lead, wool and cotton thread, the chief commodities sent from Java to Japan, were sold in Deshima at a heavy monetary loss. Silk goods only could be marketed profitably, but silk was difficult for Dutchmen to acquire. The ten Chinese junks allowed to enter Nagasaki yearly carried sufficient to satisfy Japan's requirements.

During the first half century of Dutch commercial dealings the Japan trade returned a handsome profit. Virtually no serious restrictions were imposed by either the Shoguns or the local officers. But after 1661, when Koxinga expelled the Hollanders from their Formosan forts, conditions changed. Considering that the Occidentals were not unconquerable, the Japanese began to limit Western trade.

An early edict, issued in 1671, forbade the exportation of silver from the Empire. It was a measure dictated by fear lest the white metal be completely drained away. During the first years of Dutch trading, silver had been sent to Java literally by the ton. Gold, too, was being exported in huge quantities from Japan. On this trade alone the Hollanders were making a profit of a million florins yearly.

Prices in Japan were shooting skyward; internal trade was suffering. The Shogun's economic advisers explained the financial crises as due to Dutch greed for gold. New limitations were suggested for foreign traders.

In 1685 the total volume of imports was cut by edict of the Shogun to a maximum value of 300,000 ounces of silver, an amount equal, at the high 1937 silver price, to less than $200,000. The imports must consist, it was decreed, of certain enumerated articles, of which two-thirds were piece goods and weighable commodities on which the Dutch East India Company was compelled to take a loss. The remainder was to be in silk.

Further legislation restricted Japan's exports. After the limitation on the shipments of the precious metals, Holland turned to copper as a source of profit. By exporting copper in huge quantities for use in the mints of the world, the Dutchmen were making a profit of approximately one thousand percent. The new export regulations reduced the copper exports to two thousand tons annually. After 1685, therefore, less than one-quarter of the shipments sent from Deshima to Batavia could consist of the commodity upon which Holland relied for profit.

By open bribery the Hollanders found means of circumventing the copper restrictions, but worse measures were to follow. Realizing that the Dutch would accept almost any restrictions rather than lose the hope of future gain, the Japanese in 1696 debased the currency. The weight of the gold kobang, the coin exported by the Dutch for its bullion content, was reduced by more than a third; the Hollanders were, however, ordered to accept the cheapened coin at its old rate of exchange.

One important purpose was to stop the drain of gold. Instead of the former twenty-five percent profit made by melting the kobang for recoinage the Dutch would suffer a fifteen percent loss. Gold exportation stopped at once. The need for conserving the metal basis for Japan's currency was obvious. During the period of foreign trade the nation lost more than $200,000,000 worth of gold and silver. Japan's populace was not, of course, as completely dependent upon currency as are more modern industrialized peoples, but the degree of deflation was so serious as to embarrass the national economy.

A second, perhaps much more important, purpose of the currency regulations was to halt Japan's drift toward Westernism. Influential circles in the Empire, then as well as now, were convinced that alien influence was destroying Japan's unique spiritual culture. Frivolity, extravagance, waste, and corruption, it was believed, were encouraged by foreign trade. "Nothing is thought of," said Hakuseki Arai, chief adviser to the Shogun, "but procuring foreign productions, expensive stuffs, elegant utensils and other things not known in the good old times. The greater part of our wealth has gone for things we could have done just as well without." Once the corrupting spell of foreign trade was loosed, he thought, Japan would readily return to her traditional virtue and simplicity.

Arai, a firm believer in the Confucian theory that outward manners, established by strictly observed form and ritual, would exert a salutary discipline, was battling for the classicist ideas. As the chief official of the Shogun during the era called Genroku, the fifteen years between 1688 and 1703 when Japanese society touched its nadir of decadence, he sought to stem the tide toward sophisticated modernism. By cutting down the foreign contacts, he believed, the source of corruption could be attacked. Arai did not live to see the completion of his plans, but his warnings have been heeded during all the years from Genroku to the present day.

A succession of new orders cut the export trade. In 1710 the kobang, once worth $11, was halved in its gold content, though the Dutch were again required to accept it at face value. In 1716 the total copper exports were still further limited to but sixty percent of the amount previously permitted. A further edict reduced the amount to a scant

650 tons, and in 1744 this small amount was halved. Though a slight increase was permitted soon thereafter, a final order, issued in 1790, limited copper exports to but 250 tons a year.

While these restrictions were being imposed further orders sought to limit the frequency of foreign contacts. At one time Dutch ships were allowed to arrive at will, but after 1716 two ships only were permitted yearly, and after 1743 one ship only might arrive.

Oriental etiquette required that these restrictions be couched in an attractive form. Dutch pride must not be openly injured by the blows designed to kill the trade. The official explanation of the refusal in 1790 to allow a larger copper export expresses extreme solicitude for the welfare of the merchants it was planned to ruin.

"The cause of our friendship with the Hollanders," wrote the Shogun's councilor, "is trade, and the trade is supported by copper. If the one be exhausted, the other must fail. Is it not wise, therefore, to perpetuate our friendship by allowing only so much copper to be issued as our mines may be able forever to afford? The mines are not like the hair of man which, being cut off, grows again, but, on the contrary, resemble his bones which, if taken away, cannot be replaced."

Copper, it might be added, is even yet produced in Japan at the rate of approximately sixty-five thousand tons a year. When the Shogun's councilor wrote his appealing explanation about three thousand tons were mined annually. The limitation of export to 250 tons seems to have been somewhat more drastic than was actually necessary if the explanation is to be accepted at face value.

The Dutch were, however, far from guiltless in the matter. Their briberies were notorious; the smuggling was overt. Dutch sea captains and their sailors, even the opperhoofds, or factory managers at Deshima, tried to evade the rigid customs laws. The hope of illicit profits which might run as high as seventy percent on corals, ambers, silks, and porcelains, was far too fascinating for the traders to resist, especially as the profits on ordinary commodities which, from 1600 to 1717, had averaged twenty-six percent yearly, were now dwindling rapidly.

Severity of punishment seemed insufficient as a deterrent. One opperhoofd was banished, while ten of his Japanese confederates were beheaded. During a two-year period no less than fifty smugglers were beheaded or crucified. "Among the latter were five prisoners who, upon being taken, made way with themselves, to avoid the shame of public execution; but their bodies were nevertheless preserved in salt, on purpose to be afterwards fixed to the cross."

Trusting in the Japanese courtesy toward officials the Dutch captains evolved an ingenious smuggling device. They came to Nagasaki wearing huge uniforms under which contraband might be concealed. In these cumbersome costumes they made several trips a day from ship to shore "being so often loaded down with goods that they had to be supported by a sailor under each arm." By 1776 this device was discovered. Captains and opperhoofds were made subject to search. Further orders decreed that the skipper must either stay aboard his ship or, if he chose to land, should visit the vessel only twice during his entire stay in harbor. "It was droll," writes an observer, "to see the astonishment which the sudden reduction in size of our bulky captains excited in the major part of the ignorant Japanese, who before had always imagined that our captains were actually as fat and lusty as they appeared to be."

Japanese harbor police thereafter made thorough examinations of every ship arriving. Chests were emptied and tested to discover false bottoms. Beds were ripped open and the feathers examined. Iron spikes were thrust into tubs of butter; holes were cut in cheeses, and large pointed wires were thrust through in every direction. Even eggs were broken open to discover contraband.

Under such restrictions both of public trade and private profit, many Dutchmen questioned the value of continuing a profitless enterprise. Holland was willing to endure a remarkable amount of slur and insult if, in return, the gains seemed commensurate, but the price was beginning to seem far too high.

Sumptuary laws, moreover, seriously affected even the limited amount of trade remaining. Sadanobu Matsudaira, councilor to the Shogun Iyenori, drew up a series of restrictions reminiscent of the efforts of the Romans to control extravagance. No person with an income of less than fifty thousand bushels of rice a year (the amount is approximately the same equivalent in dollars) was to be permitted to buy anything new. All were restrained from purchasing foreign goods when native articles were available. The Matsudaira laws struck directly at the marketing of imports brought in from Java by the Dutch.

Many Java merchants seriously proposed the total abandonment of commercial intercourse, following the precedent of the English factory at Hirado. But realizing how the British regretted their action in giving up a privilege whose generosity could never again be equaled, Holland was unwilling to end even a losing trade.

There were, moreover, political objections to such a radical reply to Japan's restrictive laws. Governor General Imhoff, to whom the Batavia merchants referred their problem, was quite convinced that if the Dutch withdrew, other nations would rush into Nagasaki to replace the Hollanders. The Dutch would lose a valuable outpost in the East and might, indeed, be crushed out of the Indies by pressure of rivals operating simultaneously from India and Japan. Though he was certain that the Japanese designed to drive established traders from the Empire in order to substitute merchants less skilled in Japanese intrigue, Imhoff thought that continued subservience would in the long run be beneficial to the Netherlands.

Japan can gain no advantage from total expulsion of all aliens since they will thereby be isolated from all correspondence with Europe and be deprived of advance knowledge as to the machinations of others. Our peaceable conduct and the alarm given to that country by the Russians, plead greatly in our favor; and as it will be impossible for them to find other Europeans more tractable than ourselves, they can certainly have no reason to desire our departure thence, though it may be undeniable that Japan stands in no need of foreigners.

Imhoff, therefore, counseled the Dutch to mend their ways. Accept the Japanese restrictions, he advised, "because our failures have brought us into such discredit with the Japanese that they do not any longer place confidence in our promises." Imhoff was confident that if Holland maintained the promised quality of her goods, sent better agents to Japan—"the directors of trade have been selected from a very inferior class of society"—and avoided private peculations all would be well.

What Imhoff consistently failed to realize was that, year by year, the Dutch prestige was being undermined. The willingness of Dutch officials to accept new restrictions, the readiness to undergo humiliations, and the pacifism of the Hollanders under social slights too great for any high-class Japanese to bear, marked the traders as men of no importance in the eyes of Japanese. So long as Dutchmen were content to live as underlings, servilely obedient to the whim of every minor Japanese official, contumely would be their lot.

Dutchmen, to be sure, were not aware of the insolence with which the natives had been treating them. Anxious to conform to the custom of the country, hoping never to infringe a social rule, they were wholly unaware of the degradation to which they had been steadily reduced. Beginning with the comparatively high honors granted them when trade relations first commenced, the Hollanders had drifted always downward in the estimation of their hosts. Seldom has there been a better instance of how ignorance of social codes has worked to the disadvantage of the foreigner.

For the Dutchmen at Deshima, however, the consequences were less disastrous than to foreigners who were to follow. Holland was prepared to suffer indignities, partly because they were imposed by tradition and partly because the monetary profit was a sufficient balm. Subsequent visitors from other alien nations were not prepared to accept a status of inferiority. Japan saw no real reason why other strangers should not be given treatment identical with that which the Hollanders received. The conflicting points of view were to cause culture conflicts in later years.

V

ALIENS ARE ENEMIES

DUTCH pride prevented Europeans from discovering either the unprofitableness of trade with Japan or the low esteem in which the Hollanders were held. Seldom in any nation have foreigners been so hedged by restriction. If alien traders in the United States were confined on Bedloe's Island, where the Statue of Liberty stands, with all communication with the shore rigidly controlled by government police, the situation would approximate Dutch life at Deshima. If, in addition, the chief agent were required to travel by closed car to Washington in each inaugural year under close supervision by a squad of trained G-men in order to dance before the President, the analogy would be even closer.

Japanese apologists gloss over the restrictions imposed upon the little colony of Dutch merchants in Nagasaki Harbor. Blandly they suggest that the Dutch lived in almost perfect freedom or, if any slight restrictions were imposed for police protection, that the conditions were virtually similar to those in which foreigners live in any land. The comments written by the Hollanders, or by such men as Engelbrecht Kaempfer, learned physician of the Deshima factory, differ widely from the versions offered by modern Japanese.

Deshima was an artificial island raised about three feet above the normal high-water mark by a group of Japanese land speculators. They charged the Hollanders an annual rental of 6,500 taels, or in modern values about $7,500. The annual rental, the Dutchmen complained, was higher than the actual sale value of the four-acre tract on which they were confined. In this small space eleven Europeans were permitted to reside.

Access to Deshima was rigidly controlled. No ships, except only the annual cargo vessels coming from Batavia, were allowed to approach the island. Sea gates, opened only at the time the yearly vessels came, shut off all possibility of boats illegally arriving. On the landward side a small stone causeway, closely guarded by armed troops constantly on duty, afforded the only entrance to the reservation. A high fence, topped by a double row of pikes, blocked all escape.

Hollanders arriving to take up residence at Deshima were greeted by formalities which, according to Kaempfer, made them feel that they were entering a hostile country. There was, he believed, a general conspiracy of silence to discourage Dutch curiosity. "The position occupied by foreigners," he wrote, "is as low as possible. The Japanese regard us as a race of foreigners and despise us."

"Courtesans only, but no other women, shall be admitted," a huge placard posted on the causeway read. All female servants had to be hired from the public houses of Nagasaki, a town whose seventy thousand people were well cared for by a staff of some 750 prostitutes. These girls, the only Japanese allowed to stay overnight in Deshima, were required to report daily to the captain of the Japanese guard. They were strongly suspected by the Dutch of combining espionage activities with their other tasks.

Male Japanese assistants were wholly unreliable. Not only were they searched thoroughly before being admitted to, or allowed to leave, the island prison, but in addition they were made to swear a solemn oath "to deny us all manner of communication, credit, or friendships, anyways tending to support or to promote our interest." No information concerning the language, laws, manners, religion, or history of Japan was to be transmitted to the Dutch. The oath, solemnly administered to the Japanese, was signed with each man's seal dipped in black ink and "for a still stronger confirmation, some drops of his own blood which he fetches by pricking one of his fingers behind the nail." The solemn oath had to be repeated twice a year, once at New Year's and again upon the arrival of the Dutch ships in harbor. Violation of the oaths was punishable by death.

"No Japanese," reported Kaempfer solemnly, "who seems to have any regard or friendship for the Dutch, is looked upon as an honest man and true lover of his country. This maxim is grounded upon the principle that it is against the interests of the country, against the pleasure of their sovereign—nay, by virtue of the oath they have taken, even against the supreme will of the gods, and the dictates of their conscience—to show any favor to foreigners. Nay, they pursue this false reasoning still farther, and pretend that a friend of foreigners must of necessity be an enemy to his country, and a rebel to his sovereign."

To cheat or defraud a foreigner, to lessen the privileges of an alien, or to invent new and more burdensome burdens for the Dutch to bear became, therefore, unquestionable proofs of loyalty and patriotic zeal. Stealing from the Dutch was punished only by restitution of the goods or by brief banishment from Nagasaki; malingering, and the requiring that double as many workmen as would be needed must be employed, were officially condoned. No letters could be sent from Deshima unless copies had first been entered in the governor's registry book.

"Formerly," adds Kaempfer, "when a Dutchman died, his body, deemed unworthy of their ground, was thrown into the sea, somewhere without the harbor. But of late an empty spot of waste land was assigned us for decent burial."

Accusations that the Japanese courts were rigged against the foreigners, made by the Hollanders two centuries ago, are still made today in almost identical terms. "It is a very easy matter," wrote Kaempfer, "for anybody whether native or Chinese, to make his claims upon the Dutch, but we find it very difficult to obtain justice from others. In the first case, the government is always willing to give the complaining party damages, without so much as considering whether the claim be upon the whole Company, or some of its officers and servants, and whether it be just to make the former suffer for the misdemeanors of the latter. But if we have any complaint to make, we generally meet with so many difficulties and tedious delays as would deter anybody from pressing even the most righteous cause."

More recent observers echo the Kaempfer complaints concerning the partiality of Japan's justice. Foreign business firms report that suits against them are speedily decided with generous grants of damages, but that suits in their favor are slow and niggardly. How much of the contemporary complaint is justified and how much is to be ascribed to the natural tendency of foreigners to believe the cards stacked against them is not, of course, wholly discoverable, but the similarity of comment reflects what is probably a tendency to give the native Japanese the best of all the breaks.

In other matters, too, there is close likeness between the reports made two centuries or more ago by Kaempfer and current conditions. The same intense curiosity, the same suspiciousness, the same careful watchfulness over all activities of the alien, the same reluctance to allow the foreigner to learn too much about Japan, the same polite but scrupulously reserved courtesy, the same desire to overcharge the stranger by requiring many laborers to do the work that few could perform quite as well, the same meticulous listing of every small detail of foreigners' activity—these, and the endless business of interrogation are evident today. That Kaempfer was an excellent reporter and that Japan has changed but little in two centuries are both evident. The fact that his writings made so long ago apply so exactly to present day conditions argues for his accuracy.

To term Deshima a prison is, perhaps, to give a false impression that the Dutch were subjected to total isolation. Such a solitary confinement was certainly not the case. Hollanders were sometimes free to walk abroad through Nagasaki's streets and even into the surrounding countryside in search of specimens for botany or even for mere exercise. But this recreation was not to be secured at will.

If any member of the factory staff desired to seek relief from the monotony of Deshima he was obliged to ask permission of the Nagasaki governor. Petitions were sent twenty-four hours in advance asking the governor for leave to walk beyond the narrow confines of the island. The right was usually granted but only if the Netherlander was to be accompanied by a staff of interpreters—whom the Dutch looked upon as spies—subaltern police and a comprador, or business manager. Each of the retinue assumed the privilege of taking along his own personal domestics until the train consisted of some twenty-five or thirty Japanese trailing the exercising foreigner. It was expected, too, that the Dutchman would provide a banquet to the retinue and their friends, a necessity that raised the cost of the expedition to prohibitive figures.

One consolation only came with the feast. By unwritten rule, the foreigner was free from companionship while the feast was served. This was the moment when he might be free to enter shops to make small purchases, to call upon the few hosts who might be willing to receive him, or to transact any private business which might be desired. There was but little, to be sure, that any Hollander could do in these brief minutes when the supervision was relaxed, certainly nothing of sufficient importance to justify the heavy outlay that would be required.

In the first days of the Deshima residence canny Dutchmen sought to outwit the Japanese by going abroad two or three at a time, thus dividing the expense. But Japanese were even more astute. On such occasions the number of attendants was doubled or tripled so that no saving was effected. Thus while in theory the residents of Deshima were free to wander at will, in actual practice they took almost no advantage of their so-called freedom.

On certain other occasions the Dutchmen were obliged to make compulsory trips into the town. Twice a year the opperhoofd, together with one other of his staff, was expected to visit the Nagasaki governor to thank him for protection and to entreat its continuance. On the first day of the eighth Japanese month another visit to the governor's palace was required, this time with presents. All three trips required a formidable staff of guards, soldiers, spies, and officials to be paid and fêted at the Dutch expense.

Yet another day was set apart for the inspection of the five large boats, kept at the Dutch East India Company's expense, for the lightering of ships. This too involved a numerous retinue with the provision of an expensive dinner.

The Suwa Temple festival, the Suwa-matsuri, held in honor of the patron of the city, was another occasion on which the Netherlanders were expected to come into the city. Falling on the seventh day of October, by the lunar calendar, the annual ships from Batavia were almost always in port, so that their officers and men swelled the Dutch delegation, and incidentally increased the number of attendants to be paid and feasted. Four times the Hollanders were examined and searched while en route from Deshima to the platforms on which they were ensconced to see the parades of dancers, musicians, and actors on their gaily decorated procession-cars. On innumerable other occasions they were carefully counted to see that no foreigner escaped from his proper place in line.

All this demanded heavy money outlays for affairs which the Dutchmen deemed unnecessary, especially as the Japanese appeared to accept the favors with bad grace. "All these people, though they maintain themselves and their families entirely by what they get by us and our service, yet from their conduct one would think them to be our sworn enemies, always intent to do us what mischief they can, and so much the more to be feared, as their enmity and hatred is hid under the specious color of friendship, deference, and good will." Yet it was the only way whereby trade was tolerated by the Japanese.

The Netherlanders did not know their luck. To offer homage and presents to superior officials was among the highest privileges possessed by any Japanese. No man of low estate was permitted to approach his betters. The admission, therefore, of the opperhoofd to the privilege of giving gifts to the Nagasaki governor, the direct representative of the Shogun himself, was a recognition that the Dutch chief was himself of comparatively high social standing.

The Hollanders had higher rights than those enjoyed by native merchants of Japan. Iyeyasu, in granting the original charter to his friend Will Adams had granted to the Dutch the right of offering homage directly to the Shogun. The right involved the duty of giving rich gifts to the Shogun, but it was also a sort of charter of nobility. In their ignorance of Japanese custom the Dutch almost threw their privilege away. When Iyeyasu died in 1616, the Netherlanders, following European precedent, petitioned his son and successor, Hidetada, for a confirmation of the grant.

Such an application stunned the Japanese. It was not merely a violation of the respect due to the late Shogun, now deified as "Great Light of the East, August Incarnation of Buddha," but it was a positive insult to Hidetada. Asking the son to reaffirm his father's grant implied the apprehension that he might have considered alteration or rescinding of the gift—an offense against filial piety which no true Japanese son would have considered. Hidetada felt himself insulted, but could not bring himself to deny the Dutch privileges.

For almost a century the Dutch opperhoofds repaired annually to Yedo to perform the homage. Then, partly to save the Shogun the expense of the reception and partly to reduce the Dutch prestige, the journeys were made quadrennially, though the presents were still required to be sent each year from Nagasaki.

In European eyes the official progress toward Yedo was marked by pomp and circumstance. The Dutchmen were accompanied by some thirty-five Japanese officials and by two hundred personal servants. In the train were taken all the personal necessities which the foreigners might require along the route, even to the tables, chairs, and other articles of furniture used by the Hollanders. Wines, cheese, and butter filled the packs of men and animals, while immense stores of candies, cakes, and liqueurs were transported for the delectation of Japanese dignitaries who would be met en route. Frugal Dutchmen considered that the procession was a convincing demonstration of Holland's hospitality.

To Japanese the march seemed singularly mediocre. Even the least influential of the local daimyos seldom went to Yedo with less than several thousand followers, while the highest chiefs took some twenty thousand in their train. The Hollanders were happily unaware that the Japanese regarded them as most unimportant visitors.

The trip to Yedo was, however, an occasion upon which the opperhoofd enjoyed the most honorable distinctions. Each day he was formally consulted as to where he wished to dine and sleep, though the stops were immutably fixed by custom and could not possibly be changed. Salutations of the deepest reverence greeted his approach in the high-grade *norimono,* or palanquin, in which he traveled. Each daimyo through whose lands the procession passed entertained the travelers. The honors were paid not because of the opperhoofd's high rank but because he was about to be glorified by admission into the presence of the Shogun.

With the distinction went a loss of liberty. Shrewd observers in Japan have frequently remarked that isolation is a customary accompaniment of eminence. The opperhoofd in his temporary glory was no exception. At every stop, and especially at Osaka and Miako, the Hollanders were closely guarded. The Shogun's agents were particularly careful to shield the Dutchmen from any contact with officials of the Dairi. No opportunity whatever was afforded for the Netherlanders to learn anything concerning the populace or its needs. At Arai, a chief station on the great Tokaido highway, the Hollanders were stopped and searched to ensure that they were carrying no forbidden weapons. Not the least of their worries at this stop was the intimate personal examination required to assure the Shogun's officers that no woman was included in the retinue. Should a woman be smuggled past the Arai barrier the penalty was death for all the members of the procession and for the guards who were deceived. Only women in the Shogun's pay were to entertain the strangers.

At Yedo there was even more close confinement than at Deshima. The Nagasakkya, where the Dutchmen were housed, was a polite house of detention. In the front rooms of the establishment the Japanese companions and attendants were guarded but with some slight degree of liberty, while the Dutch heads of the delegation, presumably men of rank and dignity, were shut in four back rooms until the Shogun saw fit to hold his audience. The tedium was relieved, to be sure, by incognito visits from Japanese curiosity seekers and by ladies of the court who came to nibble candy and to finger the contents of the baggage trunks. Only on one occasion, in April 1806, when a great fire destroyed some thirty-seven palaces and killed upwards of 1,200 people, were the Dutchmen allowed an opportunity to roam unattended through the city.

The Shogun's audiences could, by edict, take place only on the twenty-eighth day of a month. If, perchance, the twenty-eighth of one month was by any accident missed, the deputation would be obliged to wait a full month for the next occasion. The opperhoofd and his attendants were obliged to report at the palace at six o'clock in the morning to don the special velvet garments, embroidered with gold lace, required for the ceremony. After waiting for some hours the opperhoofd was taken into the Shogun's presence. Then, as a state councilor shouted "Capitan Oranda," or Dutch captain, the kneeling opperhoofd bowed until his forehead touched the mats. He held the posture for some minutes. Then he withdrew. The audience was at an end.

The ceremony was short and placed the Hollanders in none too dignified a position, but it was of distinctly higher grade than that which had been required in early days when foreigners were less well known. When the Dutch mission went to Yedo in 1691 the Shogun was curious about what sort of people the aliens really were. After the formal homage had been paid, the Shogun commanded that the Dutchmen play-act for his amusement. "We were made to sit upright, to take off our clothes, tell our names and ages, stand up, walk, turn about, dance, sing songs, compliment each other, be angry, invite one another to dinner, converse as fathers and sons would talk, show how two friends, or a man and his wife greet or take leave of each other, remove our perukes, dance, jump, and kiss." This sort of public entertainment continued for two hours and a half to the intense amusement both of the Shogun and his officials and of the court women who looked down upon the scene from a screened balcony. "A thousand ridiculous and impertinent questions" were flung at the unfortunate envoys.

The seventeenth century saw an end of this buffoonery. The audiences granted by the Shogun grew shorter and more formal. In return for the granting of rich presents to the Shogun and his staff the Hollanders were allowed to see the great man and to bow in obeisance but could utter no words of greeting.

A score or more of calls upon state officials, most of whom allowed the visits to be paid upon their subordinates, followed the formal reception by the Shogun. When the round of courtesy calls was finished

and the required gifts had been distributed, the Dutchmen were free
to return to Deshima in the same fashion they had come.

On neither the northward journey nor on the return was any ceremony permitted to be paid the Dairi at Miako by the Hollanders.
This Son of Heaven was regarded as "being a personage too holy to
be lawfully known by, or even thought of, by the Christian foreigners."

Japanese refrained from giving to the Dutchmen any inkling of
the Dairi's function in the administration of the government. So
reticent were they, indeed, that as late as 1860, foreigners were not informed that the true name of the Dairi's capital was not Miako, "The
Capital," but Kyoto. The word Kyoto had been imbued with too
much *mana* for foreigners to learn of it.

The best interpretation available to Westerners was a familiar
analogy. The Shogun, so the Hollanders believed, was a temporal
sovereign similar to the kings of Europe. Though the Shogun was
called in common European parlance the "Emperor" and though, as
late as 1860, he was so addressed in formal diplomatic documents, he
was in fact an autocratic military dictator nominally taking orders
from a powerless superior. The true Emperor, the Dairi or Mikado,
too holy to possess a common name, was considered as a spiritual sovereign similar to the Roman Pontiff. Thus, though the Shogun was
not in actual reality the proper wielder of all Imperial power, it was to
him, and not to the divine Son of Heaven, that the Dutch embassy
made obeisance. The Dairi lived in perfect isolation in the seclusion
of his Miako palace.

The easy analogy did not restrain the Dutchmen from trying to
unravel the tangled skein of Japan's political arrangements. Because
of the Japanese reticence and because vague data was drawn from
many varied sources, it is not surprising that the Netherlanders gained
an oddly distorted picture of the Dairi's daily life.

There is no question that the Japanese, jealous beyond all Western
understanding of the position of their sacred Son of Heaven, twisted
the truth in talking to the Hollanders. The reports which Dutchmen
learned probably bore the slightest possible relation to the actual truth,
but the important fact remains that for generations, even beyond the
time of Perry, Europeans acted upon the assumption that the Dutch
reports were accurate. The misconceptions which the Japanese encouraged foreigners to hold caused sufferings to aliens in the years to
come.

The Dairi's dignity, Hollanders were assured, became the excuse for depriving him of power. Worldly affairs were believed so wholly undeserving of the attention of a successor of the gods that for him to bestow a thought upon them would degrade him, if indeed it did not actually profane the ruler. Accordingly no business was submitted to him for consideration, no act of sovereignty was by him performed, unless it had a religious character. Once he had deigned to confer upon his ministers the assurance that they were to act in his behalf, the secluded Emperor's task in mundane affairs was virtually concluded.

His ritual duties were of far more consequence. Each day, so the Dutchmen were convinced, the Emperor was obliged to pass a certain number of hours upon his throne, immovable, lest by turning his head he bring disaster upon that part of the empire to which, or from which, he might turn his gaze. By such immobility he would maintain the whole realm's stability and tranquillity. When he had sat the requisite number of hours, he resigned his place to his crown, which then continued as his substitute upon the throne during the remainder of the day and night.

The honors paid to him were quite as extraordinary as the duties to which he was obligated, according to the reports the Dutch received. During an entire month of each year all the gods, or *kami,* of Japan, were believed to wait upon the Emperor as his attendants. During that month, named by the Japanese "without gods," no native frequented the temples, believing them deserted of their deities. The sun-goddess' descendant was receiving all the homage of the heavens.

As further dignity, and to prevent any violation of his sacred person, the Emperor was closely guarded. That unhallowed eyes should not pollute him with their glance, he never left the precincts of his palace. That his foot should not be defiled by vulgar earth he never moved except upon a litter borne upon the shoulders of his princely servants. That he should not suffer even the slightest of indignities, his hair, his beard, his nails were never cut, except by stealth while he was sleeping or pretending to sleep. By elaborate fiction these operations needful for his comfort were described as "stealing his nails and hair."

Everything about the Emperor was required to be incessantly new. No article of dress was ever worn a second time, his dining service must be new at every meal, as must the kitchen ware in which the food was cooked. None could inherit his leavings. Whatever article had been hallowed by Imperial use, even by such remote use as cooking what he was to eat, was thereby so sanctified that no human touch must afterward be permitted to profane them. To wear his cast-off clothes, to eat from his plates, cook in his saucepan, or even to taste the broken victuals from his table would call down upon the sacrilegious offender the awful vengeance of heaven. To prevent all such risk, everything that had been once employed in the Imperial service must be torn or broken or otherwise destroyed.

The cost of maintaining such elaborate state must necessarily have been overwhelming had not the Shogun, from whose budget the funds were drawn, combined frugality with reverence. Because the Emperor conferred sanctity upon whatever had the honor of his use, the Shogun, with characteristic Japanese humor, acted on the belief that it was needless to provide the sacred ruler with expensive furnishings. The Imperial glance, to say nothing of the Imperial touch, was sufficient to imbue the cheapest and the coarsest equipment with all the attributes of luxury. The Emperor, accordingly, was offered articles of the simplest and most inferior nature, such as the poorest coolies of his land might use. The budget was spared a most embarrassing drain and loyal subjects would never dare to notice that the Emperor had been slighted. Hans Christian Andersen's fable of the Emperor's New Clothes could have been history in Japan save for the fact that no clear-eyed child would venture to blurt out the truth.

Imperial aloofness was readily transferred to those who ruled in his name. The same sacredness that enveloped the Dairi also surrounded any of his agents acting in his stead. The humblest harbor policeman, enforcing the Imperial rule, demanded, and insisted on receiving, the proper homage due from a low-caste Hollander toward the agent of the Son of Heaven. Thus it was that, until the Dutchmen realized their place, conflicts of authority occurred with frequency.

Soon the Dutchmen fell into the routine prescribed by formal etiquette. Intercourse between the Hollanders and the Japanese was canalized into formal channels. No native grandee above the rank of the humblest port official ever spoke directly to a Dutch merchant. Always an interpreter was required, even in the case of the one or two opperhoofds who learned a little Japanese through illicit channels.

The interpreters were few in number and for the most part, in early days, they were incredibly inefficient. In Kaempfer's time, at the close of the seventeenth century, not one in ten of the so-called interpreters at Deshima could speak a word of Dutch. Communication was car-

ried on through signs and gestures, sometimes aided by the use of
Chinese. Kaempfer taught a young servant to read and write Dutch
better than any of the official linguists assigned by the Nagasaki government.

The post of interpreter had become a hereditary position for approved Japanese families who, knowing that no competition would be
permitted, thought it unnecessary to study the alien tongue. When,
in the so-called Kioho period, 1716–36, two Yedo youths received
permission to join the interpreter corps, the official guild of interpreters discouraged their attempt. "It is entirely useless for you to try to
learn the language," the Nagasaki linguists warned. "It is not an easy
thing to understand the Dutch speech. For instance, if we want to
ask what drinking water or wine is, we have no means of asking
except by using gestures. I was born into a family of interpreters and
have been used to these things all my life; you who live in Yedo must
not hope to learn much. It is far the best for you not to begin."

The Yedo applicants persisted. Eventually they learned some seven
hundred words of Dutch, and then they set themselves to translate
Dutch textbooks on astronomy, medicine, botany, zoölogy and science. Only slight attention was paid to Western books on ethics, morality, or art. Thus the impression was produced that the Occidentals
were interested solely in material affairs, and that the Europeans knew
nothing of "spirituality." Japan is still convinced that the chief difference between West and East is found in materialism as opposed to
purity and saintliness.

The head of the factory changed almost yearly, though a few opperhoofds might return at some later day. Hence the Hollanders, except
occasionally an insignificant under-officer, knew virtually nothing
about the country in which they were resident. The Japanese were
rather better informed concerning the inhabitants of Europe. Churyo
Morishima's *Komo Zatsuwa* (*Red-Hair Miscellany*), published at
Yedo in 1787, described the English as "fierce, intelligent, skilled in
sea fighting, and versed in various arts." The French were set down
as "kindly disposed, clever in learning, all bold spirited, and excelling
in military tactics; in their intercourse with foreign peoples they show
politeness."

The increased knowledge of Western lands was largely due to the
repeal, in 1720, of the prohibition against the importation of non-
religious books. Bunzo Aoki, the Shogun's chief librarian, continually
urged the importance of securing Dutch books, and through his influ-

ence European almanacs, astronomies, and treatises on mathematics were added to the Shogun's library. These were the chief sources through which Japanese scholars learned to calculate eclipses.

According to Genichiro Fukichi, one of Japan's pioneer news-papermen, the first Western grammar was brought to Japan about 1820. The purchaser, Sunosuke Yoshio, opened a grammar school on the strength of this one book. Eager Japanese scholars trudged nine hundred miles from Yedo to Nagasaki to study at Yoshio's school. Their plan seemed, said Fukichi, to write down the Japanese equiva-lent for each foreign word, set the characters down in a Dutch book, and then memorize the sentences irrespective of the meaning of the words. It was no wonder, he said, that it was difficult for Japanese to learn a foreign language.

All this learning was, however, for a long time of no avail. The Japanese dignitaries declined to make use of volunteer interpreters. The governor spoke to his secretary, the secretary to an underling, the under-officer to an interpreter, and the interpreter to the opperhoofd. Replies were transmitted to the governor in reverse order. The process required a vast amount of time, but short cuts were not permissible.

There was a social disadvantage inherent in the process which long remained unknown to the Hollanders. By speaking directly to the interpreters, instead of through a series of officials, the opperhoofds placed themselves upon the low level of the native interpreter caste. Thus Holland, failing to shield her dignity, lost face in Japan and marked her people as inferiors.

VI

RUSSIA BECOMES CURIOUS
1708–1742

THOUGH British eagerness for oriental trade was somewhat
stilled, other nations were moving steadily toward Eastern markets. Japan, whose apprehensions were constantly excited by the
Dutch at Deshima, was nervous lest foreigners arrive to break down
her seclusion.

Of all the foes, the most feared were the Russians. Throughout the
eighteenth century, rumors were abroad that soldiers of the Tsar
were mobilizing to attack the Empire. Warnings were frequent that
Russians were marching irresistibly across the continent of Asia en
route to the East. Settlements of Muscovites were dotting the Siberian
plains; patrols of Russian regiments were penetrating even to Pacific
shores. All this presaged, the Shoguns feared, descent upon Japan.

Americans have been, perhaps, too captivated by the dramatic incidents of the conquest of our own continent to realize the full extent
of this Russian sweep. Britons have been intent upon the steady spread
of their pioneers into unknown lands. The story of the Russian march
across Siberia still remains to be presented in full color to the English-
speaking public. Here it is enough to point out that the Russians had
achieved, in Eastern Asia, feats of exploration of untrodden lands
surpassed by the trail breakers of no other nation.

Japan feared that these movements were deliberate steps toward
annexation. Ever since the arrival of the Russians at the Sea of
Okhotsk in 1638, wild rumors borne by excited savages from the distant Kurile islands had warned the Japanese against the giant "Red
Hairs" who fed on human flesh.

Incredible though many of these rumors now seem, there was a solid basis of hard fact in many of them. Russian explorers, such as Vassily Poyarkov, deliberately traveled light, carrying guns and ammunition to shoot the little red deer of Siberia, but not hesitating, in the lack of deer, to shoot the aborigines. Poyarkov, it was alleged at a court trial in Moscow, lived upon the flesh of natives whom he shot and roasted.

These Poyarkov excesses, committed during the years 1643 to 1646, harmed the Russian cause. Peoples in the Amur River basin preferred the exactions of Chinese tax collectors to the cannibalism of Russian exploration parties. Russia's conquest of Eastern Siberia was long delayed through opposition thus created. Japan shrank away in horror from all possible association with men who lived on human beings. When, half a century after Poyarkov, Vladimir Atlassov came to Kamchatka and when, in 1706, he slowly struggled to the tip of that peninsula, the Japanese were certain that the "Red Hairs" would not long delay in crossing to the Kuriles. The distance from Kamchatka to the nearest Kurile island was but slight. In favorable weather the waters could be safely crossed in ordinary rowboats.

The fears were certainly well founded. Even before Atlassov had taken all Kamchatka he had heard about Japan. In 1694 a fishing ship from Osaka, carried out to sea in a typhoon, drifted, stripped of mast and rudder, to the Kamchatkan coast. One lone sailor, Debune, was picked up by Russian scouts. Atlassov, conversing with Debune partly in a patois built of Kamchatkan Japanese and partly by sign language, learned of Japan's wealth. Moved by cupidity, he sent a subordinate to pillage the nearby Kuriles. Then he asked his master, Peter the Great, for permission to launch an attack upon Japan.

Peter, intrigued by the idea, sent for Debune. At Moscow, in 1702, the first Japanese in Russia conversed at great length with the Tsar. Peter the Great commissioned Debune to teach Japanese to a number of Russian scholars preparatory to the dispatch of a well-planned expedition to the East.

History abounds in offering remarkable comparisons. While the supposedly "man-eating" Russians were fêting the ex-fisherman Debune and were listening open-mouthed to his extravagant reports about Japan's wealth and power, a man of far higher social status and of much broader education was visiting Japan. The reception given him was scarcely parallel to that which Debune received.

Giovanni Batista Sidotti, Italian missionary priest, was fired with zeal to emulate the work of Xavier in Japan. For two years he assiduously studied the language until he convinced himself that he was letter-perfect. Then he resolved to smuggle himself into the forbidden Empire. Taking ship from Manila, he landed at night on the rocky Kyushu coast. When daybreak came he was arrested.

The remainder of Sidotti's story is best told by Hakuseki Arai, the Shogun's inquisitor sent to cross-question the intruder.

"I heard," reports Arai, "that a wild man had come ashore. Except for a few such words as Nippon, Yedo, and Nagasaki, his language could not possibly be understood. He said he came from Roson, but the Hollanders denied all knowledge of the place and none of them could understand a word the wild man said.

"All agreed that the stranger was to be punished, but it was a time of court mourning for Tsunayoshi, so the punishment had to be postponed. The man was jailed to wait until the time was right to punish him. A year later the Government declared that it was time to investigate the man to find out why he came and why he would not accept the gift of warmer clothes from any but the people whom he called his 'disciples.' I talked with him. He said that he had come to teach his doctrine and thus benefit and save all men. He asked to have his guards removed, saying that it was not right to cause them sleepless nights. He offered to be manacled and fettered at night in order to save the comfort of his guards. Even if he should escape, he said, he could not remain unnoticed because of the difference in his appearance from the looks of Japanese. 'Why should I escape?' he asked, 'I came of my own will.'

"This seemed sad to me. I should not have thought him so deceitful. The guards, I told him, were assigned to him by order of the Government. They could not be removed.

"We wished to kill him but we could not because he said that he was an envoy of Rome, but he bore no letters to prove his ambassadorship. We thought he must have come to Japan because he had been under sentence of death for some crime at home. We asked the Hollanders about this and they said that that was probably the case.

"He did tell us about clocks and how the compass could be used, and he made a good map. We wished to know where Java was, for the Hollanders came from there, but he refused to tell us lest we go there to conquer it. He told us about his religion, too, but it appeared to be not in the least like the true way. We kept him in jail until he died in 1715."

No one now knows how Sidotti died. A grave which seems to be his bears "all the marks of those who die in disgrace," but Japanese records disclose no more evidence. Two aged people who sought to care for him were murdered for the crime of being Christians.

Debune, in "man-eating" Russia, had a happier life. As professor of Japanese, he was granted a dignified position with the savants of the Academy of Science. Few Russians were aware that Debune's accent and vocabulary were those of low-caste fishermen. Nobly born Japanese would resent the fisher dialect as keenly as a European premier would object to a diplomatic address couched in waterfront slang. Luckily for Debune's reputation, perhaps, his pupils had small opportunity to try out their Japanese. Debune retained his post at the Academy of Science until his death in 1736.

Peter the Great, impressed by Debune's boastings about Japan, ordered a reconnaissance upon the Kurile islands. Ivan Petrovitch Kosirewski, grandson of a Polish prisoner of war, volunteered to lead an expedition. Specifically he was "to investigate Kamchatka and the nearby islands, to inquire into what government the people owe allegiance and to force tribute from those who have no sovereign, to inform himself as much as may be possible about Japan and the way thither, what weapons the inhabitants have and how they wage war, whether they might be willing to enter into friendly and commercial relations with Russia, and, if so, what kind of merchandise they might be induced to buy."

There is, therefore, considerable truth in the Japanese belief that Kosirewski was a spy, but none at all in their accusation that "a Russian fleet attempted to conquer Japan." Kosirewski's little force of fifty Russians, eleven Kamchatkans, and a shipwrecked Japanese who acted as interpreter, crossed in small skiffs to the first Kurile. There, in August 1711, after a skirmish in which ten Kurile natives were killed and many others wounded, he secured what the Russians understood to be a "promise of eternal subjection."

The material gains were, however, exceedingly slight. Neither sables nor foxes, nor other valuable resources, were discoverable. Kosirewski and his men, living on swans, geese, and ducks, prepared to pass on to the next island after completing three small ships for the journey. The second island was, however, heavily armed and offered so much resistance that the Russians did not dare attack. Kosirewski sent a message ashore demanding subjection to Russia and was met by a flat refusal. "We are subject to no one," the Kurile islanders retorted, "and we pay no tribute. We have no sables and no foxes, but in winter time we catch beavers. These beaver skins we have already sold to strangers from the neighbor nations on our south in exchange for iron tools, muslins, and other needful articles. You can expect no tribute from us."

The Russians stayed two days, hoping that the Kuriles would relax their vigilance, and then returned empty-handed to Kamchatka. Again in the summers of 1712 and 1713 Kosirewski crossed again, visited three of the islands, talked with the natives, and came home to Kamchatka bearing a small quantity of silks and metals. A chart, based on information furnished by the islanders, showed the relative locations of about half the thirty-two islands, and gave the location of the city of Matsumai in south Hokkaido. But Matsumai, he warned, was strongly guarded by troops well armed with muskets and cannon.

Kosirewski's report, forwarded to the provincial governor at Yakutsk, seemed suspicious. Investigation disclosed that he had kept for his private use several thousand dollars' worth of plunder. Kosirewski, thus found guilty of embezzlement and strongly suspected of both murder and sedition as well, was dismissed from official service. But since, in the turbulent prison camp life of Eastern Siberia of the time, few crimes were ever followed by capital punishment, Kosirewski was allowed to expiate his offense by surrendering the loot and by taking holy orders. Much of his time thereafter seems to have been spent in denouncing the authorities. Eventually, it appears, the angry Kosirewski became a "peasant saint" of the Rasputin pattern.

Meanwhile his report, together with the highly inaccurate map, had been forwarded to St. Petersburg. Peter the Great, mindful of Debune's promises of wealth, read the documents and then sent out Feodor Luzhin and Ivan Yevreinov as special agents to retrace Kosirewski's course.

Just what happened on this semi-secret Luzhin-Yevreinov adventure is not wholly clear. Leaving Yakutsk at the time of the spring thaws of 1720 the envoys, guided by Hendrick Busch, a Dutch sailor, passed through to Kamchatka, built boats and sailed as far south as the fifth Kurile. There internal dissension seems to have put an end to further progress. Busch warned against anchorages in the rocky harbors of the islands. Luzhin and Yevreinov overruled the advice. The cables were badly frayed by sharp rocks, four anchors were lost, and not even a landing seems to have been effected.

The expedition came back sullen and torn by dissension. Almost immediately upon landing on the continent Yevreinov hurried back to St. Petersburg, leaving his colleagues in Siberia. Officials in the East were uneasy concerning the tales of malfeasance or of inefficiency that might have been reported to the Tsar, but when nothing came of the suspected tale-bearings, life settled back to a normal routine of frontier existence. No one, outside the inner circle of the Tsar's advisers, seems to have glimpsed the report, though it is believed that a revised map of the Kuriles was delivered at St. Petersburg when Yevreinov arrived in May 1722.

Further Russian penetration of Japan was halted temporarily until the results of the Luzhin-Yevreinov expedition could be appraised. Then, in 1725, Peter the Great, Tsar for half a century, died, leaving Russia in a state of confusion from which she was not to emerge until several years had passed. Expansion in the East came to a stop.

Japan was, however, not reassured. Sensational rumors came to Yedo from both north and south giving the most terrifying accounts of the diabolical wickedness of the giant Russian "Red Hairs." The Kurile islanders outdid fiction in their exaggerations of Russian armaments; the Deshima Dutchmen, anxious to win favor from the Shogun, corroborated all the worst slanders on the character and motives of the Tsar's expeditions.

But the same causes which first excited Russian interest soon roused new curiosities. Tribute-bearing Japanese junks, loaded with cottons, silks, and rice, were wrecked by storm and were carried by the Kuroshiwo to the Kamchatkan shores. Not every fate was as terrible as that which in 1729 befell the *Wakashima* of Satsuma. This ship, richly laden with precious stuffs and silver as a tribute to the Shogun, fell into the hands of Lieutenant Schtennikov. He, eager to take the tribute for himself, shot fifteen of the half-starved survivors of the wreck. Two men escaped the massacre and these, the aged merchant Sosa and the young pilot Gonza, trekked across the frozen wastes of Asia during two Siberian winters to report the outrage to the army chiefs at Irkutsk. Their report caused the arrest of Schtennikov, who was hanged for his heartlessness, with the Japanese as witnesses.

Sosa and Gonza were, like Debune and other refugees, sent on to St. Petersburg where their accounts of Japan's grandeur revived Russia's cupidity. The Academy of Sciences, which in all probability possessed the secret Luzhin-Yevreinov report, was already planning a grandiose scheme for the exploration of the North Pacific. Vitus

Bering, one of the Danish naval officers hired by Peter the Great, was to head a party of discoverers. With him was to sail a corps of naturalists, astronomers, historians, and other scientists to make a lasting record of the expedition.

Probably the Bering expedition found more difficulty in getting started from Siberia than in mapping out its new discoveries. Bering's galaxy of scientists quarreled like operatic prima donnas. Martin Spanberg, the Danish officer assigned to sail southward from Kamchatka to the Kuriles and Japan, faced virtual civil war among his men. Camped for three years on the shores of the Sea of Okhotsk while boats were being built, the explorers lived in two hostile camps, fortified against each other and spending their spare time, according to their records, in shouting violent abuse at each other from behind the barricades.

By June 1738, however, three small ships were finished. Spanberg's flagship, *Archangel Michael,* a sixty-footer, held sixty-three men. Two smaller ships, the sloops *Nadezhda,* under Captain William Walton, and *St. Gabriel,* under Captain Alexander Shelting, took forty-four men each. The small size of the expedition is important for, according to the Japanese, this force of 151 men spread terror throughout the northern islands.

In actual fact the Spanberg party of 1738 merely cruised among the Kuriles, making no landings whatever. After less than seven weeks' voyaging Spanberg turned back, at the island of Urup north of the Hokkaido. He gave as his reason for abandoning the enterprise "The lateness of the season, the length of the nights [the date was August 3!], the unknown waters, strong currents, lack of food, and fear of the enemy."

Before the 1739 exploration season began, a fourth ship, a fifty-footer, was added, and Spanberg and his men again set out for discoveries. They came on June 16 to Japan's main island—the first Russians to see Japan—and on the following day he received what he construed as an invitation to land. He did not dare accept.

No good ports exist in the latitude of 38 degrees where Spanberg first glimpsed Japan, so it is difficult to identify the exact spot where he saw villages, fields, and forests. It was, however, in the Mito territory of the north, a region singularly well inclined toward foreign intercourse.

Mito's ruler was, at the moment, antagonistic to the ruling Shogun. For more than a century the Mito daimyos had supported the secluded

Dairi against the "usurpations" of the Shoguns. Partly this was due to a sincere belief that all officials should be subordinate to the throne, a belief later to flower in the Meiji Restoration of 1868. Perhaps even more strongly, Mito was moved by jealousy. The Mito daimyos were distant relatives of the Tokugawa Shoguns, but felt themselves unjustly subordinated. Old laws forbade Mito men to succeed to the Shogunate. Only once in Japanese history, it might be noted, was this law violated, in the case of Shogun Keiki, the last Shogun to be appointed.

Spanberg came, then, to a seashore village in which anti-alienism was less rife than in other sections of the Empire. Fearing treachery, for Sosa and Gonza had warned him that it was a capital offense for foreigners to set foot in Japan, he refused an invitation to land. Instead he asked the townsfolk to board the Russian ships. Crowds came, headed by four "important-looking officials" with gifts of gold coins, rice, tobacco, and fish. Spanberg greeted the headmen with sweets and brandy which, he says, they seemed to relish. But when he looked at the waters round his ship he saw himself surrounded by a thousand guards. Spanberg dismissed the Japanese visitors and sailed away in haste.

Walton's ship, *St. Gabriel*—he had traded vessels with Captain Shelting—won the distinction of being the first Russian craft to land men in Japan. Separated from the squadron by a storm, Walton sighted a Japanese junk which made signs for him to follow its guidance. He came to a Japanese city which, from his description, seems to have been Kochi, on Tosa Bay, near the place where the *San Filipe* was wrecked in 1596.

The reception was friendly. Kasimirov, his mate, and seven others were allowed to land. Wood and water were provided for the ship, presents were exchanged, and a limited trade was permitted. Walton, however, objected to the guard boats thrown about the *St. Gabriel* and left hurriedly.

One further effort was made, under Spanberg's leadership, to survey Japan's trade possibilities. In May 1742 he took one ship, the *St. John,* with seventy-eight men to investigate Japanese government, politics, and commerce.

The *St. John* sailed southward toward the main island and became hopelessly lost in a fog which, for some curious reason, paralyzed the nautical instruments. Spanberg was unable to discover where he was, and then was battered by bad weather. He did succeed in landing men at Komaishi in Miyagi province on the main island and in paying a brief call to the east coast of Hokkaido. Then, becoming discouraged when scurvy attacked his crew, Spanberg turned back.

The voyages stirred immense interest in Russia, not so much because of their geographical or imperial significance as because of the intrigues that were caused. The start of Spanberg's explorations was delayed by internal strife. Those bickerings continued throughout the voyages. Eventually the Admiralty, the Naval Academy, and the Academy of Sciences were dragged in as arbiters.

Exploring parties are almost never happy families where life is one sweet harmony. Always there are petty jealousies and meannesses that would do discredit to the fictional girls' boarding schools. Spanberg's set was no exception. It is no exaggeration to declare that every officer was at odds with every other leader and that all the superiors were cordially hated by their men. Martin Spanberg made wholesale accusations that his associates were drunken louts who could not keep the records straight. He found faults enough in Walton's log to fill a sixteen-page notebook full of criticisms and corrections. Walton retorted that Spanberg ordered falsification of the logs under threats to hang his underlings if they refused to lie. Evidence was produced to prove that Spanberg had never seen Japan but that he had really visited Korea by mistake. All this the Russian savants were compelled to straighten out. Their decision was a masterpiece of tact. Both Spanberg and his critics, they declared, were right. The confusion had been caused, they said, because the two parties to the conflict had used different maps. By Spanberg's map, which they agreed was probably more nearly accurate, the expedition had been in Japan, but there was reasonable ground for the belief, they hastened to admit, that if one used the rival map, Spanberg might appear to have gone to Korea.

The trouble started probably because the crews of Spanberg's ships were made up of half a dozen nationalities. Walton and Shelting were Britishers who lost no opportunity for criticizing Russian naval weaknesses; Spanberg and Bering were both Danes; the sailors were Russians, Swedes, Kamchatkans, and assorted natives of Siberia. Many of the men were inexperienced as sailors.

Nor was there wild enthusiasm for the assignment. The captains were aggrieved because they could not accompany Bering on the trip where greater glory was anticipated, and because they knew that they were not the favored protégés of Peter's court. All knew that Spanberg had suffered criticism at the start and that his superiors in Siberia were not in complete accord with Spanberg's plans. All were anxious to end the exploration and to get back home.

In such an atmosphere of nervous tension, with officers and men alike tired out and easily annoyed, quarrels were frequent. It is probably a feat to Spanberg's credit that, in face of psychologic circumstance, he returned with information that did show a new path to Japan, that gave some vague approximation of her northern islands and that proved Hokkaido to be insular. He offered the first definite proof that Japan was no peninsula of Asia.

His activities were completely misunderstood by Japanese. Even to this day Japanese historians convey the impression that each Russian voyage was an armed expedition planned for the reduction of Japan. Though Japanese control over the chain of islands lying between Hokkaido and Kamchatka was never strong, and though the loyalty of northern daimyos to the Yedo Shogun was never absolute, Japan insists that Russian scouting of the Kuriles was a violation of her sovereignty.

The failure of the Russian expeditions, then, is set down in Japanese histories as proof that Japan has beaten back repeated Russian "invasions" of her territories. That most of these voyages were chiefly in the interest of scientific observation and for the opening of trade relations is, to Japanese, beside the point. The vaunted isolation of the Empire was at stake.

Thus, when messages came down from the north that Russians were seen along the coast, the Yedo authorities were on the *qui vive* for hostilities to happen. Time and time again the northern troops were called upon to mobilize against aggression, forts were prepared for an expected attack, the weak war junks were made ready to beat off the invaders.

Unfamiliar with the practices of sea-going ships, the Kurile guardsmen unwittingly exaggerated the power of the Russian scouting expeditions. Each whaleboat launched from the mother ship was counted as a separate man-of-war. Thus Yedo was informed that the Russian "squadrons" were of enormous size. When Walton came to Kochi his favorable reception was doubtless due to the fact that the anticipated Russian "fleet" consisted of one ship only. The fear that other ships of war were just beyond the horizon may have been an additional factor in the unwonted kindliness shown to the first Russians landing in Japan.

Sad consequences flowed from Japan's self-satisfaction. Secure in the belief that Russia had been overwhelmed and that the Shogunate was far more than a match for all the vaunted forces of the Tsar, the Japanese thenceforth treated the Muscovites as men of no importance. Russian captains, and in later days even Russian envoys, could be maltreated with impunity, just as the Dutchmen of Nagasaki could be safely scorned. For more than two centuries thereafter, insults and indignities were the Russian lot.

A further factor must be kept in mind if one would understand the fanatical opposition to the coming of the Russians. Japan was thoroughly convinced that Muscovite intruders had some special intrigue with the demons whereby evil would befall the Russian's foes. No Chinese in the Boxer days was ever more imbued with the belief that white men were "foreign devils" than were the eighteenth-century Japanese.

To cultured people in contemporary times the proof seems puerile, but to folk with slight knowledge of the world the chain of circumstances was unbroken. After each of the five visits that Russians had made to Japan's shores calamity had followed. The incidents were far too numerous, and much too impressive, to be dismissed as mere coincidence.

Kosirewski's trip, in 1713, had come upon the heels of Shogun Iyenobu's death. The bold invader had scarcely withdrawn from the empire before some twenty thousand peasants in the Musashi province, hard by the walls of Yedo, rose to destroy the homes of rich men and to rob the fields and forests.

Seven years later the Luzhin-Yevreinov semi-secret expedition broke down the barriers of Japan's privacy. Almost at once, revolt flared in the northern province of Mutsu. There was no more direct connection between the farmer rebellion and the Luzhin-Yevreinov scouting than there had been between Kosirewski and the Musashi revolt, but Japanese officialdom immediately saw the possibility of Russian influences.

Spanberg's arrival in 1738 added more detail to prove the close connection between Russian fleets and domestic insurrection. In the same year that Spanberg came, a vast uprising of 84,600 farmers marched on the Matsudaira fortress in Mutsu province with a long list of grievances against the weight of taxes imposed upon them. Long custom, to which Matsudaira gave assent, approved the levying of imposts of nearly half the total produce of small farms. Rising prices, traceable to exportation of Japan's specie by the Dutch, were making the costs of living so high that the tremendous taxes could be borne no longer. The peasants' complaints had a reasonable justification because of current economic conditions, but the Yedo officials, hearing only Matsudaira's version of the story, were not weighing causes and effects with any scientific care. It was enough to know that Russians had arrived and that revolts had then occurred. *Post hoc, ergo propter hoc.*

Next year, 1739, Spanberg came again to Mito, while Walton called at Kochi. The expected insurrection was not long delayed. At Ikuno, in Tajima province, just across the island from the port where Walton called, the greatest riot since the Shimabara massacre flared into action. The miners of the region, operating the oldest silver mines in all Japan, were goaded to despair by the Shogun's embargo on silver exports and by the steadily increasing cost of living. So numerous were the strikers that a ten-mile road was crowded with the multitudes of protesting workers. Before the demonstration could be suppressed it became necessary to call in the help of all the neighboring lords for joint action to preserve the peace.

Even the unsuccessful Spanberg visit of 1742 brought disorders in its train. At Hida, in Bingo province, ten villages appealed directly to the Shogun for relief. Before the Shogun could consider it, Anai, leader of the protestants, was seized by his superiors and was condemned to death.

Five times, therefore, Russians had descended on Japanese shores and five times there had been murmurs in the peasantry. Nor were the Russians the only foreigners who could call down disaster on the empire. The harmless priest, Sidotti, arrived almost simultaneously with the murder of the Shogun Tsunayoshi. Four thousand farmers of Echigo, across the island from Yedo, were denounced to the authorities as planning revolution. Though nothing came of the plot, the existence of disaffection was enough to show that any aliens were a most disturbing factor.

When the next foreign voyager arrived, the Graf von Beniowski in 1771, the usual revolts occurred. Ten thousand men of Kasatsu, in Hizen province, called loudly for reforms. As in the famous Peasant Rebellion of John Ball, the lord granted his consent to the demands but then, disarming the suspicions of the recalcitrants, ended the danger by punishing the leader.

Undoubtedly the great mass of the Japanese were wholly unaware of both the insurrections and of Russian visitors. News traveled slowly in feudal Japan, a fact which easily absolves the Russians of any real participation in the domestic difficulties of the Shoguns and the daimyos. But the effect produced upon the court officials and indirectly, therefore, by the orders sent out from Yedo to the coastal provinces, remains. Japan tightened her restrictions against aliens partly through the fear that foreigners would bring calamity.

The superstitions thus begun in the early days of alien intercourse long plagued the foreigners. In the larger centers of the land the Japanese, especially of the official classes, were able to accept the visitors as somewhat similar to themselves, though no true Japanese was ever quite convinced that *seiyu-jin* and Japanese are wholly equal. In the provinces distant from the capital, the more conservative farmer folk preserved the old traditions that the aliens were enemies. The strange coincidence between foreigners and catastrophe was current in the rural regions for long years after Japan was opened to trade.

VII

WASHINGTON,
WAR GOD IN JAPAN
1771–1787

BECAUSE an egocentric Polish adventurer plotted to advance his private interests, Japan took sides with the American colonists during the ordeal at Valley Forge. One year after the Declaration of Independence was signed, the Empire of the Rising Sun was praying earnestly for Washington's success.

Japan cherished no democratic principles; she had no special love for liberty. Her friendliness was sentimental. Fearing that the European despots who were busily annexing conquered territory would spread their influence to the East, Japan favored any opposition which might limit their expansion. Japanese statesmen considered that Japan had suffered injury from Portuguese and Spanish imperialists, from the rivalries of Holland and Great Britain, and from the alleged intrigues of Russians. Armies of secret agents were popularly, though quite falsely, believed to be spreading sedition throughout the Empire. Japan was prepared to give moral support to any rebellions which might weaken the strength of nations thought likely to attack the East.

Mauritz August Aladar, Graf von Beniowski, was unwittingly responsible for Japan's early pro-Americanism. A brave but thoroughly unscrupulous charlatan, an imaginative braggart who was economical of nothing but the truth, he insisted that Russia and Great Britain were planning to divide the world. For Russian aid against the Thirteen Colonies, he warned, England would allow the Tsar to take the Kurile islands, to annex Japan, and to add China to the Russian territories. Britain, in addition to reducing the rebellious colonists, would gain firmer footholds along the Good Hope route and would consolidate her gains in India.

Beniowski had himself voyaged in the East, although his exact itinerary is unknown. Few narratives are more detailed and less dependable than his recital of his wanderings. He omits all definite locations, offers no latitudes and longitudes (except one that is obviously erroneous), gives no soundings, no wind directions, no deviations of the compass, nor any other data such as one might expect from the trained navigator which he professes himself to be. It is fairly certain that he sailed from Kamchatka with eighty-seven men and nine women in May 1771, probably in a stolen ship, that he touched at Unalaska in the Aleutians, and that he then crossed the Pacific to Japan. Probably he received only the usual offerings of food, wood, and water when he came to Suruga bay, a hundred miles south of Tokyo, but his *Memoirs* give more picturesque details. By Beniowski's own story, he was greeted as an equal to the "king" and was allowed to open trade relations.

In exchange for this warm hospitality, Beniowski struck his Polish flag and hoisted Japanese colors on his ship. Then he sailed south, turned pirate, captured Takashima near Nagasaki and suffered shipwreck somewhere near the island of "Usmay Ligon" in the Luchu archipelago.

Germs of truth undoubtedly reside in some slight details of the narrative, but from the arrival at the imaginary "Usmay Ligon" onward to the end of the story, the legend is fantastic. An army of three hundred, armed only with parasols, waited upon Beniowski bearing a letter supposedly signed by a Portuguese missionary seventeen years before. (No Portuguese clerics had been permitted in Japan's territories for more than a century.)

"Stay with us," urged an islander of distinction clad in sky-blue taffeta, "and we will give you land. Daughters of nobles will be yours in marriage." Beniowski demurred, fearful that his companions "might displease the natives by caressing their women." The headman replied that no difficulty need be feared upon such score, provided the sailors touched only the girls and not the married women. "I told the company of this," says Beniowski. "The news produced a universal joy, and they immediately dispersed. I walked about. I found few who were not accompanied by young women, some of whom were real beauties."

Beniowski was again an honored guest. Seven young ladies, all garbed in white silk with blue sashes, were introduced for his inspection. "The choice would have been difficult, for there were three among them who might have disputed the preference with the most perfect work of human nature." Eventually he threw the veil over one Tinta Volanta, "luminous moon," who announced herself the grand-daughter of the holy missionary! Beniowski adds, "I kept one of the women from the ship by me for my protection."

Why he did not stay in such an Eden is not clear. "The open and benevolent character of these estimable people was such as will make me ever regret that I could not fix my abode here where the vices and wickednesses of Europe are unknown and the government is founded only upon the principles of humanity." In spite of the entreaties of his host, Beniowski sailed away, promising to return with "a society of virtuous, good, and just men to dwell upon the island and to adopt the manners, usages, and laws of the inhabitants."

The next stop of the Polish adventurer, according to the wholly unreliable *Memoirs,* was in Formosa, where he murdered two hundred unarmed natives. When the "blacks" protested, Beniowski raided a city, killing 1,156 Formosans and capturing 643 without suffering a single scratch. Formosa thereupon offered to make him king. Beniowski accepted, provided he were given 1,500 pounds weight of gold, and provided Formosa would wait two years until he could go to Europe and return. As a foretaste of what he might expect for all the remainder of his life, "The islanders became so familiar with us as to leave their daughters freely in our camp."

The fantastic oriental voyage was almost at an end. Beniowski sailed for China, en route to France to secure soldiers for his new kingdom. On October 3, 1771, he entered Macao Harbor, one of the few details in all the farrago of fiction which can be verified by other evidence than Beniowski's own. He arrived sick, penniless, tattered, and in disgrace, for one of the "women" of the party was discovered to be a male. Even hardened Macao was profoundly shocked by the disclosure.

Beniowski took passage on a French ship, though he fails to state how he paid his passage, and arrived in France in August 1772. At once, he declares, he was given command of an infantry regiment and was invited by Louis XV to set up a colony in Madagascar.

Such were the antecedents of the man who first caused Japan to think favorably of the United States. Beniowski retailed his suspicions of the imaginary Anglo-Russian plot to Comte de Vergennes, newly appointed French Foreign Minister. To De Vergennes, who had seen the actual workings of just such a plan at the time when Poland was divided, the scheme seemed plausible. At diplomatic posts in Constantinople and at Stockholm, then as now clearing houses for secret agents, De Vergennes had watched such plots mature.

Fearing an Anglo-Russian alliance, De Vergennes set the diplomatic machinery of France in motion to prevent such an understanding. To friendly neighbors he sent warning messages against the coming coalition; to Catherine of Russia he suggested the advisability of an armed neutrality rather than of an alliance that might involve the Russians in a war. France threw in her lot with Britain's rebellious colonists. England, it was hoped, would be so seriously embroiled in war that no time could be devoted toward widening the British realms.

The news was passed around the world to distant Yedo. The Dutch were carriers of gossip. Beniowski's rumors were current in Paris early enough in 1776 for the Dutch ships of that summer to convey the news to the Netherlandish agencies in Java and Japan. By April 1777, Japan was warned that British and Russians were planning an attack upon the Empire.

Japan was never loath to suspect the foreigner. Fear of impending attack has ever been rife. As early as 1613, when Saris arrived in the *Clove,* rumors were abroad that aliens intended to annex the Empire. More than a hundred suspected alien agitators were rounded up in that year for deportation to Macao. Anti-foreignism, which scoffing critics today sometimes call "espionitis," has been pandemic in Japan from the beginnings of her acquaintance with occidental visitors.

In such circumstances the scope for rumor widens. Almost every Japanese was certain that the red stuffs imported from Europe were dyed with babies' blood. "Red-faced, light-haired barbarians who had no heels and who had to prop up their shoes with artificial blocks, who ate large animals whole at one sitting and who carved up cooked eagles at their feasts" would feel no qualms at throttling oriental independence. Such men as these from Britain, reinforced by the man-eating Russian "Red Hairs" were, Japan was easily convinced, meditating evil. Holland took no trouble to disabuse the Japanese of such misunderstandings.

The inevitable result was a reaction in favor of any peoples who might oppose the Russians and the Britons. Dutch merchants at Deshima encouraged a pro-American sentiment, proclaiming that the Netherlandish people strongly favored the rebellious colonists. Nothing was said to indicate the pro-British views of Holland's king.

Even the Dutch imports of the time were chosen with a view toward furthering the friendly feeling toward the new United States. Amsterdam and Batavia, in the yearly budgets of news sent to the Shogun's officers, included generous accounts of the American progress against the tyrant Britain. Hastily drawn pictures of George Washington were prepared for distribution to the Japanese; samples of the new American colors were included in the gifts sent to the Yedo government. In consequence of the well-designed anti-British propaganda, Japan swung sharply toward America's side. George Washington became a hero to the Japanese. Many of the upper classes kept his portrait in their homes, giving it a place of honor, and continued for a century to look upon him as a mighty champion of Japan's independence.

No doubt they totally misunderstood his aims in other ways. There could be but slight sympathy in Japan for any plan of throwing off the yoke of kings or of insisting on the right of representation for all citizens. The principles laid down in the Declaration of Independence would not have been tolerated for a moment by the feudal-minded Japanese. There is no evidence whatever to show that the Dutch gossipers ever bothered with passing on the news that such a document had ever been drafted by the colonists.

Washington was, to Japanese, a foreign prince struggling to protect Japan, a far-seeing, noble general who so admired the spirit of the Empire that he was anxious to protect her life. His purity and lofty moral character they could hold in admiration, for these were qualities which Japan esteemed in her own samurai. They knew, of course, that he was not of their high lineage, but his virtues, as reported by the Dutch, seemed surely sufficient to entitle him to recognition as a minor hero. Years later it was hard to disabuse the minds of Japanese of the idea that Washington was worshiped as a war-god in America.

America itself was wholly unknown to any native of the Empire, but in her gratitude for service rendered in protecting Japan against Anglo-Russian plots, Japan was willing to grant slight concessions to the altruistic colonists if ever they should visit Japan's shores.

It was America's hard luck that no trader turned up in Japanese waters for fifteen years thereafter and then, lucklessly, at a time when anti-foreign feelings were running high. Before the eighteenth century had passed, the Stars and Stripes were borne into a harbor of the southern island, but by that time the affections of the Japanese had cooled, the admiration for her foreign helpers had faded, nor were the Dutch as warmly enthusiastic for Americans as of old. Japan has never since been as friendly to Americans as she would have been in 1777.

Connoisseurs of the ironic will not fail to note that Beniowski, whose feverish imagination had conceived the wild idea of Anglo-Russian plotting, gained but little from the canard which he had set in motion. His rumor, received and spread so eagerly by De Vergennes, repaid the inventor only a small sum. At the Colonial Office he was turned down when he applied for preferment; Franklin, it is said, gave Beniowski some encouragement, but in all probability it was but a blessing and good wishes rather than actual monetary aid.

Of this, of course, the Japanese knew nothing. They were too engrossed in watching new foreign "depredations" which seemed to confirm the Beniowski rumors. Britain, France, and Russia were dispatching expeditions to explore the Kurile islands and Hokkaido; Elias Hasket Derby's *Grand Turk,* out of Salem, was nosing into Canton Harbor with the overt approval of the French. Alien interests in the East were multiplying rapidly.

To Japanese the only possible explanation was that immediate attack was contemplated on their islands. In this they were completely justified, provided a sufficiently broad interpretation be given to the word "attack," for almost all important maritime nations were convinced that some form of commercial naval base was needed in the East. British and American whalers, searching new hunting grounds, had worked their way into the North Pacific. The long routes round the Capes, together with the devastations of fierce Pacific storms, intensified the need for harbors where the battered vessels might refit. And, since Russia guarded jealously her harbors in Kamchatka and since no ports were open in North China, only unknown ports in undeveloped regions seemed available as refuge in emergencies.

No charts were trustworthy enough for use. Holland seemed to take delight in furnishing her European rivals with false maps of the Japanese coastlines; the Russian atlases were wholly unreliable.

Even in Japan herself, as foreigners were later to discover, no true knowledge of the contours were available. Forbidden by strict legislation from engaging in much foreign exploration, the Japanese knew almost nothing of their northern islands.

Japan had voiced no claim, in fact, to the Hokkaido until the island was brought to Hideyoshi's knowledge, in December 1590, by an excited stranger, Yoshihiro Takeda, who recounted its supposed riches. Hideyoshi, always anxious to extend his sway, accepted what he considered Takeda's homage, renamed the stranger Matsumai, and appointed him governor of the hastily annexed dominion. Governors were regularly named thereafter, but the Hokkaido was regarded solely as a fishing ground and not as an essential part of Japan proper. No Japanese subject seems to have penetrated into the northern sections of the island until 1684, long after South Japan was well known to foreigners. An exploration party sent out by Shogun Tsunayoshi came back with news that it had stayed a winter on "a very large continent, between 40 and 50 degrees latitude, believed to be America." It came back, however, "without bringing the least account whatever of the country or its inhabitants."

Under the circumstances it is not surprising that nearly all the task of mapping the contours of Japan, and even of establishing the Empire's geographical position, had to be carried out by European mariners. Japan, content with isolation and hostile to alien intercourse, had slight incentive to explore. Russia, anxious for warm-water harbors, was moving southward from Kamchatka; Holland, consolidating her position in the Nagasaki area, held all approaches from the south. Any other nation seeking entry was compelled to find some new avenue for access.

France anticipated Britain in the later eighteenth-century rush to learn the truth about Japan's position. The French Government in 1785 sent out Jean-François Galaup, Comte de la Perouse, with two ships to explore the whole Pacific coast. Specifically he was told to sail from the west coast of America to find a Northwest Passage, and then, after surveying the fur trade of Canada and the whale fisheries of the South Pacific, to draw up a report on future French commercial possibilities.

De la Perouse, forty-four-year-old veteran of the war against Great Britain, hero of naval engagements in East Canada and in Hudson Bay, crossed from Alaska to Hawaii en route for Macao at just about the time when Beniowski, whose romantic tales had probably inspired the whole adventure, was dying in the Madagascar jungles. From Macao and the Philippines he moved northward, paralleling the mainland, to Korea, the Maritime Provinces, and Japan. Unluckily, after pioneering through the Japan Sea in waters that no European navigator had yet sailed, he failed to penetrate the narrow straits that lie between Saghalien and the mainland. Thus he failed to prove the separation of that island from the continent of Asia, but by sailing through the waterway that now bears his name he showed that Hokkaido and Saghalien were separate islands. The hopes inspired by the uninformed Debune that Japan might be joined by land to Asia were thus shattered by the La Perouse discoveries.

Fortunately for later explorers, La Perouse called at Kamchatka late in 1787 to dispatch a complete report of his discoveries overland to Paris. Had he not done so all the major portions of his work would have been wholly lost, for La Perouse, sailing on for the South Seas, died with all his men in shipwreck. Some scattered fragments of his vessels, found thirty-eight years later on the beach of an unfrequented island, are the only further records of his voyages.

News of the La Perouse adventures had, however, reached both Europe and Japan; the former through his messages sent home from Kamchatka, the latter by messengers from Macao to the Dutch. In accordance with the terms of the commercial concession, the Netherlanders promptly informed Japan that France was marauding along the Hokkaido shores. The news, arriving almost simultaneously with excited messages from the northern daimyos concerning the "violations" of the foreigners, convinced Japan that France had now joined the Anglo-Russian alliance to despoil the Empire. Japan never underestimated the wickedness of aliens.

Elementary principles of international fair play might, it could be supposed, have led Holland to interpret French activities in a more favorable light. Certainly there was but slight danger that, after France had been crushed in the disastrous Seven Years' War, the French might possess sufficiently important naval stations en route to the East to constitute herself a threatening trade rival. But Holland took no chances. Not even her friends the French were safe against the slanders broadcast from the Nagasaki factory. Disquieting rumors, highly colored in Dutch interests, stressed the hostile purpose of all other nations but the Netherlands.

Thus the most dire reports were circulated concerning the fate of the crew of a Japanese junk wrecked in the Aleutians in 1782. The plain facts, which must have been available to Holland through her agents at St. Petersburg, were that the Russian officials showed a high degree of humanity in rescuing the survivors and that the castaways were given posts of honor. None of this was made known to Yedo officers. All that they were told was that a Japanese vessel had been wrecked and that the crew was captured. Japan was left to draw its own conclusions.

These conclusions were inevitable. Ever since the exclusion policy had been decreed in 1636, Japan's savage law code had commanded death, or life imprisonment, to any stranger found upon her shores. Father Sidotti, certainly a harmless visitor, had been clapped into jail for eight years until he died, upon the mere suspicion that he must have been a spy. The Luzon ship of 1640 had brought sixty-one unfortunates who were tortured to their death. And since each people, in the absence of specific information to the contrary, tends to assume that every nation follows customs similar to its own, the Japanese leaped to the conclusion that the Russians must have massacred the sailors cast away upon Aleutian shores.

Japan did Russia an injustice by so thinking. The junk's crew, headed by Captain Daikokuya Kodaya, was sheltered through the winter and was offered passage home, but the Japanese protested earnestly against repatriation. The brutal law, providing that Japanese who visited a foreign land must die, was well drilled into sailor minds. Kodaya insisted on remaining in the Muscovite dominions.

Like most contemporary Japanese sailors, Kodaya was of comparatively low social status, but caste barriers were no deterrent to his progress. His quick and eager mind readily picked up the Russian language. Kodaya became professor of Japanese at Irkutsk; he was eventually sent across Siberia to be presented at the court of Catherine the Great.

He came to St. Petersburg at a most fortunate moment. Catherine was anxious to seek new contacts with the outer world. She had been meditating the opening of trade relationships with China and the East. Kodaya's audience, though no great social triumph for the Japanese, convinced her that profit and prestige were possible for Russia in Japan. She ordered a special mission to be prepared for visiting the Orient.

Kodaya, through complete misunderstanding of Western social customs, turned the audience into a bedlam. He appeared with his hair tied in three tufts hanging behind his shoulders. His coat and breeches were of silvery material, with rose-colored embroideries and with huge red buttons. The undergarment was of blue brocade. White stockings with black Persian boots completed the costume, save for the huge black hat which he carried under one arm and the great cane which he bore in the other.

On arrival before the Tsarina Kodaya's composure left him. "Around the Imperial throne," he said, "the Court ladies stood, beautiful, like snow. I was terribly confused and did not know what was said to me." He retained, however, a vague memory of the instructions given him in advance. As Catherine extended her hand in greeting, Kodaya bent over, and while Catherine awaited the polite kiss, Kodaya, whose Japanese training included nothing of public osculation, carefully licked the royal hand!

The story of the animal-like licking of the imperious lady's hand and of the tumultuous scene that followed as her courtiers rescued the astonished Tsarina must have been familiar to the Dutch. The Netherlandish ambassador could not have been ignorant of the presence of so bizarre a figure at the capital, nor of the excited gossip that flew about the palace. Court conversation, so eagerly collected by the eighteenth-century envoys, buzzed about the preparations that were undertaken for the diplomatic mission to the East. But whatever the minister reported to The Hague, no inkling of the reception to Kodaya was carried to Japan. Instead, the Deshima merchants solemnly warned the Shogun that an elaborate Russian naval expedition was about to descend upon the Empire. Transport across Siberia was so slow, and Russian preparations were so sluggish, that Holland had ample time to send couriers from Europe to Yedo before the Russians actually arrived.

That the warnings were of Muscovite attack rather than of friendly visit need not be surprising. Knowing that her real rival in the Orient would in time be Russia, Holland spared no effort to discredit the man-eating Red Hairs in advance. Japan, too, was most receptive to such news. Old memories of Kosirewski and of Spanberg were revived to prove the evil Russian motives, while the Beniowski rumors reinforced the fear that Catherine intended to reduce Japan to servitude. Japan made ready to repulse her Russian visitors.

VIII

KENDRICK, THE FIRST AMERICAN

1787–1791

NONE of the ill luck that accompanied foreign efforts to open Japan had abated. Holland's warnings of the impending Russian "raid" came at a time when social unrest in Japan was alarming the rulers.

Four abortive revolts marked the decade of the 1770's. One, at Takayama in Hida province, required the use of firearms to suppress the unruly peasantry; another, in Shinano province, caused the caging of two leaders and the exile of six other instigators of disorder. The next decade was to witness even more serious uprisings. Five rebellions broke out during the first seven years of the 1780's, beginning in Kozuke province and spreading to the neighboring Shinano. For the first time in modern Japanese history, dissatisfaction was concentrated in an important area, the district close to Yedo.

Nature, too, was dealing disaster. Mount Asama, among the most violent of Japan's volcanoes, erupted with ashes, sand, and pumice stone in September 1783. Twenty-seven villages were flooded by boiling water from the crater. Thousands of helpless Japanese were trapped and boiled to death. The catastrophe was the most serious calamity Japan had suffered since the great earthquakes of 1707 killed five thousand people.

Japan was prompt to trace connection with the foreign demons. The 1707 earthquake had been a portent that Sidotti was about to land. Another temblor, killing 1,335 at Hirosaki, hard by the famous pilgrim shrine of Iwaki-san in North Japan, was contemporaneous with a bold proposal by Tsu Matsudaira for the furtherance of foreign trade. Matsudaira had proposed the building of ships for voyages abroad, but this defiance of the exclusion edict was followed by disaster and, indeed, by Matsudaira's death. Quite obviously, to Japanese minds, the gods were distinctly hostile to his plan.

The Asama catastrophe similarly accompanied the disclosure of a secret scheme by Governor Tango of Nagasaki to import carpenters from Batavia to teach shipbuilding to Japan. Tango's plan comprised only the construction of ships for transporting copper on the dangerous voyages from Nagasaki to Osaka, but it was discouraged by Opperhoofd Titsingh because Java possessed too few shipwrights to spare any for service in Japan. Tango planned to send several Japanese to Batavia to learn the trade. This was of course a violation of exclusion and was, upon disclosure, expiated by Tango's blood.

Indeed, the conspiracy to upset exclusion implicated very high officials in the Shogunate. Tonoma-yamossin, councilor of state and uncle of the Shogun, was deeply tinted by liberal ideas. Hard-shelled conservatives, called "Frogs in the Well" because "when they look up they can see no more of the sky than the small circumference of the well allows them to perceive," saw in the Tonoma innovations a direct blow at ancient Japanese traditions. To keep the purity of Japan's national spirit a cabal of "Frogs in the Well" murdered the liberal Tonoma in the very palace of the Shogun.

Worse was to come. In 1788 a great fire devastated the holy city of Miako, making thousands homeless and, even more portentous, burning down the palace of the sacred Emperor himself.

Fire and earthquake were surely no novelties to a land which looked on Yedo's frequent conflagrations as "Yedo Flowers," nor is there to sophisticated moderns any portent in such disasters. The inner circles at the court, the wise men of the temples, were surely not stampeded into anti-alienism at the curious coincidences of catastrophe just before or shortly after foreign calls. Few new orders were sent out to fight back aliens just because a volcano had erupted.

But to other eighteenth-century Japanese, ill educated at best and completely illiterate in most cases, these were evil omens. Minor officials at remote harbors, especially at ports where strangers seldom touched, were well imbued with fear of consequences should foreigners break through the barriers. Gossip, passed from mouth to mouth throughout Japan, was wont to magnify the terrors of the "Red Hairs" and to point out, with careful attention to exaggeration, every possible connection between foreigners and danger to Japan. Coincidence was sufficient proof that cause and effect showed ominously the baleful influence of aliens.

It was at such a juncture that Americans blundered into the restricted harbors. Cheerfully unaware of the recent history of the land to which he sought an entry, without any realization of what might be the temper of the natives, and in all probability scornful of the psychologic subtleties involved, a blustering New Englander drove headlong into forbidden seas. Had he been thoroughly aware of how friendly Japan had once been, in theory, to Americans for their resistance to the supposed Anglo-Russian plot, he could not have been more confident of a welcome. In all ignorance of the social customs, the language, and the economic needs of the people with whom he sought to trade, he thrust himself uninvited and unwanted into a private port. The consequences can be easily imagined.

Certainly a more tactful mariner than John Kendrick, Boston skipper of the brigantine *Lady Washington,* might have been found to take the Stars and Stripes into Japan's waters, but surely none could have been more colorful. A former whaler and privateersman, fur trader along the British Columbia coast, and first American sea captain to round the Horn, in the famous ship *Columbia,* Kendrick was one to command attention in any situation.

Ability to make friends was not the most outstanding characteristic of the gigantic Kendrick, nor was he gifted with undue patience. If any Yankee sailor could have been described as bluff and hearty, it was the master of the *Lady Washington.*

The whole journey to Japan is one which imperatively demands a saga of the seas. Because he fell in love with Cape Verde Island life, he lingered there for six weeks while his owners thought that he was on his way from Boston to the fur-trading harbor of Nootka Sound on Vancouver island. Then, when he sailed reluctantly away to round the Horn in the *Columbia,* he came to blows with a rash second mate who dared to criticize him for his tarrying. Arriving at Nootka, he spent almost a year in idleness waiting for the Indians to bring him furs as cargo for Canton.

The indolence not only ate away the owners' profits but brought on conflict with the Spanish. Indeed, a world war was but narrowly averted. For many years the Spaniards had been claiming all the western coast of the Americas by virtue of their original discoveries in the South Sea waters. Russia and the British were staking out their claims by right of settlement and occupation. The small Nootka inlet on the west coast of Vancouver island, christened and made known by Captain Cook in 1778, became the center of hostilities.

All three nations planned simultaneously, and in complete ignorance of each other's actions, to set up settlements in the Nootka area as the base for fur trade between the Northwest coast and China.

Estevan José Martinez, commander of the Spanish warship *Princesa,* found Kendrick lolling comfortably at Nootka when the *Princesa,* with her consort *San Carlos,* dropped anchor in May 1789. Martinez, sent from San Blas in Mexico to found a Spanish settlement, challenged Kendrick's right to use the harbor, charging that the port belonged to Spain and that the ships at anchor in the harbor were interlopers poaching on the Spanish fur preserves.

Kendrick found himself in difficulties, as did his fellow captains, Robert Gray of the *Lady Washington* (Kendrick and Gray later changed vessels), William Douglas of the *Iphigenia,* and John Mears of the *Felice.* None of them had legal rights to trade in British waters, since none possessed a valid license from either the South Sea Company, nor from the Hudson Bay Company's Pacific coast subsidiaries. Two of the ships, indeed, the *Iphigenia* and the *Felice,* were pretending to be Portuguese, with false papers, dummy captains, and Portuguese consignees at Macao. Douglas insisted that no one on the *Iphigenia* could speak any other tongue than Portuguese. The elaborate pretense served a double purpose; in China it was expected to secure lower port charges, for Portugal enjoyed special favors, while in America, it was hoped, the Portuguese masquerade would enable the ships to evade the necessary South Sea Company license requirement.

Martinez was not in the least impressed by all the mummery, for to the Spaniards, Portuguese as well as British and Americans were invaders. After friendly courtesies, in which each of the skippers invited all the rest to dinner, Martinez grew more and more insistent that the vessels leave. He was loath to resort to force, fearing that war might be declared against Spain in such event, but when the captains refused in all politeness to withdraw, Martinez was obliged to issue threats. The *Iphigenia* and the *Felice* were seized as prizes, but after twelve days' detention were released on their promise to set sail; the *Columbia* set out, under Gray, on its first American round-the-world voyage. Kendrick proved, for once, a master of diplomacy.

Thinking fast, he replied to Martinez' demands by asserting that the *Lady Washington* had been damaged in a storm and that he was in port to save his ship and to cure his men of scurvy. In reality, said Kendrick, "I believe this harbor to be Spanish and I, as a good friend of Spain, agree that Americans have no right to live here, but surely Spain will not deny the common rights of humanity to ships in dire distress."

To prove his friendliness to Spain, Kendrick asked permission for his son, whom he called Juan, in Spanish fashion, to join the *Princesa's* staff of officers. In return for the favor, he agreed to bring from Canton to the Spanish ship a set of altar ornaments and seven pairs of boots for the ranking officers of the *Princesa*. Thus he gained freedom from captivity and, what was quite as much appreciated, the right to revisit the fur centers on another voyage.

The pleased Spaniards sailed away, to capture soon after, as it happened, the British ship *Argonaut*, which was to follow Kendrick to Japan. Kendrick lingered longer at his anchorage awaiting the arrival of Indians with furs. When they came, Kendrick's quick temper plunged him into more hot water. Angrily he accused two chiefs of stealing the ship's stores. When they refused to confess, he bound the men to cannon, thrusting one leg of each man down the barrel of a gun, and threatened to give the signal for firing. Luckily the true culprits, moved by some unusual impulse, blurted out their guilt. Kendrick hastened to explain that he had been joking when he threatened to blow the Indians to bits, but the chiefs were not appeased. Waiting for a favorable moment they suddenly seized the ship and almost killed the doughty skipper as he fought them back with marlinspike and dagger. Then Kendrick set sail for Honolulu, where he founded the trade in sandalwood which later grew to profitable proportions. He then went on to China.

No one fully knows what happened in that peculiar land, Kendrick never seems to have made reports to his owners, and though he made at least two successful trips, seems not to have remitted the proceeds back to Boston. We do know that he delayed for fourteen months in Canton, leisurely refitting his ship and transforming it from a sloop to a brigantine, but the delay is far too long to be thus explained. That he had an attack of fever in the beautifully named Dirty Butter Bay we also know, and we are informed that he went to jail for difficulties with the Chinese customs rules.

Kendrick had protested against the heavy bribery that was necessary in doing business with the eighteenth-century Chinese officials. Commissions, duties, presents, and just plain graft were required at almost every step. Foreign skippers protested that to observe the meticulous Chinese laws required such an outlay of cash that all the expected profits of a trading voyage were completely lost. Since the Chinese government had given a virtual monopoly of foreign trade to twelve ship brokers and since these monopolists, the so-called Hong Merchants, insisted on having the cargoes made over to themselves before they would take action, the foreign captains considered smuggling cheaper than compliance with the law.

Kendrick was one of those who sought to evade the official regulations. Since his owners had no agent or factor of their own residing at Canton, he was supposed to choose one of the Hong Merchants and to make a bargain with him before going up river to Canton. The hot-headed skipper, perhaps in ignorance that the Hong Merchant assumed all responsibility for any depredations or misdemeanors committed by the aliens within Chinese jurisdiction, refused to drop anchor at Macao. This was a double violation of the law since an alien ship, in addition to choosing a Hong Merchant, must also apply for a permit and a pilot for Canton. Without the permit to proceed, the vessel was liable to seizure.

The *Lady Washington* passed through the Typa, the usual harbor at Macao, and sailed on to Dirty Butter Bay, a small harbor ten or twelve miles distant, where Chinese officialdom was more complaisant. Kendrick's small cargo of some five hundred sealskins, worth approximately $11,000 at the current market, was thought by him to be too tiny to pay port charges of about $6,000 and a tip, or cumshaw, of approximately $4,000 more.

Unhappily for Kendrick, his vessel was spied en route to the smugglers' haven. When, therefore, he went overland to Canton, leaving his ship at Dirty Butter Bay, Kendrick was arrested for violation of the port rules and, having insufficient funds to buy his freedom, was compelled to serve his term. The ship, safely in Dirty Butter Bay, "then out of Chinese jurisdiction," swung at anchor until he was eventually freed. Kendrick was released, but under strict injunctions never to return to China.

In seeking a market for his rejected cargo Kendrick was severely limited. Next to China, the richest field for trading was in the New Guinea area, and this, no doubt, Kendrick fully intended to exploit. Twenty thousand dollars invested in coarse cutlery, calico, cottons, beads, small mirrors, and trinkets would fetch an eventual profit of twenty times that sum even in a small ship like the ninety-ton *Lady Washington*. But with sealskins as his present cargo Kendrick had no hope of taking part in such a trading venture.

According to gossip on the Chinese waterfront, Japan afforded an exceptional market for just such a cargo. Kendrick, forbidden to sell at Canton, resolved to scout out the possibility of an illegal trade with Japanese. He dared not visit Nagasaki lest the Dutch betray him as an interloper, but there were rumors of cities quite as rich and closer to the capital.

Kendrick therefore steered the *Lady Washington,* in May 1791, into Wakayama Harbor. It had been his intention to press on to Osaka or to Sakai, both nearer to the Imperial seat at Miako, but the heavy rip tides that race through the narrow straits on either side of Awaji Island were too much for the little vessel to overcome.

Never a lucky man at best, Captain Kendrick came to Wakayama under grievous handicaps. Not only was the time unfortunate, for Japan's romantic interest in America had long since cooled, but the port was probably the least well selected harbor in the Empire. Since Walton's visit with the Russian ship to Kochi in 1739 the Japanese had gained a wider knowledge of the western world. Next to Yedo itself, Wakayama was probably the most violently anti-foreign center. It was governed by the Shogun's chief supporter and by a family which was designated as the only other clan from which the Shoguns might be chosen. Instead of entering a port which might conceivably welcome alien intercourse, poor Captain Kendrick had selected a city which prided itself on its exclusiveness. Wakayama was more loyal to the Shogun than almost any other that might have been suggested. Rebellions against the exclusionist policy of the Tokugawas had not been unknown, either in the south of Japan or in the Mito provinces to the north, but Wakayama was in the very midst of territory controlled by the Kii branch of the Tokugawa family, a branch bitterly hostile to its Mito kinsfolk. The Wakayama leaders were more certain to be pro-exclusionist than any other rulers save the Yedo men themselves.

The cards were stacked against Captain Kendrick from the start, even had there been no anti-foreign feeling roused by Russian and French scouting. But bluff John Kendrick made the situation even worse. By neglecting the fine shades of courtesy expected of all strangers and scrupulously observed by the Dutchmen at Nagasaki, Kendrick set himself down in Japanese opinions as a low-caste man of no etiquette. His leisurely deliberation in transacting business would certainly have been appealing to the Japanese temperament, his whimsicalities and vacillation might have been understood and readily forgiven; but Kendrick committed a more cardinal offense in that he would not recognize the need for yielding to Japanese demands for deference. He was too dictatorial, too self-willed, too jealous of authority, to succeed in doing business with the meticulous officials of the Shogun.

But the decisive blow to Kendrick's hopes came when the Japanese discovered what the *Lady Washington* carried as her cargo. Instead of the silks and sandalwood and sugar which the Japanese desired, she was loaded with sealskins, a commodity for which Japan had then but little use and which in any case stamped its handlers as of extremely low social standing. For, in Japan then as now, only the outcasts were low enough to touch the skins or bodies of dead animals.

Kendrick was shunned thenceforth as a pariah. He could not, by the limited means of communication open to him, make clear the difference between the ways such matters were regarded in Japan and the United States. Kendrick spoke neither Japanese nor Dutch, nor was his knowledge of Chinese writing—which the Japanese might have interpreted—sufficient to convey abstract ideas of foreign folkways.

Realizing, therefore, that the interloper had no worthy goods to offer and that he had no sincere intention to comply with proper oriental etiquette, the Wakayama authorities were only too glad to compel him to retire from their dominions. Their guard boats were instructed to tow him out to sea with unmistakable warnings not again to come back to forbidden waters.

Thus ended the first American attempt to open trade with Japanese, an attempt that failed because the wrong captain sailed in an unlucky ship with an undesired cargo to the worst possible port of an unwilling Empire. Everything was hostile from the start to such an adventuring.

And yet how easily the circumstances might have been different! Kendrick was associated on that venture with James Douglas, captain of the New York sloop *Grace,* a ship that had none of the "hoodoo" traditions of the *Lady Washington*. Kendrick, too, had made profit and a reputation by opening the Hawaiian trade in sandalwood, a commodity which Japanese importers earnestly desired. But before he sailed with Douglas from the moorings in Dirty Butter Bay near Macao, he had discharged the one cargo which might have won him entry. He had remaining only the sealskins which spelled failure to his venture.

Had Douglas carried Kendrick's sandalwood in the *Grace* to some more northern port controlled by Mito men, and had he proved more pliable than the stiffer Kendrick to Japanese demands for formal etiquette, Perry's opening of Japan could have been anticipated by more than sixty years. The time was ripe for foreign intercourse, as every Japanese observer knew, provided the right man appeared with the right cargo. But Kendrick, the unbending skipper who had been jailed in Macao and ordered never to return to China under pain of death because he refused to pay tribute to the port officials, was by no means the proper agent to inaugurate a trade relationship.

Kendrick's subsequent career is quite as fascinating as his earlier experiences. The energetic skipper who, paradoxically, loved to linger in tropical surroundings, had no intention of returning to an ice-bound New England. Knowing that trade with Japan appeared impossible, he resolved to brave the Chinese wrath again, despite the order of exile that hung over him.

So, always alert to new commercial possibilities, he sought to create a new triangular trade route. The former practice had been to take New England goods to British Columbia, especially to Nootka Sound on Vancouver Island, exchange the cargo for sealskins, and then, taking the furs to China, to reload with Chinese wares. This course Kendrick sought to shorten by selling his furs to Boston-bound vessels at Hawaii. Then, loading his own ship with pearls and sandalwood, he could exchange his cargo for the Chinese products in some safe oriental port. The new route, if successful, would give him a much speedier turnover than the longer former course.

New disappointments met him in Hawaii. The three men whom he had assigned to gather sandalwood had left the islands, and no cargo had been stored for him. But Kendrick was adaptable to changed conditions. Abandoning for the moment his idea of Chinese trade, he plunged happily into the midst of a Hawaiian civil war. His side prevailed. Kendrick, to advertise his own importance, insisted that he be given a salute of seven guns.

The demand was granted readily. The salute was fired at high noon while the little *Lady Washington* was gaily decked with colors. Kendrick gave a dinner while the shots were being fired. And then came tragedy for, though the first six guns had been unshotted, the seventh, by some oversight, was fully loaded. The last shot of the salute to Kendrick's prowess crashed through the wooden side of his ship and killed him while he sat at table. It was a fitting ending to the life of an adventurer whose whole career was one of most dramatic incidents.

So much of Kendrick's career was passed in the pursuit of ends which would not be enthusiastically approved by law or ethics that, after his death, the story of his exploits was, so far as possible, kept from general knowledge. His visits to Japan, while known to fellow-captains and told in sailor yarns, received slight attention in America. Japan preserved few records of his call, while American historians were so impressed by Perry's more successful later visits that Kendrick's abortive effort was forgotten. The exploits of John Kendrick call imperatively for a full-length biography.

IX

PROHIBITING HERESIES

1792

SOON after the abortive Kendrick visit the usual ill luck attending foreign efforts to open trade was again evident. The gods, angry at the profanation of Japan, caused Unzen-dake, the famous volcano of Shimabara peninsula in Kyushu, to erupt. The summit of the mountain entirely disappeared; the volcano vomited ashes over the neighborhood; torrents of boiling water flooded the villages, and vapors, heavy as thick smoke, blanketed the countryside. Twenty-seven settlements were destroyed by the eruption.

Three weeks later these warnings, popularly believed to have been caused by the arrival of an alien ship, were reinforced by a second eruption from a neighboring crater. The lava, streaming from the orifice, flowed in a burning stream, "setting the country aflame for miles around."

Even these afflictions did not end the anger of the gods. As though to put an end forever to the thought that Japan should ever compromise with foreigners, new calamities fell upon the regions which had proved most hospitable to aliens. Within a month after the second eruption the whole island of Kyushu was shaken by an earthquake. More than fifteen thousand died in a catastrophe which reduced a whole province "to a deplorable condition and even altered the outline of the coast." The gods were obviously punishing Japan for tolerating alien ideas. Conservative "Frogs in the Well" ascribed the events to the yearnings of innovationists who had spurned the ancient virtues.

Shogun Iyenori, who had come to power five years before and who was to rule for half a century, moved quickly to avert further divine vengeance. Through his chief adviser, Sadanobu Matsudaira, he counseled thrift, sobriety, and moral cleanliness as safeguards against the anger of the gods. He warned against frivolities and luxuries, resorting to the popular Japanese practice of reform through ukase, and tightened the barriers against foreigners who might weaken the spiritual fiber of Japan.

The device of making aliens the scapegoats for Japan's tribulations is one that has been increasingly employed in recent years. By calling upon the patriotic sentiments of an intensely loyal people the administrators of the Empire have been able to restore the nation's flagging strength. Japan, in Iyenori's time, required no revolution for her spiritual revival, but then as now her resort to anti-foreignism as remedy for her domestic ills widened the gap between Orient and Occident. On numerous occasions such insularity, officially inspired, has deliberately destroyed the international comity that modern communication tends to foster.

Iyenori's restriction of the Dutch trade to one ship yearly, and his prohibition of the opperhoofd's yearly visit to Yedo indicate the growing anti-alienism. At a time when Western nations were becoming increasingly interested in oriental trade, and when wise Dutch counsel was imperatively needed, the opperhoofd was required to wait five years between his calls. But the Dutch were not alone in their exclusion from the court. Korea's envoy was no longer to be received in Yedo by the Shogun but by an under-officer at Tsushima. China could send but thirteen small junks a year.

Certain slight relaxations in the rules of foreign intercourse were, however, ordered. A new decree rescinded the death penalty imposed on foreigners who landed without permission. Foreign ships arriving in Japan under stress of storm would be destroyed only in the event that the crews resisted official orders. In all other cases, Iyenori declared, the vessels were to be interned until Yedo could issue detailed instructions. In 1792 a further decree ordered maritime police to show "outward kindliness toward foreigners." Neither rule relieved the foreigners from imprisonment pending Yedo's decisions.

These were the laws in force when the long-awaited Russian mission came to bring back Kodaya's castaways and to ask for trading privileges. Catherine of Russia hoped, as so many subsequent rulers were later to hope, that Japan would be grateful for the consideration shown to shipwrecked mariners and that commercial treaties might eventuate.

Nothing was known by Russians of the poisoned "news" which Hollanders had poured into the ears of Yedo officers. Though nothing had been told concerning the welcome given to Kodaya in Russia, the Dutchmen had been warning Japan for months that a Russian naval expedition was in progress. Japan was fully prepared to ward off the threat of conquest which the expedition presumably implied.

Sailing from Siberia in the autumn of 1792 the mission, led by young lieutenant Adam Laxman, graduate of Kodaya's Japanese language school, spent the winter at Nemuro in northeast Hokkaido. In the spring of the following year he sailed for Hakodate with his refugees. A short distance overland brought him to the town of Matsumai, now called Fukuyama, the nearest settlement on the Hokkaido to Japan's main island.

Laxman was supremely confident that his mission would win triumphant success. Though Kodaya had vainly tried to point out the probable hostility of the islanders, Laxman was convinced that he would be received as a philanthropist. His awakening was rude. Immediately upon arrival at Matsumai, Laxman and his men were jailed. Orders from Yedo had been received during the winter for the Hokkaido authorities to build strong fortifications about each important place in the south end of the island. The ruling daimyo, anxious to prove his patriotism, had in addition begun the building of ships deemed large enough to cope with the Russian squadron. He had fetched skilled navigators from Nagasaki and had trained his troops in military and in naval technique. Japan felt herself fully prepared, therefore, to match any display of strength which the "man-eaters" might display. When Laxman arrived with only one comparatively small ship and with a force of less than fifty men there was, in Japanese minds, no question but that Russia was a puny, harmless nation to be safely insulted.

Laxman made the error, which so many others were to repeat, of trying to persuade Japan by peaceful arguments to open trade negotiations. He was of too low rank to make a favorable impression upon an oriental people. His gentleness was misunderstood. No influential personage would come, so Japan reasoned, to a minor port in the Hokkaido where none but subject peoples lived, nor would any envoy of importance come with credentials signed only by the Governor of Siberia. St. Petersburg had counted on these very facts to prove the pacific purpose of the Laxman call!

Kimura, the Shogun's under-officer, felt safe, therefore, in treating Laxman with the hauteur proper toward men of low degree. Quickly he informed the unwelcome visitor that the Japanese exclusion law had suffered unwarranted violation.

"The usual penalty," Kimura went on to say, "for breaking this law, except at Nagasaki in the case of licensed Dutchmen, is life imprisonment, but since you are foreigners and do not know the law, we will not insist upon that penalty. Instead you must go back to Kamchatka and never return to Japan. You may, if you desire, leave these shipwrecked men with us, to be dealt with as the law commands, but never again, under any circumstances, must you bring back any of our subjects who are cast away. By our law, shipwrecked sailors are the property of that nation upon whose shores they may be cast."

Laxman left the castaways in Kimura's care, thinking, as would any envoy, that the men would be welcomed by their compatriots and would soon be restored to their homes. No such happy outcome followed. Kodaya and the other men brought back from shipwreck were hurried down to Yedo to appear before the Shogun. Iyenori gave them audience at a garden fête, but the occasion was not as gay as the reception had been at Catherine's court. The returned castaways were cross-examined by a fusillade of questions to discover whether the men were really spies. Every effort was put forth to trap the sailors into admissions that they had been maltreated by the Red Hairs. At the conclusion of the interview, the luckless men were hurried into life imprisonment, "without even the smallest intercourse with their families." Their memory was long forgotten; indeed, even their names remained unknown until well within the present century.

Even so, perhaps, Kodaya was more fortunate than a later countryman who, like him, became a teacher in a language school in Russia. Seiji Mayeda, a Vladivostock teacher, returned to Japan in 1907. He was immediately publicly assailed as a spy and he was assassinated in broad daylight on a busy Tokyo street. His assailant, who excused the crime on the score of "patriotism," escaped with a light sentence.

Whether Kimura's generosity in allowing Laxman a safe conduct out of Matsumai to Russia indicates a growing spirit of liberalism is a matter concerning which Japanese historians are not in full accord. Though the Russians were jailed throughout their stay in Matsumai, they were shown every civility consistent with imprisonment. They were maintained at government expense and, upon their departure, were showered with food and presents.

Japanese apologists explain that the Shogun recognized Japan's economic insufficiency and realized that foreign intercourse would prove beneficial. The law that every foreign vessel wrecked upon the coast must, if possible, be towed to Nagasaki and that every alien must be transported to that port had certainly not been followed. Perhaps, it is explained, the abundant crops and the restored welfare that replaced the disasters of the preceding year weakened the arguments of the old "Frogs in the Well" and favored the advocates of free intercourse. Certainly in Laxman's case the precept stressing "outward kindliness to foreigners" was abundantly observed.

Probably the leniency to Laxman was an accident due to division of authority. Kimura, it appeared, temporarily superseded the local daimyo, on orders from Yedo, but Kimura, armed with all the Yedo authority, was too mild by nature to make full use of his authority. Some functions he refrained from exercising, trusting that the daimyo would fulfil them; the latter, awed by Kimura's credentials, dared not intervene. Laxman escaped through a twilight zone of power.

A further conflict arises out of the Russian claim that Kimura gave to Laxman Imperial permission for a Russian ship to trade annually with Nagasaki, provided that the merchantman be unarmed and that no other port be visited. Laxman thoroughly believed that he owned such a document and, indeed, turned over an official paper to the Siberian governor who, in accordance with instructions, proudly forwarded the license to St. Petersburg.

Japan denies that any such permission was ever issued by any officer armed with sufficient authority for the purpose. Kimura's paper, the Japanese insist, was merely a certificate to Laxman allowing him an entry to Nagasaki. In short, the Japanese contend, Kimura gave Laxman only a letter of introduction. Nagasaki, as the only port to which any aliens whatever might be admitted, was the residence of officers who would have full power to treat with Russian envoys. Laxman misunderstood the introduction as a complete permission to carry on trade. When, therefore, other Russians came much later bearing Laxman's letter, the Nagasaki port officials refused to honor it because it was not carried by the man to whom it had been issued.

The Japanese explanation has the ring of truth, although in the absence of the document itself a final proof is lacking. Certainly even the Russians themselves wondered why the Tsarina failed to take complete advantage of the supposed trade license. No further step was taken by the Russians for a full ten years following the Laxman fiasco. The usual excuse for non-action was that Catherine was pre-occupied with French Revolutionary affairs and with the Polish partitions. It is quite as probable that Catherine, discovering from her scholars in the Academy of Sciences that the supposed license was not what it purported to be, felt that the time was not ripe for follow-ing up the Laxman beginning. Such a discovery might, moreover, account for the failure of Adam Laxman, despite his training in the Irkutsk Oriental School, to gain further opportunity to lead in the opening of Japan to Russian trade.

Little of this adventure seems to have been made known at the time. Rumors reaching Europe that "a Dutchman of the name of Laxman had been encouraged or permitted to establish himself in Yedo" testify to the garbled manner in which reports were spread. The confusion undoubtedly arose because Russia had no real desire to advertise her humiliation to the world. While diplomatic circles at St. Petersburg were aware that something had occurred to a man named Laxman in Japan, the name was sufficiently Teutonic for the natural assumption that he must have been connected with the Nagasaki factory. Japan had, of course, no reason to correct the mis-conception even had she known of it. Hendrik Doeff could there-fore deny that such a person as this Laxman had ever been connected with the Dutch East India Company. "In my three visits to the capital," said Doeff, "I never heard mention of such a name or such an occurrence." He used the matter as an argument to prove that Russians could not be relied upon to tell the truth about their re-lations with Japan.

If further proof were needed to convince Japan of Russia's relative inferiority, the turning back of "low-caste Laxman" in his attempt to break down Japan's isolation would have been sufficient. Subse-quent envoys were to be treated in progressively worse fashion now that Japan was certain that she could safely scorn the Muscovites. Russia had completely "lost face" in the eyes of Japanese.

No young lieutenant could have been expected to know that Japan, in the last decade of the century, was experiencing a moral revolu-tion whose announced purpose was to expel aliens and to exalt the ideals of an ancient past. To Japanese officials, fired with reactionary zeal for restoring the golden virtues of the forefathers of the land, the coming of a foreign ship spelled nothing but disaster. Ignorant Ainus in a backwoods province might have been anxious to make friends with Laxman and his men, but Japanese administrators knew that strangers were corrupting influences.

Only a few years earlier the Yedo government, through Minister of Education Hayashi, had issued an official edict, the "Prohibition of Heresies," in which every type of doctrine less than two centuries old, and every theory evolved in any land but China and Japan, were declared dangerous. Seldom has any nation decreed such thorough fundamentalism as this Hayashi edict of 1790. Even conservative theologians protested against the enforcement of the law.

The decree was, however, not merely a religious order but a momentous political document. The Tokugawa Shoguns, anxious to defend their régime against the peasant risings and against the threat of civil war from discontented daimyos, hoped to set up a rule of dead literalism which would effectively prevent the introduction of new and radical ideas. The nation was already static so far as economic development was concerned; if only the spread of new thought could be discouraged, the Tokugawa Shogunate would be firmly fixed upon the throne. Much the same theory has been professed more recently by those who would defend the present Japanese administration.

Strangely enough, the type of doctrine chosen as official thought had begun as a dynamic effort to break down the formalism which brought stagnation prior to Iyeyasu's time. Confucianism, which had come through Korea to Japan about 284 A.D., as a simple code of ethics, had hardened into a dead dogmatic code. As Dr. Tetsujiro Inouye, the famous Japanese philosopher who was martyred in 1934 for his beliefs, expressed it, when Confucianism came to Japan it had "been robbed of all its vigor, so that it was a fossil rather than a living organism." A thousand years later a famous Chinese sage, the revolutionist Chu Hi, preached the need for moral excellence rather than classic literalism and desiccated intellectual culture. Chu Hi's ideas, popularized in Japan as the Teishu system, captured the young restless leaders of Iyeyasu's epoch. The Teishu stress on gentleness, humility, and truthfulness, its search after perfection of human character as its chief purpose, became the official creed.

Iyeyasu failed to see that strict acceptance of the Teishu doctrine would in time undermine the government. Hidden deep within the tenets of the faith were reverence and loyalty for the Emperor. By insisting on the rigid uniformity of life and thought the Shoguns were encouraging ideas which kept the secluded Emperor, in whose name the usurping Shoguns professed to govern, in the very forefront of Japanese regard. Especially at Mito, where a disgruntled branch of the Tokugawas had its seat, this respect for the Emperor as rightful ruler was sedulously nourished.

But Teishu too, like any established dogma, degenerated once its position was secure. The decadence of the Genroku age when, from 1688 to 1703, the reigning Shoguns were men of superstition and of bigotry, blind votaries of a degraded faith that, in the words of Arthur Lloyd, "accorded to puppies and kittens that care which they failed to give their fellow men," reduced Teishu to the same routine formalism which it had been designed to kill. To ask Japan, as Minister Hayashi required her, to give up all new ideas and to accept only the beliefs that had been long outworn was to compel a nation to return to medievalism.

As a national policy the "Prohibition of Heresies" was unworkable. It was, in brief time, to be ignored. It never had been fully enforced in the enlightened centers of the empire. Only in the outlying fringes of the land, where royal officers administered laws with less regard to considerations of social thought, could there be real hope of enforcement. And, by the malignance of that ill luck which for generations pursued foreign efforts to be friendly with Japan, it was to just such an intellectual backwater that Laxman had brought his castaways. They were the innocent victims of an evil edict.

X

BRITONS IN THE NORTH

1791–1797

WHILE Kendrick was in Wakayama Harbor, Downing Street was pondering new plans for entering into relations with Japan. Few hopes were held that there would be great profits out of trade. No rich cargoes were anticipated, for rumors were rife that the Dutch monopolists were losing money in their enterprise. Now that the annual Deshima fleet had been reduced to but one ship a year, the Company had ceased to pay its old forty percent annual dividends. Well-informed shipping men understood that the enterprise was kept alive only by large money subsidies from the government and that the well-advertised yearly gains of $80,000 were paper profits produced by false entries in the books.

In any case Japan offered comparatively small profits to Europeans who could make larger gains within a shorter time by trading with Canton. The British East India Company argued strongly against expansion into Japan. Only camphor and copper were to be secured, the Company insisted, and neither was essential. Only a small demand for camphor was reported, while as for copper, British India provided a sufficient store. "The trade of Japan," said the Company, "never can become an object of attention for the manufactures and commerce of Great Britain."

Statesmen took a wider view. London knew the day was dawning when Britons would be trading heavily with the East. Already the Canton commerce was important and greedy glances were being cast at northern Chinese markets. If Peking could be approached from east as well as south, the London diplomats believed, a more effective pressure could be brought upon the Chinese Empire.

Over the strong protests of the British East India Company, therefore, the Privy Council perfected new plans for invading Japan's
markets. When Earl Macartney was dispatched in 1792 as the first
British envoy to China, he was supplied with credentials not only
to Peking but also to Yedo.

Again the luck ran counter to the hopes of Westerners. Macartney,
whose offer to trade was flatly rebuffed by the Chinese because, as
the Emperor replied, "We set no value on objects strange or ingenious," never had the chance to set foot on the Japanese islands.
Perhaps it was just as well for Anglo-Japanese relations that Macartney did not try his skill, for he was strangely vulnerable in Japan.
It had been he who in 1764 had concluded an entente with Russia.
Holland would have spared no effort to convince the gullible Japanese
that Macartney's arrival was proof positive that the Beniowski rumors
were well founded. Any diplomat who was *persona grata* at the
Russian court would have been under grave suspicion by the Shogun's officers.

Not a trained diplomat, therefore, but a lumbering sea captain was
the agent who endeavored to gain trading privileges from Japan.
James Colnett, another active participant in the squabbles over
Nootka, came in the *Argonaut* to seek an entry.

Colnett, though not an original participant in the Nootka Sound
controversy, was a central figure in that incident. Since his arrival
on the Northwest American coast in 1787 he had been the chief
carrier of American furs to the Canton market. His return cargoes,
it is perhaps interesting to note, were shiploads of Chinese coolies
for permanent settlement on Vancouver Island. Colnett believed that
the hardy and industrious Chinese, willing to work for exceedingly
small wages and inured to hardship, could well withstand the rigors
of pioneer life. It was a belief that transcontinental railway builders
were to revive.

Like Kendrick, Colnett was captured by the Spaniards for poaching, in July 1789, and was transported to San Blas in Mexico. The
incident almost precipitated international war. After Colnett recovered from an ailment which his second officer called insanity and
which Colnett himself described as delirium, Britain officially protested to Madrid against the treatment of the captain. Upon his
release from captivity, Colnett sailed again for China with a valuable
cargo of otter skins. He arrived in April 1791.

Misunderstandings, probably not wholly unconnected with Colnett's desire to avoid the payment of port duties, piled up. To his astonishment he discovered that a prohibition had been laid upon the sale of furs, at least so far as the *Argonaut's* small cargo was concerned. Chinese officials, angered that Colnett resorted to the bootleg harbor of Dirty Butter Bay, refused to allow the skins to be imported to Canton. The official explanation given to the skipper was that his title was not clear and that the otter fur belonged, so China suspected, to Russian owners. They suggested that the furs be sequestered pending the determination of their ownership.

Colnett, like Kendrick, cleared away in haste. Having no other possible market he also undertook to open the Japanese trade. The west coast of Japan and the Korean ports, "never before visited by a European vessel," seemed most suitable for his purpose, and so, in August 1791, he coasted the Kyushu shores. Hirado and Fukuoka proved unfriendly. Guard boats blocked all communication with the shore. Water, wood, and food were freely given, as was customary, but no pay was accepted. The harbor police rudely ordered the intruders "to be gone, refusing all suggestions of trade." Tsushima warned him away; junks spoken at sea shunned his friendly advances.

Colnett had other grievances. His charts, secured from Dutch sources, were so erroneous "as to induce the idea they were simulated on purpose to mislead." The correct depths of water were not given, channels were improperly marked, and wholly false information was supplied concerning the navigation of Korea straits.

In his published account of his adventures, written seven years after his return to Britain, Colnett is more optimistic than he was when his troubles were freshly in his mind. "An encouraging prospect of a new and friendly commerce for my country unfolded itself before me when, in a typhoon, in the latitude of 38 degrees north, on the coast of Korea, I was so unfortunate as to lose my rudder, which obliged me to put back into the port of Chusan, in the northern part of China, where my loss was repaired."

Colnett gives no further identification of his harbor of refuge but, unless he means Fusan in south Korea, it is evident that his damage could not have been extensive. Any north Chinese port would be at such considerable distance from the place of his disaster that no safe voyaging would have been possible in a rudderless ship.

No surcease of his sorrows was, however, met at "Chusan." The natives maltreated the *Argonaut* men. "To prevent the plundering of our cargo and to save ourselves from ill-usage, we cut anchor, and, baffling the pursuit of 36 armed junks, we returned to Canton."

Official circles in London knew nothing of the Colnett enterprise until after it had failed but, during the very months that he was attempting to open trade, a properly accredited expedition was sailing out from Falmouth to investigate the possibilities of harbors in the East.

News of the explorations made by La Perouse led Britain to bestir herself. Captain George Vancouver, aided by Lieutenant William Robert Broughton and by an almost unmatched galaxy of discoverers, was dispatched to the west coast of Canada to explore and to claim for Britain every hitherto undiscovered land. The imminence of Spanish settlements on the Canadian coast, the hope of preventing Russian progress down the inland waterways from Alaska, and the desire to secure a Northwest Passage, if any such existed, led Prime Minister Pitt to insist on both thoroughness and haste. The presence of the names of Puget, Baker, Johnstone, and of Vancouver himself in place-names along the western shorelines of America testify to the lasting importance of this famous expedition of capable sea captains.

Britain sought to turn the La Perouse discoveries to her own advantage. In addition to claiming the whole west coast of North America, she hoped to checkmate the Russian southward advance from Kamchatka. Broughton, now promoted to a captaincy, was ordered, therefore, to check La Perouse's course and if possible to complete a survey of the North Pacific ocean.

Broughton was an admirable selection for the task. A naval officer since childhood, captured by the Americans when but twelve years of age while "trying to cut out an enemy ship in Boston harbor," he was drilled in the unquestioning discipline of naval duty. Slow, cautious, and methodical by nature, he made himself a master mariner and became one of Britain's best surveyors. Probably, with Vancouver and Cook alone excepted, there was no better qualified officer in naval ranks for such a detailed task as that imposed upon him.

Broughton's 400-ton sloop *Providence* was no stranger to Pacific waters. Her previous commander, Captain William Bligh, of *Bounty* fame, had but recently sailed her from Tahiti to the West Indies with the first breadfruit trees ever brought to the Americas.

At Vancouver Broughton was to make another contact with important past history. There, in Nootka Sound, the great rendezvous of Pacific skippers, he fell in with the *Lady Washington,* the American pioneer ship in Japan. Kendrick had been killed by the luckless salute, but there were officers remaining on the brigantine to give Broughton information of Japan and of the probable reception which he might expect were he to try to land.

Two months after sailing from Monterey Bay for the Orient, the *Providence* came, on September 12, 1795, to the coast of Hokkaido, which he called Insu and which the Dutch termed Yeso. Broughton explains that the Dutch so named the island because of the extreme hairiness of the Ainu population for, says Broughton, "Eso" means "Esau" in Dutch and these Ainus were considered to be Esau's kin.

Broughton found no difficulty in making friends with the Ainu fishermen who sailed out to meet the *Providence,* but no information could be elicited from them concerning the island's resources. They supplied him liberally with wood and water, invited him to come ashore, and politely spread mats for Broughton and his men to use as cushions. But suddenly he noticed that the social atmosphere grew cold. The headman of the village, a minor Japanese official, had approached. With his coming, all fraternization stopped. The Japanese drove off the Ainus, warned his people against too close approach and, though politely civil, refused to enter into conversation with the Britishers. Indeed, says Broughton, "our Japanese acquaintance appeared very uneasy in seeing us so near the habitations and strongly pressed us to return to the ship. We embarked to his great satisfaction."

Two weeks were spent in cruising about the southeastern section of the Hokkaido, charting the coast and taking scientific observations of winds and ocean currents. Then, thinking that the Japanese fear might have subsided, Broughton again tried to strike up acquaintance with the natives. Some of them, including one villager who could speak a smattering of Russian, came on board to dinner and in the exchange of presents gave the *Providence* a chart of their portion of the island. Broughton believed that this chart had been drawn by Russian mariners. It is not unlikely that the map had come indirectly from the Laxman expedition.

Again the *Providence* personnel was allowed to land, this time on the shores of Volcano Bay near what is now Muroran, for wood and water. In chopping down a tree for fuel, Hans Oldsen, a seaman, was killed by the falling tree-trunk and was buried on the island.

The permission to bury Oldsen, it might be added, was the last such privilege granted to a foreigner until Perry's arrival. Even at the latter's insistence that the right of burial was a common privilege given by every civilized nation to the unfortunates of other lands, the Shogun's officers were reluctant to allow an American to be buried near the tabu city of Yedo. Broughton seems to have experienced no such difficulty.

Once the burial was over, the Japanese renewed their pressure on Broughton's men to leave. Whenever an Ainu came close to a Britisher, Broughton reports, the Japanese drove the native off. "The Japanese prevented us from acquiring the information we wished concerning the customs and manners of the people." So the *Providence* moved away, resuming her mapping of the coast and, after charting the entire south and east of the island, withdrew southward.

Broughton had every intention of continuing his chartings to include the east coast of the main islands, but a gale blew up just as he was approaching Yedo Bay. The *Providence* was unable to put in, and was obliged to proceed past the southern point of Japan. The explorers passed on toward Formosa. There, in the following May, the *Providence* struck a coral reef and sank. The men, taking the small tender of the sloop, won safely to Macao.

Again, still in the tender, Broughton set forth to check his observations and to complete his survey. By July 1797 he was again off Japan. He sailed northward and was expecting another welcome from the Ainus, but was doomed to disappointment. As he drew near to Yedo Bay, an armed ship came out from shore to meet him and, in Broughton's words, "strongly pressed us to come in." Broughton, however, sensed a hostile atmosphere. Declining the invitation, he mustered his men and read them the articles of war in preparation for an emergency. Fortunately for Anglo-Japanese relations, no direct action was taken by either side.

Even the Ainus turned against him as he lay off Matsumai in mid-August. Broughton shrewdly suspected that the smaller boat in which he reappeared caused him to "lose face." Sailing closer to the city he saw a large contingent of troops drawn up in readiness to meet the invaders. The port officials came out to inquire why the expedition had returned. "Our old friends," says Broughton, "were very anxious for our departure and strongly urged it in a very civil way." Having gained virtually all the scientific data that was needed, the chart-makers left Japan on the last day of August.

One scrap of information told to Broughton by the port authorities deserves mention for its oddity. In seeking to persuade him to leave the neighborhood, they pointed out to him that Matsumai Harbor was not well adapted to foreign trade but that nearby, at Hakodate, there was an admirable harbor. Then they added, "The Russians trade regularly at Ago-dad-dy." Probably this refers to the recent visit of Laxman and his men to south Hokkaido, but that the Japanese should even have suggested that any foreign nation other than the Dutch was privileged to trade is an astonishing statement.

From two different standpoints Broughton's expedition achieved success. He contrived to make friends with the people of Hokkaido, a feat beyond the possibilities of the *Argonaut* or any other Britishers. That he should have been presented with a chart was such a defiance of the stringent laws as to merit death for the reckless donor. Japanese who exchanged maps with foreigners a generation later were forced to commit harakiri for this offense.

Broughton's surveying also deserved congratulations. Reëxamination of the straits between Saghalien and the mainland, made by Broughton after leaving the Hokkaido on his second visit, reaffirmed the belief of La Perouse that for most vessels the waterway was not navigable, though Broughton, like La Perouse, did not complete the passage through the Gulf of Tartary. Broughton's contribution to geographic knowledge was rather on the east coast of Korea where the great bay now utilized by the Japanese as a seaport for the railways of Manchukuo still bears his name.

Again it was unfortunate that a foreign effort to learn more about Japan should have been coincidental with unrest within the Empire. Broughton's visits to Hokkaido in 1796 came simultaneously with what is now described by Japanese as the "compulsory communism" attempted by the Lord of Tau in the super-sacred Ise district. In the effort to ease tax burdens by redistribution of the lands, the small peasants found their better farms transferred to stronger hands. Broughton's arrival coincided with the peak of this agrarian unrest. "Frogs in the Well" had little difficulty in persuading the gullible that alien influence was responsible for Japan's woes. That the unrest should appear in the district to which the sacred Shinto relics were entrusted and where the goddess Amaterasu had her preferred shrine was a matter of grave moment to all true patriots.

XI

OVERWORKED SHIP'S PAPERS
1798–1803

BROUGHTON'S leaving brought Japan no reprieve from the foreigners seeking admission to Japan's closed harbors. An American pretending to be an Englishman masquerading as a Dutchman slipped past the barriers.

The new attempts stemmed directly out of European turmoils. Holland, disastrously defeated in the wars, lost most of her shipping and many of her colonies. The French Revolutionists, strongly supported by Dutch liberals, overwhelmed the Netherlands and set up a new régime, the Batavian Republic, allied to the Directory.

New wars began with Britain, and France proved unable to defend her small ally. Java was wholly isolated from the Netherlands; Deshima had no communication with any other Europeans in the world.

But Hollanders were highly resourceful folk. Trusting that the British frigates would be too busy to bother with the tiny trade in the Far East, the Dutchmen tried strategy. Instead of sending a Dutch ship from Batavia to Nagasaki, a neutral vessel was sought out. Thus, even in the unlikely event of a British cruiser's roaming oriental waters, no confiscation would, the Hollanders hoped, break up the projected trade.

So enters another of the colorful characters who abounded in the early days of Japan's foreign intercourse. William Robert Stewart, sealskin merchant who, like Kendrick and Colnett, had been jailed in China for smuggling, agreed to the assignment.

Stewart arrived in China in March 1793 from New York via Masafuera, a Chilean island near Robinson Crusoe's Juan Fernandez. He too left his ship, the *Eliza,* at Dirty Butter Bay while he went up to Canton to investigate the market for furs. Stewart bought his way out of jail by payment of $500 and then, finding that the price of furs was low, sold his 38,000 skins for $16,000. Together with the Dutch consul and Captain Amasa Delano of Duxbury, he undertook to carry sugar for Ostend but, through the lateness of the season and the unseaworthiness of the *Eliza,* the voyage turned into an ordeal.

"The *Eliza* was leaky and extremely dull in sailing," wrote Captain Delano. "I never knew a ship leak as ours did. . . . Our sugar was wet, and a large part of it dissolved and mingled with the water which was pumped out of the hold." In addition, on arrival at the Mauritius, Delano and Stewart discovered that France was in revolution and that all foreign vessels, including those of the supposedly friendly United States, were subject to internment. "It was mortifying," wrote the captain, "to see very low men, without talents or integrity, in possession of power and using it for the worst purposes in the name of liberty."

The remaining sugar belonged, of course, to Van Braam, the Dutch consul at Macao, but Stewart and Delano, fearing the confiscation of the cargo, pretended to be themselves the owners. They sold both sugar and ship, "because it was so eaten by worms that it was not worth repairing," and with the proceeds bought the big 1,400-ton Dutch ship *Hector*. The plan was to sail back to Macao with cotton from Bombay, and thus to repay Van Braam for his losses.

Bombay was reached in safety, despite the efforts of the French to lay an embargo upon so big a boat, and then a series of curious financial arrangements, worthy of more modern entrepreneurs, enveloped the whole situation in a mystic haze. Through some chicanery, in which the American consul seems implicated, the *Hector* emerged as the old *Eliza* with Stewart in command and with Delano packed off to the United States completely penniless. The ship itself was soon sold thereafter, but Stewart managed to retain the papers.

Nothing is known of Stewart during the next three years until, in 1797, he received the commission to sail still another vessel, again called the *Eliza* of New York, with the original *Eliza* papers, into Nagasaki Harbor.

His instructions were peculiar. So long as the *Eliza* was at sea the vessel was to fly the Stars and Stripes. Since his papers indicated that he was en route from New York to China, he would, it was believed, be safe from capture by any enemy of Holland. Then, as he drew close to Nagasaki he was to erase from the document the words that said that his destination was China and he was to write in "Nagasaki" as a substitute. Hoisting Dutch colors he was to sail boldly into harbor and was to pretend that he was Dutch until such time as, emerging, he would again amend his papers and resort to the American status.

To carry out the complex deception, Stewart was carefully coached in necessary etiquette. As soon as land was sighted he must set up a table under an awning, place cushions for the port officials, adorn his ship as if for holiday, and fire the requisite salutes.

The regulations, Stewart was informed, were standardized by long-established custom. No trading was to be attempted until a special messenger from Nagasaki to Yedo brought back the Shogun's permission but, in the interval of waiting, port authorities would take an inventory of the cargo and the crew, noting down the age, the stature, the name, and the status of every man aboard the ship. These lists would later be checked ashore, and woe betide the ship concerning which the slightest discrepancy might be discovered.

Stewart was further warned to consent to the transfer ashore of his sails, guns, arms, and ammunition, was informed that rules required his hatches to be sealed, and that they should, on no account, be opened except by permission of the governor and in the presence of a governmental agent.

Strict injunctions were given to the Americans that they must not light candles while on board, and that they must work silently. No one, it was impressed upon him, must be allowed to go ashore, nor should any Japanese be permitted to board the ship except the few men officially designated as provision merchants. No money was to be paid to these vendors until the permits came down from Yedo, even though a period of some three to four months might elapse.

When trade should finally be permitted, Stewart was informed, the bills for food and fuel would be presented. After payment had been made, six men from the *Eliza* would be allowed to go on shore to buy and sell for a four-day period. This was the time, according to the Batavia authorities, when the Dutch residents at Nagasaki would be let in on the secret that the vessel in the harbor was a substitute sailing under false Dutch colors.

The whole affair, now that a century and a half has passed since the concoction of the scheme, seems impossible of successful outcome, and yet the surprising fact is that the deception really worked. Probably the canny Dutchmen at the factory ashore became aware that the

Eliza was no Hollander long before Stewart told the facts, but it was to their interest to keep the secret. And there is evidence to show that certain native port officials winked their eye at flagrant violations of the usual formalities.

Two factors operated in favor of the masquerade. Japan was anxious for the cargo to be landed now that two years had elapsed since a Dutch ship had brought silks. A vessel, especially if American, sailing under Dutch suggestion, would not be lightly turned aside. Stewart, better coached than the skipper of the 90-ton *Lady Washington,* and far more tactful in his nature, so well ingratiated himself with the port officials that he received a special invitation to return once more to Japan to trade privately.

A second, and perhaps more potent, cause lay in the intrigue carried on between the daimyo of Satsuma and Heer Hemmij, the chief of the Dutch factory. Satsuma, never too loyal to the Shogun, hoped to secure cargoes for his private use and especially to gain foreign guns for possible emergencies. By allowing Stewart to bring a special cargo, in addition to the two Dutch ships now permitted by the Shogun, the daimyo would gain a partial independence from the central government at Yedo. Hemmij willingly fell in with Satsuma's intrigue. In the report sent back to Java, Hemmij specifically asked that Stewart might be sent again to Nagasaki.

Stewart safely sailed away in the *Eliza,* carrying the distinction of having been the first foreigner, except a Chinese or a Hollander, to conduct commerce and come back with a return cargo since the closing of the gates in 1637.

So successful had been the stratagem that in the following year, 1798, Stewart sailed again in an *Eliza.* Again the elaborate deceptions were employed, and again he was allowed to set foot in Nagasaki city. But to his dismay he found the Dutch settlement half burned and Hemmij vanished. New officials were in charge who seemed reluctant to give details of what had happened, but eventually Stewart learned that Hemmij had overreached himself in his negotiations. Instead of dealing with the Prince of Satsuma, Hemmij had confided in Shigehide Shimadzu, who claimed to be an advocate of free foreign intercourse but who was also the Shogun's father-in-law. Hemmij had been denounced and killed.

Disconcerted by the news and worrying concerning his own fate, Stewart finished up his trading with undue speed and set out for Batavia. But in his haste to clear the harbor, he ran his ship upon a rock. Divers, sent down to investigate the damage, were overcome by the fumes of camphor from the hold.

Amateur Japanese engineers were more successful. Kiemon Murai, chief of the fishermen, fastened fifteen junks to each side of the ship and then, by using oars at a moment when a stiff breeze and a spring tide favored the feat, dragged the vessel from the rocks and towed it to a shelving beach. For his achievement Murai was ennobled by his chief, Daimyo Narifusu Mori of Choshu, and was allowed to wear the two swords of a samurai. As a special crest, in memory of his aid to "Dutchmen in distress," his insignia included a Dutch hat with two crossed pipes.

But Stewart's troubles were not ended. His salvaged *Eliza* sailed again, but a month later, in July 1799, came limping back to port, dismasted and disabled. Rumors reported that the dismasting was no accident but that Stewart had been visiting forbidden harbors in South Japan, trading with the Prince of Satsuma, and that he had himself damaged his ship in order to conceal his secret dealings.

The rumors in all probability were slanderous. Stewart, though by no means above such double dealings, was too uneasy over the possibility that he, like Hemmij, might be punished by the Shogun. So scared was he, in fact, that on entering Nagasaki Harbor and sighting a strange ship in the distance, he lost his nerve. Certain that the oncoming vessel was a British man-of-war looking for Dutch merchantmen, Stewart was too terrified to make the necessary changes in his papers. Instead of again amending his well-worn documents he tore them into tiny bits and threw them into the sea. He was taking no chances on adding forgery to his other accusations.

The new arrival was no British frigate, but a second American ship, chartered by Batavia under much the same terms as Stewart's own arrangements. For a fee of 30,000 Spanish dollars, a sum slightly larger than the equivalent in contemporary American coin, James Devereaux of Salem had agreed to sail the 200-ton *Franklin* on the yearly venture. He was bringing one hundred and twenty-five tons of sugar, fifteen tons of cloves, a ton of elephants' teeth and some miscellaneous material such as cotton yarn, chintz, tin, pepper, and sappan wood, together with one hundred pounds of "mummie," a medicinal bituminous drug much prized in the East as a sovereign remedy. He was to bring back the usual cargo of copper and camphor.

Captain Devereaux' instructions, still preserved at Salem, are quite as specific as were those given to Stewart on the occasion of the first

Eliza's voyage to Japan. The Hollanders were not now, however, so insistent upon his flying the Dutch flag. "It is immaterial what the colors are," the canny Netherlanders pointed out, "so long as they are neither Spanish nor Portuguese." Evidently the Japanese were none too highly regarded by the Batavia authorities.

Aboard the *Franklin* came one of the most powerful officials ever to administer the Dutch factory at Deshima. This was Hendrik Doeff, a man who for chicanery and for resourcefulness was more than a match for the redoubtable Stewart himself. When, in late November 1799, the *Franklin* and the luckless *Eliza* sailed off simultaneously to Batavia, Doeff was already sufficiently acquainted with the situation to give Devereaux secret orders to report the attempted Satsuma irregularities to Javanese authorities.

Perhaps the wily Stewart learned of Doeff's betrayal, for the *Eliza* never reached Batavia. Disappearing into the night, Stewart sheered off toward Manila. Then, wrecked on the Luzon shores—though he seems to have recovered a remarkable proportion of the *Eliza's* gear—Stewart borrowed a new brig, loaded it with goods bought on credit, and hastened back to Nagasaki. Stewart's plan was to arrive earlier than the expected time, to sail under Dutch colors, to skim the cream of the trade, and to escape before the regular Dutch vessel should arrive.

It is not, indeed, unthinkable that Stewart's scheme was actually conceived in collaboration with the opperhoofd. Doeff also had a flair for the dramatic and a zest for extra-legal trading. Certainly when Stewart came back to Nagasaki in the new brig which, having destroyed the *Eliza* papers, he renamed *Emperor of Japan,* Doeff lent every possible assistance. To calm the fears of Japanese officials that Stewart might really be a Britisher masquerading under a false passport, Doeff invented a new classification of peoples. Americans, he told Japan, spoke a language similar to English, but were of wholly distinct allegiance. "They are," said Doeff, "Englishmen of the second chop," a pidgin English phrase implying an inferior quality.

Doeff assisted the "second chop Englishmen" to load a cargo well in advance of the customary sailing time. Probably the Nagasaki governor was by no means anxious to retain a ship in port which presented so many peculiar problems as did this *Emperor of Japan.* Mistakes in judgment by Japanese officials were too often expiated by compulsory suicide. But in spite of hurried efforts by both the governor and Doeff, the ship delayed too long. Before Stewart cleared the harbor, signal guns were heard at sea. Coast guards reported the arrival of a new ship. Stewart's *Emperor of Japan* was compelled to lie at anchor until the mystery was cleared.

The new arrival, it soon appeared, was the 900-ton *Massachusetts,* formerly of Boston but now chartered by the Dutch East India Company. Launched at Quincy expressly for the China trade, she was the largest vessel ever built in the Americas at the time of her launching in 1789. The ship was indeed familiar to Stewart, for it was the vessel in which his old companion, Amasa Delano, had come out to the East. But Delano and his associates had found the vessel rotten and badly ventilated, and they had sold her to the Danes. The latter evidently chartered her to the Hollanders at a decided profit, for the Dutch East India Company was paying $100,000 for one voyage to Japan.

The arrival was decidedly inconvenient for both Doeff and Stewart. Aboard the *Massachusetts* was Inspector Walther Waardenaar of the Dutch East India Company bearing news that Stewart was no longer *persona grata* to the Dutch. But Doeff, obliged to concoct new schemes quickly to guard Stewart and to save his own reputation, persuaded Waardenaar to resort to guile. To arrest the errant Stewart, Doeff warned, was fraught with danger to the entire Dutch establishment, for the Japanese would exact vengeance on all foreigners. Waardenaar was advised instead to redistribute the personnel of the two ships and to delay until the vessels were well out to sea before imprisoning the interloper. Waardenaar agreed. Stewart, after persuading Captain Hutchings of the *Massachusetts* to put in at Manila so that he might repay his debts before standing trial at Batavia, made good his escape.

Believing Stewart safely out of the way, the Dutch continued their plan of sending American-chartered ships. No one was really deceived by the scheme when the brand-new *Margaret* of Salem sailed into Nagasaki on Sunday morning, July 19, 1801, "flying 20 different colors and entering the harbor of Nangasacca with much ceremony." Few difficulties were placed in the way of trading, either for the Dutch East India Company's interest or on private account by the members of the ship's company.

From the standpoint of international good will, as it later developed, the Japanese did well to welcome the *Margaret*. Captain Samuel Derby, part owner with John Derby and Benjamin Pickman, was a member of what was probably the most influential shipping family in America. George Cleveland, his clerk, was later to become president of Salem's powerful Commercial Insurance Company. Thomas West, Samuel Rea, Joseph Preston, Israel Phippen, Anthony Caulfield, all of whom were officers or sailors, became ship captains of importance. Japan, by allowing these men freedom of trade and of sight-seeing in Nagasaki, stored up an abundant good will for herself in America. She made friends who helped spread desirable propaganda in Japan's best interests.

Cleveland, whose *Journal* is an admirable source for information on the visit of the *Margaret* was not, to be sure, a perfect observer. In his Yankee ignorance he did not know that the "lady of the house" who came to drink tea with the foreigners when Merchant Facquia gave a dinner was probably not best described by such a title. Her deportment was sufficiently proper to allow Cleveland to write, "She appeared to be a modest woman"; but Salem society might have suspected a flaw in her character had they known the usual Japanese customs. Nor were the "exhibitions of dancing and tumbling" in the tea-houses all that they superficially appeared. The great crowds that thronged to see the strangers as they strolled the streets at the Feast of Lanterns were not wholly moved by admiration of the "fine young men in the bloom of youth" who comprised the *Margaret's* crew. Luckily Cleveland could not understand the muttered comments of the curious natives.

The tidy New England business man was horrified, however, at the minuteness of examination deemed necessary by the Nagasaki officers, and by the multiplicity of detail required to clear the imports. "It took a number of days," Cleveland complains, "to put through business that could not have been an hour's work in Salem." He protested the extortionate prices demanded for food in Deshima, but was placated when informed that the foreign foods required by aliens were not produced by Japanese. And when the return cargo came down to the docks and Cleveland saw the trays, writing desks, knife boxes, and tea caddies "packed in boxes so neat that in any other country they would be considered cabinet work," he was completely charmed. These articles were for private trade; the Dutch East India Company received camphor, soy sauce, sake, and small bars of copper. Early in November the *Margaret* sailed back for Batavia after a visit of more than three months' duration. The American ship *Samuel Smith* and the Dutch vessel *Matilda Maria,* arriving in Japan in 1802, were equally well received.

By this time Stewart came again into the story. Having had a taste of the profits to be derived from commerce with Japan, he had no intention of settling down to a normal, quiet existence. He took passage to Calcutta, painted there a glowing picture of profits to be made in Nagasaki, pointed out the freedom from the heavy port dues demanded in most oriental harbors, and asked the Bengal merchants to entrust him with a cargo. He had little to say concerning the fact that copper, which India also produced, was Japan's most marketable export. His intention was to specialize on other articles.

So persuasive was Stewart, who now declared his real nationality to be British, that the Calcutta merchants loaded the ship *Neptune* for him and then filled the *Frederick,* under Captain James Torey, as a second venture. The two ships, observing all the required formalities, rode into Nagasaki Harbor in 1803. Stewart, knowing Japan's fear of Britain, flew the Stars and Stripes from his ship. It was the first time that the American flag had been displayed in these waters.

Stewart knew his Japanese psychology to perfection. Just before leaving Canton for Japan, he painted out the *Neptune* on the bows and counter of his ship, and painted in the name *Nagasaki-maru* in both English and Japanese. As in the case of his earlier venture, *Emperor of Japan,* he hoped that the delicate attention to Japanese sensibilities might return him dividends. Because he knew also that the Dutch East India Company frequently brought in curiosities as gifts for the local rulers, Stewart brought a special present for the Shogun. This was the offering of a camel and an Indian buffalo, the first of their species to be imported to Japan. The importation of living animals was, as it happened, forbidden to the Dutch by a specific edict of the Shogun made in 1668, but either Stewart was unaware of the prohibition or he counted on the naïve curiosity of the people to permit a violation of the law. His venture proved extraordinarily successful, in so far as the welcoming of his animals was concerned. After some demurring because of the supposed need for transporting the huge pets to Yedo in a litter, as presents usually were carried, a compromise was reached with custom. The camel and the buffalo were moved partly by water and partly by their own locomotion.

The substitution of the animals was not only a novel touch but, as Stewart had anticipated, a decided saving in expense. Dutch vessels from Batavia had been accustomed to offering gifts that mounted in value to upwards of $3,000 for the Shogun and to more than that for the inferior officers. The expenses of transporting the gifts exceeded $5,600 a year; a sum, it might be added, more than five times the annual salaries of the Company officials at Deshima. Counting all expenses for presents and their transportation, the Dutch East India Company had paid, for one voyage, more than $12,000 as good-will gratuities. The salaries and table expenses of the company officials in that same year were approximately $4,000. Seeing the success of the Stewart economy plan, the Company was soon to follow his example. Dogs, horses, and even an elephant were to be substituted for more costly goods.

The Torey-Stewart expedition had an unequal reception. Torey, lacking Stewart's flair for the dramatic and lacking also Stewart's personal contacts, was made to leave immediately upon his arrival. Probably his display of the Union Jack roused too many hostile recollections. Leaving Nagasaki he sailed south to Kagoshima Bay, charting the island's shores. His *Journal* and a valuable chart were sent "with laudable public spirit and regard for his profession" to England.

There was less decisiveness concerning Stewart. Although his vessel flew the American ensign, the Nagasaki authorities still credited him with Dutch connections. Even Waardenaar, Stewart's former enemy, was none too sure that Stewart was an independent trader. He asked Stewart to exhibit his credentials.

Then Stewart resorted to boldness. Declaring to the Japanese that he had been specially commissioned by "Prince Thomas Jefferson," daimyo of Virginia and Shogun of the United States, he demanded that a place be set aside for an American trading factory either at Nagasaki or preferably at some spot more convenient to Yedo.

To make the demand sound sweeter to Japan, he professed no desire for the copper which Japan was now not anxious to export but said that he was asking only for the drugs and dried fish of which Japan possessed a surplus store. Had Stewart's proposals been accepted, the Dutch would have been compelled to accept a similar restriction and to handle only exports for which the Dutch had little need.

The Dutch response, when Japanese authorities inquired what Holland thought of such a curious suggestion, was to warn Japan against American aggression. It was pointed out that the United States was no longer Holland's friend but was consorting with Russians in the seal hunting of the North Pacific and that Elias Derby's *Grand Turk* had been escorted to Canton, on the first American voyage to the Orient, by two French men-of-war. Nothing was said to show that this escorting had been accidental or that the United States had since been on the verge of war with France. The impression was allowed to rest that the United States was hand in glove with other Western nations who had evil designs on Japan's wealth.

Luckily, moreover, for Waardenaar and the Dutch, the presence of Torey's British ship in company with the *Nagasaki-maru,* and the fact that both hailed from a British port in India, gave strength to the suggestions that the Americans were leagued with England in a plot against the safety of Japan.

So closely were the ships identified, in fact, that for years thereafter historians regarded Stewart as a Britisher under the alias of Torey. The error seems to have stemmed from Sir Stamford Raffles, British conqueror of Java, and was perpetuated by Richard Hildreth's *Japan As It Was and Is,* long a standard text on Japan's foreign relations prior to Perry. Subsequent writers on Japanese affairs, including Japan's own historians, continued the mistake.

The Dutch warnings given Stewart proved effective. Repudiated by both Netherlanders and Japanese, Stewart returned to China empty-handed, leaving both camel and buffalo in Nagasaki as memorials of his visit. Thus, so far as Japan was concerned, ended the commercial career of a seafaring genius who never allowed legality to interfere with his pursuit of profit.

Holland continued to use neutral American ships in the trade to Deshima, relying on the "second-chop English" explanation.

American flags were seen again at Nagasaki, in the annual visits of Dutch traders in 1806, 1807, and 1809, but Japan's brief friendship was at an end. Small hospitality was shown the captains on arrival. The ships were surrounded by guard boats, the men were forbidden to land and, save for the necessary Dutch freights brought to Deshima, intercourse was forbidden.

XII

REVOLTS ATTRACT RUSSIANS
1804–1805

BECAUSE the Tokugawa Shoguns created a static social situation wherein the local daimyos were so cowed that organized civil war became well-nigh impossible, and because the intrigues of domestic politics did not embroil the Empire, foreigners overestimate the peacefulness of Japan's existence under Tokugawa rule.

Discontent was boiling. A peasantry, oppressed by taxes that often exceeded fifty percent of its total income, rose in frequent protest. Forty insurrections flared within a century and a half. Several of these were, to be sure, merely minor quarrels of only local interest, but many of the rest were major risings against extreme taxation. On three occasions, in 1733, 1754, and 1764, more than two hundred thousand rebels defied their feudal masters. In other years, in scores of different localities, mobs of ten thousand men were rioting. Guns were trundled into place to shoot down peasants at the same time that Massachusetts Minute Men were gathering at Lexington.

Behind Japan's closed doors a cycle of misfortune was wreaking havoc. The nation was shifting from a purely agricultural to a mercantile economy. Prices for farm products were declining, but at the same time there was an actual increase in the cost of growing rice. Money was becoming necessary. Small farmers who once bartered with their crops for the small amount of necessary outside goods now needed coin to pay their debts and satisfy their tax-hungry daimyos. Peasants were regarded as no higher than the beasts; indeed, as one contemporary author writes, the farmers seemed little better than the seeds. "Like sesame, the harder you press for oil, the more oil you squeeze."

Farm population was declining, partly because independent culti-
vators were driven from their holdings to seek work as landless city
laborers, partly because of natural calamity. More than a million rural
lives were lost through famine, pestilence, and flood during the six
years after 1780. Large areas of farm land in the relatively infertile
north and east ceased to be cultivated.

Japan was well aware of the true cause of her decline, but took
little effective action to prevent the causes. Statesmen sought instead
to remedy the ills by ukase. For a century and a half, down to the time
of Perry, the Shoguns strove to rivet feudalism by compelling farm
folk to return to their lands. Forcible resettlement seemed safer to the
Shoguns than exerting effective pressure on the selfish daimyos. No
real improvement was secured; economic conditions steadily dete-
riorated.

Children, so earnestly desired and so deeply loved by Japanese, became regarded as a hindrance. Child brokers roamed the countryside
buying the unwanted for resale to those who sought cheap labor.
Infanticide was frequent, though strictly forbidden by a Yedo edict.

None of these phenomena has wholly ceased, even in the far more
efficient Empire of today. The famines that ravaged northeastern
Japan in the first years of the 1930 decade brought many of the same
evils, particularly in the sale of young girls to the city brothels. The
same malnutrition, disease, and death that followed eighteenth-
century famines still trail their evil influence. So, too, the frequent
tenant-farmer risings of the modern era reflect the eighteenth-century
disputes. Rimei Honda, who wrote, in the last years of the eighteenth
century, that Japan was at a standstill and that her culture was completely dead, is echoed in the writings of contemporary publicists.

Parallel, too, are accusations that Japan's ills are wholly due to
Westernism and to foreign instigation. Such explanation has invariably captivated oriental thinkers. Always it has been popular to
ascribe misfortune, whether caused by statecraft or by natural calamity, to the evil influence of foreign thought. Alien ideas were at
extremely low ebb after Japan's famine eras.

Virtually no news of the uprisings percolated to the West. Japan
was never anxious for foreigners to know details of her internal weakness. The Dutch, immured on their prison-like island were never
specially concerned with Japan's social problems. The outer world
was unaware that a hundred thousand farmers, in Aomori, the province closest to Hokkaido, marched unarmed upon a fortress to pre-

sent an eighteen-clause petition against the misrule of the local lord, or that, in another province, sixty thousand rebels burned their oppressors to death to make their protest more effective. No news leaked out from Tajima when the farmers and silver miners of that province rebelled in such a mighty mass that a ten-mile road was filled solidly from end to end with mutineers.

The unrest in the rural regions confirmed the Shogun's opposition to increase foreign intercourse. Nations seeking to annex new lands almost always pose as liberators of the peoples whom they wish to conquer. If aliens were allowed to enter Japan's empire it was certain, so the Shogun reasoned, that the disaffected farmer folk would rally to the foreign standards.

Least of all were the Japanese anxious to admit Russians, yet it was Russia which began to knock most loudly upon Japan's closed gates. Rumors reached Nicolai Petrovich de Rezanov, chief of the Russian-American trading monopoly, that there was civil strife in Japan. Most probably these rumors were of farmer insurrections that broke out in central Japan as an aftermath of the great eruption of Mt. Asama, though five other rebellions in the last two decades of the eighteenth century may have been contributory factors to his news. In any case Rezanov misunderstood the causes of unrest. Believing that the Emperor and Shogun were at war and that accordingly the "spiritual and temporal powers" were at odds, Rezanov prepared to avenge the repulse of Laxman.

The intervention was construed by Russia as a proper activity for Rezanov to undertake. By the terms of his monopoly, his Russian-American Company, successor to all previous trading ventures, could concern itself with all Asiatic interests from Siberia southward to Japan. Probably the Tsars would ratify whatever action he might take, for Rezanov had induced the Russian Imperial Family to invest heavily in his stock.

A forceful personality, well worthy to be included with the galaxy of exciting people who pioneered in Japan, Rezanov led a life of wild adventuring. His subtlety and diplomatic skill, which proved so successful in winning favors from Catherine and her successor Paul, were to prove themselves unequaled at a later date when Rezanov, to save his starving settlements in Alaska, bamboozled the Spanish of the California garrisons into provisioning their Russian enemies. Rezanov used his power of persuasion on the governor of California and won the heart of the daughter of the San Francisco commandante, "the most beautiful girl in New Spain," as stepping stones to his success.

Such was the man who, prior to his appearance in America, sought to set up Russian intercourse with Japanese. As aide upon the expedition he secured Adam Ivan Krusenstern, young Esthonian naval officer who was eager to lead a Russian expedition round Cape Horn. Sailing from Kronstadt in two English-built ships in August 1803, Rezanov and Krusenstern first carried the Russian colors into Southern waters. The vessels parted company in Hawaii. The *Nadezhda,* carrying the envoys, went on to Japan. In October 1804, they put in at Nagasaki to demand an audience.

Russian prestige suffered in the aftermath. Oriental practice required petitioners to wait a long time until the Shogun should have ample opportunity to consult with his advisers and to prepare a proper answer. But, to reduce the Russians to an especially low level in the eyes of Japanese, the Shogun's answer was unconscionably delayed. For six long months the Tsar's ambassadors were kept waiting under conditions of an intolerable ignominy. Far from being treated as representatives of an equal sovereign, the Russians were virtually kept incommunicado. "Our stay here," writes Krusenstern, "was literally a confinement. It was impossible for us to obtain even the slightest information. Only the lowest class of interpreters came on board."

For six weeks the Russians were not permitted to leave the ship, not even for the purpose of rowing about the harbor for exercise. Then, after repeated protests from Rezanov, a tiny "walking ground" was set aside on shore. The place thus grudgingly afforded contained but a single tree and not a blade of grass, and was effectively fenced in by a thick bamboo hedge. Two guard houses kept watch over the Russians as they used this athletic field, and guard boats surrounded the ship's skiff as it took men ashore for exercise.

"The barbarous intolerance," Krusenstern protested, "even went so far as to forbid our forwarding letters by the Dutch ship about to sail for Batavia. Rezanov was permitted to send a report provided the message merely said that all were well. Even then the Japanese government insisted on having a translation of this in the Dutch language so close that every line of the letter in both Russian and Dutch should end with the same word. We were not allowed to visit the Dutch factory nor to have the Dutch visit our ship."

Anxious in every way to conform to the Japanese requirements and to keep peaceful relationships, Rezanov even consented to the removal of the powder and arms from the *Nadezhda*. This was an insult to a man-of-war against which Krusenstern protested as vehemently as was possible in the face of his superior's complaisance. So shocking was this disarmament to a naval officer that, in the instructions later issued to American warships en route to Japan, the Washington officials expressly ordered that no such insult should be permitted by our officers.

Rezanov, the ambassador in command, was not however a naval man. Because the Russians were allowed to keep their swords—but only after a protracted argument—he thought that all would be well and that a surrender of other munitions would be a graceful act of acquiesence to the Japanese conventions. The next step was to disabuse his credulous mind. Governor Nabeshima of Nagasaki ordered seven huge ships and many small guard boats to picket the *Nadezhda*. On land, simultaneously, the daimyos guarded all approaches to the city.

With a military quarantine thus established, Nabeshima evidently thought it safe to allow the Russians to take up a residence on shore, but only under the strictest supervision. Six weeks after his arrival, Rezanov was permitted to take nineteen Russians and five Japanese, returned after having been shipwrecked in the Aleutians in 1796, to the place allotted for detention. This, the so-called "Megasaky," was an old fish warehouse situated on a narrow tongue of land extending into the harbor. On three sides deep water washed against the walls; on the land side only a narrow path, effectively controlled by bamboo barriers and guardhouses, led toward the mainland. Both land and sea were closely fenced and gated. Any skiff from ship to shore was made to pass along a narrow lane of bamboo canes sunk into the water. Double locks, the keys to which were held by the governor and his chief lieutenant, had to be opened whenever a boat wished to pass, nor were the gates ever allowed to remain open for a longer period than five minutes at a time.

The Megasaky itself was also closely guarded by armed watchers. The unfortunate Ambassador and his men were kept shut within the building. Air and light were supplied them through a window one foot square and closed by double lattice work. Here they were to stay until word came from Yedo as to the reception of their request for an audience. Meanwhile no association was permitted with the Nagasaki natives. Indeed, the Japanese were not even allowed to look at the captive Red Hairs, who were being treated as culprits and inferiors.

Krusenstern, aboard ship, was having similar difficulties. After parting with the *Neva* at Hawaii, the *Nadezhda* had been hit by a typhoon. The ship was leaking, and her copper plates were badly in need of replacement. Permission was requested to move the vessel into the inner harbor where she would be safe and where the needed repairs could be accomplished. But, with gentle Japanese humor, the request was denied on the ground that Chinese junks were already in the inner harbor and that it was unfitting that "a ship of war with an ambassador should lie in the same road with a merchantman." Not for two months was the repair work possible. The ship had to be pumped steadily.

Meanwhile the Russians were protesting because the interpreters and governors were not frank in their discussions. "Invariably," says Krusenstern, "they sent us false reports. The promises they made were empty words. We knew that it was possible to send a message to Yedo and to receive an answer within thirty days. Sometimes the round trip could be made within three weeks. But the interpreters assured us that three months was the time usually required for this."

A curious plot was developing while the Russians marked time. The five Japanese castaways turned against their rescuers. Krusenstern had already noted, during the first days of the voyage, that the refugees, except for one old man of sixty, were lazy, dirty, ill humored and addicted to passionate rages on slight provocation. He gave them extra rations of food and water, and made allowances for the psychological disorders that shipwreck and exile might have caused. But suddenly he was informed that one of the castaways had written a private letter to the governor, alleging that the Russians were brutal, that they were "the most bigoted of Christians," that force was being used at the Megasaky to compel conversion to the Christian faith, and that the sole purpose of the Rezanov mission was to inflict Christianity upon Japan. Then, having written the complaint, the Japanese tried to slash his throat.

No Russian surgeon was allowed to tend the wound. Japanese doctors were quartered in the Megasaky ostensibly to treat the would-be suicide, who now was lamenting loudly that he had been mistaken and that he wished to die for his unkindness to his Russian friends. From January 16, when the suicide attempt was made, until

February 19, when the governor's envoys returned from Yedo, the physicians remained in constant attendance.

The denunciation of the Russians as oppressors caused Rezanov to shift his plans. Twice he had been requested by the governor to surrender the castaways, but each time Rezanov insisted on retaining his waifs until he could himself offer them, dramatically, to the Shogun in person. After the revelation of the Japanese letter of accusation, Rezanov was only too anxious to be rid of his embarrassing charges. But now the governor refused to accept responsibility, probably because removal of the men from the Russian Megasaky would entail the withdrawal of his spies.

The castaways remained in close captivity, therefore, for seven months after their arrival in their native land. No information is available as to their final fate when they were eventually turned over to the Japanese on the last day that the Rezanov-Krusenstern expedition remained in Nagasaki. The laws of 1636 decreed death to those who should return from foreign travel.

Eighteen weeks elapsed after the arrival of the *Nadezhda* before word came from the Shogun that his envoy would soon be ready to receive the Russian Emperor's petition for friendship. To Rezanov, who anticipated a trip to Yedo to interview the Shogun and to present the gifts sent by the Tsar, the shock was stunning. His sovereign was not treated as an equal but as a minor prince with whom an underling might deal.

Governor Nabeshima endeavored to soften the blow to Russian pride by informing Rezanov that the envoy sent from Yedo was a man of most exalted rank, so eminent, as Nabeshima awe-strickenly declared, that "he could gaze upon the Emperor's august feet." All lesser men, Nabeshima explained, must keep their gaze upon the floor. Rezanov, with his own ideas concerning the Tsar's omnipotence, was not appeased. Happily for his own conceit, Rezanov never knew that Toyama, the Shogun's representative, was merely one of the sixteen ordinary, or junior, *metsuke* who assisted in government affairs. Toyama was of no higher rank than was Kimura who had met Laxman.

Six more weeks passed before this heralded clerk consented to receive the Russian embassy. Raging inwardly because of the inhumanities with which he had been treated and because of the wholly unnecessary delays in starting the negotiations, Rezanov resolved to counsel retribution to the Tsar. He could not refuse to meet the Shogun's agent but he could, and did, mature his plans for vengeance.

Even on the state call of courtesy the Russians suffered indignities. Seven Russians, headed by the ambassador, were sent by small boat and palanquin to meet the Shogun's messenger at Ohata. Armed ships surrounded the barge in which the Russians traveled, while on shore heavy canvas curtains were hung along each side of the narrow roads. The Japanese explained blandly that these were to protect Rezanov from contamination from the gaze of low-caste peasants. To Rezanov, the real interpretation seemed that Japan was anxious to prevent espionage.

At Ohata the reception was not excessively enthusiastic. When Rezanov presented the trading license brought by Laxman to the Tsar, the Japanese refused to recognize the document. Rezanov was flatly told that the Shogun refused permission for Russia to buy "even the least thing." As a token of his esteem, the ruler of Japan would give to the *Nadezhda* sufficient necessities to last the ship two months, but no pay would be accepted. The presents sent by the Tsar could not possibly be accepted. Such acceptance would involve a return gift from the Shogun to the Tsar and would necessitate a special mission from Yedo to St. Petersburg. No such mission could be sent because "it is contrary to the laws of the Empire for any Japanese to quit his country." The *Nadezhda* must prepare to sail at once, never to return. No Russian ship should ever come again.

In his anger Rezanov took action which still further lowered Russian prestige. The gifts, spurned by the Shogun, could not be carried back to Russia so Rezanov gave them to Toyama as a personal present. In return Rezanov received a gift of rice and floss silk. The exchange of courtesies, begun by Rezanov with insufficient thought as to their diplomatic import, was interpreted by Japan as a confession that the Russian Tsar considered himself on an equality only with one of the Shogun's junior officers. Russia thereby recognized, according to the super-patriotic Japanese, that the Yedo ruler was far superior to the sovereign of the largest land in Europe.

Japan was unquestionably anxious to discredit the Muscovites in revenge for Russian violation of Japan's sovereignty in the northern islands and in punishment for the murders of Japanese sailors cast away on Russian coasts. The Shogun's men were never too considerate of foreign feelings and were invariably oversensitive in detecting slights to Japan's national honor. But, in addition to these special reasons for the repulse of the embassy, there were causes springing out of the clash of national cultures. Asia and Europe were living in radically different diplomatic worlds.

Judged solely by the standards of conventional Western theory, Russia had just ground for grievance. An imperial ambassador, representing the inviolable person of the Tsar, had been grossly insulted. By all the rules of polite international relationships, an ambassador, standing in the stead of his sovereign, enjoys the same immunities as does his master. Accepted diplomatic technique assures the ambassador an immediate personal access to the head of the nation to which he is accredited.

Japan flagrantly violated these conventions. Not yet past the old oriental notion that an envoy must be an agent of espionage, she piled insult upon Rezanov and jailed the envoy and his suite. These in themselves were actions amply sufficient to justify hostilities. Had Europe not been engrossed in the death struggle against Napoleon, war might easily have resulted.

In Japan's view the incivilities were further warranted by Rezanov's own actions. He refused, said the Japanese, to make the proper bows to Nagasaki port officials, though this charge seems dubious in the light of Rezanov's complaisance in the disarming of his ship. He declined, Japan alleged, to make obeisances which he and Krusenstern believed indecent, and would not pay proper deference to the Shogun's agent. These might possibly have been overlooked, Japan has since insisted, had not Rezanov sought data for the use of coming conquerors. His intense curiosity concerning Japan's natural resources, his keen interest in the coast defenses, his insistence that the Russians be permitted to walk freely through the city, and above all his arrival in a vessel suitable for war, convinced Japan that Russia meditated an assault.

Why else, the Japanese reasoned, should Russia and Great Britain take such careful soundings along the coasts or be so meticulous in their queries about wind and water conditions? Japan sent out no exploration parties, manifested no unusual interest in the affairs of neighbor nations. Pure scientific interest was a pursuit wholly foreign to the static mode of life.

It was defensible, therefore, in the Japanese view, to mislead the alien in every fashion possible. Pleased when it was learned that the *Nadezhda* had arrived from the well-charted eastern coast and not from the jealously guarded Sea of Japan, the Nagasaki authorities tried to dissuade Rezanov and Krusenstern from going home the western way. The waters were too shallow, Russia was informed; rocks were too plentiful; the channel much too tortuous for safe navigation. Indeed, there really was no outlet by any water route save that along the southern and the eastern coasts. Besides, the natives who dwelt on the shores of the Sea of Japan were savages who thought the killing of all strangers a religious duty. All this misinformation was solemnly retailed to Rezanov to dissuade him from making undesired discoveries.

Japan's insistence merely stirred the Russian curiosity. Rezanov and Krusenstern were all the more resolved to check the accuracy of the details. For, if Japan were really linked by land to the Asiatic mainland, as Debune had declared, and as this Nagasaki information seemed to show, a Russian military descent would be facilitated; if not, the geographic data would be invaluable for Russia's navy.

When, therefore, the *Nadezhda* sailed, the Russians intended to penetrate the forbidden waters. Japan informed Krusenstern that the strait between Korea and Japan was only a mile wide—the information was decidedly inaccurate—and warned the Russians that they must not, on any account, approach near the Japanese shore under penalty of death.

Before going back to Russian soil, Rezanov ordered landings in Hokkaido, scouting, it appears, for suitable landing places for a future Russian force. As in the case of Broughton's ship, the Ainus proved friendly and anxious for trade in minor articles, but Japanese officers stationed in the district again drove off the Ainus from association with the foreigners and issued commands that the *Nadezhda* clear away at once. One of these officials, it appears, had met Laxman and knew a few words of Russian, but even he was adamant against fraternization with the visitors. "He would not," writes Krusenstern, "accept even a trifling present or a glass of Japanese sake. He earnestly requested us to sail immediately, else Matsumai would send a large fleet against us from which we could expect no mercy."

A junk spoken at sea proved more companionable. The two ships drew close. The captain traded sake, rice bread, and tobacco for Russian presents, and wished that he could procure some of the good Russian cloth. But, despite the strong urgings of the Russians, the cloth was not accepted lest the officers on shore, seeing the evidence of trading, "would infallibly strike off the heads of all."

Rezanov, returning to Russian territory, found the Tsar's orders sending him to the Americas. But before sailing from Kamchatka for Alaska, Rezanov drew up commands for vengeance on the Japanese. Knowing from his observations that neither Ainus nor Japanese in Hokkaido possessed guns and that troops were few, Rezanov believed that a force of two cutters, with perhaps twelve guns and a hundred artillerymen as a landing force, could reduce the island to subjection. "Two cutters could sink the whole Japanese fleet even if 100,000 men were sent against us," he told the Tsar.

Russo-Dutch relationships were certainly not improved by the Rezanov affair. Doeff, in all the controversies, ranged himself firmly on the side of Japanese officialdom. On the very first night of the *Nadezhda's* arrival, Doeff and a small group of his assistants boarded the Russian ship as temporary interpreters. He counseled complete disarmament and an abject surrender to Japan's demands for proper obeisance, but the Russians, proud of their mission as personal representatives of their monarch, refused the latter and only partially acceded to the disarmament demands. Doeff took credit to himself for having prevailed upon the Japanese to allow the *Nadezhda* to anchor inside the harbor.

No other fraternization took place between the Russians and the Dutch. Doeff averred that Japanese feared a possible foreign confederacy against the Nagasaki natives; Rezanov was equally positive that Doeff was busily engaged in spreading false rumors about imminent Russian attacks. One of Japan's special agents confessed that "the Dutch designedly infused suspicions into our government against Russia and England. There was an agreement, the Dutch said, between Russia and Great Britain to divide the East. England was to come by sea and Russia by land. Proof of this was to be seen in the British acquisition of India and in the Russian conquest of Siberia. Broughton's explorations, it was represented to us, were further proofs of the aggressive tendencies of Russia and Great Britain."

Evidence, convincing to both British and Russians, was found in the contents of a letter discovered on a captured Dutch ship bound from Batavia to Amsterdam. In this letter, which the Dutch declared a forgery, the Batavia Council's secretary reported to his head office that the interpreters at Nagasaki had "turned everything to the advantage of the Dutch and had given the Japanese such an idea of Russia that they had dismissed Rezanov with an answer which would make the Russians think no more of sending ships to Japan."

European circumstances played wholly into Japanese hands during the course of this Rezanov visit. Japan was completely unaware that Russian attention would be so riveted on the Napoleonic activities that almost any incident in the remote Far East would be dwarfed by comparison. But, had the Tsar been less interested in the European war, and had he been more free to turn all his might against the insulting Japanese, a war for the reduction of Japan might easily have eventuated in consequence of the insults heaped on Rezanov.

An odd commentary, incidentally, on the Rezanov affair is the report that Yedo was completely displeased at Nagasaki's treatment of the Russian Embassy. "A former Shogun had, indeed, beheaded a Portuguese embassy but had neither degraded nor insulted it."

XIII

BEARDLESS LADS ATTACK JAPAN
1806–1808

REZANOV'S reports, reaching St. Petersburg soon after the disastrous Russian defeat at Austerlitz, were temporarily pigeonholed until the Tsar could reform his legions, but Siberia was much more free to take punitive action against the villainous *makakas* of Japan. Rezanov, prior to his departure for America, commissioned two young naval officers to lead an expedition.

Lieutenants Nicholas Alexander Chvostov and Gavrilo Ivanovich Davidov, two lads in their early twenties, who had won praise for pioneering a new route from St. Petersburg to the Pacific, were the instruments of Russia's vengeance. While Krusenstern pursued his circumnavigation of the globe, the first Russian to emulate Magellan, these young men were sent to avenge the Nagasaki insults.

The reputation caused by the irresponsible depredations of these two young men in their senseless assaults on insignificant fishing villages has been inflated out of all proportion to their actual accomplishments. For years following their deeds the Chvostov-Davidov "atrocities" caused Japan immense indignation. As late as 1882, the chief of Japan's Geographical Society, Admiral Viscount Buyo Enomoto, wrote a series of articles tracing the origin of Russo-Japanese hostility to the effects of this punitive expedition set in motion by Rezanov's revenge. Rezanov ordered Chvostov and Davidov with two small men-of-war to take Kushunkotan, the chief Japanese settlement in south Saghalien. This was territory claimed by both Japanese and Russians. A raid here would, it was believed, cause fewer complications than a descent upon a village where Japanese had stronger rights.

145

The two young officers carried out their commands with an alacrity which might have been expected from ambitious youngsters seeking, in a far-off corner of the globe, to prove their eligibility for more desirable promotions. Arriving at the tiny town of Kushunkotan in 1806, they fired what is described in Japanese manuscript accounts as "poison-smoke-guns." Then, landing an armed force of perhaps sixty-five men, they pillaged the storehouses of rice, took eight Ainus and one Japanese soldier captive, and set the town afire. Before they left, they nailed upon the torii of the Benten temple, far enough removed from any building to escape the flames, a copper plate inscribed with a message to Japan.

The message complained that the Japanese had forbidden trade, since Krusenstern and Rezanov could not even buy a fan or snuffbox while at Nagasaki. It went on to say that if ever Japan desired to change its mind and thus avert future unpleasantness, the Russian settlements in Saghalien or in Kamchatka would be glad to hear of it. If Japan refused the invitation, the tablet threatened, the ships would come again to ravage every Japanese settlement in Saghalien. The notice warned Japan that Urup and Yetorup, the two largest Kuriles, were under Russian sovereignty.

To the Yedo government this tablet was an open declaration of hostility. Three thousand men were mustered and after being well equipped, were sent northward to Hakodate. The Great Northern Highway was, according to the picturesque Japanese accounts, thronged with warriors and with supplies for use in war against the Red Hairs.

The boys must certainly have written a more imaginative report than a bare description of this heroic adventure or there would have been an end to their exploits, but in the spring of 1807 these two daredevils were back again at their Homeric tasks. This time they fell upon Naiho, the ten-year-old Japanese colony in Yetorup, where a thousand Ainus and three hundred Japanese, including five women, carried on a precarious fishing venture. By no conceivable interpretation could the town have been considered an important economic center, but two hundred Russian troops attacked it. After firing their muskets in most menacing fashion, they went off with booty, consisting of the spare clothing of the colony. Five Japanese were taken captive, names and sex unknown.

Next the daring Russians appeared before the somewhat larger town of Shana, too small for any map, where Matsudayu Toda and his two hundred men sued for mercy. While the peace negotiations were in progress, seventeen Russian sailors met a group of six Japanese and, terrified lest this be ambush, fired upon the six. Two Japanese and one Russian, the interpreter, were killed, and so the Russians, fearful of being overwhelmed, retreated in good order.

Japan, elated beyond all reason by this victory over the fearsome Red Hairs, celebrated by a party of thanksgiving but forgot to set a guard. At night the Russians landed, breathing vengeance, surprised the Japanese and took all the spare rice and sake of the city. In addition, as a lasting trophy of the engagement, the Russians uprooted the ornamental spears set before the gates of the headman's house, and burned the village to the ground. Toda, shamed before his people, committed harakiri.

Then the doughty Russians withdrew, loaded down with battle glories, but leaving behind two men as killed or missing. They were, as it later appeared, as yet unharmed, lying drunk in the seclusion of a shed. They were found there by the Ainus and the Japanese, and before they waked to give more trouble, were speared to death. Then their heads were cut off and salted, and sent down to Hakodate, together with their arms and uniforms.

Not waiting to ascertain the fate of their missing comrades, Davidov and Chvostov sailed back to Saghalien. After destroying another tiny village, they fell with glee upon two junks and burned them to the water's edge. Finally they found a ten-pounder brass cannon which seemed a fitting trophy to take home. It was, by some curious chance, an old Korean gun captured in 1597 by Hideyoshi's invading force, but it was hauled away in triumph to be taken to Kamchatka as a memorial.

The two youngsters could not resist one last defiance. Though the gesture meant a slight deviation from their direct course, they ordered a side trip to Rishiri, an island off the northwest corner of the Hokkaido. There they landed their prisoners with a message informing Japan that the depredations were "a specimen of Russian power in return for your refusal to listen to our Tsar's request for trade." The message ended with a threat to take away all Japan's northern provinces unless trading privileges were granted.

Yedo was informed that her garrisons had been attacked by "five hundred Red Hairs, each eleven or twelve feet high." Kozo Hirayama, a northern swashbuckler who had not been present at the fighting, offered to avenge Japan by leading an expedition "to conquer Russia with a band of a thousand convicts. The ugly barbarians are no more than animals. If they are animals, then in attacking them it is impossible to apply the rules which are usually practiced."

The proposal was seriously debated by the Shogun's Council. Sadanobu Matsudaira was asked for expert opinion of the Hirayama plans. He wrote a memorandum to the Shogun approving it in part. "If there should be contemplated an attack upon the Empire of Russia, it would be possible to arrange an unexpected descent upon her dependencies, the Kurile Islands or Kamchatka, with a small number of soldiers. However, if instructions should be issued to proceed to the harbor of the capital of Russia and capture it, it would scarcely be possible to carry these out with one or two ships." Japan closed the incident by issuing an official proclamation forbidding all mention of the events, but the proclamation did not imply forgiveness or forgetfulness. No one, except poor Toda, shamed into ceremonial suicide because he was overpowered by a stronger force, seems to have come off from this sophomoric enterprise with any honors.

By one of the strange coincidences that mark Japan's early international intercourse, the next Russian flag to come into a Japanese port arrived at Nagasaki almost simultaneously with the Chvostov-Davidov activities in the North. It came under false pretenses.

The ship, the new Boston-owned *Eclipse,* commanded by Captain Joseph O'Kean, was a typical interloper. Manned by a crew inveigled from competing ships by a promise of high wages and by an immediate cash bounty of $20 to be spent in port before sailing, the *Eclipse* had cleared from Canton in May 1807 for Kamchatka, the northwest coast of America, and the South Seas. It was a curious itinerary, to be sure, and one that promised little profit. One wonders, too, concerning the difficulty poor O'Kean must have had the night before he sailed in rounding up his roaring crew from their $20 spree ashore!

Once at sea, the mystery was cleared. O'Kean, it appears, had arranged with the Russian-American Company to try to open trade at Nagasaki. The *Eclipse* carried tea, silk, sugar, rice, and the brownish-yellow cotton cloth called nankeen for sale in the forbidden ports. The Russian-American officials, in their ignorance, supposed that Japan would buy tea and rice, of which Japan possessed a surplus store. Not daring to venture a Russian ship to Nagasaki, the Company chartered O'Kean's American vessel for the purpose.

There were other serious irregularities about the *Eclipse*. Certain sailors, lured off other ships, signed articles under false names to prevent impressment by roving British men-of-war. The *Eclipse,* passing Macao, skulked for safety into out-of-the-way channels until danger was deemed past. Then the ship steered straight on its hopeless voyage to Japan.

O'Kean, blissfully unaware of the past history of Russo-Japanese relations, stood into Nagasaki Bay on June 6, proudly flying the Tsar's colors. He was astonished when an immense fleet of small boats rowed out to take possession of his ship. Halfway up the bay, Doeff came out to meet the new arrival, warning him that Japan was much exasperated because of "some outrages lately committed by the Russians upon the islands." Doeff urged strongly that the Russian flag be hauled down and that the Americans fly their proper colors. He also insisted that the Muscovite supercargo, the only Russian subject among the twenty-eight men of the ship's company, be kept out of sight.

The *Eclipse* was not wholly frank in its dealings with the Japanese authorities. Asked to surrender all his powder, O'Kean gave up only six or eight kegs, assuring the port officers that he had no more. Told that he might have excuse for coming only if in need of water or provisions, he ordered several water butts in the hold to be started and hoisted on deck empty. When a plentiful supply of water was sent off in small boats and in tubs, he emptied the supply on deck, stopping the scuppers and allowing it to run off at night. Evidently he believed that the guard boats, anchored about the ship, kept very indifferent observation.

Convinced by the third day that nothing was to be gained by a further stay, O'Kean got under way. A hundred boats towed him five miles out to sea, refusing pay for this service, as well as for the water, fish, vegetables, and swine provided for the stores, and left him, "waiving their hats and hands." The *Eclipse* sailed through the forbidden straits of Shimonoseki, and O'Kean reported his failure to the Company at Kamchatka.

Chvostov and Davidov had meanwhile returned to Russia, where they died in a foolhardy, schoolboy-like attempt to leap across an open drawbridge in the dark. Death was probably a happy escape for the swashbuckling heroes of the Kurile islands, for Russia soon learned exactly what had happened on the northern islands and realized that the boys had dealt the Tsar's ambitions a killing blow. St. Petersburg promptly disowned Russian responsibility for the raids.

Chvostov and Davidov, it was at once proclaimed, had no official standing. True it was that they were navy lieutenants, but at the time of their descent upon the Japanese settlements, neither officer was on navy duty. Both were acting solely in the interests of the Russian-American Company which, it was stressed, had no official connection with the government.

Indeed the disavowal tried to clear the Russian-American Company leaders too, since several of them had intimate connections at the court. "The directors of the Company," Russia declared, "were not persons of any great distinction in Russia but even they had not sanctioned the illegal proceedings." Chvostov and Davidov, and the irresponsible local officials in Kamchatka, were wholly to blame.

"These local officials," Russia said hurriedly in order to make the disclaimer seem more real, "are all rogues. None but vagabonds and adventurers ever enter into the Company's service as fur collectors. Often they are criminals. In both Kamchatka and America they tyrannize to an inexcusable degree over the natives. Their idleness, drunkenness, and debauchery are notorious enough but, to make it worse, the Company agents seduce and stimulate them to drink brandy to excess."

These were the men, Russia endeavored to suggest, who had been guilty of atrocity, not the accredited agents of the Russian Imperial Government who sought to save the fur traders from hunger, vice, and squalor. Japan should judge the Russians by noble officers like Laxman and Rezanov, not by the fur-trading scum.

Japan remained wholly unconvinced. Russia's excited protests probably never even reached the Shogun's ears, since the only channel open between Yedo and St. Petersburg was subject to Dutch censorship. All that Japan knew was what she had seen and heard when Russian exploration ships spied the coast, and when the hated Red Hairs landed to ravage the undefended settlements. Russia remained a nation to be feared.

To guard against future outrages, a stricter guard was placed upon the northern islands. The daimyo of Matsumai was not compelled to die because, in obedience to the Shogun's orders, he had been at Yedo, but he was degraded from his high estate. Evidently incapable of properly defending his dominions, unable to safeguard the

subjects entrusted to his care, his lands were reduced to a small holding. Matsumai, the Hokkaido, and the Kurile Islands were henceforth transferred to direct rule by the Shogun. Any subsequent
invasion by the Russians would be a matter for national warfare
between the Shogun and the Tsar.

Great Britain very narrowly escaped accountability for the
Chvostov-Davidov deeds. Again, through sheer coincidence and ill
luck, the long-feared Anglo-Russian alliance seemed corroborated.
War conditions had of course delayed the annual Dutch ship from
Batavia to Deshima. Japan had no means of knowing that Napoleon
and the Tsar, sitting on their raft in the river Niemen, had concluded
a peace treaty. So far as Japanese officials knew, Russia and Great
Britain were staunch allies against the Dutch. Not until the yearly
ship arrived with European news would Japan cease to suspect that
England might avenge the wrongs done to Rezanov or that the
British might increase the harm that Chvostov and Davidov had
done. Under these misapprehensions of European politics a major
catastrophe was but narrowly averted. An incident involving still
another beardless youth was about to take place in Japan. Had it
been handled in more clumsy fashion, a world-wide war might
readily have been precipitated.

Early in October 1808, while Deshima waited for the long overdue
annual ship to come up from Batavia, a sail was sighted by the watch-
men on the hills. In accordance with custom, word was rushed down
to the new governor, Dzusho Matsudaira, and he, following the usual
formalities, assigned officers to board the merchantmen. With them
were to go two Dutch clerks from Doeff's headquarters.

To the Hollanders the arriving ship seemed strange. The trim
lines were much more graceful than those of the usual commercial
ship; the sails set too well and were too smartly handled. These
omens might be overlooked, for, because of war conditions, Batavia
had been hiring foreign vessels of unusual styles in order to evade
the vigilance of British cruisers. This new vessel might prove another
of the American chartered ships, but even so, it seemed too lightly
laden.

The Dutch uneasiness was amply justified. As Matsudaira's harbor
boat drew near the stranger, the new arrival demanded its surrender.
Faced by a force of bluejackets, "waving swords, pistols, and lighted
matches," the Nagasaki men gave up without a struggle. The Netherlanders were hauled aboard the ship. The Japanese boatmen leaped

overboard and swam for safety. When haled before their master, they nervously explained that they had really wished to fight but that they had refrained "lest it cause the governor too great anxiety."

Word was brought ashore from one of the captured clerks. His message said simply: "A ship is arrived from Bengal. The captain's name is Pellew; he asks for water and provisions."

Secretary Tokuyemon, chief adviser to the governor, suggested· that the captives be recovered by a stratagem. "I shall go alone," he said, "obtain admission on board by every demonstration of friend- ship; seek an interview with the captain and, if he refuse to deliver the prisoners, stab him first and then myself."

Knowing nothing of the true identity of the invader, Doeff ad- vised against precipitous action. The caution was undoubtedly wise, for the vessel turned out to be an English man-of-war, the 38-gun *Phaeton,* a crack ship which proudly boasted itself to be one of the "Saucy Channel Four." Its commander was Fleetwood Broughton Reynolds Pellew, a smooth-cheeked lad of less than nineteen years who, according to Tokuyemon's official report, "sat all day and night upon a chair and moved no more than a mountain." Under his command were "350 picked men as ferocious as lions." He had come to intercept the two Dutch merchantmen who had left Batavia for Deshima. Having missed them on the sea, he tried to pick them up at their anchorage. He was astonished to discover that they had not as yet arrived.

Pellew would not have yielded to any threat of force. Like Brough- ton, a naval officer from the age of ten, he had spent his adolescent life in dominating a cringing crew that dared not raise objection. He was hard-boiled in his beliefs concerning the inferiority of Ori- entals. Confident that he knew "how these people should be man- aged," he would brook no interference. Arbitrary and impetuous, and with no real understanding of the world, he preferred stern dis- cipline to open-mindedness.

Steeped in the conviction that Britishers were closely allied with Russians for the subjection of Japan, the Nagasaki officers antici- pated an attack. Perhaps, they thought, this Pellew may have come to exact vengeance for the treatment of Rezanov and Krusenstern. These fears were intensified when, on the day following the kidnap- ping of the clerks, a second message came ashore.

The note was terrifyingly stark. "I have ordered my own boat to procure me water and provisions. If it does not return with such before evening, I will sail in tomorrow early and burn the Japanese and Chinese vessels in the harbour." The messenger added a verbal appendix to the written message, "The captain states that unless I return this evening with the provisions, the Dutch prisoners will be hanged without mercy."

Matsudaira, who was certainly no coward, resented Pellew's imperious demands. But, anxious to gain time to perfect his defenses, the governor accepted Doeff's suggestion "to amuse the young commander with promises" while troops were being mustered. A small supply of water, wood, and vegetables was sent to the *Phaeton* together with a note explaining that more substantial supplies were not immediately available but that they would soon be sent.

Meanwhile a council of war was called. The daimyo of Omura proposed that three hundred fireboats surround the ship and set it ablaze. Doeff suggested sinking stone-laden barges in the narrowest portion of the bay so that the *Phaeton,* bottled in the harbor, could be sunk by gunfire from the shore. Matsudaira himself preferred direct attack, by barges filled with lancers, bowmen, and soldiers with matchlocks. Tokuyemon, realizing the helplessness of Japan's warriors against the 38-gun frigate and fearing that Doeff's plan would permanently impair the harbor, won a compromise arrangement whereby the Omura fireships could be combined with the stretching of an iron chain across the harbor.

The plans could not be carried through. Matsudaira met insuperable difficulties. The guard houses were unexpectedly short of men. Of a thousand soldiers presumably on duty, less than sixty were actually at their posts. The rest had taken leave without permission, a breach of discipline for which their lord, then absent in Yedo, would be compelled to suffer.

Matsudaira's military aide showed marked reluctance to take active steps, though with true Japanese indirection he fell back upon a better excuse than mere unwillingness. "I have no inclination for such a task," he said, "besides I have no garments suitable for such a most important work." Matsudaira sentenced the mutinous subordinate to imprisonment and transferred the order to another military man. But he, informed of his assignment, pleaded with the governor, "to think of the anxiety my poor mother would suffer if I take the field." Baiyei, the official physician, summed up the situation when he reported to his chief that everyone at headquarters was suddenly sick. "Their loins are out of joint through cowardice."

Matsudaira was only too well aware that, under the strict lash of Japan's customs, no alternative remained for him save detention of the ship or ceremonial suicide. The law required him to intern all alien ships arriving in his district. If Pellew's vessel should escape, after sending ultimatums to Japan, Matsudaira would pay for the violation with his life.

The need for victory was all the more acute because the Dutchmen were representing the intrusion as another proof of Britain's definitely hostile intent against Japan's freedom. Pellew's impetuous high-handedness was in itself sufficiently tactless for Doeff's purpose, but by misrepresentation and exaggeration, perhaps even by deliberate deceit, the opperhoofd fanned Matsudaira's fear. The presumed Anglo-Russian Alliance was dinned into receptive Japanese minds, and the need was stressed for instant action.

"I warned the governor," wrote Doeff in his *Recollections,* "that the east wind, which had blown for some hours, was fair for the Englishman's escape, but it was expected that he would wait for a further supply of fresh water, which had been promised him."

Pellew, perhaps sensing something of the plot, took advantage of the fair breeze and slipped out of harbor before the hostile preparations were complete. His departure was well timed. Scarcely had the *Phaeton* vanished beyond the horizon before the summoned troops arrived. Chikuzen sent eight thousand men, eighty of the guard ships came, and word was received that the fireboats were in readiness. A clash that would most certainly have brought on war with Britain and in all likelihood would have developed into a struggle for the forcible opening of Japan's ports to European commerce, was averted by the margin of but a few hours. Pellew, who almost certainly could have fought his way clear from the harbor forts, was not the man to minimize any aggressive action against a British man-of-war. His report of armed attack upon the *Phaeton* would most certainly have been sufficient to have driven Great Britain into action.

Instead of opening Japan, however, the *Phaeton* incident probably kept the Empire more tightly sealed. Japan was firmly convinced, by Dutch insinuation and by British action, that the nations of the outer world were intent upon assailing her integrity. Stricter orders were dispatched from Yedo for the close guarding of the coasts.

In this aftermath, however, Matsudaira was to have no share. Disgraced by the intrusion of the ship, dishonored by its escape, the outwitted governor prepared for the only step which he could now

honorably take. No sooner had the *Phaeton* cleared the harbor than
he sat down to write a report to Yedo. Generously he sought in his
report to save his subordinates by pre-dating their activity, "in order
to convey an impression of promptitude." Yedo was given to understand that they had actually accomplished all that they were ordered
to perform. It was a considerate, and a most unusual, gesture. Half
an hour later, before the *Phaeton* was wholly out of sight of the
guardsmen on the cliffs, Matsudaira committed harakiri. His two
under-officers and ten subordinates, unwilling to escape responsibility
by his action in pre-dating the report, followed him in death.

Certainly the harakiri was the best escape from Yedo's certain
wrath. The penalty for incompetence was transfixion. Matsudaira
would have been manacled and corded to a cross. Then, as he hung
helpless, a spear would have been thrust upward through his body
from the right side to his heart, the point emerging above the left
shoulder. A second spear, struck from the left, would have completed the dispatch. For more than three centuries such was the fate
of governors who failed their sovereign.

Indeed, when Britishers eventually were admitted to Japan, the
Japanese interpreter informed the visitors that Matsudaira had actually been transfixed. It was the same interpreter who told Admiral
Sir Edward Belcher that Pellew had landed to take bullocks by force.
Then, said the interpreter, "The *Phaeton* sailed away and never
returned, which made our Emperor's heart very sore." The impression given was that Japan had regretted the loss of Britain's friendship!

Matsudaira's suicide safeguarded the family name. The daimyo of
Hizen, held responsible for the failure of his men to guard the forts,
was jailed for a hundred days. Then he asked permission, as a further
sign of contrition, to grant Matsudaira's young son a present of 2,000
kobangs, approximately equal to $10,000, for educational expenses.
The Council of State, pleased with Hizen's thoughtfulness, granted
the petition readily but added an additional favor. "To spare the
daimyo of Hizen the trouble of making further application, he is
permitted to repeat the gift annually." The permission was equivalent to a command, so young Matsudaira, later to win high favor at
the Yedo court, was thus assured a permanent pension.

XIV

JAILED IN A BIRD CAGE

1809–1813

FOUR years elapsed before the Japanese could retaliate against the Russian Red Hairs, but the delay did not reduce Japan's vindictiveness. From the earliest days of her intercourse with foreign peoples, the Japanese capacity for vengeance has been noted with amazement by her visitors.

Following the Chvostov-Davidov expedition, Captain Vasily Mikhailovich Golovnin, a thirty-year-old naval officer, was withdrawn in 1807 from his volunteer service with the British fleet and was ordered by the Tsar to make a survey of the Pacific shores. Sailing around the Cape of Good Hope he reached Kamchatka in October 1809. He was assigned the sloop *Diana* for a careful study of the Sea of Okhotsk, the southern Kuriles, and the Japan Sea.

The dominating reason was, in all likelihood, the heavy cost of marketing Kamchatkan furs. For more than a generation Russians had been buying sealskins on the Kamchatkan shores for approximately thirty rubles each, but by the time the furs had been transported nearly one thousand four hundred miles across deserted steppes to Kiatchka on the Sino-Siberian frontier and then another eight hundred miles to buyers in Peking, the price had quadrupled. If an easy sea route could be discovered between China and Kamchatka, or if a shorter land trip could be found, the Russian trade would leap. The opening of a new market in Japan was also an important item of the Golovnin enterprise.

All went well on the first stages of the expedition. Golovnin mapped out the Okhotsk areas and then, on July 4, 1811, sailed through the straits between the Hokkaido and Kunashiri. Signal fires were observed on shore, but the Russians took little heed. On the next morning the *Diana* was fired on from shore batteries. Golovnin promptly anchored and, with six seamen and a Kurile interpreter, pulled toward the beach in a small boat.

Despite his signals assuring the coast guards that he was bent on peaceful mission, cannon blazed from half a dozen different points. Luckily, says Golovnin, the Japanese were poor shots so that, though the balls passed close, no harm was done. He considered returning the fire, even aiming his small fieldpiece at the fort, but thought better of it since he was without authority to open war.

Returning to his ship, Golovnin ordered a cask sawed in two. In one half, he set a glass of fresh water, a piece of wood, and a handful of rice "to show our need"; in the other, he placed a few small coins, some cloth, crystal beads, and some pearls "to show that we would pay, or exchange, for what we might receive." Then the casks were set adrift for the coast guards to seize.

The gesture was understood. Soon the Japanese piled a quantity of goods along the shore and retreated into hiding. Golovnin sent his chief officer, Captain-Lieutenant Rikord, ashore to load the wood, rice, and dried fish brought down by the natives and to leave "articles worth more than the cost of the supplies" in exchange. He also left a letter to the governor asking for an interview.

Again the overtures seemed well received. A Japanese calling himself Koosma, in Golovnin's phonetic spelling, "came out waving a crucifix." He suggested that Golovnin and the governor meet in a conference in small boats in the harbor. Koosma explained that the Japanese were friendly, but that they had fired because of fear. The governor proved affable, assuring Golovnin that no harm had been intended to the visitors. The cannon were fired, the governor alleged, because the *Diana* had failed to salute the small boat sent out from shore to meet her. "He was excusing his own conduct," Golovnin adds, "because no such boat was sent." Golovnin, realizing that Japan could not understand why a foreign nation should fit out a ship for exploration purposes unless there were a secret design of conquest hidden in the background, assured the governor that the *Diana* had put into Kunashiri in distress. He was, said Golovnin, en route to Canton. Neither side was telling the full truth.

After these preliminaries, Golovnin prepared to leave the island, but just as he sailed, his casks came back to the *Diana*. In them were all the payments he had made for his provisions, the governor observing the law by supplying the visitors with necessities but without accepting any articles whatever in exchange.

On July 11 Golovnin again put into port, this time to call upon the governor for an official explanation. Landing with three officers and four seamen, he walked with a supply of presents to the castle, unarmed except for the sidearms and a small pistol for use "as a flare in case of fog."

The reception was peculiar. The governor, richly dressed, was accompanied by four hundred men, all supplied with muskets, spears, and bows. Golovnin hastened to deny all connection with the Chvostov expedition. The disclaimer seemed to be well received. The Russians were then subjected to intense cross-questioning which Golovnin parried as best he could. He was none too accurate, for when the governor asked how many men the *Diana* carried, Golovnin doubled the actual numbers. Then, seeing that sabers were being passed about among the Japanese guards, the Russians fled for safety.

"They threw oars and wood at us and shot after us. We escaped to the shore but, on arriving at the place where we had left our boat, we found it stranded by low water. The Japanese closed in on us and took us prisoners."

The next stage was a seven-hundred-mile journey, partly by land and partly by water, to the provincial headquarters at Hakodate. Golovnin had an admirable opportunity to inspect the countryside, studded every two miles with a prosperous village, but was kept under close watch lest he escape.

We were all placed on our knees and corded in the cruelest manner, with cords about the thickness of a finger: and yet this was not enough; another binding with smaller cords followed, which was still more painful. The Japanese are exceedingly expert at this kind of work; and it would appear that they conform to some precise regulation in binding their prisoners, for we were all tied exactly in the same manner. There were the same number of knots and nooses, and all at equal distances, on the cords with which each of us were bound. There were loops around our breasts and necks, our elbows almost touched each other, and our hands were firmly bound together: from these fastenings proceeded a long cord, the end of which was held by a Japanese, and which on the slightest attempt to escape required only to be drawn to make the elbows come in contact, with the greatest pain, and to tighten the noose about the neck to such a degree as to produce strangulation. Besides all this, they tied our legs in two places, above the knee and above the ankles:

they then passed ropes from our necks over the cross-beams of the building, and drew them so tight that we found it impossible to move. . . .
We were bound so fast that a child, without the least risk, could have
led us where he pleased. The Japanese, however, did not think so lightly
of the business. Each was led by a cord, by a particular conductor, and
had also an armed soldier walking by his side. In this manner we moved
onward, one behind the other.

The cording was in full conformity with ancient Japanese practice.
The prisoners of the *Kastricoom,* a century and a half before, had
been treated in identical fashion. Nor has the practice completely
died. Americans arrested in Osaka in 1935 were led through the city
streets firmly corded in much the same manner as Golovnin was tied
in 1811. On none of these three occasions were the prisoners convicted of a crime; in each case they were being escorted to a formal
examination before a magistrate.

Golovnin's trip resembled a procession. After the first week the
more annoying cords were loosed so that walking was made fairly
comfortable. Every effort was made to keep the Russians from wet-
ting their feet when crossing streams. Guards brushed off the annoying gnats. Save for the ropes and watchfulness, it might have been
a march of triumph.

Two Japanese from the neighboring village proceeded first, walking
side by side, and carrying staves of red wood, handsomely carved; their
office was to direct our course. These were relieved, on entering the next
district, by two new guides, carrying staves of the same description. The
guides were followed by three soldiers. Next came my turn, with a soldier
on one hand, and on the other an attendant, who, with a twig, kept the
gnats and flies from fixing on me. Behind me was a conductor, who held
together the ends of the ropes with which I was bound. We were followed by a party of Kuriles, carrying my litter, a plank about four feet
long and two and a half feet broad, covered by matting in order to
shelter it from the rain and supported by twigs from a pole borne on
the shoulders of the Kurile. After them came another party destined to
relieve the others when they became fatigued. The whole retinue was
closed by three soldiers, and a number of servants carrying provisions
and the baggage of our escort. The party must have amounted to between one hundred and fifty and two hundred men. Each individual had
a wooden tablet suspended from his girdle, on which was an inscription,
stating with which of us he was stationed, and what were the duties of
his office.

By July 20 the prisoners were turned over to soldiers of the Imperial army, men so richly garbed that Golovnin mistook them for nobles of exceptionally high rank. These now escorted the Russians through villages almost wholly Japanese—the former towns had been Ainu or Kurile in population. On entering Hakodate, August 7, Golovnin and his men passed through streets crowded with spectators who looked on the Red Hairs with friendly eyes. "There was," writes Golovnin, "not one malicious look, no hatred and no insult." Golovnin and his men were lodged in prison, "in small compartments, exactly like bird cages, six feet square."

Brought before the Hakodate governor for examination, Golovnin was informed that he was jailed in retribution for Chvostov's proclamation annexing the Kuriles. He was cross-examined, with each question and answer carefully written down. Japanese "who said that they had been to Russia" told Golovnin that the local Hakodate officials were wholly convinced of Golovnin's innocence but that the Shogun's court believed him guilty. One great proof of his guilt, said Kamajiro, one of the interpreters, was that Golovnin claimed to be Russian but that Golovnin's hair was not in the least like that of Laxman, a real Russian, who had been to the Hokkaido earlier. Laxman's hair had been tailed and powdered, Kamajiro explained, whereas Golovnin's hair was straight. "Has a religious change occurred in Russia?" Kamajiro inquired. He was astonished when Golovnin assured him that religion and hair dressing were not allied in St. Petersburg.

For eighteen days thereafter the prisoners were confined to their bird-cage cells, in a dark building which Golovnin thought must have been a converted barn. Golovnin's cell was six feet wide by six feet long, with a ceiling eight feet above the floor. The only furniture was a bench too short for him to lie upon at full length.

"Mine was a palace compared to the others," Golovnin wrote. "I had a door and two windows, the others had to crawl through a narrow aperture. They had no sunlight in their cells. They were always in complete darkness."

Golovnin's guards assured him, however, that he was not in prison, "because we had fire, tea, tobacco, sake, and better food in our 'oksio' than in the real prison, the 'ro.' But the same guards and the same strict discipline were required in both." Golovnin was not at all convinced that he was being treated well. The tea was especially bad, he thought, and the food much worse than that he had been given during the procession time. He amused himself by writing a formal letter in Russian to warn any future prisoners of the injustices they might expect.

On the eighteenth day a note came from his comrades on the *Diana,* announcing that they were returning to Okhotsk for reinforcements but assuring their commander that they would never quit the coast of Japan until all the Russians were released. The Japanese who brought the letter insisted on a full translation before the baggage accompanying the message was delivered. When the Japanese learned that a rescue was contemplated, Golovnin and his comrades were transferred to a safer jail at Matsumai. The change, carried on by a procession in which the corded prisoners were escorted down long lines of spectators, put an end to a wild hope cherished by Golovnin of breaking through the wooden spars that barred his cell and of escaping to the seaboard.

At Matsumai the Russians were given two attendants who were survivors of the Chvostov raid. They had been carried off from Saghalien, according to their story, and kept a whole winter in Kamchatka. These men, evidently feeling sorry for their captives, endeavored to ease the Russian loneliness by providing the prisoners with three pictures of Japanese belles "to look at for consolation."

A long winter ensued, after which more freedom was accorded to Golovnin and his men. By April they had gained some slight facility in Japanese because of mutual language lessons exchanged with a young scholar named Teske, who was assigned them as interpreter. Teske possessed the usual Japanese curiosity and, in return for information about Russia, told them much concerning Japan. Golovnin's volume on Japan is largely based on data filtered through the medium of Teske's language lessons.

Teske confirmed the European suspicion that the Dutch deliberately instilled fear of Russia and Great Britain into the Japanese mind. It was through him that Russians first learned that Beniowski had warned of a secret Anglo-Russian alliance to divide the world. Teske also said that the Shogun resented the killing of the men left behind by Chvostov. "Their premature death deprived us of much important information."

The new liberty to wander under guard revived the Russian hopes of making an escape, but there were new fears stirring. One of their own officers, young Lieutenant Moor, showed signs of turning pro-Japanese in hopes, Golovnin thought, of being made the chief interpreter for Yedo. In discussing the proposed break for freedom, Moor's opposition had to be discounted, and when the others broke jail and fled across country, Moor was left behind.

After a week of wandering, during which the plan of escape proved completely hopeless, the Russians were recaptured. No special punishment was inflicted upon them for their attempted runaway, though they were removed from their comparatively palatial jail to the common cells of ordinary criminals. The same round of visits by official interpreters was resumed. Among them was a Japanese astronomer from Nagasaki who was, he said, a special friend of Doeff.

The visitors brought news of the Napoleonic wars, especially the report that Moscow had been captured by the French. Golovnin, as a true patriot, refused to believe the story. Since the city was entered by Napoleon in September 1812 and since Golovnin declared that he was informed of the capture during the summer of that year, it is evident that the Golovnin story, written after his return to Europe, cannot be implicitly relied upon as to actual details.

Late in the summer of 1812, Captain Rikord returned. Sending an ultimatum ashore, he announced that unless his chief was at once released, the *Diana* would blockade the port. Japan refused to release the prisoners until Rikord produced an official letter disavowing the Chvostov raids. Rikord at first refused, sending a castaway ashore with a second ultimatum. As the man landed, gunshots were heard ashore. The castaway was never again seen by the Russians. Three days later, a second castaway was sent ashore but came running back to report that he had been kicked out of the castle. Still another castaway, whom the Russians called Leonsaima, went to verify this treatment and returned with news that all the Russian captives had been killed. Sent ashore again to bring a written statement of the Golovnin fate, Leonsaima completely vanished.

Rikord then put the blockade into effect. Not many vessels used the little harbor off which the *Diana* stood guard, but the vigil resulted in the capture of several unimportant coastal ships. Then a larger ship was taken. This was a merchantman, plying between Yedo and the Kuriles, via Hakodate. Its captain, Kahei Takadaya, one of Japan's leading business men, fell in perfectly with Rikord's plans. Announcing that the captives had been taken to Matsumai, the prisoner agreed to go back to Kamchatka with the *Diana* and asked four of his own men to go as hostages aboard the Russian ship in place of the castaways. The remaining waifs were accordingly set free, in hopes, says Rikord, that they would spread pleasing information about the Russians. Takadaya and a girl with whom he had been traveling wintered in Kamchatka with the Russians. Two members of his crew died during the stay, a matter that caused Takadaya inconsolable grief.

In June 1813 the *Diana* appeared again at Kunashiri Bay with the required letters of assurance and disclaimer. Rikord was passed on to Hakodate where Golovnin and his men were jailed. Takadaya, acting as intermediary, secured permission for Rikord's guard to land with muskets. He explained Rikord's refusal to remove his shoes on entering the governor's audience chamber. "Boots," said the diplomatic intermediary, "have been taken off. Shoes are merely leather stockings."

After feastings and compliments, the formal disavowal of Chvostov, sent by the governor of Irkutsk, was delivered in a box covered with purple cloth. Orders were immediately sent to Matsumai to release Golovnin and his men, so two years after their capture the Russians were set free. With the released prisoners was sent a letter reiterating Japan's insistence on seclusion. Golovnin was asked to deliver it to the commanders on the Russian coast.

In our country the Christian religion is strictly prohibited, and European vessels are not suffered to enter any Japanese harbor except Nagasaki. This law does not extend to Russian vessels only. This year it has not been enforced, because we wished to communicate with your countrymen; but all that may henceforth present themselves will be driven back by cannon balls. Bear in mind this declaration, and you cannot complain if at any future period you should experience a misfortune in consequence of your disregard of it.

Among us there exists this law: "If any European residing in Japan shall attempt to teach our people the Christian faith, he shall undergo a severe punishment, and shall not be restored to his native country." As you, however, have not attempted to do so, you will accordingly be permitted to return home. Think well on this.

Our countrymen wish to carry on no commerce with foreign lands, for we know no want of necessary things. Though foreigners are permitted to trade to Nagasaki, even to that harbor only those are admitted with whom we have for a long period maintained relations, and we do not trade with them for the sake of gain, but for other important objects. From the repeated solicitations which you have hitherto made to us, you evidently imagine that the customs of our country resemble those of your own; but you are very wrong in thinking so. In future, therefore, it will be better to say no more about a commercial connection.

In October 1813, the *Diana* sailed away, but not before a gala night had been spent by the ship's crew. Takadaya, overjoyed at being permitted to return home after his winter's exile in a foreign land, and grateful for his escape from the laws requiring him to suffer for his absence, clamored for permission to treat the crew. As the owner of ten ships he knew the needs of sailors, as he pointed out to Rikord. "Sailors, captain, are all alike, whether Russians or Japanese. They are all fond of a glass, and there is no danger in the harbor of Hakodate." For the first time in nearly two centuries, an evening of free revelry was enjoyed by white sailors in a Japanese port town.

Takadaya had, it appears, surmounted a high obstacle. On arrival at Hakodate he had been heavily guarded and forbidden all communication with his friends. The Hakodate governor, however, was a friend, and having a letter for the merchant from his only son, contrived to break the law in Takadaya's favor. Not a word was said to Kahei but, in sending him with a note from Golovnin to the *Diana,* the governor contrived to throw the son's letter toward him as though it were a piece of waste paper pulled from his kimono sleeve by accident with the Golovnin message. Then the governor pointedly turned his back to give Takadaya time to pick up the forbidden missive. Takadaya seems to have been restored to full favor.

Golovnin, returning to Siberia with the *Diana,* went overland to St. Petersburg with his reports. He was almost immediately dispatched to circumnavigate the globe. Sailing from St. Petersburg in 1817, he rounded the Horn to Kamchatka, and then continued via Good Hope until, in September 1819, he again reached Russia. Promoted to a vice admiralcy in the Russian navy, he set himself to compile a very exhaustive account of his adventures in Japan, prefacing the three-volume narrative with a full account of Japan's geography, the character of its people, their religion, government, and laws, the principal products of the Empire, and its population. He has much to say concerning the morality of the Japanese and of the extent to which infanticide had spread. In short, Golovnin in his *Memoirs of a Captivity in Japan* performed exactly the service which had been asked in vain of Kosirewski, Spanberg, Laxman and a number of others. He died in 1831.

XV

ONLY DESHIMA IS DUTCH

1813–1815

TO a nation like Japan, which had suffered no important political changes for more than two centuries, the kaleidoscopic shifts in European power were incredible. A description of the new American people as "second-chop Englishmen," as Doeff had dubbed them in a flash of inspiration, was understandable. Japan, too, had social castes, but there was little in Japan's long history to explain how one sovereign power might be absorbed by a rival of equal antiquity.

Such a complication was now presented for Japanese consideration. As part of her operations against Napoleon and the French allies, Britain sent an expedition against Holland's Far Eastern possessions. Java fell in 1811 to a British fleet. In his capitulation, Governor Jansens gave the British governor, Sir Thomas Stamford Raffles, title to Java and its dependencies, a description embracing the Dutch factory at Deshima.

The consequences of the fall of Java affected Japan for years to come. For the first time since the establishment of the factory, Nagasaki was cut off from intercourse with Europe. Even in the grim days following the Stewart visits, there had always been communication either by Dutch ships or by Americans, but the carrying of the war into the East disrupted all normal intercourse.

The last act of the Napoleonic drama was carried on in Europe while the Dutchmen in Japan remained in almost total ignorance of the events. "No one," writes Doeff, "but a resident of this period at the factory can form a conception of our state of mind. Separated from all intercourse, close prisoners in a spot which ships seldom ever pass, much less touch at, knowing nothing, guessing nothing of events in the remainder of the world; uncertain whether for the next ten or twenty years, or to the end of our lives, a ship of our country would ever greet our sight; living under the constant inspection of a suspicious nation which, treating us it is true with kindness, and allowing us to want for nothing which they could supply, could yet never consider us as countrymen; this was a sad lot, and sadder prospect."

News of the Golovnin capture and detention did, to be sure, relieve the monotony in 1811, especially when Doeff was invited by the Japanese authorities to give his opinion as to the disposal of the Red Hair captives; but Hollanders had never been anxious for Russian arrival in the jealously guarded Japanese market. Golovnin's successor, Rikord, brought the unwelcome news of the Moscow fiasco, which did not tend to make the exiled Dutchmen more jubilant. Doeff records the gloom that settled over Deshima.

Our hope was now fixed on 1812 but alas! it passed away without relief, and without intelligence either from Europe or Batavia. All our provision from Java was by this time consumed; butter we had not seen since 1807 (for the ship *Goede Vrouw* had brought us none in 1809). To the honor of the Japanese I must acknowledge that they did everything in their power to supply our particular deficiencies. . . . The police agent or inspector, Dennozen Sige, among others, gave himself much trouble to distill gin for us, for which purpose I supplied him with a still-kettle and tin worm which I chanced to possess. He had tolerable success, but could not remove the resinous flavor of the juniper; the corn spirit, however, which he also managed to distill, was produced in perfection. As we had been deprived of wine since 1807, with the exception of a small quantity brought by the *Goede Vrouw,* he likewise endeavored to press it for us from the wild grape of the country, but with less success. He obtained, indeed, a red and fermented liquid, but it was not wine. I for my own part endeavored to make beer. With the help of the domestic dictionaries of Chanel and Buys, I got so far as to produce a whitish liquor, with something of the flavor of the white beer of Haarlem, but it would not keep above four days; seeing that I could not make it work sufficiently, nor had I any hope of imparting to it its due bitter, so as to remain longer drinkable.

Doeff's pictures of the policeman trying to make gin, of the Hollander's wry faces as they taste its pitchy flavor, of their delight at the sight of a red and fermented liquid and their sorrow when they found that "it was not wine," and of the perishable excellence of the book-directed brew stir the sympathies of readers after the lapse of more than a century and a quarter. But other distresses and privations were to come.

Our greatest deficiencies were in articles of shoes and winter clothing; we procured Japanese slippers of straw, and covered the instep with undressed leather, and thus draggled along the street. Long breeches made we with an old carpet which I had by me. Thus we provided for our wants as well as we could contrive. There was no distinction among us. Everyone who had saved anything threw it into the common stock, and we thus lived under a literal community of goods.

In the summer of 1813, the fourth year of separation from the world, signal guns announced the arrival of two merchantmen. The ships flew the Dutch flag and hoisted the private signals agreed upon when the *Goede Vrouw* had departed from Nagasaki. Doeff and his small band believed the isolation ended.

After its curious experiences with William Robert Stewart, Nagasaki was prepared for almost any kind of ship as its annual trading visitor, but the coming of the *Charlotte* and the *Mary* in 1813 offered a new thrill. Japanese harbor police were not surprised to find the ships' officers speaking English rather than Dutch; the closing years of the eighteenth century had made such talk familiar. Nor were they taken aback when the skippers whispered that the two ships were really American vessels sailing under Dutch colors; similar deception had been necessary in past years.

That something was not in order seemed, however, evident when Walther Waardenaar, Stewart's old enemy, who seemed to be in a position of command, declined to exhibit his credentials. Waardenaar preferred, he told the port authorities, to confer first with opperhoofd Doeff. Ordinarily such an irregularity would not have been permitted, but Waardenaar was an old acquaintance, and the harbor police temporarily waived the strict enforcement of the rules. Waardenaar was rowed ashore to Deshima to present his message in person.

Doeff was not startled at the appearance of his old friend. He expected a recall and, indeed, was eagerly awaiting his return to Holland. Waardenaar's arrival was not wholly unexpected, although it was unusual to replace an opperhoofd by a man of such experience. The shock came when Waardenaar presented the Batavia letters. Doeff's recall was signed "Raffles, Lieutenant-Governor of Java and its Dependencies." The document was written in English, not in the customary Dutch.

"Who is Raffles?" Doeff inquired. Then he learned, for the first time as he declared, that Java had been surrendered to the British and that Holland itself was no longer in existence. Possibly Doeff was not, in reality, so uninformed as this implies, for Raffles, Golovnin, and Rikord all declare that Japan was quite aware that Java had fallen into British hands, but it is more than possible that while the news may have been known at the Shogun's court, no inkling had been given to the factory at Deshima. Waardenaar explained that the fiction of American ownership was invented in order to avoid any such experience as that of Pellew's *Phaeton*. Waardenaar had no desire to suffer an imprisonment like Golovnin's. He asked Doeff to assist the enterprise since Doeff too was now, by treaty, British.

The two ships, *Charlotte* and *Mary,* it was explained, were sent by the British not so much to secure copper and camphor as to gain an insight into Japan's commercial possibilities. Raffles, it appears, was by no means willing to undertake a trade that would, according to his opinion, result only in the exchange of British woolens for copper "which we already have in abundance."

Raffles did hope that, by continuing to send the yearly ship to Nagasaki, a definite political advantage might be secured, even at a monetary loss. "Might we not," he asked, "expect from the Chinese a more respectful and correct conduct than has been customary with them, if they knew that we were in some measure independent of our connection with them? Is it not important that in case of our actual exclusion from China there should be a channel open for our obtaining commodities with which we are at present supplied by that country?"

Nothing was known in Java about the current state of the Nagasaki factory. Doeff's privations were unsuspected by the head office at Batavia, but because he had already served more than double the usual period of time, a new opperhoofd, Heer Cassa, was sent out, in the *Charlotte,* to replace him. As commissioners to audit the accounts, Walther Waardenaar, former inspector who now, like Cassa, was British by allegiance, and Dr. Daniel Ainslee, an English-born physician, were added to the Cassa entourage. Dr. Ainslee was to remain as resident medical officer after the *Charlotte* and *Mary* returned with Doeff to Batavia.

Doeff declined to relinquish his authority. Calling in the five chief

Japanese interpreters he told them, in the presence of Waardenaar, the news that Waardenaar had brought and then added that, though Java had been captured, he disbelieved the news about Holland's being annexed to France. The two ships in harbor he disclosed to be British and not American.

Panic seized the interpreters, remembering the compulsory suicides that had followed the unauthorized visit of the *Phaeton*. They were afraid to tell the governor of their mistake in identifying the arrivals as Americans, lest the ships be burned and the crews massacred, and even more afraid not to tell that the strangers were British lest the penalty be their own death.

Doeff suggested an escape from the dilemma. This was to suppress the whole history of the conquest and to do business under the customary conditions. The interpreters were to announce that a successor had been sent to Doeff, in the person of Heer Cassa, but that the Batavia governor requested, as a personal favor, the temporary continuance of Doeff as opperhoofd. This would permit Doeff, after so many lean years, to gain a profit for himself. Doeff would buy the cargoes, sell the imports, and collect a return consignment to sell to English agents. The Dutch flag would continue to fly from Deshima. The little prison island in Nagasaki Harbor would now be, in fact, the only spot in the whole world which still professed Dutch rule.

The curious arrangement was accepted, though with many misgivings. The ships, unarmed in accordance with Japan's harbor rules, could not resist attack. To avoid confiscation and disaster, the English captains agreed to pretend to be Americans, though the United States was then at war with England. Waardenaar, rather than incur the rancor of the deceived harbor police, went through with the arrangement. Cassa, promised full pay for comparative idleness, postponed his leadership. He did not, however, purpose to remain in Nagasaki during the delay. Instead, he told the Japanese, he was obliged to return to Java with the ship and would return the following year.

This first trading venture, under the Raffles régime, was scarcely an overwhelming financial success for anyone but Doeff. The cargo taken to Japan cost at Batavia $273,000. Other expenses, including the repayment of a debt of $48,000 owned to Japanese since 1809, swelled the total costs of the trip to more than $370,000. In return for this expenditure, the venture brought a gross return of only $342,000, a deficit of some $28,000 on the voyage. Doeff, on the other hand, made a double profit on the deal.

The British traders, moreover, were under the necessity of carting back to Java an elephant which Raffles had sent as a present for the Shogun. This animal, as uncommon a rarity as the camel which Stewart had introduced, was refused by the Japanese on the ground that the transport of the beast to Yedo would involve more cost than they were prepared to pay. The elephant, and its Sumatran mahout, stirred intense interest in Japan. Even in the distant North where Golovnin was confined, detailed descriptions of the animal and of its strange caretaker were circulated.

In 1814, the following year, but one ship was sent from Java, and this, in all probability, not to seek commercial profit but to persuade Doeff to cease the pretense of Dutch rule. Cassa, returning on the ship, brought news of the Pan-European alliance against France and of the Dutch insurrection by the House of Orange against French rule. In his private instructions to Cassa, Raffles said that Britain would return the Netherlandish possessions if Holland coöperated with the British.

Doeff had no intention of yielding the one independent spot of Dutch soil in the world. He held the upper hand by his control of the interpreters through whom all news must pass from Europeans to the Japanese officials. So long as they were loyal to his interests no interloper could displace his rule.

But Cassa had not spent the year in idleness. In the interval between his first departure and his return on the *Charlotte* in 1814, he discovered the weakness in the Doeff position. Equally adept at intrigue, Cassa urged two of the interpreters to advise the Japanese against prolonging Doeff's stay in Nagasaki. If they would so advise the Shogun, Cassa promised, he would protect their secret.

The counter-plot against Doeff might have been successful had Cassa held his tongue. He made the mistake of confiding too freely in certain of the tea-house girls sent to the Dutch factory for entertainment of the visitors. They, as it happened, were in Doeff's pay, so the opperhoofd was forewarned of danger. By threatening to disclose the whole truth to the governor of Nagasaki—an action that would have brought death to all concerned—Doeff checkmated his opponents. Cassa was obliged to quit Japan again, leaving Doeff master of the situation.

For three years more he carried on as chief of the small settlement, in a splendid isolation. No further British ships were sent north by

Raffles, nor could any trade be conducted. Doeff was again supported by the largess of his former customers.

He was not, however, allowed to remain idle. Ten Japanese interpreters were assigned to him for assistance in compiling a Dutch-Japanese dictionary. He was an ideal choice for such a task, since he possessed not only the friendship of the natives and an advanced knowledge of the language, but also a thorough understanding of Japan's manners and customs. His, too, was the necessary patience and assiduity needed to clarify the numerous double meanings of Japanese characters and to illustrate usage by appropriate examples. Some 2,500 pages of closely printed information were compiled.

Only one copy of the work appears to have been contemplated by the Japanese authorities, for deposit in the Yedo library for the use of interpreters of Dutch scientific works. But Doeff, with his customary foresight, wrote out a copy privately for himself. This, he hoped, could be taken to Holland as the manuscript of the first Japanese dictionary ever to be published in a European language. Unluckily the manuscript was lost when the ship on which he took passage to Amsterdam foundered at sea. The original rough draft of the volume, found at Deshima by Overmeer Fischer in 1829, was later used for Dutch publication. It led to a violent accusation by the aged and embittered Doeff that Fischer was plagiarizing Doeff's labor.

The quarrel, curiously enough, coincided with the appearance of an extremely odd dictionary published in Batavia in 1830 by Walter Henry Medhurst, an English missionary to China. Medhurst knew no Japanese and hence entrusted the bulk of the labor to a Chinese assistant who knew neither Japanese nor English. The resultant volume, a lithographed publication based on the Doeff-Fischer notes, was the chief source for information about the Japanese language until after Perry's time.

Even with the arrival of his relief, Jan Cock Blomhoff, in 1817, Doeff's intrigue did not cease. Proud that a restored House of Orange had sent him the Order of the Lion for keeping the Dutch flag flying, Doeff prepared to return home to enjoy his private profits. It was, however, necessary to intercede with the Japanese authorities to break the rules in Blomhoff's favor. The new opperhoofd, relying too confidently on his semi-diplomatic status, had brought from Java his young wife, their infant, and a Javanese nurse. Because the rules were strict against the introduction of "unnecessary persons" into the

factory and especially against the importation of foreign women, the
Nagasaki governor flatly refused to allow the wife and nurse to land.
With what seemed a most unnecessary cynicism, Blomhoff was informed that there were tea-house girls available at any time upon
proper application, and that special permission might be secured to
let these girls stay over night in the factory buildings. Blomhoff appealed to Doeff for the retiring opperhoofd's influence to secure suspension of the regulations.

Doeff, pleased that the days of carpet trousers, straw sandals, and
pitchy gin were ended, and that he could at last leave Deshima, tried
to help his successor. Suggesting a special ruling on the matter, Doeff
arranged for a provisional landing of the women. The required
physical examinations, made to guard against smuggling of prohibited articles, were conducted with what Doeff regarded as "the
utmost forbearance and decency."

Yedo, however, refused to make any exceptions even in the case
of a wife or nursemaid for an opperhoofd's child. When the 1817
ship, the *Vrouw Agatha,* cleared for Batavia in December, Doeff was
accompanied by the deported women.

Perhaps the moralists might use the Doeff career as a convenient
text for sermons on the futility of intrigue. Resident in Japan for
more than nineteen years, during most of which he was virtually an
independent sovereign of his little realm, Doeff enjoyed greater opportunity for knowing Japan than had any of his predecessors. He
was well aware of the probable cash value of that information, and
was fully alive to all the possibilities of making private gain through
secret arrangement with his hosts. Stewart and other American sea
captains found him receptive to suggestion that they and he, without
the knowledge of the Dutch East India Company, might come to
some amicable agreement for unauthorized trading. Cassa and Waardenaar had been his unwilling accomplices in keeping Deshima free
from control by the nominal superiors in Java. On one voyage alone,
the 1813 venture, Doeff is believed to have piled up a private credit
balance of some $25,000 while the Company was losing a larger sum.
Now that he was sailing back to Holland, Doeff took with him a
sufficient store of curios to stock a museum of his own. This, together
with his bank balances and with the profits expected from the publication of his dictionary, would assure him a comfortable living for the
remainder of his days.

None of these plans were to mature. After nineteen years of association with the tea-house ladies, Doeff married a young Dutch girl from Batavia. In the voyage home the ship was wrecked, Doeff losing his papers, his collections, his cash, his bride, and all his possessions. The memoirs which he later wrote, in 1833, after an absence of sixteen years from Japan, still represent the best source we possess for appreciating the difficulties under which aliens tried to conduct business.

It is interesting, moreover, to note that the publication of the Doeff memoirs led to a revived interest in Japan. Reviewers of the more scholarly British periodicals dug deep into the dust to exhume ancient writings on Japan, and to give them a long-delayed notice. Volumes published half a century or more before the appearance of the Doeff volume thus gained an attention greater than that granted them at their first appearance. Doeff's writings not only awakened interest in Japan but set the tone for popular beliefs about the distant nation.

XVI

BRITAIN ASKS ADMITTANCE
1816–1818

O THER nations, knowing nothing of Holland's isolation in the
East, were not above fishing in the troubled waters. Commodore
David Porter, sent out during the War of 1812 to safeguard American
whalers from attacks by British men-of-war, conceived a scheme for
blasting Japan open. After all, he suggested in a letter to Secretary
of State James Monroe in 1815, if Decatur could compel a treaty of
amity with Algiers, why could not an envoy with a frigate and two
sloops enter into friendly agreements with Japan?

Monroe was inclined to fall in with the Porter plan, but there were
political dangers to be heeded. Too many opponents of the Administration were fearful lest the impetuous Porter, excited by his share in
the Algerian successes, by his escapade in rounding Cape Horn without orders, and by his brashness in annexing Nukahiva, largest of the
Marquesas Islands, might aspire to something approximating a dic-
tatorship. Monroe, anxious to run for the Presidency with the harmo-
nious support of every faction in the nation, dared not support Porter
too openly. Instead of backing the plan to open Japan, Monroe temporized by having Porter recalled to Washington as a member of the
new board of naval commissioners, a post which Porter held throughout the "Era of Good Feeling." America's opportunity to open Japan
was temporarily postponed.

Britain was less restrained. Now that the fear of Napoleon was
completely calmed, with France crushed for the moment and all
Europe gasping for economic breath, England was free to try a new
adventure. The East always interested the Manchester merchants,
and though Japan was not a primary concern in view of the some-

what pessimistic reports sent back by Sir Stamford Raffles, no possible customers could be overlooked.

Much more was hoped from China. Macartney's repulse was far distant, and the tea trade profits were bulking larger. London statesmen saw an opportunity for capturing the China trade.

Early in February 1816, therefore, a British Embassy, headed by Earl Amherst, nephew of the Lord Jeffrey Amherst of American fame, left on a mission to the East. Two ships, the frigate *Alceste,* commanded by sixteen-year-old Captain Murray Maxwell, and the small sloop *Lyra,* under Captain Basil Hall, comprised the squadron. After landing Amherst on what was to prove an abortive effort, at Tientsin, the two ships were detailed to pioneer along the coast of West Korea and then, voyaging along the Ryukyu, or Luchu, islands, were to pick up Amherst at Canton. Amherst, it was planned, would go overland from Peking to South China.

Hall's account of the expedition is one of the classic tales of marine discovery, noteworthy not only for its narration but for the piquancy of its style. Though he touched at no port on the main islands of Japan, his comments on the aloofness of the unsocial Koreans and on the rudeness with which they rebuffed alien overtures provide a parallel to incidents already noted by strangers in Japan. They would, he wrote "give anything on condition of our going away." They would accept neither money nor presents in return for the bullocks and poultry supplied to the ships. Though, like the Japanese, they were intrigued by glass tumblers, they dared take none so long as any of their officials were in sight. Two men to whom wine glasses had been given came back breathlessly to return the presents and hurriedly returned to the village, evidently to report to some overlord. Another Korean, finding himself alone, smuggled a wine glass in his sleeve.

Precisely the same story might have been told by almost any foreign visitor to any hitherto unopened Far Eastern port. Evidently the embargo against intercourse with strangers was much more sweeping than could be explained by merely a Japanese Shogun's whim. Korea, like Japan, was secluded both by its ruler's choice and by the desire of its commoners.

Hollanders had already been victims of Korea's desire for isolation. When, in 1653, a Dutch ship was wrecked on Quelpart, an island in the Korea Straits, thirty-six survivors reached the peninsula safely. They were at once taken prisoner and were sent to Seoul in chains.

The king kept them as curiosities, together with a huge red-bearded Dutchman, named John Wettevree, who lived at the royal palace as a sort of Korean Will Adams. Each year, when the Tartar envoy came to Seoul to collect the annual tribute, the Hollanders were hidden from his sight. Then, one year, two of the Dutchmen eluded their jailer, and appealed to the Tartar envoy for permission to go with him to China. The request was refused, perhaps because Korea paid a huge bribe to the Tartar for his silence, and the men were kept in jail until they died.

The other Hollanders were banished from the capital. For years they lived as beggars, badly treated and in rags. Eleven died in a famine. After thirteen years of hand-to-mouth existence, eight men escaped in an open boat, and were picked up by a Dutch merchantman. No news was were gathered concerning the fate of the remaining castaways.

This experience seems to have strengthened the Korean policy of complete exclusion. When Hall landed, the natives trembled with fear and "drew their fans across their own throats, and sometimes across ours, as if to signify that our going on would lead to heads being cut off."

Hall's party was troubled, too, by Korean etiquette, just as alien visitors were often embarrassed in Japan. Three days after their arrival, they met a boat whose chief distinguishing characteristics were a huge blue umbrella and a band of music. Under the umbrella sat a fine, patriarchal dignitary whose full, white beard covered his breast and reached below his waist. The grandee's blue silk robe flowed magnificently about him; his hat measured a full three feet in diameter. He carried a slender black rod tipped with silver, with a small leather thong at one end, and a black crêpe bow at the other.

The chief knew no language but Korean; none of the Englishmen could speak any foreign tongue; and the Chinese interpreter proved utterly incompetent. The chief and the British skippers carried on a stream of speeches during the course of a full day. No one had the slightest idea of what was being said, but Hall guessed that the chief was asking medical advice for a sick friend. The Englishmen offered to send the ships' doctors ashore to treat the invalid, but, when dawn brought the chief again, a "very sickly companion" was introduced. The medicos demanded that the new arrival show his tongue, hold out his pulse, and submit to an extremely delicate personal examination. No ailment could be discovered, but from the air of grave propriety with which the chief and his friend submitted, the English-men came to the uncomfortable conclusion that "they evidently con-sidered the whole scene as a part of our ceremonial etiquette." It developed, then, that the sick man was, in reality, the court scholar come to act as interpreter. The chief spent most of the second day in close inspection of the ship, taking accurate measurements of every portion of the ship and all its armament. "As he went along he took samples of everything that he could easily put into his sleeve, which served him instead of a sack, so that when he came upon deck, he was pretty well loaded."

So well was the chief served that Hall and Maxwell were deter-mined to pay a return visit to the official headquarters ashore. The chief was dismayed, making the usual motions of drawing his finger and his fan across his neck and, when the Britishers insisted on landing, breaking down in tears. What happened to him after the two ships weighed anchor is not known, but Hall, in spite of re-sentment at the chief's "pitiable and childish distress," was evidently worried over "the painful uncertainty which hangs over his fate."

Hall, too, made a searching comment applicable not only to the *Alceste-Lyra* expedition but to all other efforts to open trade with secluded foreign peoples:

We have frequently remarked that the sailors make acquaintance with the natives sooner than the officers. This seems the natural effect of the difference in our manners. On meeting with natives, we feel so anxious to conciliate, and to avoid giving offense, that our behavior, thus guarded and circumspect, has an air of restraint about it, which may produce dis-trust and apprehension on their part; whilst, on the other hand, Jack, who is not only unreflective and inoffensive himself, but never suspects that others can possibly misconstrue his perfect good-will and unaffected frankness, has an easy, disengaged manner, which at once invites con-fidence and familiarity.

From Korea the two ships sailed on September 1816, on a voyage of discovery along the Luchu archipelago, the long chain of islands stretching from Kyushu to Formosa. Present-day world travelers, sticking closely to the steamship lanes, find it difficult to appreciate the interest that sailing masters once took in these small bits of land. A century ago this Luchu, or Ryukyu, chain was of intense importance. Small ships, caught in the frequent typhoons of the Tung Hai, or Eastern Sea, kept close watch lest they be caught upon

the Luchu rocks. The residents, it was understood, were often kind
to shipwrecked navigators, even furnishing them, as in Pinto's case,
with junks for return to the Asiatic mainland, but there were rumors
that the kindnesses alternated with barbaric savagery. Too many
ships had disappeared, too many crews had vanished without further
word, while navigating in these waters.

The port of Napa, on Okinawa Island, largest in the archipelago,
seemed especially desirable. Maritime nations cast envious eyes on
a harbor so close to the continent of Asia. A naval station here
would, it was believed, command the ocean route to central and
north China. England, until she gained the island of Hongkong, was
anxious to annex the town; Russians and Americans also coveted
the port.

Few foreigners had landed willingly upon the islands, though
Beniowski claimed to have visited at "Usmay Ligon," and though
Broughton had refitted somewhere in the Luchus. The expedition of
the *Alceste* and the *Lyra* was, therefore, in every sense a voyage of
discovery to find final evidence concerning the ownership, the resources, and the trade possibilities of the Luchu chain. If the findings
proved favorable, Great Britain was prepared to announce annexation of the islands.

Upon arrival, Hall and Maxwell learned that the Luchus sub-
scribed to the usual Eastern policy toward foreigners. Instead of
welcoming the Britishers with open arms, the Luchu natives were
aloof and even sullenly hostile to the strangers. There was no
violence displayed against the Englishmen but only, Hall believed,
because the Luchu natives were virtually unarmed.

The islanders were no more anxious for Englishmen to land than
were the Koreans or the Japanese. Time and time again the voyagers
delicately insisted that walks ashore would benefit their health;
indeed the sixteen-year-old Captain Maxwell declared that shore
trips had been prescribed by his physician, but each time the
islanders turned the matter aside.

All the resources of Eastern etiquette were employed to keep the
Britishers aboard their ships. The Luchu men, it was asserted, were
of such inferior grade that no such honor as an English visit could
possibly be granted. Then, when Hall and Maxwell pointed out that
custom required a call of courtesy upon the ruler of the island, the
response came quickly that the Great Man really lived a thousand
miles away. This, as it happened, was completely true, in so far as

the sovereign of the islands resided either at Tokyo or at Peking, according to whatever view one took of Luchu allegiance, but the Britishers believed, with perfect justice, that there was also a local chief.

Eventually, after much polite resistance, permission was allowed for a shore visit, but only on condition that the walk must be confined to the beach and that the Englishmen must neither go into the town nor wander into the countryside. Careful watch was kept at first to see that the strangers did not break the promise, but in time the restrictions were gradually loosed, and by the end of the visit comparative freedom was accorded. Never during the entire stay, however, was complete liberty of movement allowed.

Meanwhile the islanders roamed at will over the two ships. Laughing, good-humored interpreters broke down the barriers between natives and foreigners, especially after the English discovered that copious draughts of sweet wine were very welcome gifts. When they had scouted out the way, two other men, Madera and Anya, came out to the ships to note down every possible detail of British speech and manners. From the beginning Hall suspected that the two later comers were men of rank masquerading as low-caste islanders, a suspicion which later proved amply justified.

Madera's actual rank was not disclosed to the British, but Hall's suspicions were aroused at the deference showed him by the Luchu natives. When the "mighty prince," Shang Pung Fwee, bearer of a red-paper visiting card measuring four feet long by one foot wide, came in state to visit the ship, all other Luchuans quailed before him. Madera, however, though always respectful, was fully at his ease. His real position, as was later learned, was as the Shogun's *metsuke,* or resident, at the court of a protectorate.

Somewhat shamefacedly, Hall confessed that the general Luchu attitude was in striking contrast to the boisterousness of the English. The grave Luchu propriety, as compared to British hilarity, Hall hoped, was due "to their looking upon us as their superiors, and vice versa; but even admitting this, which we were sufficiently disposed to do, it is no excuse for us."

The ribaldry was, however, confined to the forecastle. From the very outset of the oriental cruise, Hall and Maxwell agreed to conduct negotiations in an atmosphere of dignity. Distance and reserve appeared essential in dealing with the Asiatics, the captains thought, for "the Chinese and their dependents invariably repay condescension with presumption." The policy was popular among British diplomats in the East, for it seemed to them to suit the oriental psychology. Certainly it impressed the Nagasaki natives when Pellew, the boy captain, assumed an air of unapproachable dignity. In later years it was to be adopted by Commodore Perry in his dealings with the Shogunate.

The *Alceste-Lyra* expedition returned with pessimistic reports concerning trading possibilities. Hall denied that the Luchus could ever be important to foreign merchants, since they neither produced goods of value nor were rich enough to buy alien articles. He did, however, stress the availability of the islands as a naval base. His suggestions for establishing supply stations in the Luchus were to inspire both British and American commanders. His volume, published almost immediately after his return, excited wide interest, particularly because of his helpful information for the guidance of any foreigners who might later visit Napa.

Hall's report of the Luchu "island paradise" rekindled British interest in the East but definitely killed the hope that profits could be found at Napa. Golovnin's misadventure certified that no gains were possible in the Hokkaido. Torey's return with news of Stewart's activities proved that interloper merchants could not break into the Dutch preserve at Nagasaki. The time was ripe for voyaging in Eastern waters, but no good haven seemed available.

Again the Russians indirectly aided in furthering alien efforts to open Japan's harbors. Because the Okhotsk merchants failed to welcome Captain Peter Gordon in his 65-ton brig, *The Brothers,* Japan received another caller.

In May 1817, Gordon, "mariner, missionary and militant reformer," sailed from Calcutta for Okhotsk. His full experiences in that remote northern port remain unknown. Gordon, returning to Calcutta with an empty ship, reported only that, "as all the merchants had left town," he stored his cargo and came home. He was too full of fuming indignation to explain himself in more detail.

At Calcutta, Gordon learned that Hall was just returned from adventures in the Luchus. Fearing a second rebuff at Okhotsk, Gordon conceived the scheme of attempting a commercial call upon Japan. He loaded *The Brothers,* accordingly, with two types of cargo; one a complete set of samples of English goods available for export to Japan; the other a consignment for Siberia. Thus, if the Japanese refused to trade, a profit might yet be won by sailing back to Okhotsk.

None of this strange plan was made known to Gordon's Calcutta associates, lest he face competition from rival merchants. Not even his six shipmates were aware of what their skipper planned. Gordon, knowing that a journey to Japan would not require great deviation from the normal course to Okhotsk, felt no need to seek advice from other sources.

Gordon's background amply prepared him for the great adventure. The son of a sea captain, he had heard exaggerated sailor yarns of the Dutch traders; as navigator along the closed coasts, he had gazed curiously at the forbidden shores. Then, coming to the Okhotsk waterfront, he heard wild tales of the riches of Japan and of the reception given Russian merchantmen who dared to enter. The stories of such adventures were not tempered by insistence upon truth.

Repulsed in Russia, Gordon's imagination played with the plan of reaping profits in Japan. He resolved on two bold steps. Knowing something of the long-distant history of Will Adams, Gordon believed that a direct appeal to Yedo, at the very gates of the Shogun's palace, would prove more effective than a visit to some minor daimyo at a provincial outport. He sailed his brig direct to Yedo Bay.

The second daring plan was also drawn from the past experience of other traders. A temporary visitor, Gordon was convinced, would not be welcome. But if, thought Gordon, he could land within the Empire and if he could stay long enough to learn the language, he might achieve success. The plan was probably based on the report that Lieutenant Moor, Golovnin's aide, was offered an official post as chief interpreter. Such report was current in Okhotsk, though there was little authentic basis for the rumor. Gordon hoped to turn the chief interpretership into a medium for winning trading privilege.

In looking back upon the scheme, a twentieth-century historian finds interest in the cleverness with which Gordon made his plans. With shrewd psychology, the twenty-seven-year-old skipper suspected that the Yedo officers would be much more tolerant than the rule-ridden, tradition-governed, provincial authorities. In the strict etiquette of Japanese administration no under-officer dared attempt an individual action; Yedo governors could be more free to cut red tape. His desire to make a permanent home in Japan pleased the proud rulers. Gordon was no diplomat, but his eagerness to learn the native language was a highly diplomatic gesture. No other hopeful trader had been so thoughtful of Japan's sensibilities. The Japanese, to be sure, would not be anxious to dispense the secrets of their cryptic tongue to any alien, but they would be flattered by the foreigner's proper deference.

Choosing his time skilfully, Gordon sailed *The Brothers* into Yedo Bay toward dusk of June 17, 1818. The number of coasting junks and fishing smacks hastening to reach port before nightfall gave him sufficient cover to enable him to slip unobserved into the harbor. Without being recognized as a stranger, he sailed directly for the capital, hoping, as he said, "to be at the gates of the Shogun's palace by daybreak."

Luck turned against him, as it happened, for calm came in the night. The brig drifted close to rocks and Gordon was compelled to drop anchor two miles from a cluster of small villages. At dawn he was seen from the shore and he was immediately challenged by swarms of small boats from the nearby towns.

Later in the morning two officials rowed out to inspect the brig. From their elaborate decorations and from their great gravity, Gordon assumed that they were of high Imperial rank and so, acting with the studied deference which he had learned to be essential, he asked leave to send a letter to Yedo.

The officials were equally polite but wholly non-committal. Accepting Gordon's letter, but refusing every offer of small mementoes, they pointed out that *The Brothers* was in great danger from wind and tide in such an exposed position. They advised the Englishman to remove the brig into a nearby bay where it would be more sheltered. A pilot and two small boats towed the ship into the more secluded Shimoda Bay. Then they asked Gordon to surrender his arms, ammunition, and spare sails, to unship his rudder and to send it ashore, and finally to dismantle the brig completely. Gordon yielded to all the requests except the suggestion of total dismantling, refusing this on the clever plea that it would occasion too great a loss of time when he should be required to sail away.

The Brothers was safely moored in secluded Shimoda. The usual guard boats were set to watch the ship. The vessel was encircled by twenty small boats, roped to each other only a few yards distant from the interloper. Beyond this cordon lay twenty larger boats, besides two or three large armed junks each equal in size to *The Brothers*. "Our floating guard often numbered a thousand men and never less than half that number. It was incredible how good a lookout they kept and how narrowly all our actions were watched." Gordon remarked that sketchers were continually occupied in drawing every detail of the brig's equipment.

During the whole of the first day of captivity, visitors flocked to inspect the ship, coming in such crowds as to inconvenience the Englishmen. After the first day, however, the guards forbade strangers from approaching, though the shore was crowded by curiosity-seekers, "a very great majority of whom were females." On the fourth day, June 21, two interpreters arrived, one a perfect master of the Dutch language, the other partially acquainted with Russian, and both speaking a little English.

The conversations were conducted in Dutch and covered a wide range of topics. Learning that the brig was British, the inspectors asked if *The Brothers* belonged to the East India Company, and whether Britain and Holland were still at war. Gordon gave them full details of the Congress of Vienna, of the land settlements that had followed Waterloo, of Napoleon's surrender and his exile, and of the restoration of the legitimate monarchs.

The interpreters were particularly anxious to learn of Russia's plans. They had heard, undoubtedly through the Dutch, that Golovnin was to be appointed governor of Okhotsk. They desired explicit data from Gordon, who, they were told, had just returned from that region, as to whether this appointment would mean war against Japan. Until Gordon told them all that he knew about Okhotsk, they refused to give any information about trade possibilities or about the probable answer that Yedo might return to his appeals.

"I am inclined to think," Gordon writes with shrewd insight, "the Japanese rather dread the neighborhood of one so intimately acquainted with their northern possessions. So suspicious did the Japanese appear to be of the intention of Russia respecting their detention of Captain Golovnin, that were I to assign any specific cause for not being allowed to trade, independent of the national policy, it would be the wish on the part of the government not to give umbrage to Russia by conceding to others a favor which had been denied to them; indeed this was assigned as the true cause of our dismissal in a manner almost official."

The wait for Yedo's answer required a week, during which *The Brothers* was visited daily by the inquisitors. They required minute details concerning the birthplace and family history of every man aboard the brig, cross-examined Gordon on the entries in the log, and then checked the duration of the voyage by carefully counting the number of bucketfuls of water needed to refill the casks.

Always they were friendly and polite, though they held forth no hope that he would be allowed to trade. His private opinions concerning Russians may have proved a contributory factor in the good reception, for Gordon was outspoken in referring to the Russians as "rude, deceitful and ignorant, much addicted to excessive drinking and to unlawful and beastly pleasures." This was just the type of information which the Japanese preferred to think was true. Gordon endeared himself by sweeping condemnations of the Red Hairs.

Certainly the whole series of negotiations was carried on in an atmosphere of friendliness. "I never was in a country," Gordon writes, "the inhabitants of which conducted themselves with so much propriety as the Japanese. They were not only polite and affable toward me but invariably so toward each other."

Gordon's proffered gifts of garden seeds, of sheep, pigs, and goats, of newspapers and of books about geography were all refused. Japan's laws, he was informed, were strict against receiving any goods from foreigners; a fact already abundantly clear from the similar refusals shown to virtually every previous arrival in the Empire.

On the eighth day of the Shimoda stay, Yedo's answer was announced. It was a flat refusal. "You have applied for permission to trade. We are desired by the government to inform you that this permission cannot be granted, as the laws of Japan interdict all foreign intercourse with the exception of that which exists already at Nagasaki with the Dutch and Chinese. The government consequently desires you to sail with the first fair wind."

Gordon had made so favorable an impression that the refusal was somewhat softened. An official statement, evidently prepared in advance, was read to him from a second document not presented to him for his keeping. The laws of Japan, he was informed, were so strict that they permitted of no exceptions. A similar request thrice made by Russia, at the visit of the *Eclipse,* by Rezanov, and at "Matsumai in 1813," had each time been refused. "It is better not to return," the officials said, "because you can get nothing by it."

Comedy was not lacking at departure. Gordon was asked by the port officials to signal when he would be ready for the towboats to lead him out to sea. He answered that he would display some sort of flag to show his readiness. But when the time came for departure, after he had received his munitions and his spare sails and had re-shipped his rudder, he found no suitable ensign for the signal. All he had on board, he says, were the British merchant flag and the jack, neither of which he cared to display so long as he was in a state of semi-captivity. Accordingly he hoisted to his masthead one of his smaller spare sails. The officials came off posthaste to inquire what Gordon meant by such irregularity. Had anyone of less personal charm than Gordon been responsible, it is likely that the supposed insult to Japan might have been followed by grave consequences.

Thirty guard boats towed *The Brothers* out to sea. No sooner had they cast off than multitudes of small boats flocked about to revisit Gordon's ship. So numerous were the throngs on board, writes Gordon, "that I was glad to see a guard boat pull toward us for the purpose of dispersing the crowd. As soon as the people recognized the boat they fled in every direction, but when the guard boat went away, many of them returned. Some two thousand people came on this and the next day, all eager to barter for trifles." They fingered his samples eagerly and assured him that commercial relations might be opened were the English to visit Nagasaki. Gordon was convinced that Japan would offer an admirable market for woolen exports from Britain, since the Empire had no sheep and since the winters were too cold for silk or cotton clothing.

How far Gordon varied from an accurate appraisal of Japan's attitude may be judged by the Japanese aftermath of his adventure. At the very moment when he was weighing anchor, convinced that the Empire was prepared for foreign trade, the Yedo government was issuing a decree that all inhabitants of the seacoast towns should be carefully instructed in the shapes and sizes of foreign ships, lest other interlopers sneak into the harbors in the midst of fishing fleets. Noburu Watanabe, better known under his literary pen name "Kwazan," was urging that official notice boards be used to train the public in the appearance of foreign ships and alien flags.

Gordon's visit did, however, tend to break a long-established prejudice. For the first time since the Beniowski visit, a British caller violently denounced the Russians. Gordon's anti-Muscovite prejudice, caused doubtless by his rebuff at the "deserted" Okhotsk, may have been discounted by the suspicious Japanese as insincere, but his evident emotion weakened Japan's conviction that every Englishman was a warm friend to every Russian Red Hair.

So, too, they welcomed Gordon's vehemence against the English East India Company, that nest of "wholly unconstitutional, utterly anti-Christian, and totally abominable" rogues whose actions, he insisted, were "worse than those of French jailers, Cossack frontier guards or the officials of any barbaric nation in the world." Gordon did not succeed in opening a private trade for his own benefit, but he did break down the belief that Britishers were a united people intent only on the destruction of Japan. The fiery sea captain, who retired from oriental seas to live in London's "Cut Throat Lane," made entry to Japan a little easier for future independent traders.

XVII

HARASSING THE COAST
1819–1830

NO one now knows all the events that ensued along the coastline of Japan during the two decades following Gordon's departure. At least three callers came, all English and all with a
certain spirit of friendliness. All were turned away. They went with
angry memories, insisting that Japan was a nest of robbers who
would stop at no action to hurt the foreigners.

Evidently there were other arrivals of whom few records are
preserved. These must have been unpleasant characters who occasioned violent receptions, but who they were and what they did,
or whether they were guilty of any crime save that of asking wood
and water, is not now discoverable. Legends lend a hint, but folk-
lore is unreliable as evidence. In such affairs as those of the forgotten men, formal Japanese history is wholly untrustworthy. Loyal
authors blend patriotic color into the deeds of their own people, and
paint the alien in less attractive hues.

So numerous were the frequent squabbles between the Japanese
authorities and whaling crews who violated Japanese seclusion that
official interpreters were stationed at strategic spots along the coast.
Watch towers were erected on all high hills to discover the approach
of foreign ships. If, according to the strict Japanese law, "a vessel
shall be discovered from a nearer watching place, it shall be im-
puted as a crime to those in charge of the more distant post. The
governors thus guilty of negligence shall be deprived of their offices."
Ships so discovered were seized and, "after placing a strong guard
on board, without allowing a single person to land, were sent in all
safety to Nagasaki."

The rules were strict but often quite unworkable. Occasional foreign vessels slipped past the watchers and penetrated into harbor. A foreign ship arrived, for instance, according to gossip of the graybeards, in 1823, close to the port of Mito in Hitachi province. At once the coast guards were mobilized, but, when the Shogun's soldiers went aboard, the foreign ship was found to be a peaceful whaler. Yet this whaler, according to frenzied reports from Narinaga a twenty-six-year-old fisherman who boarded the ship, was heavily armed. Its name and nationality, its movements and its muster roll are matters not now known. The Mito reports do not disclose whether the vessel actually came into port or whether it was lying in the open sea. Above all, there is silence as to whether the "guns, swords, and other weapons in profusion," of which Narinaga speaks, were really war material or merely the gear employed in ordinary whaling operations.

The whaler's coming was indicative that Japan's isolation could not be prolonged indefinitely. By 1820, nearly $20,000,000 was invested in the North Pacific whaling industry. The ships were passing close to Japan's coast and, being small in size, were caught in sudden sea disasters. Lacking the ability to call for aid, and lacking steam power to move them into safer waters, the whalers sought whatever refuge was quickly available. If Japan refused the appeal of seamen in distress, the greater perils facing them upon the ocean would force the seamen to risk a fight ashore rather than certain sinking in the open sea.

How many sailors actually sought refuge in Japan only to meet death or long-term imprisonment cannot be discovered. The loss of certain unreported ships, last seen off the Japanese coast, may be due to foundering or to inhospitality. Sailor rumors told wild tales of how ships were confiscated and how crews were executed, but seamen's yarns are frequently exaggerated. Yet even if the Japanese be given all the benefit of every possible doubt, sufficient proof remains that Japanese were brutal, inhumane, and violent in their treatment of castaways.

Captain Gibson's experience at Otsu, a small Hitachi fishing village, is typical of such occurrences. Twelve English sailors, arriving in a whaler in June 1824, appealed for food and water. The villagers, accustomed to believing that foreigners lusted after power, accused Gibson of lying. "I did not like it," wrote an Aizawa samurai, "that he should conceal the real purpose of his coming." The Britishers were jailed so that they could be cross-examined. Then, when it became evident that all the whalers actually required was a supply of vegetables, pork, and chicken for the sick, with fuel and water for the galley, and that Gibson was willing to pay handsomely for the supplies, the men were released. They had been jailed for nineteen days.

Meanwhile the vessel had been carefully searched. The ship was found to be armed with thirteen harpoons, undoubtedly for whaling, and with four guns, each five feet in length, "with innumerable bullets." Gibson endeavored to explain that these were harpoon guns for sinking the barb into the whale, but Japanese refused to credit the explanation. "Outwardly," they reported to the daimyo, "they are mild and peaceful men but really they are untruthful and full of wickedness."

Rumors of the hostile intentions of the Englishmen spread in all the countryside. Hio Fujita, a firebrand samurai of nineteen years, called together his fellows and organized a plot "to lie in wait and slay all the foreigners as a service of the highest importance to our country and as a manifestation of our 'Yamato Damashii.'" He was disgusted at what he termed the "weak policy" of the daimyo's council in allowing the whalers to go free. Unfortunately for his plan, the ship sailed just prior to his arrival.

Even then the ill repute of the Gibson ship was not at an end. In forwarding a formal report of the incident to Yedo, mention was made that the ship had sailed to sea, but that "cannon were fired all day from the ocean." The implication is that the town of Otsu was bombarded, but the truth more probably is that the cannon shots were harpoon guns fired in the hunt for whales. The official report magnifies the affair into a raid by "many ships" to "pillage the town." The Japanese counted each ship's boat as though it were a separate vessel. In giving the ship's nationality, a bit of history is added which casts light upon the trustworthiness of Japanese reports. "It seems as though the English were subject first to Russia, but, as her power increased, she became superior to Russia."

Undoubtedly other incidents of similar nature are to be discovered in the local records. There is, for example, a well authenticated instance of a British whaler which called somewhere in the vicinity of Kagoshima in the same year that Gibson's ship was at Otsu in Hitachi province. The Japanese, in writing some years later, reported that a shipload of foreigners landed men to rob Tanegashima, the island where the discoverers first landed, and that the bandits were taken prisoner. The men thus caught may have come from either the *Tobey,* lost in 1822, or from the *Lady Adams,* which vanished in 1823. Save for the roll of missing ships during the 1820 decade, no other trace tells of the identity. Nor is it certain from the Japanese report that its nationality was necessarily British, though coast gossips agree that the ship was of English registry.

Matters such as these, while they cannot enter formal history, colored Japanese opinion. Some such special circumstance must have been responsible, for instance, for the issuance of a formal decree, the "Ochi-harai-Rei," in April 1825, in which it was "strictly decreed that English ships coming into Japanese waters should be fired on and driven away. Should any foreigners land anywhere they must be arrested or killed, and if the ship approaches the shore, it must be destroyed." Dutch ships also, since they might possibly touch at ports other than Nagasaki, were warned to exercise great care in shaping their course, "lest they meet with misfortune."

Probably the direct reference to British ships, rather than to alien ships in general, was inspired by the unknown crew who tried to steal the Tanegashima cattle, but the next formal visit by a British vessel was from a man-of-war too powerful for the coast defenses of the isolated region where it called to offer adequate resistance. Captain Frederick William Beechey, one of Britain's most famous explorers, entered Napa Harbor in 1827 to check the reports of the "Island Paradise." He gained a distinctly unfavorable impression.

Beechey experienced a reception almost identical with that accorded Hall and Maxwell. He was supplied with food and water, for which no payment was accepted, but when he asked permission to exercise his men ashore, the Luchuans attempted to refuse. "After a great deal of trouble" the sailors were allowed to land, but none of the Britishers were permitted to visit Napa, though the city was in sight and close at hand.

Anya, one of the officials who knew Hall, came down to Beechey's *Blossom,* but flatly disclaimed at first any knowledge of Hall or of any foreign ship. Under the influence of copious drafts of sake, his curiosity overcame his prudence. Remembering that the boatswain of the *Alceste* had been accompanied by his wife, Anya inquired if "ship got womans?" When Beechey answered in the negative, Anya replied, in surprised fashion, "other ships got womans, handsome womans." The slip convinced Beechey that Anya had not been speaking truthfully in denying the arrival of foreign vessels. Anya, taxed with the deception, cheerfully admitted the truth.

"I was also a little vexed," wrote Beechey, "to find that neither Anya nor Isaka-Sandu, who was also of our party and who is mentioned by Captain Hall, made the slightest inquiry after any of the officers of the *Alceste* or the *Lyra,* by whom they had been treated in the most friendly manner, and for whom it might have been inferred, from the tears that were shed by the Luchuans on the departure of those ships, that the greatest regard had been entertained. The only time they alluded to them was when Mrs. Loy recurred to their imagination."

Grateful remembrance of foreign visitors is not the strongest trait in Japan's psychology, but there is, in addition, another explanation for Anya's silence concerning former British arrivals. Special credit is supposed to accrue from first adventurings in untraveled regions. Down to the present day, residents in out-of-the-way portions of the Empire will assure the new arrival that he is the first foreigner to set foot in the region. Beechey may have been complimented, in Japanese fashion, by his native guest, as a pioneer and a discoverer. To the Englishman, however, Anya's refusal to remember former friends seemed like a combination of ingratitude and of crude deception.

Just why the Luchu men failed to ask after the health of their acquaintances is more difficult to fathom. The men at Matsumai were most solicitous to learn about Golovnin; Nagasaki Japanese inquired about foreigners known to the southern ports. There is, in all probability, a more flattering explanation to be found than Beechey's belief that Anya was hard-hearted and deceitful.

Beechey looked upon the Luchus as anything but an earthly paradise. The liberality displayed in granting food without receiving payment in exchange was interpreted as cunning knavery. "They are consummate adepts in all the arts of dissimulation; smooth, hypocritical, false, and at the same time jealous in a high degree; always attempting to accomplish their object, and commonly succeeding, by means of cunning, cozenage, and deceit, lackered over with an outer covering of fair-seeming urbanity and plausibility, which seldom fail to impose on those with whom they have to deal." Hall had seen, it was implied, only the external varnish without glimpsing the coarse material which the varnish seemed to smooth and gloss.

Hall's conclusions concerning the lack of money and of armament in the Luchu economy were also upset by the Beechey expedition. Far from being non-resistant pacifists, Beechey learned, the Luchu islanders possessed a store of cannon and muskets. He saw no arms in the possession of the natives, to be sure, but relied upon the statements of his interpreters—the same men whom he so roundly denounced for their willingness to lie!—and upon the sight of three square buildings which, because of their platforms, parapets, and loopholes, he took to be forts.

Perhaps his heaviest blows against Hall's accuracy were leveled at the belief that Luchuans were so gentle that their heaviest penalties consisted only of a slight tap with a fan. Beechey learned upon inquiry that the codes of punishment were sanguinary. "For great crimes the reward was death; for less aggravated offenses the body was loaded with iron chains, or the neck locked into a wooden frame, or the culprit was enclosed in a case with shaven head exposed to the scorching sun, or the hands and feet were bound, or quicklime was thrown into the eyes." Confessions, always exacted in oriental countries, were extorted by dividing the finger joints, or clipping the muscles of arms and legs with scissors.

One is almost tempted to believe that the devil or an inquisitor had invented these atrocities; there being scarcely any other supposition on which we can account for a refinement in cruelty such as that which is at length found to prevail among the people of Luchu, and which, unquestionably, would reflect no discredit either on the place of punishment below, or on the best imitation of it that has ever been got up above.

In short, as the reviewer of Beechey's account in *Blackwood's* succinctly puts the case, "The worthy inhabitants of Napa-kiang and its vicinity are the most egregious liars that the world ever produced."

The notorious British convict brig *Cyprus* met in 1830 a less happy reception. Captured by mutineers while the captain and crew were unaccountably absent on a pleasure trip, the brig wandered somewhat aimlessly over the Pacific. Nine men, few of whom had ever enjoyed previous sea experience, navigated the vessel to a port in South Japan. Refusing to receive a boarding party, the brig was bombarded by shore batteries and was badly crippled. The mutineers fled in their leaky craft, but somewhere near the Luchus the *Cyprus* sank. Five luckless convicts, taking to a longboat, rowed safely to

China, where they were arrested and were sent back to trial in England. The men were convicted again, of mutiny and piracy. It was a sad end, though thoroughly deserved, for men who triumphed over the perils of the sea.

Such attempted "raids" as these, and others of which no record is preserved, intensified Japan's fear that foreigners were seeking to invade the Empire. Internal incidents seemed to prove that organized conspiracies were afoot. Dr. Phillip Franz von Siebold, for example, for five years physician to the Dutch factory at Deshima, was detected in what was termed a spying plot.

The German-born Von Siebold had never been fully trusted by the Japanese, though they made full use of his medical skill and profited by the establishment of his Nagasaki hospital. When he departed from Japan in 1828, his ship was cast ashore by a typhoon. The cargo was reëxamined and maps of Japan and the Hokkaido were found. Von Siebold was also caught with a Japanese costume embroidered with the Emperor's sacred chrysanthemum crest.

Von Siebold was imprisoned for two years. Thirty-five of his Japanese friends, including the official astronomer and the Shogun's personal physician, were jailed for complicity. The astronomer had exchanged the maps for a set of Russian books and a map of Australia; the physician had given the clothes to Von Siebold in exchange for "lessons in ophthalmology." Before the incident was considered closed, several of the prisoners were forced to commit harakiri. Von Siebold, after the imprisonment, was banished from the Empire. He was officially declared a Russian spy.

These unfortunate events are now forgotten. A monument in Von Siebold's memory stands in a Nagasaki park, but the inscription does not mention his imprisonment, nor the alleged espionage.

The Empire's worries were increasing. Central Japan was torn by domestic insurrection. A daimyo near Amano-hashidate, one of Japan's most sacred sites, levied heavy taxes a year and a half in advance of the proper date. Disaffection spread to five nearby provinces. Even Ise, shrine of the Emperor's ancestors, was smirched by civil war. A force of 120,000 farmers fought against their lords. Unlike most other risings, these riots were partially successful. Perhaps in consequence, agrarian disputes were almost yearly occurrences during the first years of the 1830 decade.

The unrest was coincident with new worries concerning the isolation policy. Britain and America were both reaching out to tap the Eastern trade. With the swift rise of the whaling industry, the rapid increase of Chinese commerce, and the exploratory spirit of the period, it was becoming increasingly difficult for the long chain of islands covering the Asiatic coast to retain its inviolability.

England, securely established in its naval stations round the Good Hope route, was not immediately interested in the opening of Japan, but the United States, accustomed to the Cape Horn passage, and experienced in the voyage to Hawaii, turned her attention to finding better harbors in the East. Larger vessels, filled with the machine-made products of the Industrial Revolution, called for wider markets. Sea captains were speculating on the possibility of cutting in upon the Dutch monopoly. Japan, despite the pessimism of the Deshima merchants, was an inviting field for exploitation.

The project was no novelty. David Porter's plan had been discussed for fifteen years and, though the scheme had temporarily been shelved, the traders had not abandoned hope.

John Quincy Adams revived Porter's suggestion. For two decades he had been curious about Japan. As minister to Russia at the time of Golovnin's return, he learned much about the odd Empire which defied the Tsar; as trade commissioner to England and as envoy there when Hall and Maxwell were discussing their expedition to the Luchus, he acquired new interest in the Orient. The troubles of the whalers were a constant care to any Secretary of State and to a President. Adams urged that "it was the duty of Christian nations to open Japan, and that it was the duty of Japan to respond."

Adams' term as President expired before definite action could be taken, but the demand for extending American commerce was enthusiastically endorsed by Andrew Jackson, his successor. In order to prepare the way for better trade relationships with Asia, the Jackson administration inspired a series of special missions to conclude trade treaties "with all the powers whose dominions bordered on the Indian ocean."

Since it was deemed essential to prevent advance news of the project from leaking to European nations, special secrecy was enjoined on all participants. The leader of the party, Edmund Roberts, a sea captain of Portsmouth, received no formal instructions until his ship was well at sea, though Roberts, the nephew of old Josiah Roberts, first officer of the famous *Massachusetts,* was well aware of the nature of his task. But even Roberts knew only that he was to tour the East to sign treaties with Siam, Muscat, and Cochin

China; the Far Eastern extension was not particularly mentioned to him.

Ostensibly Roberts was captain's clerk to David Geisinger aboard the sloop *Peacock* and, lest even this assignment imply too much to eager eyes, Roberts assumed his task two months before the *Peacock* was due to sail. Roberts suspected, but did not definitely know, that his real orders were locked in the *Peacock's* strong box. Four months after leaving Boston, while the ship was off the coast of Africa, far removed from any possibility of foreign espionage, Roberts opened the box. It contained blank letters of credence for use in oriental courts. Roberts was instructed to gather all the data that could be possibly secured, but he was warned "to be careful in obtaining information respecting Japan, the means of opening a communication with it, and the value of its trade with the Dutch and Chinese." This was his first formal intimation that the United States contemplated a voyage to Japan.

The expedition proceeded under explicit directions intended to prevent the American dignity from insult. Roberts was expressly commanded not to go to Japan in a warship lest it, like Rezanov's *Nadezhda,* be submitted to "the degrading dignity" of being disarmed. A coasting vessel was to be chartered for the purpose.

Two other restrictions were also imposed. Roberts was warned not to spend any unnecessary amount of money—an instruction so vague that he dared spend no money whatever—and he was not to visit Japan until he had successfully concluded treaties with Muscat and Siam.

These treaties, the first American agreements with any oriental peoples, were complete in 1833. Roberts returned home with them, hoping to receive more definite instructions concerning the cost of his Japan adventure, and then set out again for the East. He promised "much further and varied information, to be derived under more favorable auspices and more intimate knowledge of Eastern forms."

Whatever advantage might have been derived for the United States by the almost furtive departure of the first voyage was now lost. The intent to travel to Japan became common property. This time Roberts traveled in state, as was befitting a messenger carrying ratified copies of treaties between the United States and the proud nations of the Orient. Two ships sailed from New York in April 1835 to escort the envoy. They came a year later to Bangkok, exchanged formal ratifications of the treaty, and then started for Yedo and for China.

Again, ill luck intervened. Roberts died at Macao in June. No such contingency had been anticipated. The official instructions were so drawn as to apply only to Edmund Roberts and to no other agent. Now that the envoy was dead, the American naval officers were entirely without instructions concerning an expedition to either Peking or Yedo. The new commander, Commodore Edmund P. Kennedy, considered that he had no other alternative than to sail back to the United States for further orders. The expedition was a failure.

In all probability, Kennedy had some special enterprise in mind. Naval captains of his day, accustomed to acting on their own responsibility because of their inevitable absences from their superiors, were not customarily so helpless. A messenger hurried back to Washington might readily have served the same purpose that was served by Kennedy's return. The mystery of his failure remains to be solved.

XVIII

JAPAN REFUSES CHARITY
1831–1837

WITH the opening to white settlement of British Columbia, following its discovery in 1774 and its surveying by Vancouver in 1792, new contacts between Asia and America were made inevitable. The fur trade which brought Kendrick, Colnett, and Douglas across the Pacific dropped in importance, but increasing commerce caused scores of energetic sea captains to explore the Asiatic waters.

For centuries, the travel tide had flowed from west to east. Asiatic fishermen, caught by storms in their clumsy junks off the Japan coast, were carried helplessly across the sea. Steady northeast monsoons blew dismasted vessels directly off shore into the strong flow of the Kuroshiwo, or Japan Current. This Kuroshiwo, setting strongly northward at the rate of ten miles per day, ferried hundreds of wrecked ships to America.

Whether derelicts drifting in the Kuroshiwo were cast upon the shores of Kamchatka, as were the junks of Debune and Sosa, or came to British Columbia, depended upon luck. Somewhat north of Tokyo the Kuroshiwo splits. One branch flows to Kamchatka; the other, following the forty-fifth parallel, goes eastward to the Aleutians and America. The men whom Laxman and Krusenstern attempted to repatriate were rescued from this latter current.

How many sailors were thus carried to the shores of North America can never be ascertained. But, because the cruel 1636 edict required that Japanese coasting vessels must be unfit for the open sea, hundreds of wrecked ships must have been caught in the Kuroshiwo following the sudden storms that sweep over Japan toward the end of each year. Records covering less than a century show that more than half a hundred junks were thus brought to the American Northwest Coast. These were the fortunate ones; very many others must have foundered on the way. Even today, when steam and radio and more accurate forecasting of the weather have reduced the toll of shipwreck, trawlers from Japan occasionally drift across the Pacific, and the glass floats for fishing nets used off the Japanese coast are frequently picked up in British Columbian waters.

After the settlement of the Northwest area, the chances for safety for such sailors as survived the trans-Pacific drifting were greatly increased. Dr. John McLaughlin, chief factor for the Hudson Bay Company, and governor of Fort Vancouver, took special interest in caring for such castaways. A man of deep religious sentiments and of warmly hospitable impulses, he combined his humanitarian ideas with a keen appreciation of possible commercial advantages. Though he never set foot in Japan and, in all probability, was ill informed about the Empire, he was anxious to open trade relations with a people whom he believed to be anxious for Canadian furs.

To John McLaughlin is due the credit for an inspiration which eventually resulted in a special expedition to Japan. The story, never before told in its entirety, is a saga of adventure, filled with incidents of hardship and of heroism. Starting from a tiny, straw-thatched village of the Inland Sea, the luckless participants crossed the Pacific during fourteen months of suffering and starvation, underwent shipwreck on the rocks of Cape Flattery in what is now Washington State, were enslaved by the Indians and then, by means which seem more imaginative than real, were eventually rescued by McLaughlin's men.

In June 1834, three years and a half after the adventurers had set out from Owari to carry tribute to the Shogun at Yedo, three survivors of the original fourteen sailors were brought safely into McLaughlin's camp at Fort Vancouver. These three waifs, Iwakichi, Kiukichi, and Oto-san, (whose name was originally Otokichi Yamamoto), are the first Japanese actually known to have set foot in North America. Other parties of wrecked Orientals had unquestionably preceded them, in days before the white men came to the Pacific coast, but no records survive to give their names.

McLaughlin kept the men in camp until the middle of November, seeking by sign language and by scraps of broken phrases to learn something of the islands from which the waifs had come. Then, as Captain Darby of the brig *Eagle* was about to sail for England, McLaughlin entrusted the Japanese to Darby's care. The men, he told Darby, were to be supplied with every necessity, and the amount was to be charged to the Company's account.

To the Governor of the Hudson Bay Company McLaughlin sent a special letter outlining his plan for making an effective use of the three shipwrecked sailors.

As I believe they are the first Japanese who have been in the power of the British nation, I thought the British Government would gladly avail itself of this opportunity to endeavor to open a communication with the Japanese Government, and that by these men going to Great Britain they would have an opportunity of being instructed, and would convey to their countrymen a respectable idea of the grandeur and power of the British nation.

If, McLaughlin concluded, the Government would not make such use of the men, private individuals would, he was sure, underwrite the cost of their return.

McLaughlin's plan was not approved in London. After only a week there, the three men were sent off to Macao, by way of Good Hope, while a mild rebuke was dispatched to McLaughlin. "It would have been better," the Company wrote its chief factor, "to have sent the men no further than the Sandwich Islands."

Thus Iwakichi, Kiukichi, and Oto-san, though not the first Japanese to circumnavigate the globe (the Krusenstern refugees had preceded them), became the first of their nationality to attempt a return home after visiting America. The effort was not their own; they were but pawns in a scheme to open trade relations.

The United States had already made two false starts. Neither Porter nor Roberts ever glimpsed the shore line of Japan. The third attempt, begun exactly a century ago, seemed at the time to promise more fruitful outcomes.

Dr. Karl Gutzlaff, chief interpreter for the Superintendent of British Trade at Macao, and Dr. Samuel Wells Williams, head of the American Board Mission Press at Canton, were instigators of the plan. Starting with the idea that they could learn sufficient Japanese from the shipwrecked mariners to translate the Bible, the two men evolved the idea of a peaceful expedition to Japan. By returning the unfortunates, three from America and four from Manila, they thought, in common with so many other hopeful men of other nationalities, that they would be welcomed by the Japanese. In gratitude the Japanese might break down the interdict against trading with the West.

The plan captured the imagination of other foreigners. Dr. Peter Parker, head of a Canton hospital, hoped to take Von Siebold's place as a resident physician in Japan. Charles W. King, a young merchant, planned to investigate trade possibilities. Missionaries desired an entrance to a new field.

The seven Japanese were pawns in this new effort, and indeed knew nothing of the deeper implications of the scheme. They were the tools of ambitious aliens who, although sincerely anxious to establish good relations with Japan, exploited the homesickness of men who had already suffered greatly in their exile. Iwakichi, Kiukichi, and Oto-san were well aware that return from foreign voyaging spelled death under the traditional laws; probably they were acquainted with the 'longshore gossip concerning the fate of previous exiles who had dared to come home. But such was the force of homesickness, and such their longing for return, that they were willing, albeit with dire forebodings, to participate in the attempt.

In the spring of 1837 the fast-sailing *Morrison,* a 564-ton brig commanded by David Ingersoll, sailed from Macao with thirty-seven persons for Japan, "having no apprehension of a worse reception than had been accorded to Broughton, Colnett, Torey or Gordon." Nine days later they sighted land at Luchu, "much like the southern shores of Rhode Island by its soft beauty, its very moderate height, its dusky verdure, its bareness of wood, and the conformation of its shores."

At Napa the hills were crowded by masses of curious spectators, but none came off to meet the ship until a full hour had elapsed. Then Anya, who knew Hall and Beechey, rowed to the ship. He seemed gray and sad, King reported, and had lost most of his command of English. Again, as on the occasion of the Beechey call, he at first denied that any other ship had come to Napa, but eventually he "remembered" the other incidents. No other Luchuan remained alive, he said, who had associated with Captain Hall.

Food was given grudgingly, perhaps because the *Morrison,* after so short a passage, stood in no need of refreshment. King's request for Luchu fruit was refused on the score that a recent typhoon had ruined the entire crop. King believed, probably with justice, that the explanation was a subterfuge to prevent trade either with the islanders or with the seven Japanese junks anchored in the harbor. It is probably also true that the poverty-stricken condition of the island discouraged the presentation of food stuffs to a ship as well supplied as the *Morrison*.

The *Morrison* was no pleasant place to linger. "Shortly before sailing," Williams reports, "the ship had discharged a cargo of rice. Some had escaped into the limbers of the hold where it underwent partial fermentation and decomposition, sending off an effluvia which was exceedingly offensive. This, being partly composed of nitric acid and ammonia, united in the hold with the lead in the paint and changed the plate and silver to a dull black. The salt in the seawater also decomposed and gave off muriatic acid which affected the gold of our watches. The hot air from the hold caused faintness and coughing. The water pumped from the ship threw off an insufferable odor of ammoniuretted hydrogen."

Even had the Napa folk been inclined to sociability, these physical conditions would have discouraged polite intercourse. The *Morrison* leaders were anxious to go ashore to escape the odors of their ship and to explore the island. Against the orders of the islanders, they insisted on wandering afoot "for health and propriety." Williams and his companions scattered bright new nickels among the crowds that thronged curiously about them and, much to the jubilation of the Americans, pressed a United States flag upon the people.

Probably Williams had some vague idea that this acceptance of a flag was close to an actual annexation of the Luchus, for he began almost at once to speculate upon the possibility of turning Napa into an entrepôt where Americans might meet Chinese and Japanese traders upon equal footing. Napa, he believed, might in time become a second Singapore. If it could be brought under American administration and become a port of call for Yankee clippers en route for China, this harbor in the Luchus might even rank with New York or London as a commercial center.

Much preliminary work would be required, the *Morrison* men were well aware, before this collection of poor bamboo huts, "not equal in appearance to a fourth-rate Chinese town," could be converted to a metropolis. Nor was the harbor perfect. Safe enough against east winds, there was in the small anchorage too slight protection against westerly gales. Before there should be any definite commitment to Napa as the American naval station in the east, more surveys were suggested.

Reuben Coffin of Nantucket had discovered, in 1823, a group of uninhabited islands, now called the Bonins, lying about eight hundred miles eastward from the Luchus. Supposedly first found by Sadayori Ogasawara in 1593, they had been a convict settlement for the Japanese, but in Coffin's time they were literally *muninto,* or uninhabited. Coffin reported his discovery, but Beechey forestalled the United States by raising the Union Jack over the islands in 1827. Certain waifs and strays, especially shipwrecked sailors, disorderly mariners marooned by their skippers, and South Sea islanders, had drifted to the islands and had set up a form of rule which Beechey had placed under British protection. Now, when Napa seemed to have its drawbacks, the American sloop *Raleigh* was dispatched from China to visit the settlement and to scout its strategic possibilities. The prospects were unfavorable for European colonization, but Britain, and latter Perry, flirted with the plan of sustaining the settlement on account of its nearness to Japan. Nothing came of the suggestion. In 1880, the islands were formally annexed to the Tokyo prefecture. They have since gained great importance both as a cable station and as an outpost for Japanese defense.

Undoubtedly the foreign interest in strategic possessions must, because of the loose conversations of the *Morrison* people, have become known to the Luchu officials. Orientals are never slow to suspect espionage, and the members of the *Morrison* expedition were none too clever in their concealments.

Suspicion was aroused because of the peculiar actions of the men aboard the *Morrison*. Dr. Peter Parker, anxious to introduce the comparatively new practice of vaccination into the Japanese Empire, was making extravagant assertions concerning the preventive qualities of the operation. The Luchuans were, however, loath to volunteer as subjects, so Parker resorted to guile. As one old graybeard, who seemed to be a physician, was inquiring concerning the methods of inoculation, Parker seized the old man's arm and, before the old gentleman could break away, inoculated him in three places.

To Parker the whole affair seemed an excellent jest, as indeed it seemed to the other visitors. "The whole surrounding assembly burst into a hearty laugh to see how the reynard had been taken; and the old man perceiving his predicament, enjoyed the joke with his countrymen." More probably, however, the laughter was dictated by considerations of face-saving, for the report of the affair, as related in Japan, was far from humorous. The incident was accepted as proof of the evil intention of the *Morrison* mission.

Suspicion became a certainty when the Napa port officers suddenly learned that seven members of the *Morrison's* crew were Japanese. Nothing had been said about them, lest the castaways suffer inconvenience from persistent questioning. The Americans had failed to reckon with the impatience of their own wards.

Fired with excitement at their arrival at a port of their own country, even though it was the fabulously remote town which had once marked for them the ends of the earth, the castaways were not content to hide. Kiukichi and his friends, hearing once more the beloved syllables of their native land, and seeing again the blue-and-white striped standards of the Satsuma daimyo, crowded to the decks. They chattered gaily with the crews of the coasting junks that lay inside the harbor, boasted happily to the Napa officers of how they soon would be home safe again with tales that would astound their friends, and made lavish promises of all the gifts that they would give the gods in thankfulness for safe return.

To suspicious Japanese, mindful of the previous visits of armed ships, this boast of sudden wealth meant merely that the seven waifs had sold their native land. Craftily they suggested that Kiukichi and his mates return to Satsuma aboard one of the native junks. When the offer was refused, a fast junk was at once dispatched from Napa for Japan, bearing warnings that a foreign ship was on its way to force an entrance to the Empire and that seven Japanese were plotting in the aliens' interest.

Of this, however, the *Morrison* was unaware. King had seen the junk depart, but he was deceived into thinking that it was taking sugar north to Satsuma. Williams paid so little heed that he did not deem the incident worth mentioning in his elaborate narration of the voyage of the *Morrison*. Yet the clearing of this junk spelled failure for the *Morrison* adventure. It was carrying the news that the foreigners were not only poisoning the Luchu islanders by force, but that the aliens were deliberately lying to the officials about the motive of the cruise.

King and Williams were convinced that they were behaving with great cleverness in thus concealing their true intentions. Williams was banking heavily upon the hope that Japan's exclusion policy might have weakened during the long period which he supposed must have elapsed since a foreign ship had touched at any port but Nagasaki. He was wholly unaware of any trade attempts since Gordon was repulsed. He counted on the influence of Japanese curiosity and on the nature of his errand in returning the strays to secure at least a courteous reception. Though he had no thought of opening a trade immediately, he was careful to carry a great variety of patterns of cotton and woolen fabrics as a bait for future commerce.

King subtly prepared his defense for violating Japan's seclusion. He chose Yedo as objective, partly because Gordon had been favorably treated there, but also because it was the seat of supreme government "where the highest assurance could be obtained for the future safety of the returned Japanese and a decision given as to American intercourse without reference." It was also, King was quick to see, a port "where the question would more probably be settled on principle and not after long custom and local prejudice."

If our approach to the capital should be treated as criminal, it could be replied, that not having been included in the law which confined foreign trade to Nagasaki, we had not offended by entering any other port. Besides, we could suggest to the Japanese that there is much wisdom in the old proverb, "divide et impera," and that their fears took a wrong direction when they suggested regulations which must aid foreigners to conspire together, if so disposed, by placing them in close and constant contact.

The course was then set straight for Yedo. It was the first American ship to carry the Stars and Stripes into Yedo Bay, though not, of course, the first vessel of its nationality to visit Japan. Warned by flares along the headlands that the Japanese were watchful, the ship dropped anchor at Uragawa twenty-three miles below Yedo, on July 30, 1837, to await the coming of the port officials.

In preparation for the expected visit of the officials, King and his associates prepared a packet of four letters, written in Chinese, to explain the coming of the *Morrison,* to introduce the castaways, to list the presents to be offered, and to record the cargo carried.

"The American merchant King," said the covering letters,

respectfully addresses His Imperial Majesty on the subject of the return of seven of his shipwrecked subjects. He is come to this honorable country from Cap-shuy-moon in China, in a ship of three masts, called the

Morrison, commanded by Captain Ingersoll, having on board a physician, naturalist, etc., etc.

Seeing the distressed condition of the shipwrecked men I have brought them back to their country, that they may be restored to their homes, and behold again their aged parents. Respectfully submitting this statement, I request that an officer be sent on board to receive them, to hear the foreign news, to inspect the register of my vessel, to grant supplies and permission to trade. I also request, if there be any shipwrecked Americans in your country, that they may be given up to me, that I may take them home with me on my return.

The second letter was adroitly written to appeal to Japanese prejudices in every possible fashion. Its emphasis, and indeed its suppressions, are excellently made.

America lies to the east of your honorable country, distant two months' voyage. Its western parts are not yet cleared, but are still inhabited by savage tribes. On its eastern side, where the people are civilized, and from which we come, it is separated from England and Holland by a wide ocean. Hence it appears that America stands alone, and does not border upon any other of the nations known to the Japanese. The population of America is not great, though the country is extensive. Two hundred years ago it was entirely inhabited by savages; but at that time, English, Dutch, and other nations went there, and established colonies. Their descendants increased gradually, and sixty-two years ago they chose their first President named Washington. That high office is now filled by the eighth President. Within the space of sixty-two years America has been twice invaded, but its people have never attacked other countries, nor possessed themselves of foreign territory. The American vessels sail faster than those of other nations, traversing every sea, and informing themselves of whatever passes in every country. If permitted to have intercourse with Japan, they will communicate always the latest intelligence.

The laws of America are just and equitable, and punishment is inflicted only on the guilty. God is worshipped there by every man according to his own conscience, and there is perfect toleration of all religions. We ourselves worship the God of peace, respect our superiors, and live in harmony with one another. Our countrymen have not yet visited your honorable country, but only know that in old times the merchants of all nations were admitted to your harbors. Afterwards, having transgressed the laws, they were restricted or expelled. Now we, coming for the first time, and not having done wrong, request permission to carry on a friendly intercourse on the ancient footing.

The presents, comprising a portrait of Washington, a telescope, a pair of globes, an encyclopedia, a collection of American treaties, an American history, and the like, were accompanied by a written list to which was added a special offer. "Languages of nations differ, and perhaps ours, though much more extensively spoken than the Dutch or Portuguese, may not be understood in your honorable country. If so, and at your request, one of my party shall remain in Japan a year to teach our language." The list of merchandise on board was closed by a request to have free intercourse with the native merchants, so that future cargoes might be made to suit, in all respects, the Japanese tastes.

A final note, from Dr. Parker, told of the medicines brought to Japan, "the wonderful efficacy of which, as well as the singular skill of their employer, could only be known by experience." Parker offered to stay in Japan a year without exacting any fees for any practice he might be permitted to treat.

The initial reception was, however, far from friendly. As the ship sailed up Yedo Bay, guns were fired from the headlands. The shots fell short. The castaways endeavored to explain that these were intended as salutes or as messages of warning for the port officials. The Europeans were less hopeful, wondering if Japan intended to open hostilities even before the *Morrison's* message was received.

When the mists that covered Yedo Bay cleared away at dawn and the adventurers saw solid shot dropping near them in the water, the worst suspicions were aroused. But soon thereafter firing ceased, and peaceful little boats thronged round the huge green-painted foreigner to marvel at its size and gossip at the hugeness of the hairy-handed *seiyu-jin*.

Many came aboard in curiosity, touched all the furnishings in awe, and pulled out little measuring devices to take notes on every possible dimension. Questions by the hundred were popped at Gutzlaff when they found that he could speak their language, albeit with an odd provincial accent. The customs men, who came aboard according to fixed rule to search the ship for contraband and to prevent the importation of strange women, went officiously about their task, wrinkling their brows and muttering strangely when they saw Mrs. King. To every question concerning the possibility of landing the refugees but one answer was returned, "Wait until we hear from Yedo." All the visitors, officials or civilians, were polite, accepting all the little presents that the *Morrison* would give, but offering nothing in return but one small fish and a cask of water.

The next day brought a surprise. Suddenly, with no warning, a hail of cannon shot poured in from guns hauled overnight to the hills. One shot struck the gunwales and ploughed up the deck. Other missiles whistled through the rigging. All too evidently the petitions were refused. After an hour of such constant fire, the *Morrison* reluctantly weighed anchor and set off down the coast. Gunboats, filled with thirty or forty men, pursued the ship, firing steadily from small swivel guns mounted in the bows.

The *Morrison* sailed down to Kagoshima, hoping for a more enthusiastic welcome. There two of the Manila men were put ashore, for this was their home province, and messages were sent to the port officials. Replies came back that all was well and that the foreigners would be allowed to land as soon as the daimyo could see the vessel's papers.

The port officials and the chattering fisher folk who flocked about the brig were unaware that Yedo had sent orders to refuse access to the new arrivals. While the local magistrate, receiving the sworn statements of the happy castaways concerning their good treatment by the Westerners, was exclaiming, "Truly these benevolent foreigners must be more than human," and while the port folk were exchanging what Iwakichi called "sweet words," the daimyo of Satsuma was mustering his legions.

The Americans could not appreciate the terror with which the coming of the *Morrison* inspired poor Satsuma. Too many dangers loomed over the daimyo's head for him to welcome alien traders. Satsuma was suspect. Only a generation earlier, a former lord narrowly escaped punishment for seeking private trading with the double-dealing Stewart. No daimyo in the Empire had as much to lose by the entry of aliens as had this lord; no province would be so hard hit by the establishment of foreign naval bases in the Luchus. The rejection of King's appeal for trade was a foregone conclusion.

The answer was not long delayed. Troops marched quickly into camp along the hills. All round the ships the guard boats turned sullen, and the fishing smacks sheered off in haste. Then cannon shots were fired from several coast batteries. For eighteen hours the bombardment continued until the *Morrison* weighed anchor.

The expedition was a failure, not worth, said Williams, the $2,000 laid out for the trip. The Japanese were taken back to Macao where some were set to work in Williams' printing plant, and others taught their language to earnest missionaries. Students of these teachers were later to be interpreters for Perry's expedition.

As usual, the foreigners arrived at just the time that domestic unrest was again reviving. The crops of 1836 failed, owing largely to a typhoon of thirteen days' duration, and for this and other reasons, six somewhat scattered provinces were in revolt. At Kokura near Kagoshima, the castle of Daimyo Ogasawara was burned. In Osaka, Heihachiro Oshio, a scholar who sold his books to buy rice for the starving, led a riot which required government troops for its suppression. In Bingo, Echigo, and Settsu provinces, small risings, led by Oshio's disciples, caused trouble for the authorities. These, following the difficulties in Kai province of 1836, rendered the Shogunate exceedingly unwilling to tolerate the presence of aliens who might add fuel to the rebellious flames.

King heard of these rebellions, but did not consider them important. His scepticism was somewhat shaken when, on looking down into the hold, he saw a party of hungry Japanese sitting around a huge basket of bread and a large bowl of molasses, greedily gulping the "Yankee collation," but he saw no connection between the incident and the news of famines in the interior of the island.

King was more concerned with what he believed to be a narrow escape from a confinement as long and as painful as that which Golovnin had endured. He was quite certain that he and his companions on the Morrison had been guilty of no breach of native law, but he was convinced that his ship was being penalized for the depredations probably committed by unknown American whalers somewhere on the Japanese coast. He also believed that he was the victim of false reports sent from Macao to Deshima. It is more likely that he himself was partially responsible for the hostile greetings because he refused at Napa to give honest explanations for the presence of his Japanese waifs.

King's comments on the repulse of the Morrison are shrewd and sensible. Immediately upon his return to Macao in August 1837, after his two weeks' futile effort to negotiate with Japan, he drew up an elaborate report urging American intervention.

I will not conceal my fears that the easy repulse of the "Morrison" will tempt the officers on the coast of Japan to riddle every American ship which distress or any other cause may carry within the range of their guns; for, be it remembered, the officer has only to report that he had evidence of hostile designs, and his cruelty and falsehood are sure to be rewarded by imperial favor.

The people, King remarks in echoing so many early observers, are friendly to foreigners and board the ships with confidence when permitted to do so. "But should the canaille of Japan get a taste of American plunder, the friendly might be outnumbered by wreckers and robbers."

I look up on the injury done to the American flag, in the treatment of the "Morrison," as an occasion too valuable to be lost for bringing national influence to bear on the point where private effort has failed to make any impression. . . . I propose, then, that a small naval force (say two sloops and a tender) shall be directed to pass the summer of 1839 on the coasts of Japan; the commanding officer, or rather the accompanying envoy (for I am afraid of military men) being furnished with the views of the government on the late treatment of the national flag, and with its ultimatum on the point of future intercourse. This ultimatum should embody security for the kind reception of the vessels and seamen of both nations in each other's ports; the admission of an American minister to the court of Yedo; the necessary exequatur for such consuls as may be appointed to care for our seamen, and some other like provisions.

The ultimatum, King foresaw, would be rejected even though it were wholly free from "the suspicion of mercenary motive." The United States should then resubmit the ultimatum together with an "exhibition of the defenselessness of Japan, its immense coast line, its exposed capitals, its feudal weaknesses, its entire dependence, in fact, on the very moderation and good will in our own and foreign nations."

As a final step King approved the declaration of war. He knew that a blockade of Yedo would convince the Shogun of his helplessness. But because suffering would fall upon the innocent lower classes, King disapproved that plan of coercion. He favored instead blockading Kagoshima as a step toward the entire emancipation of the Luchus. This would end the Empire.

"Every friend of Eastern Asia and of man will celebrate the day of its dissolution; and every American, familiar with the subject, will rejoice if his own country may be the emancipator, provided only that it be done at the call of clear, unquestionable duty."

King, it is well to point out, foresaw that England would within a year or two strike at the Chinese Empire "for the protection of an article which it is a shame even to the Chinese pagan to consume." Fearful that this would involve the fall of Japan to British arms, he urged American action while there was yet time. His volume closes with an odd peroration:

I am tired of hearing every allusion to American influence in behalf of E. Asia answered every day, as it now is, by men of all nations— "O, your government will never do anything here." I would silence the taunt, I would disappoint the sneer. I would not involve my country, by any means, in vast experiments of doubtful issue; but have her send out her light troops; at least a picquet guard, a spy or two; if in the war upon eastern despotism she cannot maintain the "line." And if her interference fails to do good, or if the time come when peaceful means, her moral power and generous attitude, are exhausted, and one single life must be perilled, let her call off her men of war, and let the blood of the missionary flow. For him to *die* is gain.

King's foresight was appreciated at Washington. Almost immediately upon receipt of his "advice," Secretary of Navy James K. Paulding ordered Lieutenant Charles Wilkes to set out with three ships for Japan. Wilkes reached Hawaii safely but soon lost one of his ships, the *Peacock,* in a storm. The *Vincennes* and the *Flying Fish* thereupon gave up the proposed Japan visit.

XIX

HOLLAND ADVISES HOSPITALITY
1838–1845

THE bare recital of the *Morrison's* experience fails to indicate the influence that Westernism was beginning to exert. Japan was ever sensitive to new ideas; she always alternated between a love of foreign fads and an intense anti-alienism. The *Morrison's* arrival, while superficially quite as barren of results as Wells Williams believed when he complained that the venture was not worth its cost, led to important national decisions.

Conservative opinion had prevailed when the brig was sent away. Fearing that some dark motive lay behind the visit of the huge ship, the reactionary forces strongly counseled resistance against the foreigners. One daimyo proposed to torture the castaways into telling all the truth about the alien intentions; another wished to arrest the captain of the ship in order to question him about his hidden motives. While the *Morrison* swung at anchor waiting for Japan's decision, the Shogun and his leading daimyos argued over policies. Only the fear of foreign guns prevented another Golovnin incident.

Reform was in the air, but the *Morrison* came a few months too early. Farmer unrest, culminating in six great riots within three years' time, prevented the acceptance of "dangerous ideas" from the Occident. With a violent rebellion of ten thousand farmers brewing in nearby Otsu, the Shogun dared take no chances.

Yet foreignism was becoming popular. Noboru "Kwazan" Watanabe, once violently anti-alien, swung suddenly to advocacy of Western thought. Joining with Nagahide "Choei" Takano in the formation of the Shoshi-kai, or Old Man's Club (the original members were all under thirty years of age), he demanded free foreign intercourse. Foreign art, alien geography, and outside history, he warned, must be understood by Japanese if they were not to fall behind in culture.

The Old Man's Club was not moved by love of foreigners but by fear of foreign force. Japan, as Watanabe pointed out, was helpless to resist aggression. Old-fashioned rifles, such as were provided by the Dutch for Japan's use, wooden forts, and cotton curtain barricades would not resist the heavy guns of foreign frigates.

Takano ridiculed the Shogunate for inefficiency. In a famous booklet, *Yume Monogatari* (*Story of a Dream*), he lashed the Yedo officialdom for its intolerant short-sightedness and for its narrow exclusionism. With rare prophetic power Takano suggested that Japan begin a program of expansion. If emigrants were sent to uninhabited Pacific islands, a dual purpose could be served. The burdens of domestic farmers would thereby be lightened, and the dangers of agrarian rebellion be reduced; the islands, too, would provide naval bases from which Japan's future fleet could operate. Such protection was essential, Takano thought, to guard against the enormous British armaments. According to Takano, England possessed in the Pacific a force of 25,860 warships.

Only one important daimyo, Masayoshi Hotta, lord of Bitchiu, supported the pro-foreign policy. The Old Man's Club was assailed as a hotbed of sedition financed by Dutch subsidies. The colonization program, so anticipatory of the present Japanese expansion in the Pacific, was an especial target of attack. Conservative patriots denounced a plan that would remove loyal Japanese to regions far from the direct protection of the gods. Takano's house was searched. When a Dutch book on Christianity was discovered, Takano was jailed. He remained a prisoner for seven months. Later, like Watanabe, Takano was forced to commit harakiri.

Shozan Sakuma took up the battle for reforms. Never an advocate of alien entry, he was keenly interested in securing reform of Japan's administration. Boldly he told his daimyo that classic learning was obsolete and that Western science was essential knowledge for Japan. He gained his knowledge from Peter Parley's *Universal History,* bought at an exorbitant price equal to his total income for fifteen months. The Deshima merchants who sold Sakuma this childish volume of silly unctuousness pretended that it was the most scholarly volume ever published in the West!

In an elaborate memorial, published in 1841 after Watanabe's suicide, Sakuma presented an eight-point program for reform. He asked a ban on copper exports so that more metal could be used for casting cannon. He begged for modern forts and better ammunition. Ships, he declared, should be built on occidental models, in order that food could be safely brought to Yedo. An up-to-date navy and an efficient ocean-going merchant marine were recommended. Schools were suggested, even for remote rural communities, to instruct the people in "national ideals." Strict justice was demanded, and a congress of feudal lords was urged.

The military suggestions were accepted, and Sakuma began to hope that general reform was possible. Spending his days in teaching gunnery and philosophy, and his nights in learning Dutch, he imagined that Japan was ready for modernization. To his astonishment, he was attacked as unpatriotic, sacrilegious, and treacherous. His emphasis on nationalism earned him the hatred of the Shogun; his suggestion that horses should be shod in foreign style with nails and paring of hoofs caused the fervent Buddhists to call him "a fiend incarnate," worthy of the name "Akuma," or devil, rather than his own. A facile comparison of his suggested reforms with those of Peter the Great invited the accusation that he was a Russian spy. Sakuma was assassinated by fervent isolationists.

Few inklings of these ferments seeped to foreign lands. The outer world was almost wholly ignorant that seething forces were at work to modify Japan's traditional stagnation. To Europe the sealed Empire seemed a static state.

Because we are accustomed in these modern days to elaborate news reports concerning Japan's domestic happenings, it is difficult for us to appreciate the dearth of knowledge in the times of our great-grandfathers. It seems incredible that for thirty years the London *Times,* the best informed of all contemporary newspapers, carried no authentic news regarding the secluded Empire. From 1814, when the Raffles efforts failed, almost a generation passed without trustworthy news items.

Excluding the report of the Golovnin captivity sent from St. Petersburg, there were, during the thirty years ending in June 1844, but three dispatches printed from Japan. They indicate the ignorance of well-informed Englishmen concerning Japanese affairs. In 1823, the *Times* published a brief article describing Japanese paper handkerchiefs; two years and a half later, in November 1825, the supposed ideals of Japanese honor were set forth in some detail. Eight years elapsed before any further mention was made about Japan. The silence was broken by a remarkable "story" which declared that the Shogun required all young people to grow to a certain specified height "or to suffer the bastinado until they do." Japan did not again enter the English news for ten and one-half years.

Magazine articles were little more complete. Most of them took the form of book reviews of works by travelers, some more than half a century old. Volumes by Dutch opperhoofds, such as Doeff and Fischer, were the only writings available, and these were based on extremely scanty data concerning any phase of Japanese life beyond the walls of Deshima. The English East India Company did, to be sure, recommend the publication of certain of its ancient documents, more as a means of cleaning out its files than as a medium for extending information, but the Company records gave little material later than the closing of the Hirado factory in 1623.

The lack of enlightenment concerning the true condition of Japan was exceedingly unfortunate, but the Japanese were but little better served in their information of the West. The Hollanders kept Japan abreast of many of the newer discoveries in science, particularly in matters of medicine and warfare, and provided a brief summary of current events, colored in Dutch interests. Neither Orient nor Occident knew much about the other at a moment when each was anxious for a better understanding. Japan completely misunderstood the foreigner and suspected his motives; the alien, equally, failed to understand the Japanese, and looked upon him as of radically different type than that of normal men.

Only through occasional castaways could the internal happenings of the Empire be learned, though these waifs were for the most part illiterates who knew little of events beyond their own small villages. From eight shipwrecked sailors, who had drifted half a year in the Kuroshiwo, the outer world heard of a great famine in 1838, during which hungry peasants lived on the bodies of their own dead relatives. Others reported the promulgation of a new edict in 1842, rescinding the 1825 rule that foreigners should be attacked on sight. It tightened the surveillance of the coasts.

The new law, issued through Tadakuni Mizuno, head of the Great Council at Yedo, evidently was inspired by fear of British naval power. Japan, anticipating that England's attack on China in the Opium War might be followed by an assault upon Japan, counseled its coast guards "to act in accordance with the gracious principles of humanity." The new regulations decreed that "even foreigners, when, driven by stress of weather or other misfortune, they come to seek provisions and water, shall henceforth not be driven away, but be accorded such supplies as they may need and only thereafter be required to sail away." The rules insisted, however, that "on no account shall foreigners be allowed to land." If the alien ships resisted the invitation to depart, the coast guards were commanded to use force to drive the ships away.

The concession did not satisfy the hundreds of navigators then thronging the eastern seas. By the decade of the 1840's "not scores but hundreds of vessels spread their canvas within full view of the coast." Rumors were insistent that whalers were being imprisoned and put to death for landing on Japanese territory.

One ship, the *Lady Rowena,* it was declared as early as 1854, landed men to destroy a Japanese town on the east coast of the Hokkaido. Much effort has been expended to track down the origin of the *Lady Rowena* report, since no authenticated case is known of any ship which deliberately pillaged a Japanese town without provocation. The rumor is customarily ascribed to a supposed advertisement in the *Sydney Gazette* of February 1842, wherein the master of the *Lady Rowena* warns fellow mariners against visiting Japan. Thorough search of the *Sydney Gazette* files for the period failed to discover the notice, nor are there records in the customary maritime mediums of the time referring to the event. Strangely enough, there appears to be no Japanese version of the incident, though recent publicists make much use of the supposed affair as an indication of Japan's justification for her inhospitality. Had the *Lady Rowena* been seriously at fault, it is unlikely that the Great Council would have been willing, within a few months of the supposed outrage, to issue the 1842 order relaxing the old severities. How the story of the *Lady Rowena* rose into popular currency is difficult to understand.

Europe displayed such interest in Pacific affairs as a result of the Opium War and the booming whaling industry that, by 1844, even Holland was convinced that her commercial monopoly was drawing to a close. William II, the king of the Netherlands, sought to anticipate his trading rivals by concluding a formal treaty with Japan well in advance of any other Western nations. He ordered Captain Koop of the Dutch Navy to sail in the *Palembang* to Nagasaki with a letter to Shogun Iyeyoshi relating "to matters worthy to be treated of between king and king."

Calling Iyeyoshi's attention to the calamities that had befallen China, William adds:

Such disasters now threaten the Japanese Empire. A mere mischance might precipitate a conflict. The number of vessels sailing the Japanese seas will be greater than ever before. How easily a quarrel might occur between the crews of these vessels and the inhabitants of Your Majesty's Dominion.

This, All Powerful Emperor, is our friendly advice; ameliorate the laws against foreigners, lest happy Japan be destroyed by war. We give Your Majesty this advice with honest intentions, free from all political self-interest.

By the best interpretations, the letter was not unduly tactful in its suggestion that Japan was helpless, but to patriotic Japanese the note seemed almost an ultimatum. William II, according to Japanese opinion, had sent a studied insult to the honor and the arms of the Empire.

Captain Koop was not allowed to take his message to Yedo. The local governor of Nagasaki, assisted by another such *metsuke* as those who interviewed Laxman and Rezanov, conducted all negotiations. Yedo's answer, dated eleven months after the letter was received, was a flat refusal. Iyeyoshi, even then, did not send a personal reply but through four daimyos expressed his "deep appreciation" of the "sincere loyalty" expressed by the Dutch sovereign. William's solicitude was noted, and his suggestions were deemed "worthy of adoption" but, the reply pointed out, the strict letter of the ancestral law could not be broken:

Posterity must obey. Henceforth, pray cease correspondence. If not, although it should be attempted a second or a third time, communications cannot be received. Letters from Your Excellencies also will have the same treatment and will receive no response. Nevertheless the trade of Your Excellencies' country will remain unchanged. In this also the ancestral law will be carefully observed. Pray communicate this to Your Excellencies' Sovereign.

The reply, discourteous as it may have been both in its content and in its delivery, was wholly in line with Japanese custom. It had not been lightly drawn. Its portent was so well understood that the creation of the modern Japanese Navy dates from the deliberations in the Cabinet over William's message. Count Awa Katsu's *History of the*

Japanese Navy holds William's letter to be "in large degree the cause of the political changes of succeeding years." Japan had, moreover, the experience of witnessing the arrival of two foreign ships, one British and the other American, in the weeks just prior to the drafting of her formal answer to the Dutch request.

The Empire was very wide awake to the necessity for keeping abreast of alien developments. News filtering through the careful Dutch censorship of Deshima was expanded by the Yedo officials to such degree that minor movements of unimportant ships became magnified into hostile mobilizations of foreign squadrons for the reduction of Japan. The tendency toward exaggeration was aided by the scraps of information seeping to Japan by way of Chinese trading junks which brought distorted reports of developments, not only in their own nation but abroad.

To suppress the growth of foreign thought, drastic action was required. When Heishiro Yokoi, adviser to Daimyo Matsudaira of Echizen, wrote a daring poem extolling Christianity as a religion "better than any that existed in Japan" and decrying the system of primogeniture on the ground that an incapable heir ought to be replaced by an adopted son chosen if necessary from a humble family, the only answer was assassination. The tottering Tokugawas could take no chances on what might turn out to be a new rebellion. Thirteen peasant insurrections between 1830 and 1842, the last one enlisting ten thousand rebels in Omi on the Echizen frontier, could not be disregarded.

The need for watchfulness against alien entry came into bold relief with the polite but insistent effort of Captain Mercator Cooper, skipper of the 440-ton American whaler *Manhattan* of Sag Harbor, to effect an entry in April 1845. Cooper was cruising off the southeast coast of Japan when he came to the comparatively barren land then called St. Peter's Island. He steered toward it, hoping to find fresh turtle for his mess, but seeing a broken pinnace drawn up on the strand, he went inland. There he startled eleven persons in uncouth dress, who fled in dismay. When he overtook them, they prostrated themselves on their faces. "They were alarmed and expected to be destroyed."

Cooper learned, by signs, that they had been shipwrecked many months before and that they had been unable to put to sea in their damaged pinnace. His offer to take them to Yedo was gratefully accepted.

"I had two great and laudable ambitions in view," Cooper admitted, "to restore the shipwrecked sailors to their homes and to make a strong and favorable impression on the government."

A day or two later, the *Manhattan* sighted a sinking junk from which he rescued eleven other sailors. A gale sprang up the next morning and, Cooper believed, the junk sank in the storm. He with his twenty-two wards, went on to Japan, sighting land somewhere north of Yedo.

Cooper was much more fortunate than the majority of his predecessors. The fisher folk gave him a warm and friendly reception, were pleased with his visit, and offered no objection to his landing. He sent one of his waifs to Yedo with a letter stating his wish to come to the capital with the remainder of the shipwrecked men. Then, while awaiting a reply, the *Manhattan* sailed off to explore the coasts.

Cooper was caught in a storm and was blown off his course for such a distance that he required a week's sailing to return to the point from which he had started. Then, sending two more messengers to Yedo to repeat his original request, he sailed straight for the capital.

His reception was unusual. As he entered Yedo Bay, a barge came out to meet him with a personage who "from his rich dress appeared to be an officer of rank and consequence." Word was given Cooper that his messengers had arrived safely and that the "Emperor" had granted permission for the *Manhattan* to sail up to the capital. He was towed "within a furlong of the capital."

The traditional crowd came off to visit the American. People of all ranks "from the governor of Yedo to the lowest menials, clothed in rags" crowded to the decks. Though Cooper and his men were forbidden to land under penalty of death, the interpreters, who spoke Dutch, a few English words and "more intelligibly, by signs," informed him of everything he desired to know. The rescued Japanese were allowed to go ashore, but on taking leave "they manifested the warmest affection and gratitude for his kindness. They clung to him and shed tears."

The future of the men is, of course, unknown. Strict interpretation of the rule issued in 1636 would have required capital punishment for the returning sailors, and knowledge of this fate may explain the tears and the reluctance to take leave of Cooper's ship. The captain was convinced, however, that special exception was being made for his charges.

Once the castaways were landed, the attitude of the officials changed. Officers were kept on board the *Manhattan* and three circles of guard boats, the nearest so lashed together by hawsers that their sides touched, were thrown about the ship. Nearly a thousand armed ships, with troops whose weapons glittered in the sun, kept watch by day and night.

On one occasion Cooper detailed some of his sailors to lower a damaged whaleboat to the water. Immediately the Japanese seized their swords, drew their fingers vigorously across their throats, and pointed both to Cooper's crew and to themselves. They would not even permit Cooper to restore the boat to the davits but insisted on performing the task themselves.

For four days the *Manhattan* lay at anchor with all necessary food provided. Then Cooper was told explicitly never to come again to Japan, "for if he did he would greatly displease the Emperor." The guards told Cooper that Japan was quite convinced that he could not be "bad hearted" for he had come so far out of his way to restore poor sailors to their native land. "The Emperor thought well of his heart and had consequently commanded all his officers to treat him with marked attention." Indeed, the day before the *Manhattan* was to sail, the Emperor sent Cooper his autograph which Cooper describes as "like a half grown chicken which had stepped into muddy water and then walked two or three times deliberately on a sheet of coarse paper."

Cooper was also presented with a passport, probably the first and only one of its type ever issued by Tokugawa Japan, in which he was commended to the care of Holland and which asked all Dutch ships to help him in whatever way they could. The passport stated explicitly that Cooper had not been allowed to set foot on shore and that he had received no knowledge of the products of the country. Then the *Manhattan* was towed twenty miles out to sea, and would have been pulled farther had he not protested. The whaler passed on to Kamchatka.

In all likelihood the courtesy extended to Cooper in allowing him to approach so close to Yedo—if Cooper's report is to be accepted at its face value—was a generous return for Cooper's consideration in sending two messengers to Yedo in advance to ask permission for the violation of seclusion laws. It is quite possible, however, that after Cooper's return from his whaling ventures in the North Pacific, his memory proved somewhat fallible on details and his interview may have erred on the side of optimism. Whatever may be the complete truth of the visit, and there are no other testimonies than Cooper's own, the fact remains that the kind treatment accorded to the *Manhattan* brought much comfort to other whalers forced by stress of circumstance to venture close to Japan's shores.

The reception of the *Manhattan* is of especial importance because it seemed to emphasize the point, already suggested by the *Morrison* men, that the Yedo officials might be more amenable to new ideas than the Nagasaki officers. In all events, it was now evident that the delay required before word could be sent to the Shogun and an answer returned would be a matter of but days at Yedo but of months at any other port.

Certainly Mercator Cooper enjoyed a happier reception than did Sir Edward Belcher, captain of the British surveying frigate *Samarang* when he arrived at identically the same time at Nagasaki. As he drew near the anchorage, after having explored the Luchus and various outlying islands, guard boats, "each of a beautiful model, elegantly painted and equipped with light and picturesque canvas," drew about him warningly. From the deck of one of the boats, which Belcher took to be a quarantine craft, an officer stretched out a long staff to which a box was attached. In the box was a letter, worded in Dutch and French, ordering the *Samarang* to anchor at a designated spot and not to leave until further orders should be received.

Belcher, a peppery Englishman who had sailed with Beechey and who was experienced in oriental tactics, was not to be commanded.

Intercourse with remote countries has taught me that to yield to any inferior authority, especially of the Tartar breed, is to reduce one's own standard very materially. I went on past the harbor master. Then I sent a letter in Chinese saying that I was at a loss to understand their want of attention in not sending me an officer of proper station. Unless such an officer should be sent, I declared that I would land at once.

The proper officer arrived and arranged for a ceremonial visit to the Nagasaki governor. The *Samarang,* according to the Japanese, had been long expected because the Dutch had told them, two years before, that such a survey ship was voyaging to the East. When Belcher informed them that he intended to remain but four days "they seemed disappointed." The Japanese suggested that he remain two weeks until Yedo had time to send a proper message. Meanwhile, they said, he could purchase fresh provisions for his ship.

Belcher believed, however, that treachery was afoot. The guard boat crews were troublesome and, on one occasion, "made suspicious movements toward me with some coils of very gentlemanly white cord." Remembering the experience of Golovnin, Belcher doubled his guards. He kept an active eye upon the throng of strangers who crowded the decks curiously, with fans to be autographed and with innumerable questions to be answered. The one interrogation which roused Belcher's ire was the inquiry as to why the British had waited so long before coming to Japan. It was identical with the query asked of the *Return* in 1673.

Belcher mentioned the experience of the *Morrison* and was blandly informed that the *Morrison* had "attempted clandestinely to break through our laws and had landed illegally as a smuggler." Pellew's experience was also misrepresented to him as an attack upon the city. Belcher suspected that his hosts were not being wholly sincere in their replies.

The fear intensified when, in spite of promises, the Japanese made excuses for not supplying the *Samarang* with fresh food. "They would not give us bullocks because, they said, the bullocks were 'too tired' and had been too hard worked. It would not be right, they said, to kill animals that had labored so faithfully. They thought it sinful to eat a working beast."

Finally, when fresh regiments came from the North to take their places on the guard boats, and when new scaling ladders were brought to the side of the *Samarang,* Belcher was convinced that a night attack was planned to take the *Samarang* by storm. He saw great guns concealed beneath mats and counted vast stores of arms distributed to the watching troops. He resolved to leave at once.

Refusal of the authorities to take pay for the vegetables and fuel supplied the ship, in spite of their agreement to receive money at an agreed-upon rate, seemed to Belcher a corroboration of his fears. He left Nagasaki completely satisfied that, though the officers were friendly and polite, hostilities had been planned.

None of this preparation for warfare had been seen by Cooper at Yedo Harbor, though Cooper had been kept prisoner aboard the ship, while some of Belcher's surveyors had been allowed to land upon a barren island to take observations. The difference in treatment may be due to Cooper's care in sending advance warning of his coming and to his polite requests for entry. The difference in nationality may have been a contributory factor, and the nearness to the central court is also a possible explanation. But the coming of two ships of different nations in one year was a striking illustration of how seclusion was drawing to its close.

Indeed, the high-handedness was no true indication of Japan's private indecisions concerning foreign policy. At the very moment when Cooper and Belcher were being denied admission to Japan, the Great Council of the Shogun was discussing the advisability of opening the Empire, and at least one daimyo was planning a trade treaty, with the tacit approval of the Shogun himself.

The breach in Japan's ironclad exclusionism was being forced at Napa in the Luchus, Hall's famous "Island Paradise." For two years Belcher had been surveying in Luchu waters and had forced from the Resident the right to "wander as he pleased." The population was not warmly friendly for, by Luchu edict, all people were obliged to withdraw from the presence of the British when the foreigners roamed ashore, but the reception was not openly hostile. Indeed an official document, signed by Ching-yuen-kin, the acting mayor of Napa, besought Belcher "that a stop be put to surveying in order to set at rest the minds of the people." But when the British declined to leave, the Luchuans made no effort to compel them to depart.

Instead of freedom from foreigners, the Luchuans found that other aliens were arriving. Admiral Cecille arrived at Napa with a French squadron of three ships in 1844. He bore with him a long document, purporting to be signed by Louis Philippe as "Emperor of the French," asking that Luchu grant to France rights identical with those that China had given to European nations. The Luchu authorities, terrified at the thought of what their Satsuma overlords might think of such an action, declined to agree. "We are too poor, and we have no surplus for trading," they replied to Cecille.

The Napa prefectural record of this French call presents peculiar features. According to this official version Cecille landed a hundred marines, leaving thirteen hundred more warriors in reserve upon his ships, and insisted that Luchu sign a treaty similar to the agreement "already signed with the United States." Cecille produced a document "sanctioned by the French Emperor," which, he said, must be at once accepted. "Even the slightest modification is out of the question." Then he rose and left, ignoring the tears and pleadings of the Luchu natives. Ten days later he returned with 230 men, all brandishing swords. Luchu signed the treaty.

Napa followed Japanese advice. Fujita, the Satsuma resident, had fled to the hills, in order that the connection between the Luchus and Japan might not become public. It was the Resident's usual practice upon the arrival of Chinese embassies, for Peking still asserted suzerainty over the archipelago. When Cecille withdrew to his ships, Fujita reappeared and advised Luchu to sign the treaty. If, he thought, the treaty were accepted under duress and in the name of a Chinese Emperor who possessed no real authority over the islands, the Japanese overlords would not be bound by its terms.

Satsuma, when the reports arrived, was less indignant than the Luchuans anticipated. Nariakira Shimadzu, heir to the Satsuma daimyate, realized that the outlying Luchus could not be defended by Japan's small ships against the French and British men-of-war. Believing that isolation must necessarily end, he advised his father to ask the Shogun's permission to open Luchu to trade.

Yedo debated the request with mounting excitement. The more conservative statesmen counseled the removal of Nariakira as heir to Satsuma, but surprisingly the rector of the University, Hayashi, and other influential advisers believed that a modified opening of the Empire, in distant Napa, might satisfy the foreigners and provide Japan with needed European goods without violating Japan's cherished seclusion. The Mito daimyo, realizing that such a privilege would provide his Satsuma rival with military and commercial advantages not available to the other Japanese nobles, fought to prevent the grant.

The Shogun yielded to Satsuma, but only on condition that the permission to open Napa be kept secret and that the Shimadzus "be careful to avoid future trouble." Both France and England landed missionaries on the Luchus, the British representative being Dr. Bernard John Bettleheim, converted Hungarian Jew, who opened a medical mission at Napa in 1846. The French priests left after two years' residence, during which they gained no converts; Bettleheim, the so-called "Nammin-nu-Gancho" (the man whose spectacles were mirrors), opened his English Free Hospital, introduced vaccination, translated the New Testament into Japanese and, though he too failed to acquire converts, was regarded as the pioneer of Western civilization in the Luchu archipelago. A monument to his memory was set up by the Japanese in 1926.

With the withdrawal of the French missionaries, however, the foreign interest in the Luchus temporarily subsided. The secret treaty made by the Satsuma daimyo was allowed to lapse. The slight breach made in Japan's exclusion laws was immediately closed, with no further effect than the granting to Bettleheim of permission to continue his residence at Napa. He remained until the arrival of the Perry fleet in 1854.

Bettleheim thus became the first alien in modern history to penetrate the seclusions of Japan's remote possessions. Not even at the present time are aliens encouraged to settle in the Luchus or in other Japanese dependencies. Increasingly, pressure is put forth to crowd out foreigners, whether business men or missionaries, from the nation's periphery. The reasons now given in Japan for allowing Bettleheim to stay at Napa are far from flattering to his memory.

XX

THE AMERICANS ARE INSISTENT
1846–1847

THREE separate streams of influence now converged upon the Washington authorities to urge an opening of friendly relations with Japan. Missionaries, eager to invade a fresh field where converts were anticipated in large numbers, echoed the demands of the *Chinese Repository,* the admirable Canton monthly of Wells Williams, for making Japan secure for Christianity. Williams prepared, through the assistance of the exiled castaways, copies of the Gospels in vernacular Japanese. He was anxious to spread the Word. Medical men, too, were ready to assist with practical measures of social service work. Williams and Parker and Gutzlaff urged with all their might that Japan be opened to development.

Diplomats and naval men hoped to redeem themselves from the two failures already suffered. Now that Britain had gained entry into China and that the arrival of Americans was but a matter of months, the need for naval bases was becoming evident. Roberts had failed because his instructions had been so narrowly drawn that transfer of his credentials had been impossible; Wilkes had let slip an opportunity because of time limits placed upon his traveling by inelastic Navy rules. Both State Department and Navy were ready to prove their true efficiency.

The third, and probably the most potent influence, came from the merchant interests. King's story of the repulse of the *Morrison* was widely read. His outline on methods to be pursued won ready acceptation. Almost immediately after King's report was received in the United States, Aaron Haight Palmer, of Baltimore, director of the American and Foreign Agency, endorsed the plan. In letters to in-

225

fluential statesmen, Palmer pointed out that steam vessels would soon be employed upon the Eastern runs and that coaling stations would be needed in the Luchus or Japan. Trade circulars, stressing the ability of Americans to supply modern machinery and to offer a steamship service that would be more regular in schedule and far quicker in service than the sailing ships employed by Netherlanders, were prepared for distribution in the East. Fourteen of these documents were slipped into Nagasaki during the five years from 1842 to 1847. A final argument insisted that Americans would soon be trading in great numbers to the East, for a Panama Canal would offer the United States a quicker and a cheaper service to Japan and China than other nations could present.

Palmer's ardent advocacy of entering into friendship with Japan received support from Caleb Cushing, President Tyler's special commissioner to China. After landing at Macao from the American ship *Brandywine* in February 1844, Cushing negotiated the first American treaty ever signed with China. He conceived the idea that Japan might be induced to follow the Chinese example, and sent a message to Tyler asking for permission to carry through the project to completion. Tyler had but little expectation of success, but he forwarded the necessary credentials through Secretary of State John C. Calhoun, for "full power to treat with the Japanese authorities." But as Cushing had left China before Calhoun's letter arrived, no action was taken on the matter.

American action had hitherto been taken by executive decree but, in February 1845, Congress urged the administration to secure trade and friendship with Japan. Largely as a result of the lobbying of missionaries, military men, and merchants, Zadoc Pratt, a New York Congressman, introduced a joint resolution asking for the opening of both Korea and Japan to American trade.

Pratt's arguments were based on considerations of commerce and of justice. Japan seemed to offer trade potentialities but, even more heavily in Pratt's mind, was entitled to recognition by the United States because of her high degree of culture. Korea, he seemed to think, was less promising a field, but the attempt to open that nation "will not entail additional expense and we can send the same ambassador there whom we send to Yedo."

With a population exceeding 50,000,000 (about thrice as numerous as the United States) the Japanese Empire combines a degree of civilization and power that may well render it respectable and formidable among the nations of the earth. That civilization, even judging from our imperfect knowledge concerning it, places Japan in advance of several nations with which our government now maintains diplomatic and commercial relations. Industry and many of the useful arts are practised by them with a degree of success unsurpassed in some of the European nations with which we are on terms of polite intercourse. Japan has internal trade, great markets, numerous coasting vessels and well conditioned roads. The power of the government may be estimated from the statement that the army ordinarily consists of 100,000 infantry and 20,000 cavalry which force may be increased to 400,000 in time of war. Jeddo is reputed to be one of the largest cities of the world. . . .

Another year will not elapse before the American people will be able to rejoice in the knowledge that the Star Spangled Banner is recognized as an ample passport and protection for all who, of our enterprising countrymen, may be engaged in extending American commerce into the countries into which it is now proposed to dispatch suitable diplomatic and commercial agents on behalf of our government.

The Pratt resolution led to quick action. In April 1845 Secretary of State James Buchanan wrote to Alexander H. Everett, who had succeeded Cushing, a letter granting Everett full power to negotiate a commercial treaty with Japan just as soon as he had exchanged the ratifications of Cushing's Chinese treaty. This time the instructions were made elastic so as to provide for possible eventualities. In case any accident, of weather or disease or death, such as invalidated the previous efforts of Roberts, Wilkes, or Cushing, should prevent Everett from fulfilling his duties, the credentials could be transferred to some other agent qualified to carry through the task.

Commodore James Biddle, commanding the *Columbus* and the *Vincennes,* was ordered to take Everett to Macao or Canton.

In an especial manner you will take the utmost care to ascertain if the ports of Japan are accessible. Should the Commissioner [Everett] incline to make the effort of gaining access there, you will hold your squadron at his disposal for that purpose; and should he decline to do so, you may yourself, if you should see fit, persevere in the design, yet not in such manner as to excite a hostile feeling or a distrust of the Government of the United States. The policy of the United States is avowedly pacific.

The permission to transfer credentials proved to be a wise addition, for Everett was taken ill and was obliged to leave the ship at Rio de Janeiro. Commodore Biddle thereupon took over the diplomatic mission as well as the command of the two ships. He went on to the East, visiting Manila where twelve men of the *Columbus'* crew died of cholera, and arriving at Macao on Christmas Eve 1845. He called at Amoy, Ningpo, Shanghai, and the Chusan Islands, and then, on July 7, 1846, sailed for Japan. It was by chance, the same day on which Commodore John Drake Sloat was hoisting the American flag over California at Monterey.

Agitation had not ceased, meanwhile, in America. While Biddle was calling at the Chinese port towns, Palmer was writing to President James K. Polk, on January 31, 1846, reiterating his request for an attempt to open Japan. Palmer had progressed to the point where he was listing the personnel to be sent on such a mission and was drawing up a proper list of presents to be given to the Japanese. His first choice as envoy was S. Wells Williams, chiefly because of Williams' *Morrison* experience and his presumed knowledge of the native tongue.

Palmer, it is now evident, was speaking with authority when he pleaded for American action in helping to open Japan. As director of the American and Foreign Agency he conducted an exhaustive correspondence with many oriental governments and princes, searched the records of foreign trade associations and scientific societies, and was thoroughly conversant with the work of missionaries and explorers in the East. But, even more, he had traveled to Europe and had been given free access to the files of official sources in England, France, and, significantly enough, Holland.

There is reason, then, to believe that Palmer was a special agent for foreign interests, especially for the Dutch, who were by now convinced that monopolistic policies were no longer profitable. Holland had learned from its experience in Java that greater profits could be secured through unlimited commerce than were to be gained from exclusive trading rights. The Netherlandish government was persuaded that a similar prosperity would be furthered by opening Deshima to other nations than itself.

"The Dutch are no longer opposed to the intercourse of foreigners in Japan," Palmer wrote to Secretary of State John M. Clayton. "There are strong reasons for believing that the king of Holland, if officially requested by our Government, would readily, as an act of national comity and courtesy, interpose his friendly mediation with the Japanese Government for the opening of a privileged port or ports to American commerce."

Whether he spoke similarly by the book in urging the use of the Luchus as a haven for American whalers and as a coaling station for merchantmen and warships in the East is less certain, but there is no doubt but that he voiced the opinions of officials in high authority when he made his suggestions.

So convinced were members of the presidential Cabinet by Palmer's plans that Secretary of the Treasury Robert J. Walker wrote in an annual report, "The opening of commercial intercourse with the Orient would revolutionize in our favor the commerce of the world, and would more rapidly advance our greatness, wealth and power than any event which has occurred since the adoption of the Constitution."

Biddle's arrival at Yedo Bay on July 20, 1846, came at a most inconvenient moment for the Japanese. The Shogun's Great Council was sufficiently concerned with the surveying activities of French and British naval men, and with the presence, by secret treaty, in the Luchus of the missionary men. There was no desire to complicate Japan's foreign difficulties by the arrival of still a third alien people.

But there were other reasons for Japan's regret that Biddle chose just this moment to arrive. Two months earlier, on May 27, an American whaler, the *Lawrence* of Poughkeepsie, had struck the rocks off the Kuriles. Three boats were launched, but because of stormy seas the captain, first mate, and several of the crew were drowned. One boat only, containing Second Mate George Howe and seven sailors, floated successfully. After a week's rowing, during which one man died, the survivors reached the Hokkaido. During the last four days of the struggle, they had been wholly without food. On June 3, while eating seal meat, their first hot food since the wreck, they were captured by sixty swordsmen.

For a year the men were kept in jail. Then, on May 31, 1847, they were transferred to the dark and filthy hold of a junk where they stayed three months more without seeing light or breathing fresh air. They were taken to Matsumai.

Again the unfortunates were jailed in what Howe describes as "a roofed box" and were taken out only when they were compelled to spit on a crucifix. One man escaped, but was overtaken and was "almost cut to pieces by swords." No medical attention was given him; no one was permitted to go near him. He died in jail two days later. Eventually, after another eighteen months' imprisonment, the survivors were sent from Nagasaki in a Dutch ship to Batavia.

The story of the privations of the *Lawrence* men caused violent indignation both in England and America. The anger was intensified when it was learned that other shipwrecked sailors had similarly suffered. Not the least repulsive feature of the outrage, to Americans who might otherwise have forgiven the Japanese, was the realization that the *fumiye,* supposedly long since discarded, was still employed as a routine in Japanese prisons.

The *Lawrence* survivors were in jail at the moment when Biddle arrived at Yedo Bay. The Japanese, although quite certain that no news of the imprisonment could possibly have leaked outside Japan, were in a quandary. Yedo was uncertain whether it would be better to release the prisoners to Biddle, and thus violate the law, or to conceal the presence of the captives and perhaps subject the city to bombardment if Biddle should learn the facts.

When the two ships sailed into Yedo Bay, the Japanese harbor master, "with a Dutch interpreter," (meaning a Japanese who knew the Netherlandish language), boarded the *Columbus* in some trepidation to discover how much Biddle really knew and what might be his purpose in the unannounced call. The Japanese had long expected an American arrival, but this visit came as something of a sharp surprise. Relieved of worry when the Commodore announced that he "came as a friend to ascertain whether Japan had, like China, opened her ports to foreign trade, and if she had, to fix by treaty the conditions on which American vessels should trade with Japan," the officers asked that the request be reduced to writing and said that they would refer the matter to their superiors.

The customary guard-boat routine was followed, with the usual throngs of Japanese on board the ship's decks. Biddle's tidy naval soul was outraged by the freedom of the visitors and by their persistent poking into details of guns and stores and rigging, but he allowed the investigations to continue "in order to show a friendly disposition." Permission for the Americans to land was peremptorily refused. "The Japanese objected to our boats passing between the *Columbus* and the *Vincennes* but as I insisted upon it they yielded." Biddle flatly refused, perhaps in accordance with the orders given Roberts, to surrender the guns, muskets, and swords of the warships.

Five days elapsed, in which the Americans were kept cut off from the shore, before Biddle issued an exasperated request for an answer to his appeal for friendly relations. Two days later, on July 27, a suite of eight officials brought him a formal refusal, couched in the usual terms stating that Japan would trade only with the Chinese and the Dutch, that all foreign intercourse must take place at Nagasaki, and that while Japan admitted that it differed from other lands in such matters, "each nation has a right to manage its own affairs in its own way."

"The Emperor positively refuses the permission you desire," the answer concluded, "and earnestly advises you to depart immediately and to consult your own safety by not appearing again upon our coast."

The relations were none too cordial during the week's delay. Biddle's boats, using the time to take soundings of Yedo Bay, were dogged by swarms of guard boats. His requests for water brought only two hundred gallons the first day, and less on the second. Biddle then threatened to detail his own men to go ashore for a proper quantity, unless a larger amount was sent. In the next two days twenty-one thousand gallons were furnished.

The climax was reached on July 28th, the day when the Shogun's answer was received. Biddle was invited to board a Japanese junk to receive the reply. He demurred, thinking that it was more courteous for him to have the letter delivered on his own ship, but when the envoy insisted, Biddle decided to gratify the Japanese. Then came "an occurrence of most unpleasant character."

"At the moment that I was stepping on board, a Japanese on the deck of the junk gave me a blow or push which threw me back into the boat. I immediately called to the interpreter to have the man seized, and then returned to the ship." The Japanese followed him to the *Columbus* and there delivered the Shogun's letter with profuse apologies for the mishap. An offer to punish the culprit in any fashion Biddle demanded was declined by the Americans.

Biddle, ignorant of the Japanese language, was unaware, until his vessels reached Macao, that he had been further insulted. The Japanese reply disclosed rudeness and incivility. The note, according to an official dispatch sent to Secretary of State Buchanan, was "prepared with an evidently studied and intentional disregard for the rules of courtesy." It was unaddressed, undated, and unsigned.

Everett, who by now had recovered from his illness and had made his way to Macao, said in a supplementary message to Buchanan, "The attempt of the Commodore to open a negotiation was perhaps not made with all the discretion that might have been desired and has placed the subject in a rather less favorable position than that in which it stood before." He promised to renew his own efforts for a treaty.

On July 28, 1846, the day before the Americans left Yedo, Cecille's two French warships sailed into Nagasaki Harbor "to let the Japanese know that the French, too, had great ships of war." The liberality shown at Napa was not repeated in Japan proper, especially in the presence of the Dutch. Cecille reported that the French were treated with extreme rudeness. They were surrounded by guard boats, and refused all access to the shore. Cecille curbed the insolence by his own studied hauteur, but realizing that he would gain nothing, after a forty-eight-hour stay, he withdrew from the port.

Biddle's seeming complacency in the face of insult and injury was in strict compliance with his instructions, but the effect was a lowering of American prestige among the Japanese. One of the American captives from a wrecked ship, protesting to his guards against brutality, was laughed at for his objections. "At Yedo," his tormentor said, "a common Japanese soldier knocked down an American officer and the Americans took no notice of it. Why should we take any notice of poor sailors such as you?"

So certain were the Japanese that neither Americans nor British would resent the treatment of their shipwrecked subjects that, in 1847, following the friendly calls of warships of two nations to Japanese ports, the usual harsh treatment was accorded to twenty-seven survivors of the British brig *Catherine*. Captain and crew were jailed in the same fashion as the *Lawrence* men had been.

News of the treatment of unfortunately shipwrecked men, as revealed by the sufferings of the *Lawrence* castaways, intensified the feeling in America that the time was more than ripe for definite protection to be given to Western sailors in the Eastern seas. Aaron Palmer's pleas for action grew more earnest than before. Not now content with the appointment of consuls to Japan, he asked, in a letter to Secretary of State John M. Clayton, that a blockade be declared of Yedo Bay until such time as Japan might be willing to see reason. The suggestion had been originally made by King, but had been discarded as unfair to innocent civilians.

Backed by a sheaf of memorials from merchants of Baltimore, New York, and other eastern cities, he asked for a full and ample indemnity for all American sailors who had been unjustly treated, for guarantees that future castaways should be granted proper care, for the enforced opening of ports to trade, and for the establishment of coaling stations and full whaling rights.

The two formal calls by the *Manhattan* and the *Samarang* in 1845, followed in 1846 by the visits of Cecille and Biddle and by the wrecking of the *Lawrence,* were indications that foreigners were not long to be strangers in Japan. France, England, and America were meditating official applications for admission; Russia was considering a new attempt to enter into Japan's harbors. The Germans, new arrivals in the East, were cruising in the straits of Matsumai.

Perhaps because the Russian memory was too clear concerning the fate of Laxman, Rezanov, and Golovnin, perhaps because she still feared retribution for the Chvostov raids, the Russians thought of surreptitious entry. The Russian-American Company fitted out a brig, *Grand Duke Constantin,* to sail under Gavrilov to explore the Gulf of Tartary, the Sea of Japan, and above all to start a trade with some northern port, preferably Hakodate or Matsumai. Gavrilov was given strict instructions not to let the Japanese suspect that he was sailing under semi-official auspices. He was to pass himself off as non-Russian, even to such minor matters as the use of Virginia tobacco in his smoking outfit rather than Russian tobacco, and was cautioned that neither he nor any of his crew should speak any other words than English words.

The vessel was dispatched in 1846, but though it is certain that it never reached Japan, no evidence is available to indicate just where the *Grand Duke Constantin* voyaged. Gavrilov entered the mouth of the Amur, opposite the northern end of Saghalien, but seems not to have penetrated far along the river. He died soon after, leaving no journal and a very insufficient log of travels.

In the next year, 1847, Count Nicolai Nicolaevich Muraviev-Amurski, new governor-general of Siberia, undertook an extensive secret survey of the North Pacific. He too chose a Russian-American Company captain, Nevelski, as his agent, and through him gained a reliable chart of Saghalien, the Amur region, and the nearby Kuriles. Suspecting and dreading Britain above all other rivals, Muraviev-Amurski endeavored to create a Russo-American Alliance in the East. The Crimean War ended his hopes in this direction, and he turned his attention to acquiring friendship with Japan.

XXI

THE NAVY DEMANDS FREEDOM
1848–1850

TRADERS might be scorned, missionaries might (like the famous Dr. Benjamin Bettleheim of the Luchus) be so completely isolated that there could be no possible contact with the natives, but American whalemen were not to be mistreated with impunity. Some of them, no doubt, fully deserved punishment for their violation of Japanese law, for whalers on a lark were never too meticulous about preserving law and order, but the United States Navy was intent on seeing that they received full justice.

America was, it is certain, looking for a good reason for intervening in Japan's affairs, especially if commerce or strategy might be furthered by her interference. But over and above all cynicism and beyond all question of national gain, there remained the firm conviction that Japan was violating the rules of international courtesy and that she owed a duty to humanity.

The American opportunity, several times frittered away by poor judgment and handicapped by departmental red tape, was to appear during the late years of the 1840 decade. On half a dozen excellent occasions excuse for the United States to force its way into Japan's affairs presented itself. The injuries to American seamen provided fitting reason why angered naval officers could burst into the closed harbors to demand redress and to secure assurances of future fairness to our citizens.

Fifteen men from the New Bedford whaler *Lagoda* suffered the worst of all the Americans who entered Japan prior to Perry. Their story is one of privation similar in many respects to that of Golovnin and his men. News of their difficulties, seeping through the channels of Dutch trade, brought down upon Japan a minatory visit from an

American man-of-war and led to their release after almost a year's imprisonment.

The underlying cause of their arrival in Japan remains uncertain even after a thorough naval inquiry. The ship, one of the most famous whalers in the New Bedford annals, left New England in August 1846. According to one story, she struck a shoal in the fog in June 1848 near Matsumai. Five boats were launched, but two were swamped, drowning thirteen of the crew. The other boats reached shore successfully. Another, and more probable, account relates that the fifteen men who landed in Japan were deserters from the ship who could no longer endure the ill treatment of their officers. The fact that the *Lagoda* eventually returned to New Bedford in June 1849 and that she continued in whaling service until 1890 seems convincing evidence that the striking on the shoal was no fatal blow.

Both stories agree that the fifteen men, eight Americans and seven Hawaiians, reached the Hokkaido after two days in their small boats and that they were at once imprisoned. They were given water but no food and were not allowed to sleep until the authorities of the small coastal village had safely transferred the prisoners to the Matsumai officials. Matsumai informed them that they would be given a small boat in which to leave Japan, but soon the captives learned that this was a false promise and that they were being held for transfer to Nagasaki.

The thin wooden walls of the Matsumai prison were but a slight barrier to the sailors. Two of the men, John Bull of New York, the chief mate, and Robert McCoy of Philadelphia, broke through their prison bars and fled to the mountains, but were recaptured and placed under stricter guard. McCoy and John Martin of Rochester then cut an eighteen-inch hole in the roof and fled once more. They were lost in the woods and, again captured, the Americans were punished by being caged in a small box, barred on all sides but open to public inspection. They were fed through a hole "just being enough to pass a cup" and were kept in this close confinement for ten days.

The men were young, restless, and, according to the Japanese, violent. "They quarreled habitually among themselves and gave much trouble." To prevent a further escape, the three fugitives were transferred to another prison upon a junk in the harbor. They spent seventeen days in a cage measuring twelve by ten feet, barely high enough for the three men to stand erect, and supplied with one small window. McCoy complains that they nearly suffocated with the heat. They asked forgiveness, promised not to attempt escape again, and were restored to their companions. All were taken to Nagasaki, preparatory to being sent home by way of Batavia.

Soon after, McCoy again broke through his prison walls. Japanese jails, he told his comrades, might do well enough for Japanese but could not hold Americans. When again retaken he was corded, as the *Kastricoom* crew and Golovnin had been, placed in a sort of stocks and was repeatedly examined under suspicion of being a spy. For three weeks he was kept in solitary confinement until, after a four-day hunger strike, he was restored to his mates under a strict parole.

Much of the trouble seems to have been occasioned by the accident that one of the prisoners possessed a name which the Japanese thought ominous. John Bull stirred the Japanese suspicions. Over and over again he was accused of being a British spy. Whether this accusation was due to the use of "John Bull" as a nickname for Britishers or whether, as McCoy suggests, the Hollanders, who by now had heard of the plight of these Americans, misled the Japanese, is probably unimportant. From McCoy's account, however, it is evident that the fate of the prisoners would have been more endurable had not the accusation of espionage been lodged against them.

McCoy did not believe that the Dutchmen were friendly. He especially resented a message sent by the opperhoofd, Jan Levyssohn, who warned the Americans to be quiet and patient and to show a proper behavior toward those who had them in charge.

Bull, McCoy, and Jacob Boyd of Springfield then plotted to burn a hole through the floor of the prison and to escape from their captivity by digging under the board fence of the prison compound. The attempt was successful, and the three men made their way to the seashore. No ships were in sight and, not daring to show themselves at any settlement, the men lived for two days on raw turnips. Then they were discovered, corded, with the ends of the ropes extending into the guardroom of the jail, and placed in the stocks. The cage to which they were transferred was so small that they were obliged to enter it upon their hands and knees and they could not stand erect. It was "offensive, filthy and full of lice."

The three Americans protested against the treatment but were answered by the governor's reply that all were spies and that there was no redress for people of such type. McCoy threatened that the American government would use force to compel fair treatment and would demand punishment. It was on this occasion that the answer was returned that if a high ranking American naval officer could be pushed off the deck with impunity, the United States would do nothing for common sailors.

The food supplied the prisoners seems to have been sufficient, though the sweet potatoes, rice, fish, and seaweed were more acceptable to Japanese than to American palates, but the prisoners suspected that the meals were poisoned. Thirteen of the fifteen captives were, at one time or another, attacked by "cramps in the stomach," and three of them died. McCoy says that one victim, Ezra Goldthwaite of Salem, had been perfectly well until he was suddenly seized by fever and delirium. For ten days Goldthwaite was left naked, without medicine and without attention, until he died on January 24, 1849. A few days later John Waters of Salem was attacked with identical symptoms and died suddenly. One of the Hawaiians, unable to endure the imprisonment, committed suicide. His body was allowed to remain in the cage for two days after his death.

The accusations against John Bull were, meanwhile, becoming more serious. So convinced were the Japanese that he was a secret British agent that he was condemned to solitary confinement in a cell much smaller than those of his shipmates. His prison was a "grated crib, six feet high in front, and three feet high in the rear. It was six feet long and four feet wide. Bull was 5 feet 10½ inches high. He could not stand up except in the very front of the cell. There he remained ten days. He was not allowed to speak. He tried to do so on one occasion and was poked by a stick."

By the time of Goldthwaite's death, news of the captivity of the Americans had been received in Canton, through information sent by Levyssohn through Robert Browne, the Dutch consul at Canton, to United States Commissioner John W. Davis. Davis at once informed Commodore David Geisinger (who as captain had taken Edmund Roberts to the Orient) and Geisinger ordered Commander James Glynn to take the eighteen-gun corvette *Preble* "to the Bay of Nangasaki to obtain the release of the fifteen seamen." If necessary, Glynn was empowered to proceed to Yedo and to communicate with "the Imperial Court." "You are instructed to make a firm, temperate and respectful demand of that Court for the immediate release, and surrender to you, of the above-mentioned prisoners. You are to ask if other prisoners are in Japan. You are to be conciliatory, but firm and you are not to violate the laws or customs."

Glynn received his orders on January 31, 1849, two days after news of the captivity had been brought to Canton. He sailed in twelve days, but smallpox compelled the *Preble* to return. Not until March 22 was his quarantine lifted. Nineteen days later he called at Napa, and on April 17 he arrived at Nagasaki. Disregarding the warnings of Japanese officials who advised him to leave at once, Glynn insisted on an immediate audience with the governor.

Three documents were delivered to the American commander ordering him to exercise care that none of his officers or crew should leave the ship or discharge any guns, that he was to anchor his ship, and that he was to answer a questionnaire concerning the name of his ship, its tonnage, the number of the crew, its port of departure and the date it sailed, and whether he had any wrecked Japanese aboard the ship. Unless he observed the requirements strictly, Glynn was informed, "very disagreeable consequences might result."

Glynn wasted no time in preliminaries. As soon as the Japanese officials arrived, he protested against the guard boats that surrounded the *Preble* and demanded an immediate response from the governor on his request for an interview. When, after a week's delay, he received only the promise of "a speedy answer," Glynn threatened to take direct action. If the prisoners were not delivered to him by the following morning, April 25th, he would leave Nagasaki immediately to report to his superiors that Japan refused to give them up. The result of such a message, Japan was informed, would mean a visit in force from American warships to take the men away.

The Nagasaki authorities were faced by a dilemma. If they refused the Glynn request, war would certainly result; if they yielded, they would violate the law requiring that all important matters must be referred to Yedo for decision. In either event, it seemed, their heads would be in danger.

So they compromised. Knowing that the original intention had been to keep the prisoners at Nagasaki until such time as a Dutch ship should come from Java and then to return the men to their homes by way of Batavia, Governor Ido found a method for escape. All that was necessary, he decided, was to surrender the captives to the Dutch in advance of the usual time. If the Hollanders then saw fit to give the men into American care, that would be the Dutch responsibility. Ido drew up a memorandum for Glynn, stating that, as all shipwrecked mariners were sent home by the Chinese or by the Hollanders, this special sending for them could not be permitted. Thus he kept his record clear in case Yedo should object. Then having scrupulously observed the law, he turned the surviving captives over to the care of Levyssohn. The opperhoofd immediately sent them to Glynn. The *Preble* sailed from Nagasaki on April 26.

As Geisinger reported to the Secretary of the Navy, "The release and surrender of these seamen, under the circumstances, is probably the first time in which the stubborn policy of the Japanese had yielded to the demand of foreigners."

Five weeks after the clearing of the *Preble,* another British surveying ship, the *Mariner,* under Commander Matheson, appeared in Yedo Bay. The usual guard boats appeared with the customary warning, in Dutch and French, requiring Matheson to leave immediately. Matheson refused to depart but, after being watched all night, asked for permission to pay a formal call upon the governor. He was informed that such a call would be so repugnant to Japanese law that the governor would be executed if Matheson landed, or indeed if the *Mariner* moved higher up the bay. Matheson finished his observations, went to Shimoda Bay on the other side of the Ise peninsula, charted the shores and, after a week, during which he was closely guarded, sailed from the harbor. His ship was kept supplied with fish during the visit, and guard boats were provided to tow him out of sight of land.

Shipwrecked sailors continued to be jailed. Survivors from Captain Carter's *Pocahontas,* of New York, wrecked off the Kuriles in 1848, and from the British whaler *Edmond,* Captain H. H. Lovitt, cast up on the Hokkaido in 1850, were caged in the holds of junks for transportation to Nagasaki. The *Edmond* men were carted through the Nagasaki streets in cages, a small cage being provided even for Lovitt's pet dog. The men were taken to the town hall, were compelled to step upon a bronze crucifix set in the doorway, and were kept in confinement until a Dutch ship arrived in December 1850, to take the prisoners to Batavia.

The rigid observance of the strict letter of the law was shown by the treatment of the corpse of an *Edmond* sailor. One of the men had died by drowning when the hold of the prison junk flooded. The body was boxed in salt and was carried the entire length of Japan by land and sea to Nagasaki for official examination. After it had been inspected at the Nagasaki town hall, the dead body was granted burial.

In sharp contrast to the treatment of foreign seamen wrecked in Japan was the consideration shown by aliens toward unfortunate Japanese. Among a score of instances, the case of Manjiro Nakahama offers a fair comparison to the way that shipwrecked sailors were caged in Japan.

Nakahama, a fourteen-year-old fisher boy of Tosa, was caught with four companions in a sudden storm in January 1841, and was swept into the Kuroshiwo. Six months later, Captain William H. Whitfield, of the New Bedford whaler *John Howland,* found the boys living on a semi-desert island in the Pacific. He took the waifs to Honolulu, where all but Nakahama remained. The boy went on with his rescuer to Fairhaven, Massachusetts, where he remained six years, under the name of John Mung, and where he attended school. Whitfield took him on whaling voyages and then, when Nakahama's education was complete, allowed him to take passage for Honolulu.

At Hawaii, Nakahama found three of his companions (the fourth had died), and all the party sailed aboard a whaler for Shanghai. When the ship drew near the Luchus, the Japanese were provided with a whaleboat and were allowed to leave the ship. They made their way safely ashore, giving the impression that they were just come from Japan and, after six months, ventured to return home. Nakahama endeavored to explain that he had not been outside the Empire, but the ruse was discovered and he and his companions were jailed for thirty months.

Shortly before Perry's arrival, Nakahama was released and, because of his perfect English, was commissioned as official interpreter. In July 1917, his memory was honored by a Fairhaven celebration at which Ambassador Kikujiro Ishii was the principal speaker.

Glynn reached New York July 2, 1851, at just about the time that Nakahama's party was arriving in the Luchus. He sensed the need for naval bases in the Orient. The United States, as Glynn was well aware, could not indefinitely rely upon using Macao as its oriental naval station, both because Macao was a Portuguese possession and because the rising strength of Hongkong, across the harbor, was a potential menace to Macao's safety. His brief call at the Luchus was sufficient to convince him that Napa was a better base for the American fleet. He pressed the idea for a Napa base, and for an immediate commercial opening of Japan, by streams of letters addressed to Congress, to commercial agencies, to the public press, and to his superiors in the Navy Department. Glynn desired to be appointed leader of an expedition to secure a treaty with the Japanese. Perhaps he was too eager in his campaign, more probably the ironclad Navy rules of precedence were too strong for him to break. Glynn met opposition from an officer of higher rank and, being a mere commander, was tactfully passed by.

Commodore John Henry Aulick, sixty-four-year-old son of a Hessian soldier, was also anxious for the assignment. Thoroughly familiar with the situation, for he had sailed with Biddle to claim Oregon and had served four years on the Pacific, he was about to be dispatched as chief of the East India Squadron. He was a thorough student of naval affairs and one whose originality was not to be disputed. Appointed as an officer at twenty-two, with no previous experience of the sea, he had asked for leave of absence before entering upon his duties. Then, gaining a furlough, he shipped as sailor before the mast of a merchantman. He concealed his rank almost a year until the voyage was complete. As the ship stood in toward harbor on the return trip, the skipper ordered Aulick, in what the young man thought a too peremptory tone, to man a boat to pull the officers ashore. Aulick went below, donned his naval uniform, put his warrant of appointment in his pocket, and came back on deck to demand the same favor for himself.

As a commodore, where Glynn was but commander, and as close associate of the powers in control of the Navy Department, Aulick outranked Glynn, especially as the appointment to head a mission to Japan might be construed as in the line of duty for the East India station.

Almost immediately upon receipt of news that the brig *Auckland* had brought shipwrecked Japanese sailors to San Francisco in March 1851, Aulick rushed to Daniel Webster, then secretary of state, with a scheme for using the waifs as an instrument for winning access to Japan. Undoubtedly he was well aware that the same device had been employed several times before by almost every other nation with Pacific interests, but the cloak of philanthropy was much too attractive to be discarded.

There was, on this occasion, no thought of limiting the appeal for good relations to a gentle request. Merchants, missionaries, and naval strategists were convinced that only ruthless dealings would win results. The commercial interests were hoping for huge profits. They were unaware that the Dutch trade, which had averaged $100,000 yearly on sales to Japan and $280,000 annually on purchases from that country during the 1820 and 1830 decades, had now fallen to about two-thirds those sums. One estimate, widely accepted in 1851, anticipated a yearly trade of "at least $200,000,000."

President Millard Fillmore was outspoken in his insistence that considerations of humanity required an opening of Japan's closed harbors. "It was so exclusive," he declared in speaking of the Shogun's government, "that it refused succor and help to those accidentally cast upon its shores. Shipwrecked whalers were treated with great cruelty and some of them were carried about in wooden cages until they perished from exposure and starvation."

Secretary of the Navy William Alexander Graham, famous in the annals of the service for his reorganization of the coast survey, the reform of navy personnel, and for furthering the exploration of the Amazon, also demanded that Japan consent to admitting foreigners.

The long interdict which has denied to strangers access to the ports or territory of that country, and the singularly inhospitable laws which its government has adopted to secure this exclusion, having been productive, of late years, of gross oppression and cruelty to citizens of the United States, it has been thought expedient to take some effective measure to promote a better understanding with this populous and semi-barbarous empire; to make the effort not only to obtain from them the observance of the rights of humanity to such of our people as may be driven by necessity upon their coasts, but also to promote the higher and more valuable end of persuading them to abandon their unprofitable policy of seclusion, and gradually to take their place in that general association of commerce in which their resources and industry would equally enable them to confer benefits upon others, and the fruits of a higher civilization upon themselves.

Graham was not, however, content with making a general statement that Japan was unjust in its treatment of shipwrecked mariners. He went further to insist that the Empire must open its gate for the benefit of all mankind.

These events have forced upon the people of America and Europe the consideration of the question, how far is it consistent with the rights of the civilized world to defer to those inconvenient and unsocial customs by which a nation, capable of contributing to the relief of the wants of humanity, shall be permitted to renounce that duty; whether any nation may claim to be exempt from the admitted Christian obligation of hospitality to those strangers whom the vocations of commerce or the lawful pursuits of industry may have incidentally brought in need of its assistance; and the still stronger case, whether the enlightened world will tolerate the infliction of punishment or contumelious treatment upon the unfortunate voyager whom the casualties of the sea may have compelled to an unwilling infraction of a barbarous law. These are questions which are every day becoming more significant. . . . The day has come when Europe and America have found an urgent inducement to demand of Asia and Africa the rights of hospitality of aid and comfort, shelter and succor, to the men who pursue the great highroads of trade and exploration over the globe. . . . The opening of Japan has become a necessity.

These were theories which, however curious they might sound from a Carolinian states' rights supporter, were warmly greeted by the expansionists. The nation had but recently spread to the Pacific and was witnessing a rapid settlement of California and Oregon. Transcontinental traffic, chiefly across Panama and Nicaragua, added to the growth of a Pacific merchant marine, and concentrated attention upon the Orient. England's success in opening China to the world's commerce, by whatever questionable devices, inspired demands that Japan, too, be made available for exploitation.

Chance, which intervened so frequently in the history of Japan's alien intercourse, now operated for once in occidental interest. The Shogunate, worried over the increasing frequency with which whalers were visiting Japan, asked the Dutch to send a circular to every foreign government. On April 30, 1851, ten days before Aulick's visit to Secretary Webster, the State Department was handed a memorandum from the Dutch Legation reminding the United States that trade was still forbidden with Japan.

Foreign vessels are excluded from Japan by the Government of that Empire. It was, nevertheless, determined in 1842 that if such vessels should be cast upon the shores of Japan by storms, or come there in want of provisions with a view to asking for such commodities, water, or wood for fuel, those articles should be granted to them on request. For fear, however, lest this determination, prompted as it has been by feelings of humanity, should give rise to any false interpretation, the Government of Japan has solicited that of the Netherlands to inform the other powers that the above mentioned resolution does not infringe upon, or otherwise imply any modification whatever of the system of separation and exclusion which was adopted more than two centuries ago by the Japanese Government, and since the establishment of which the prohibition against allowing any foreign vessel to explore the Japanese coasts has been constantly in force.

Aulick probably was unaware, when he talked to Webster on May 9, 1851, that this circular had been delivered by the Dutch, and that the Fillmore Cabinet was already deeply interested in the Japanese adventure. There had been talk, in line with the Jackson policy of asking civilians to be responsible for trade agreements, of ordering Consul General Joseph Balestier of Singapore to undertake such a mission. But with the Shogun's defiant notice that exclusion was to be continued, and with news that Glynn had won a point by threatening to bombard Nagasaki, the Aulick request seemed reasonable.

On May 30, Aulick was handed a letter of credence authorizing him to act as American envoy to negotiate a treaty with the Shogun. His instructions from Webster added a new detail for, when Aulick received the orders of the Secretary of State, he found that he was to get the right for coaling stations for the Navy. "Coal," said Webster, "is a gift of Providence deposited in the depths of the Japanese islands for the benefit of the human family."

These, too, were strange words for a Cabinet member of one isolated nation, priding itself on lack of complications with its neighbors, to use regarding a second isolated people. A Whig subscribing to strong Hamiltonian ideas might endorse the thought that central governments could control mineral resources in the interests of social welfare, but Webster would unquestionably be horrified at the use to which his words might now be put by advocates of New Deal theories. Statesmen use a different language when they talk of international affairs than that which they employ in the heat of political debates.

Aulick's embassy was not to have plain sailing. The *Susquehanna, Plymouth,* and *Saratoga* cleared from Old Point Comfort for the Orient on June 8, 1851. The last two ships were sloops, but the *Susquehanna* has the distinction of having been the first American war steamship to clear for Eastern ports.

Aboard the *Susquehanna* were two American envoys, Robert C. Schenck, minister to Brazil, and J. S. Pendleton, chargé d'affaires to Argentina. A third passenger, and one destined innocently to cause trouble for Aulick, was Chevalier S. de Macedo, Brazilian minister to the United States, returning on brief furlough to Rio de Janeiro.

Somewhere on the route to Rio, false impressions spread about the *Susquehanna* that Aulick had declared that he was personally paying for De Macedo's passage, since the Brazilian government refused to do so. The envoy rose in wrath, reported to his superiors at Rio, and had them send a burning protest back to Washington. Letters mailed back to the Navy Department also intimated that Aulick was taking his son to the East, without authority, at the Navy's expense.

No one now appears to know who was responsible for the canards. Secretary Graham, baffled by the accusations but not daring to refuse credence to the Brazilian government, took the only step possible by ordering Aulick supplanted in the command. The fleet sailed onward to Macao, stopping to pay an official visit on the Sultan of Zanzibar, but when it reached the China coast, found that its mission was temporarily postponed until the new leader, Commodore Matthew Calbraith Perry, should arrive. The accusing letters were received in Washington in November 1851. Perry was given the command November 18. It was his first official inkling of his consideration for the post.

Aulick, dismayed at his displacement, sent a letter to the Washington authorities demanding a court of inquiry to clear his reputation, but his demand was deemed unnecessary. By the time that Aulick's letter was received—it was mailed from Macao in February 1852— the charges had been sifted and found baseless. He was reinstated as an officer, though not restored to his command. Soon after he was promoted, but was presently retired for age. Edward M. Barrows, biographer of Perry, insists that Aulick was "literally gossiped out of his command," but he asserts that Perry was no party to the plot.

Though the method of removal may be justly criticized, calm judgment recognizes that Aulick was ill suited for his task. The *Auckland* castaways were vehement in their accusations that Aulick treated them with brutality. The statements may not be true, as far as Aulick is concerned, but no doubt exists that the officers of the *Susquehanna* allowed the crew to mistreat the refugees.

"Our cabins," wrote a Japanese, "were cramped and stuffy. On one hot day we went on deck and lay down in the shade with the sailors. The officer of the watch kicked us with his heavy boots and drove us down below like a herd of swine."

Aulick, in the Japanese view, "was too accustomed to dealing with greedy and cringing Chinese and had just come back from Fiji where he had negotiated with natives who had killed and eaten American sailors." This portion of the statement is certainly ill founded, for the *Susquehanna* had made no such voyage. It may equally be true that the Japanese was inaccurate in stating that Aulick, too, had kicked them. "We could not complain," the castaway continued, "because we did not know the language."

Second thought at Washington had, meanwhile, swung the Cabinet to the belief that a separate mission, distinct from the East India Squadron, would be more effective than a naval visit in full force. They were not convinced that a civilian envoy would be preferable, but a special envoy, even though accompanied by warships, was deemed more suited for the task.

The plan was held in something like abeyance for four full months. Aulick was dismissed in November 1851, and though Perry was called into conference and was assured of the appointment, no formal orders were presented to him until March 24, 1852. Meanwhile he was gathering material, studying the situation, and drumming up support. And meanwhile, also, news of his intention to visit Japan was being told to British and to Dutch diplomats who lost no time in hurrying the warnings to their own respective capitals. Holland informed Japan that the United States was on the way long before Perry actually steamed into Japan's waters.

XXII

THE SCHOLARLY SEAMAN

WHEN Glynn took the *Lagoda* men aboard the *Preble* in Nagasaki Harbor, he found another castaway among the number.
The instructions given Glynn by Geisinger called for the surrender of
any other shipwrecked Americans who might be present in Japan.
Glynn included this demand in writing his ultimatum to the Nagasaki governor, and Ido, anxious to observe the letter of the law, included the extra waif.

The new arrival, Ranald MacDonald, sometimes styled the little
Chinook, was probably of much more permanent importance than all
the *Lagoda* prisoners combined. His influence upon international relationships, exerted indirectly, was so powerful that every subsequent
diplomatic understanding, every treaty, and every issue where interpretation was required, was filtered through a mind that had been
trained by this one man. Together with Nakahama and the pupils
of the three castaways who taught Japanese to white men in China,
the interpreters whom Ranald MacDonald trained in English were
for many years the sole intermediaries between East and West.

He came in search of adventure and of international understanding, deliberately risking death in the desire to know the hidden
empire better. Priding himself on being through one parent the descendant of Noah, through a clan that had a private boat upon Loch
Lomond throughout the Flood, he was convinced that on his
mother's side he was linked with the lords of Eastern Asia.

MacDonald was born "in the salmon running time" of 1824 at
Astoria, then part of British Columbia. He was the son of John Mc-
Donald, chief factor of the Hudson Bay Company, and Princess
Sunday, daughter of the great chief Com-Comly. By virtue of his

descent, "the little Chinook" Ranald claimed to be the rightful ruler of the whole Northwest Coast.

Ranald led a lax existence during the early years of his life. Princess Sunday died soon after his birth, and his father married again, leaving Ranald to the care of the Chinooks. In his seventeenth year young MacDonald walked to the Great Lakes and thence to St. Paul, where he enlisted on a Mississippi river boat as deckhand. At New Orleans he shipped for New York.

The little Chinook was a lad of bizarre ideas. Desirous of a berth aboard an ocean ship, he conceived the bright idea that he would be more welcome if he applied rudely dressed for the position. He appeared in buckskin shirt, heavy wool trousers tucked into his fur-trimmed leggings, and a coonskin cap with a tail at the back of it. It was an odd garb in which to go to sea, but Ranald was a powerful young fellow with some knowledge of seafaring life, and he was signed on for a voyage to London. From England he seems to have sailed for India, and then in a ship carrying kegs of specie to Southern California. In later years he hinted darkly that his officers aboard this ship scuttled the vessel for its gold and threatened the crew with death if ever they disclosed the crime. Then he sailed aboard a slaver which was chased by a British man-of-war, and from which the Negroes were made to walk the plank, so that when the ship was overtaken "our decks were as clean as a hound's tooth." Another Cape Horn voyage took him to Lahaina in Hawaii in the autumn of 1847.

Unhappy love affairs brought him to Japan. The thickset, straight-haired, dark-complexioned boy proposed marriage to a blonde Canadian, only to be rejected scornfully because he was part Indian. It was the first time, seemingly, that the idea had been brought home to him that his royal ancestry was not universally admired. The shock was disillusioning, and MacDonald turned to morbid introspection on matters of race relationships.

The outcome of the disappointment was the resolve to try an entrance to Japan. Long drawn to contemplation of that country because it lay across the water from his own native region and, more strongly, because he had met and sympathized with the Japanese waifs who were succored at his father's factory, MacDonald, like so many in the old Northwest, had come to believe that the Japanese were the ancestors of the Chinook Indians. He decided to seek out the land of his own people.

In looking back across the youthful career of Ranald MacDonald, one now sees a number of portents which, though they had no real connection with his effort to invade Japan, might seem to lovers of coincidence to foreshadow his connection with that Empire. The fort in which the little Chinook was born had, six years before, been formally annexed to the United States by the then Commander Biddle. Ranald went to school to a pedagogue named John Ball, whose name was very similar to that of one of the *Lagoda* men. He himself had met the three survivors of the junk wrecked off Cape Flattery in 1833, and had seen Iwakichi, Kiukichi, and Oto-san enslaved among his mother's people. At Honolulu he had heard tales of Denzo and Goyemon, survivors of the *John Howland* refugees, if indeed he did not meet them personally. For one who, like Ranald MacDonald, possessed a strong streak of mysticism, the coincidences took on an importance far beyond their actual worth.

His scheme was simple and ingenious. He shipped before the mast with Captain Lawrence B. Edwards, of the Sag Harbor whaler *Plymouth,* for a cruise from Honolulu to the Japanese whaling grounds. The understanding was that MacDonald, working on the usual share profit agreement, would be free to leave the ship whenever and wherever he desired so soon as the cargo was complete, and that he might use his share of profits to buy a whaleboat and supplies. The *Plymouth* sailed from Honolulu in company with the *David Paddock,* which was later to be wrecked off south Saghalien.

Like so many other sailors of his time, MacDonald had an eye for future naval needs in the Pacific. Sailing past the Luchus, he came to Quelpart Island at the entrance of Korea Straits. Its position seemed to him admirable for an American naval depot. "Fortified and held by a naval power it might be made the Malta of the great Eastern Asiatic Archipelago, and even of the vaster Northern Pacific —the Greater Atlantic of these latter times. Russia may take it. That rising power has grasped all it dare of the Kurile chain, but that, nor even her Vladivostock (ice bound in winter) does not, and cannot secure her anchorage in the Junk thronged seas of China and Japan." MacDonald's hope was that the United States might establish control over the island.

On June 27, 1848, while the *Lagoda* men were suffering imprisonment, the *Plymouth* completed its cargo, and MacDonald applied for permission to depart. Captain Edwards was loath to carry out the obligation, fearing disaster for his friend, but the little Chinook insisted. The captain's private boat, built especially for Edwards' use, was sold to MacDonald and was stocked with a month's provisions and with such necessaries as sails, a quadrant, clothing, a revolver, two water casks, "one cask containing animal flesh," a large amount of bread, and half a hundred books.

The last named were an exceedingly important part of Ranald's plan. He desired to present himself as a castaway and to rely on Japan's humanity for protection. Too many stories were current among sailors of the cruelty inflicted on common sailors, and even on such officers as Golovnin, for MacDonald to place too complete trust in this device. If he could arrive as a scholar in distress, he thought, there might be greater hope for a successful entry.

I knew that such freight, so strange for a mere castaway from a whaling ship, would naturally excite suspicion; but I had my story, ready, for the nonce. Themselves even of the middle and lower classes, being a people of literature and books, I thought I might pass on this score. The sequel proved so. In fact it was *that* that saved me: for seeing me ever reading, a man of books, they drew to me: the books magnetized them: and they (books and Japanese) made me their teacher.

MacDonald left the *Plymouth* five miles off the northwestern coast of the Hokkaido, in a dense fog. He came to a small rocky island where he landed and spent a Robinson Crusoe life for four days, living on beef, biscuit, and chocolate, until the *Plymouth* was so far off that there would be little suspicion that he had parted from that ship. Then, on July 1, he made his venture.

MacDonald was an admirable stage manager. North of his temporary refuge was the island of Rishiri off the northwest Hokkaido cape. He steered for this island, maneuvered until he sighted in the distance a small village which he later found to be called Notsuka, and then prepared for discovery. His design was to present himself as a scholar in distress and so, having first capsized the boat in practice (losing his rudder by so doing), he came within five miles of the town. At dawn of July 2 he was discovered from the shore. The Ainus launched a skiff to meet him. MacDonald pulled the plug of a hole in the bottom of his boat, let his craft half fill with water, plugged the hole, and was found in a supposedly sinking boat wholly absorbed in studying a ponderous volume of mathematics.

The Ainus were impressed. As soon as they spied the studious stranger they began to bow reverently, rubbing their palms together and then raising their hands toward heaven. After this they stroked their beards from chin to breast and uttered guttural sounds in respectful salutation. MacDonald gravely acknowledged the greeting, inquiring politely "How do you do?" and raising the right arm. The Ainus, says MacDonald, "did not seem to be afraid of me but to be wonder-struck."

He took full advantage of their wonder, ordering them by signs to fasten the boats together and to row him ashore. Whether because he knew the proper code of conduct for scholars or because he stumbled by accident upon the idea that he should proceed with dignified leisureliness, he rebuked his escort for undue haste, and gained abject apologies. "To avoid further hurting their feelings, I stooped as if to adjust my sandals, but they would not allow me to do so—doing it themselves and appearing to be glad of an opportunity of performing an act of kindness to me; the rest of the way they adjusted their pace to mine.

"When I got amongst them first my feeling was that I had got into a nest of pirates of Tartars, with their heavy beards, uncombed long hair, and unwashed faces; they looked uncouth and wild, both in person and dress, comparing very unfavorably in this respect, with the clean, refined and cultivated Japanese."

The feeling of fright was short lived. MacDonald was put under close guard—though he was permitted, on his first day only, a short walk out of doors—but was given courteous attention. Togoro Shinagawa, a samurai, was placed as guard, and proved in MacDonald's words "a point of interrogation." Within a short time he and the castaway were exchanging language lessons; each of them, as Shinagawa explained, in defiance of the law, wrote down the foreign words. The samurai went so far as to show to his captive a colored map of Japan. But before disclosing the chart Shinagawa led MacDonald to a distant section of the unfrequented shore, where he peered intently over the long grass to see if spies were about. He was concerned, MacDonald discovered, that he too might be the object of suspicion.

The friendliness was not to last. MacDonald was ordered one morning to stay within doors and "by way of impressing me with a due sense of my position, they placed mats before my windows: a proceeding which rendered my then present and future dark indeed." Soon afterward half a dozen officers arrived to question him. MacDonald informed them that he was a voluntary deserter from his ship, because he and his captain had quarreled. He and all his be-longings were carefully measured, and notes were solemnly written. Then he was ordered to take his place in a march to the provincial capital.

"Curtains of cotton, striped, of various colors, were put up along each side of the street or way on our line of march. Why these cur-tains were so used I never could find out. If intended for conceal-ment from my view they certainly did not answer the purpose, for I could see over them." MacDonald was four inches taller than his captors.

For thirty days MacDonald was jailed at Pontomari on Rishiri, guarded by Shinagawa and by Shonusuke Miyajima. He was al-lowed to leave his cage but three times during the month, each time for a bath. Then he was escorted to a junk and was ordered to occupy a small cell which could be entered only by crawling upon his hands and knees. It was with great difficulty that he could sit erect, even when cross-legged. "I told the officers about it, and asked them to give me permission to go out; but they objected to this. I suffered a great deal of pain."

The next stop was at Matsumai where MacDonald went to jail again, remaining in a cage from September 6 until October 1. "In re-gard to creature comforts I certainly had no reason to complain but on the contrary, they were, all, aboundingly kind and ever kindly to me." He was, however, under no illusions as to his fate if he should try to take advantage of his jailers. They showed him ropes with which he might be bound, and an iron rod, an inch and a half in diameter, with which prisoners would be beaten if they should at-tempt to escape. His jailer, the same man who guarded the *Lagoda* men, pointed out a patch of new boarding over a hole in the roof and told MacDonald, who had known nothing of the story, that fifteen Americans had made their escape by that opening. "They had been caught, hand-cuffed, dragged back, and had their throats cut," according to the report given MacDonald.

From Matsumai he was taken, through streets curtained in pure white, to a seagoing vessel which, he was told, would take him to Nagasaki. The ship was bristling with armament. On the quarter deck "was a forest of spears, upright, with glittering steel heads, shin-ing shafts, ornamented with gold and silver and mother of pearl, and appended were elaborate sheaths, of finest fur, for the spear heads."

At Nagasaki he was given over to the care of Einosuke Moriyama, a young samurai interpreter whose piercing black eyes "seemed to search into the very soul." Moriyama was well drilled in English, though his pronunciation was peculiar, and spoke Dutch, as Levyssohn charitably said, better than Levyssohn himself. He had been the interpreter for the *Lagoda* men and was to be an intermediary between the Japanese officials and Glynn, Perry, and Townsend Harris.

Evidently Moriyama was friendly to MacDonald. His advice to the little Chinook, when the time for examination arrived, was extraordinarily helpful. MacDonald was taken to the palace of Governor Ido and was asked to tread upon the *fumiye*. "This image," said Moriyama, "is the Devil of Japan." Then MacDonald was led before the governor for examination.

Ranald recoiled from the dirty mat upon which he was told to kneel and kicked it aside but, at Moriyama's whispered request, consented to kneel upon the bare floor. He refused, however, to kowtow when Ido entered.

Curious to read my fate at the hands of His Excellency, I looked him fearlessly but respectfully, full in the face. So did he me. I had just quickly, before that, looked around, and saw every one, even the soldiers, flat on their faces, the hands being placed upon the ground, and the forehead resting on them. They all remained in this position for quite a time, say ten or fifteen seconds during which, in dead silence, the Governor and I stared at each other.

The governor did not insist upon MacDonald's obeisance, but complimented him upon his "big heart." Then, having asked the customary questions concerning Ranald's identity and his reasons for coming to Japan, he posed the dangerous interrogations. "What," asked the governor, "do you believe in respect to God in Heaven?"

MacDonald promptly recited the Apostles' Creed, but when he drew near the phrase, "And in Jesus Christ, his Only Son, born of the Virgin Mary," Moriyama quickly interrupted. In translating MacDonald's speech, Moriyama omitted all mention of Christ or of the Virgin and, in addition, warned MacDonald, *sotto voce,* not to speak of the Bible. "It is not a good book in Japan," he told the prisoner.

Four more examinations, at intervals of approximately a fortnight, followed, each repeating very carefully the questions already fully answered. MacDonald's quadrant was an object for special attention, for the Japanese feared he intended to use it for surveying the coast. They were anxious, also, to learn if he had influential friends likely to demand his release. MacDonald was of the opinion that ordinary seamen might be imprisoned for life without any opportunity for returning home in case no one cared sufficiently about them to undertake inquiry. He thus accounted for the total disappearance of such ships as the *Tobey* in 1822 and the *Lady Adams* in 1823. MacDonald was careful to state that he was a citizen of both Britain and America so that the officials might think him a man of first ranking.

MacDonald's cell at Nagasaki was seven feet by nine and was located in a prison whose grounds were guarded by a six-foot stone wall topped by broken glass. For seven months he was given everything that he desired, save room to move about and liberty, and, as he confesses, never received a harsh word or even an unfriendly look. He was, according to Levyssohn, suspected of being either a missionary, probably because of the many books he carried, or a spy.

MacDonald's affability and especially his Japanese-like appearance won him warm friendships. His prison cell became a social resort to which Japanese officials repaired daily to discuss world news, though they studiously refrained from conversing on their own national affairs. Students, officers, and priests came to stare at him as though he were a curiosity. One of his guards brought his wife, his daughter, and three other women to hear "the Lion roar," as MacDonald expresses it, but this was evidently too great a liberty. MacDonald never saw the guard again and was informed that his head had been chopped off.

No one told MacDonald that there were other Americans imprisoned in the city, but from comments dropped by his visitors, he began to suspect that other white men were jailed at Nagasaki. His Japanese friends came to him with certain sailor terms, such as "shiver my timbers," and demanded translation into colloquial Japanese. He was, therefore, not surprised when, on his surrender to the Dutch for transfer to the *Preble,* he met the *Lagoda* survivors. He had evidently followed in their tracks from the Hokkaido southward, and indeed possessed a wooden spoon carved by one of them and left at Matsumai.

Ranald MacDonald's imprisonment brought results greater than the jailing of other mariners, for MacDonald, by virtue of his keen ear for languages, was utilized as a teacher of interpreters. During his entire stay at Nagasaki, a class of fourteen Japanese linguists took daily lessons from him. He found them quick to learn and eager to converse. Though they were obviously frightened of the jailers and of each other, because almost anyone might be a spy prepared to denounce them for revealing Japan's secrets, they were ready to discuss details about the government and the military forces. MacDonald did not dare press his inquiries to great lengths lest the accusation of espionage against him seem to be well founded.

The growing intercourse between Japan and the Western nations made the need of trained interpreters apparent. Hitherto a few scholars, trained by the Dutch, were ample to attend to the few ships that called at scattered intervals at Japanese harbors, but now when ships were calling at the rate of two or more a year, and visiting at ports other than Nagasaki, better interpreters were necessary.

MacDonald's school, though actually little more than a conversational forum, served to satisfy this need. The men who talked to him might not be able to speak English fluently and might become confused with consonants like "l" and "r," but they were able to grasp the gist of ordinary conversation. Their training at the feet of "Ranarudo Makudonaruto" gave the Japanese a real advantage when the time came for discussions with English-speaking foreigners. All unaware that Moriyama and his mates were able to understand spoken English, Glynn and Perry and Harris conversed freely with their aides in conversational asides. MacDonald's alumni listened unobtrusively and passed on the private comments to their superiors. The Japanese, on the other hand, were able to speak privately without fear of being understood. The sailor dialect of Japan, passed on by the castaways to their missionary hosts, was far more different from cultural Japanese than was the MacDonald language from good English. Had the American visitors been other than forthright naval men who were anxious to use force to win their way, if that should become necessary, Glynn and Perry might have had a harder time. But since the whispered comments were suggestions that the guns be put to use, the secret sayings were even more convincing than the soft words of the spokesmen. The fact that bluff sailormen were advocating bombardment while the diplomats were spreading salve may have given Japan the firm belief that foreigners were two-faced and not wholly frank, but at least it won the foreigners the right to enter.

To this degree, then, credit for the opening of Japan is to be given Ranald MacDonald almost as much as to the admirals and the envoys. Yet, even in Japan, his name has grown dim with the years. For decades his exploit was almost entirely forgotten. Publishers in America failed to see the merits of the memoirs that he wrote. Only within the past dozen years has his service begun to win recognition. He died in Oregon in 1894 after suffering shipwreck off the coast of India, undergoing hardships in the Australian gold rush, running pack trains in Canada, and keeping an inn along the Columbia River.

MacDonald is another of the pioneers into Japan whose memory has faded. For all her ancient tributes to his service, Japan has allowed the little Chinook to be forgotten. In the annual services held in honor of those "who helped Japan," MacDonald's name is rarely mentioned.

XXIII

PERRY REFUSES TO GO AWAY

THE world was well aware that the United States was making a new attempt to open the closed Empire. The use of armed ships to compel trade had already been foretold by William II to the Shogun, and though the Americans were insisting that no force would be employed, the world's diplomats were much too blasé to believe that Fillmore meant exactly what he said. Nor were they reassured when Fillmore pointed out, "It is obvious that this attempt could be made by no power to so great advantage as by the United States, whose Constitution excludes every idea of distant colonial dependencies." The American naval officers' designs upon Napa were too widely known.

England helped the enterprise by sending eighty of her latest charts for Perry's use; Holland issued public orders to her officials to assist the expedition in whatever way they could. Perry, however, was none too confident that the Dutch were wholly sincere in their professions of support. He was especially antagonistic to the suggestion that Philip Franz von Siebold, once jailed and later exiled from Japan, should be attached to his expedition as interpreter. Perry thought him too conceited and too self-important.

The Americans did not intend to suffer a rebuff. Though the need for force was not anticipated, the United States determined to send so strong a fleet that its very threat of power might be overwhelming. Biddle's experience, in contrast to that of Glynn, was sufficient to prove that no good could come from a mere polite request for trading privileges. Perry was assigned eleven ships, two of them fresh from the shipyards, as concrete arguments for American entry.

Almost everything went wrong with the projected plans even be-

257

fore Perry could clear from the United States. Presidential politics were partially responsible, for, as 1852 was an election year, Washington was torn by conflicting ambitions. Fillmore was fighting for renomination against Daniel Webster, his Secretary of State; Graham of the Navy Department was pulling wires for a vice-presidential candidacy; the remaining members of Fillmore's largely Southern cabinet were striving to make political alliances that would hold them in their shaky seats. Perry's official superiors were willing to support his expedition, but their chief interests lay, for the moment, in domestic politics.

War scares also threatened. Fishermen's rivalries on the Grand Banks led to conflicts in which Canadians attacked Massachusetts fishing smacks, while New Englanders looted Canadian coastal villages. British warships took some sixty American hostages. The Administration, harried by Congress in the heat of an election campaign, detached Perry from his preparations for a flying visit to the St. Lawrence region to investigate the difficulties. Nearly two months' delay elapsed before starting the trip to the East.

Not until the election was over was Perry free to sail, and then with but one ship, the *Mississippi,* of the promised flotilla. Six days after his administration had been repudiated at the polls, Fillmore bade farewell to Perry. The Commodore crossed the Atlantic, rounded Good Hope, touched at Ceylon, and arrived at Hongkong in April 1853. In China, Perry transferred his broad pennon to the *Susquehanna* and with two other ships sailed on May 23 for Napa. His personnel had been increased by the addition of Bayard Taylor as master's mate and of S. Wells Williams as interpreter. Williams was never fluent in Japanese and had not spoken the language for nine years, but he dug out his old phrase books and brushed up on the more usual salutations. He never became a proficient conversationalist in the language. So noticeable was his error in the too-frequent use of one word in particular that the Japanese nicknamed him "Tadashi San," or "Mr. But."

The special service rendered by Wells Williams was in acquainting Perry with the niceties of oriental etiquette, always heretofore misunderstood by those who sought to open trade negotiations. As an old China hand of twenty years' experience he could warn Perry against too democratic treatment of the officials. Perry was advised to surround himself with pomp and ceremony, to assume a high bearing worthy of the mighty fleet under his command, and to match the dignitaries of Japan by parallel grades of naval officers. The Commodore was to hold himself so aloof that he would speak only with nobles of the very highest station.

When, therefore, two Luchu officials rowed out through the rain to meet the Americans at Napa Harbor, Perry loftily refused to let them board his ships. The crestfallen visitors, one of whom was the mayor, retired in dismay but as Williams predicted, returned next day in greater state with a boatload of presents. Again they were refused, since Williams and Perry hoped to force the Regent, Sho Rai-mo, to make the first overtures.

Williams may perhaps have pressed the need for haughtiness too firmly for, in common with many foreigners in Chinese ports, he held Orientals in considerable contempt. A thwarted botanist who had never, since his arrival at Canton in 1834 at the age of twenty-one, been able to indulge his scientific tastes, he had become intolerant and impatient of the unscientific "rabble" among whom he was obliged to live. Evidently he doubted whether Easterners could be included among rational folk, for he was capable of writing in his *Journal* such passages as "the vessel and its inhabitants must have amazed them if they have human ideas," and "to talk about the principles of international law being applicable to such people is almost nonsensical; they must first be taught humanity and self-respect." To Williams, the aged worried Regent of Luchu was "an imbecile."

Nevertheless, when Sho Rai-mo, the "imbecile," rowed out to the *Susquehanna* to pay the formal call, Williams was helpful in arranging the reception. As soon as the official barge was seen approaching, he advised Perry to arrange an impressive welcome. Two high officers in their most elaborate dress uniforms were stationed to escort the Regent to Perry's private quarters. The band played gaily, and, as the Regent set foot on deck, a six-gun salute boomed forth. To Luchu officials, unaccustomed to the sound of cannon, the noise was frightening.

Williams suggests, however, that Sho Rai-mo, "the imbecile," scored a point on Perry when, at the formal reception, a peace pipe was passed about which Perry puffed politely and thereafter "seemed half stupefied at times." Perhaps the pipe was charged with opium, though Williams, in an unwonted passage of loyalty to his chief, suggests that Perry's daze was probably due to "amazement at his novel position."

When the Americans landed, the Luchu inhabitants, whom Williams thought subhuman, were somewhat more courteous than the Westerners. They fled in fright at the American approach, probably because of orders from their superiors, but Williams and his companions had no hesitancy in forcing entry into Luchu seclusion. On one evening Williams, anxious to inspect the interior of a Japanese junk, paid an uninvited visit to a vessel in the harbor. "We were," he writes, "endured rather than received." The Japanese offered neither tea nor pipes, and refused to sell souvenirs to their unexpected guests. When Williams left the boat, the captain politely returned him a handkerchief which Williams had given as a present. Williams, the supposed expert in etiquette, evidently did not realize the offense he had committed in thus calling without permission, but was indignant that a number of Luchu ruffians had dared to follow him to the junk. "Some day they may get roughly handled for their impertinence," he warned.

Again Williams and Chaplain Bittinger, his comrade on the junk visit, forced their way into a Buddhist temple while service was in progress. "The party," he records, "gave us a cold reception. We did not tarry."

The incidents, caused by one who prided himself on his expert knowledge of oriental courtesy, reflected little credit on the Americans, but Williams, in common with so many of the aliens resident in the East, was none too careful in considering the feelings of the common people. For officials the etiquette was well observed; for the masses the usual Western tendency was to use the same haughtiness that oriental upper classes themselves employed.

Williams played no favorites, however. He was fully as hostile toward Dr. Bettleheim, the British missionary who had lived at Napa since 1846, as toward the poor Luchuans. Bettleheim, according to Williams, was scarcely responsible for his own actions. "I have received a letter," wrote Williams in his *Journal,* "the oddest mélange I have ever read. . . . Bettleheim talked a great deal, and his way of making signs and motioning with his face was very much disliked and wrongly interpreted. I hardly know what to think of the man for he whisks about in his opinion like a weathercock. . . . He heaps a deal of ill-will and contempt upon himself by his conduct. . . . He has contrived to get the suspicion and actual dislike of almost everybody."

Although the Regent paid the first call, the play for position was not at an end. The delicate question remained as to where the return visit should be made. With oriental astuteness, the Regent suggested that Perry attend an elaborate banquet at the Mayor's house, a plan which would have put Perry, in oriental eyes, in the position of receiving favors from an under-officer. Perry replied that he must first call on the Regent at the Regent's palace.

Landing parties, meanwhile, went ashore to find a suitable coaling station. As the marines approached, the natives fled. Bayard Taylor, in charge of one party, returned to the ships to declare that the Luchuans were utterly incapable of friendship. The novelist had painted a landscape of a Luchu valley but had learned nothing of the people.

Not even a house was procurable, by diplomatic methods, for American use. Perry seized the conference room and, by stationing guards at the door, held possession of a headquarters on the island. The action was high-handed and was not in accordance with approved ethics, but it served to convince the Luchu authorities that the United States was prepared to use pressure.

During the negotiations the Satsuma Resident, Ichiki Seiyemon, who had replaced Fujita after the Cecille visit, was in constant attendance. This time the Satsuma representative did not withdraw to the hills, as Fujita had done, but was present in disguise. Donning Luchu dress and posing as a language student, the Japanese took careful mental notes for an elaborate report to be sent home to Satsuma. Perry's willingness to use force was thus made clear to Japan long before the Commodore's actual arrival.

By June 6, a full week after the Regent's visit to the *Susquehanna,* the long-drawn dispute over the return call came to an end. Perry was permitted to present himself for his courtesy call at the Regent's palace. He went in full state. Two full companies of marines, with bayoneted muskets, escorted him in their best blue-and-white dress uniforms. Happily, the colors seemed to the Luchuans to be those of the Satsuma overlords. The uniforms were construed as a delicate tribute to Japan. Two bands played martial music. Perry traveled in an elaborate sedan chair, made by the *Susquehanna's* carpenter, and hung with heavy red and blue curtains. "We made some display with our thirty naval uniforms, our forty musicians, our one hundred marines, and our two brass field pieces drawn by eighty sailors," wrote an attendant officer.

The display was intended less for the edification of the Luchuans than for the impression upon Japan. Perry was well aware that full reports of his activities at Napa were being forwarded by fast junks to the daimyo of Satsuma, and probably to the Shogun. The knowledge may have been responsible for Perry's decision to dress his men in heavy blue-and-white uniforms, instead of the more comfortable lighter tropical dress. The greater the pomp and ceremony in which the envoy appeared, the more effective would be the impression produced upon Japan. Perry's meticulous attention to detail, and his insistence upon receiving every honor due an envoy, were caused by his desire to be received at Yedo as an equal, not as a suppliant.

In order that there might be ample time for full accounts to be conveyed to the overlords, Perry turned aside from Napa to make a flying visit to the Bonin islands. Leaving Napa on June 9, he sailed for Port Lloyd, then capital of Peel Island, largest of the archipelago. He reached there six days later.

At the Bonins, Perry's actions might easily have led to war between the United States and England had either nation realized the future importance of the little islands. Their ownership was in dispute. Three nations claimed possession. Japan, relying upon an elaborate early eighteenth-century forgery, believed that the islands had been discovered by daimyo Ogasawara in 1593, but had a more tenable claim through an actual discovery made in 1670 by Chozaemon, a storm-tossed orange merchant from Kyushu. No real possession had, however, been effected. Captain Coffin of Nantucket, arriving in the whaler *Transit* in 1823, took possession of the Bonins for the United States, but no steps for effective American colonization followed his call. Two years later an English whaler, the *Supply,* came to the harbor of Port Lloyd. Its captain nailed a board to a tree, claiming the islands for Great Britain, but he too left no colonists.

Beechey's rediscovery in 1827 led to more permanent settlement. On his arrival at Port Lloyd, he found two stranded English sailors living under miserable conditions. "For eight months they had not shaved, nor paid any attention to their dress. They were very odd-looking beings." But, because they were from a British whaler, their presence seemed sufficient for Beechey to reaffirm the *Supply's* claim. He replaced the old notice board with a substantial copper plate announcing that "H.M.S. 'Blossom,' Captain Beechey, R.N., took possession of this group of islands in the name of and on behalf of His Majesty King George, the 14th June, 1827."

On his visit to Honolulu soon afterward, Beechey told the British consul, Richard Charlton, of his claim to ownership. Charlton secured a schooner, loaded it with supplies, and sent a colonizing party of five white men and thirty Kanakas, together with an unreported number of women, across 3,300 miles of open water to take formal possession of the islands. The little colony was unquestionably under British protection, but because one of the whites was Genoese by birth, another Danish, and two American, Perry took the curious position that Britain had no valid claim to ownership. "The Americans," said Perry, "were as two to one, compared with the three others, who were subjects of different sovereigns." This strange interpretation received the commendation of the new Secretary of the Navy, James C. Dobbin, when Perry reported his actions to Washington.

At the time of Perry's arrival, Nathaniel Savery, a former Cape Cod whaler, was the only living survivor of the Charlton colony. Perry, therefore, disregarded Britain's claim, since Savery was American, just as the Commodore ignored the Japanese settlements of an earlier date, and as he paid no heed to Russia's claim through the arrival of Captain Luetke of the Tsar's navy, in 1828. Perry recognized Savery as an independent owner. By paying him $50 for a large tract of land for use as a naval coaling station and by making Savery the squadron's agent, Perry tried to give the transaction a sort of official status.

In writing, however, to Sir George Bonham, British trade superintendent at Hongkong, Perry put a different color on the matter. "The transaction," he told the protesting Britisher, "was one of strictly private character . . . to withhold the only suitable position in the harbor for a coal depot from the venality of unprincipled speculators who might otherwise have gained possession of it for purposes of extortion." He said nothing of his plan to turn Port Lloyd into a naval base and a port of call for mail steamers plying between California and China.

It would be interesting to speculate on what different turns Far Eastern history might have taken had such a strategic center remained in either British or American hands, or even in the type of bi-national arrangement which Perry seems to have favored as a second choice to American ownership. As an air and submarine base, and as a cable center, the Bonins might have exerted a powerful influence on recent oriental affairs. But, as it happened, both the United States and Britain resigned their claims to Japan. The presence in the Japanese Navy of a sailor named James Grey, during the campaign against Tsingtau in 1916, called new attention to the abandoned British colony that had once tried to settle in the Bonins.

When he believed that sufficient time had elapsed for full reports of his splendor in the Luchus to be relayed to Japan, Perry returned to Napa to begin the final stages of his great adventure. He found, to his astonishment, that the "imbecile" had been dismissed in disgrace, and that new officials were in charge. Again Perry was obliged to delay, this time for five days, until the prince, the new Regent, three treasurers, and the mayor could be informed that the Americans "had prepared goblets and awaited the light of their presence" at a banquet. Then Perry sailed, on July 2, 1853, with his two steamers, *Susquehanna* and *Mississippi,* towing two sailing ships toward Yedo.

If Perry hoped that his firmness at Napa would impress the Yedo officers, he was disappointed. American aloofness might impress colonials, but it was ignored at the capital. No sooner did the squadron enter Uraga Bay, near Yedo, on July 8, than guard boats gathered. Soldiers were mobilized upon the hills; signal guns boomed from the shore; canvas barricades were again erected.

Perry had two alternatives. Either he could repeat Biddle's conciliatory friendliness, ignoring the minatory gestures of the soldiers in the guard boats, or he could emulate Glynn and threaten force. He chose the latter. Ordering his vessels stripped for action, he stationed sentries along the gunwales with orders to repel all boarders. No Japanese, he announced, was to come on board until a high ranking official should arrive to bid the Americans welcome.

One Japanese was knocked into the water by an American guard, but no other violence was necessary. Before general hostilities broke out, an official barge pulled to the *Susquehanna,* bearing Saboroske Nagashima, vice-governor of Uraga, and a Dutch-speaking interpreter. Perry, by Williams' suggestion, declined to notice the visitor. Only the very highest Japanese officials, the interpreter was informed, could talk to the Commodore, but rather than disappoint a vice-governor, Perry's assistant would condescend to speak with Saboroske. Lieutenant John Contee, Perry's chief aide, began the first negotiations with the Japanese.

Perry's expedition, by this small bit of snobbery, won a higher status than that gained by any previous applicants for treaty privileges. Contee increased the American prestige by refusing to answer Saboroske's questions concerning the American armaments or the personnel of the ships. These, he loftily informed Saboroske, were secret matters. "American national vessels are never described to foreigners."

Saboroske, accordingly, shifted the conversation to other topics. He inquired formally why the ships had come and was politely told that the squadron brought a friendly letter for the Emperor from the President of the United States. Saboroske expressed his thanks and offered to receive the letter himself "so that the Americans would feel free to depart." Contee praised Saboroske's considerateness, but replied that the Americans were bound by strict orders to deliver the letter in person. Saboroske expressed his sorrow that Japanese custom rendered this impossible, and Contee answered they dared not disobey the instructions of their President. Saboroske then suggested that the letter be delivered to the proper authorities at Nagasaki, and Contee pointed out that strict orders compelled the Americans to go up to Yedo if the Emperor could not be seen at Uraga.

The parley was a fencing match of polite stubbornness with the silent naval guns always in reserve as powerful American arguments. The conference was deadlocked, just as Williams had anticipated. The Americans were anxious to discuss the matter with someone of higher rank than a mere vice-governor. Contee, finding himself making no impression, temporarily dropped the issue of the letter, but turned to the presence of the guard boats. He asked that they be withdrawn. "They are useless," he said, "as we shall not go ashore." Saboroske, realizing that the Americans were willing to give their promise not to violate Japan's shores, nevertheless suavely explained that the boats were ringed around the American ships only for the protection of the foreigners. Contee then threatened to open fire unless the boats were ordered off. When American guns were trained against the guard boats, Saboroske sent the boats away. Then he too left, to bring a higher official.

While the Americans waited, guards were posted by either side. The next morning, Yezaimon Kayama, governor of Uraga, appeared with Saboroske and two interpreters. Because of his more exalted station, Perry detailed two higher officers than Contee to receive Kayama. It was very evident that Kayama hoped to correct his subordinate's unfortunate beginning, for he too insisted that any message from foreigners could be transmitted only through Nagasaki. He repeated Saboroske's statement that the Americans must clear away. By Japanese law Kayama was entirely correct, but Perry had no intention of yielding. Neither Commander Franklin Buchanan nor Commander Henry A. Adams, the new American spokesmen, would recede from Contee's stand. They told Kayama that if Japan assigned no person of sufficiently high rank to receive the Presidential letter, Perry would go ashore with an armed force and carry the message to the Emperor at Yedo.

Nor would they agree to recall the surveyors who had been sent out from the American ships to chart the harbor. Japanese laws, they were rightly informed, prohibited the taking of soundings and the charting of the coast. Adams and Buchanan retorted that American laws commanded the activities. The surveyers moved well up the bay. Perry's purpose was to hasten the answer of the Japanese by making a threat to their capital. Flag Lieutenant Silas Bent found himself surrounded by forty-five Japanese guard boats, each manned by ten armed soldiers brandishing their swords. Had it not been for the close presence of the *Mississippi*, Williams declares, hostilities would have begun.

Agreement was eventually reached, after Kayama had exhausted every trick of dilatory diplomacy, that Fillmore's letter would be delivered to a high court official at a special pavilion to be erected for the purpose at Kurihama, a suburb of Uraga, provided that "no conversation can be allowed and as soon as the documents are delivered, you will leave." The ceremony was set for July 14. Almost a week had been consumed by the Japanese in trying to avoid the reception of the message.

Buchanan led the way in his barge, flanked on either side by Japanese boats containing Kayama and Saboroske, whom the Americans were now calling, because of his elaborate costumes, "Jack of Trumps." Buchanan was the first to go ashore, landing on a temporary wharf built out from the beach by bags of sand and straw. A hundred marines, in dress uniform, marched up the landing to form in double line facing the sea; an equal number of sailors followed. Then a salute of thirteen guns from the *Susquehanna* announced the departure from that ship of the Commodore, who thus made his first official appearance in Japan.

The setting was carefully arranged. As the American procession, composed of big men carefully "selected for effect upon the Japanese," advanced toward the council hall, they marched through a long lane screened by canvas walls in front of which were stationed files of soldiers with brilliant banners. Near the center of the crescent-shaped walls were nine tall standards, with broad scarlet pennons. The reception hall, forty feet square, was hung with fine violet cloth stamped with the Imperial symbols. A red felt pathway led across a white carpet floor to a raised platform on which sat the silent figures of the Imperial envoys.

Daimyos Toda of Idzu and Ido of Iwami rose and bowed gravely as Perry entered, bearing the scarlet-wrapped and gold-inscribed rosewood box in which Fillmore's letter was contained. The Commodore opened the box, displayed the contents, laid them, together with translations in Dutch and Chinese, upon the lid of the box, and stepped back, his mission accomplished.

Fillmore's letter is of immense importance in the diplomatic history of the United States and of Japan, but its actual wording is comparatively unimportant. Beginning by assuring Japan that Perry was of high rank and that he was under orders to assure the Japanese that the United States had no other motive than the desire for friendship and commercial intercourse, the letter states that Perry was under strict orders "to abstain from every act which could possibly disturb the tranquillity of your Imperial majesty's dominions." Fillmore then assures the Emperor that the United States cannot interfere in the religious or political concerns of any foreign nation, points out that each nation might profit by trade, and suggests that if the Emperor were unwilling to repeal his laws against foreign trade, he might suspend them for five or ten years to see how the experiment worked.

The essential features of the letter appear in two important paragraphs, couched in conciliatory but unmistakable terms.

I have directed Commodore Perry to mention another thing to your Imperial majesty. Many of our ships pass every year from California to China; and great numbers of our people pursue the whaling industry near the shores of Japan. It sometimes happens, in stormy weather, that one of our ships is wrecked on your Imperial majesty's shores. In all such cases we ask, and expect, that our unfortunate people should be treated with kindness, and that their property shall be protected, till we can send a vessel and bring them away. We are very much in earnest in this.

Commodore Perry is also directed by me to represent to your Imperial majesty that we understand there is a great abundance of coal and provisions in the Empire of Japan. Our steamships, in crossing the great ocean, burn a great deal of coal, and it is not convenient to bring it all the way from America. We wish that our steamships and other vessels should be allowed to stop in Japan and supply themselves with coal, provisions, and water. They will pay for them in money, or anything else your majesty's subjects may prefer; and we request your Imperial majesty to appoint a convenient port in the southern part of the Empire, where our vessels may stop for this purpose. We are very desirous of this.

Ido and Toda made no verbal answer to the request, but signed to Kayama to receive a document containing their reply. The answer was curt and noncommittal.

The letter of the President of the United States of North America, and copy, are hereby received and delivered to the Emperor. Many times it has been communicated that business relating to foreign countries cannot be transacted here at Uraga, but in Nagasaki. Now it has been observed that the Admiral, in his quality as Ambassador to the President, would be insulted by it; the justice of this has been acknowledged; consequently the above mentioned letter is hereby received, in opposition to the Japanese law.

Because the place is not designed to treat of anything from foreigners, so neither can conference nor entertainment take place. The letter being received, you will leave here.

Perry had had no expectation of a more complete reply, for in the preliminary conversations it had been agreed that an answer might be long delayed. Kayama had suggested that the formal response be forwarded to the United States through the Dutch or Chinese traders, but Perry arranged to return in the spring of 1854 for the Shogun's answer. "With all the ships?" asked the interpreter. "Probably with more," said Perry.

Perry was, however, unprepared for the sharp order to depart which the Shogun's emissaries gave, following their reception of the Fillmore letter. He feared that too prompt a sailing might destroy his prestige by giving an impression that the Americans had been expelled. So, having entertained Kayama and the Jack of Trumps at an elaborate feast at which wine flowed freely and having studiously given greater gifts to the Japanese than they gave him—so that the Americans might not seem niggardly—the ships weighed anchor. But instead of standing out to sea, the Black Ships went up the bay toward Yedo. Perry sailed until he could see the wharves of Shinagawa, the south suburb of Yedo, in the distance.

The Jack of Trumps hurried back to the ship, begging earnestly that the ships go no farther. He pointed out that the Americans had agreed to leave. Contee answered that the agreement was to leave the shore, but not the harbor. Good humor was restored by a further exchange of presents, the Americans receiving several crates of poultry and three thousand eggs in return for a box of garden seeds.

Perry put about and sailed for Napa on July 17. He arrived eight days later.

The long-suffering Luchu natives were again Perry's diplomatic laboratory. Knowing that his actions would be reported to Yedo, Perry brought pressure on the Regent by a threat of force. If Yedo knew that Perry was ready to use his guns, it was believed, Japan would be more willing to prepare a friendly answer to the American request for commerce. Contee and Williams were sent ashore with a "threatening expostulation at being treated so unfriendly, disallowed access to the markets and shops, followed into every corner and lane by spies and held at arm's length in a way we would not admit was right nor submit to, if a change was not made means would be found to bring it about on a return to Napa." Williams added, conversationally, that the spies must be withdrawn. "Our officers might carry pistols and hurt some of them if they persisted in tagging after and constantly interfering wherever we went."

The poor Regent was dismayed. He tried to placate Perry by a formal dinner, but the Commodore refused to eat until he had talked business. Then the Regent pleaded Luchu poverty as an excuse for refusing to grant a site for a coal depot, explained that typhoons would destroy any buildings that might be erected, and that thieves would steal the coal. The excuses were unfortunate. Perry replied that if the authorities neglected to provide the buildings, American sailors would be detailed to do the work and that an armed guard could be stationed to protect the property. Perry concluded by threatening to move with his marines to the Shui Palace unless his demands were quickly granted. The Regent gave in completely to all the American demands.

Nothing was said, of course, about Perry's fixed determination to annex the Luchus. Armed by a letter from Secretary of State Edward Everett in which President Fillmore was quoted as saying, "It is highly desirable, probably necessary for the safety of the expedition that you should secure one or more ports of refuge. . . . You are most likely to succeed in the Lew-chew islands. . . ." Perry was intent on taking Napa as a base. He wrote to Washington asking permission to annex the port.

It is self-evident that the course of coming events will ere long make it necessary for the United States to extend its territorial jurisdiction beyond the limits of the western continent, and I assume the responsibility of urging the expediency of establishing a foothold in this quarter of the globe, as a measure of positive necessity to the sustainment of our maritime rights in the East.

I shall continue to maintain the influence over the authorities and people of Lew-chew which I now command, but it is important that I should have instructions to act promptly, for it is not impossible that some other power, less scrupulous, may slip in and seize the advantages which should justly belong to us.

While waiting for the license to take the Luchus, Perry moved to hold his Bonin Island rights. He directed the *Plymouth* to visit the settlement, to hoist the American flag over the coal depot, though not over the islands as a whole, to fire a seventeen-gun salute, and to bury a copper plate. Captain John Kelly carried through the instructions, though at the cost of a boatload of fourteen men lost in a rough sea outside the harbor of Port Lloyd. The *Plymouth* call was later an effective argument against the claims of Russians who arrived a few months later with four warships. American warships were dispatched to Port Lloyd in 1854 and 1855 to reinforce the Savery guard upon the islands.

Perry went back to Hongkong, certain that he had fulfilled his mission. Japan was not yet open, but the essential preliminaries had been passed. By refusing to concede, or to retract his demands, by insisting on his dignity and by a diplomatic show of force, he had progressed to a more advanced point than had any other visitor since the closing of the ports two centuries before. It was a foregone conclusion that Japan would be obliged to yield to the American desires.

XXIV

JAPAN IS OPENED

PERRY'S presence on the China coast was imperatively required. The Taiping Revolt, with its threat to foreign lives, terrified the alien traders. Sheaves of letters were hurried to the Commodore, asking him to rush to the treaty ports to protect Americans. Perry's private preference would have been to linger in the Luchus, leaving to the British the unpleasant task of intervening in Chinese domestic difficulties, but the needs were much too pressing for Perry to gratify his wishes. He arrived in China in August 1853.

Other complications contributed to Perry's worries. Both the trade commissioner and the consul assumed the right to order his movements. Gifted with but little tact, and prone to quick flashes of temper, Perry found himself embroiled in constant quarrels. Had he not been compelled to remain in readiness for the protection of American lives and property, Perry might have fled from the scene to a more peaceful anchorage at Napa, but the Taiping Revolt dragged on. Perry was obliged to stay in China until January 1854.

Russians, French, and British meanwhile seemed ready to anticipate Perry in Japan. Admiral Count Euphemius Poutiatine, commanding a Russian squadron, sailed into port with a suggestion that the United States and Russia join in a coöperative effort to open Japan for trade. Count Poutiatine, it was later learned, was fresh from a call at Nagasaki where he had pressed a demand for "more neighborly intimacy, precision of the Saghalien boundary, and the opening of Japanese ports for trade." His request, presented more as a demand than as a polite request, had been refused, but Poutiatine was not discouraged. He asked Perry to lend him eighty tons of coal, so that the Russians might steam along with the Americans on the return trip to Japan. Perry flatly refused, and Poutiatine departed on what seemed to Perry a mysterious mission. Perry feared that the Russian intended to seek coal at some other port and to hasten to Japan before the Americans could return to Yedo.

In November 1853, moreover, the French frigate *Constantine,* which had been lying close to Perry in Macao Harbor, mysteriously weighed anchor and hurried out to sea. The activity, in all probability, was due to news that Russia had presented an ultimatum to the Turks and that the Tsar was mobilizing for war. France, realizing that a Russian squadron in the China Sea might catch French merchantmen unawares, sought to keep Poutiatine under observation. But Perry, whose dispatches on European affairs were not so complete as those of his French and Russian colleagues, thought only that the foreigners were trying to conclude treaties with the Shogun before the Americans went back for an answer.

Similar explanations undoubtedly account for the otherwise baffling movements of a British fleet of four ships under command of Admiral Sir James Stirling. Perry was confident that Stirling too was endeavoring to cut into America's Japanese preserve. In no other way could he account for the seeming willingness of his fellow commanders to abandon their nationals in China for mysterious movements at sea.

In January 1854, therefore, Perry hoisted anchor and left for Napa with three steamships, *Powhatan, Mississippi,* and *Susquehanna.* Three frigates and three supply ships were also to be included in the party after rendezvous was completed at the Luchus. At the very moment of departure, Perry received orders to leave one of his steamers behind for use on the China coast, but Perry refused to carry out the order. He preferred to run the risk of courtmartial, on the plea that the order came too late, rather than weaken his second Japan expedition.

Perry sailed for Napa in high spirits. There was an ironical element in his cheerful salute to a small group of British warships whom he passed in harbor, for their commander, Admiral Sir Fleetwood Pellew, had been the boy captain whose call at Nagasaki in the *Phaeton* almost half a century earlier had been barren of productive consequence.

Perry was not intending to come away empty-handed. If Japan refused a treaty, he was prepared to annex Luchu "upon the ground of reclamation for insults and injuries committed upon American subjects." His announcement of the contemplated annexation caused embarrassment at Washington. President Pierce hurried back a message refusing to approve the plan. "It would be rather mortifying to surrender the island, if once seized, and rather inconvenient and expensive to maintain a force there to retain it."

At the Luchus, Perry's anger flared. The natives persistently declined to sell the Americans needed supplies. Perry asked for fresh fish for breakfast and was furnished with a blue-slate crane. The Commodore drafted a letter to the Regent, protesting in strong terms against the policy of evasion, subterfuge, and espionage which the Luchuans continued to pursue.

A further hitch occurred at Napa because of the receipt of a letter from Duymaer van Twist, governor-general of the Netherlands Indies, conveying a Japanese plea for postponement.

Iyeyoshi, the Shogun reigning at the time of Perry's former visit, had died suddenly, the letter declared. "This event, according to Japanese laws and customs, makes necessary the performance of many and continuing ceremonies of mourning, with respect to the succession to the throne. During this period of mourning, no business of any importance can be transacted. The letter of the President of the United States can only be taken into deliberation when the period of mourning is over." Under these circumstances, the Japanese warned through Van Twist, the visit of the American squadron "might create broil." Perry was asked to delay his arrival.

The Commodore did not hesitate. He had already heard of Iyeyoshi's death through the Poutiatine officers, and, through Williams, had made exhaustive research into oriental customs. In China, it was discovered, the period of mourning lasted only seven weeks. "The successor to the Imperial throne assumes the government immediately, and public business is never interrupted." Perry thought it peculiar that a man whose health had been good in July should have died so suddenly within a month or two. He even suspected that the news might be false. In any event, he decided, the conclusion of a treaty was so vitally important that he would run the risk of a rebuff.

The enlarged American squadron sailed into Yedo Bay at a most inconvenient moment for Japan. February 11, the day when the fleet was sighted from the shore, was Japan's most sacred holiday, the Kigen-setsu, or anniversary of the accession of their first Emperor, Jimmu, in 660 b. c. No day could have been less suited from the Japanese point of view for Perry's Black Ships to advertise Japan's helplessness against outside aggression. The arrival on Kigensetsu was a bitter blow to Japan's pride.

Again the Japanese resorted to a policy of evasion and delay. Protracted wranglings marked almost every step of the negotiations. Upon his arrival, Perry instructed the junior officers, who would meet with the harbor police, to insist that the American fleet anchor far up Yedo Bay. The Japanese authorities countered with the suggestion that the fleet withdraw to Uraga, twenty miles down the bay from Perry's preferred anchorage. After two days' delay, Perry moved the ships to his own selected region. Guard boats were thrown about the ships, communication with the shore was forbidden, and Perry was politely ordered to withdraw from such close proximity to Yedo. He answered by moving up to Kanagawa, almost at the Yedo city limits.

The difficulties were not over. Perry, losing his temper at the delays, thundered to his intimates that the Japanese were savages, liars, fools, and poor devils who could not be trusted, and then, said Williams, "denying all of it by supposing that they were worth making a treaty with."

Partly, no doubt, the troubles were intensified by the poor quality of the interpreters. Wells Williams had long since given up all idea of acting as intermediary, realizing that the Dutch-speaking Japanese were better at translation than he could be. All the business was, therefore, carried on in Dutch, although a few Japanese essayed a few words of sadly mangled English. Manjiro Nakahama, it appears, was too valuable as a secret spy to be publicly employed as an interpreter. He was assigned to attend the Japanese agents so that he might overhear the comments of the Americans. The latter, unaware of his complete knowledge of English, talked freely of their plans.

Three weeks after the arrival of the fleet, the Japanese called in, as reinforcement, "a new and superior interpreter newly arrived from Nagasaki." This was Einosuke Moriyama, friend of Ranald MacDonald and interpreter in the *Preble* case. From the moment of his coming, relationships improved.

A gala reception was arranged ashore for the delivery of the new Shogun's reply to the Fillmore letter. Two high daimyos, a privy councilor (Hayashi of the University), and a chief treasury official were to represent the Shogun, with six lesser daimyos as attendants.

These were personages of sufficiently exalted rank to warrant Perry's personal appearance. The Americans arranged to meet the Shogun's mission with appropriate ceremony.

On the 8th of March, about 900 officers, seamen and marines, armed to the teeth, landed, and with drums beating and colors flying, were drawn up on the beach, ready to receive the commodore. As soon as he stepped on shore, the bands struck up, salutes were fired, the marines presented arms, and followed by a long escort of officers, he marched up between the lines and entered the house erected by the Japanese expressly for the occasion. Thousands of Japanese soldiers crowded the shores and the neighboring elevations, looking on with a great deal of curiosity and interest.

The house was a plain frame building, hastily put up, containing but one large room, the audience hall, and several smaller rooms for the convenience of attendants. The floor was covered with mats and a number of painted screens adorned the sides. Long tables and benches, covered with red woolen stuff, placed parallel to each other, three handsome braziers filled with burning charcoal on the floor between them, and a few violet colored crepe hangings suspended from the ceiling completed the furniture of the room.

After the Americans were shown to their places the Japanese commissioners entered the hall. Both sides bowed politely, inquired after each other's health, and paid the customary compliments. A long silence ensued. It was broken by the solemn withdrawal of the silk-gowned Japanese to a private apartment.

The Americans had come in expectation that a banquet would be served. Some of them, unable to handle chopsticks, had been sufficiently foresighted to equip themselves with knives and forks for the expected feast. They were chagrined to find that the refreshments consisted of nothing more substantial than tea, candy, sponge cake, oranges, and sake.

After the refreshments, the Americans were invited to meet with the Japanese in more intimate quarters. Councilor Hayashi, head of the Japanese commission, formally presented Perry with the Shogun's answer to the Fillmore letter. It proved to be a polite request for delay though it professed desire for friendship. Since Iyeyoshi had died, the answer pointed out, Japanese custom prevented further action from being taken until a more direct application could be had to Iyeyoshi's successor. The new Shogun, Iyesada, had sworn to obey the laws of the Empire, and because the laws against foreign intercourse were among the oldest of the nation, the oath forbade his immediately violating the custom. The American ships would be supplied with food, fuel, and water and would be allowed to leave at once.

Perry did not realize at the time the nature of the answer he had received. He thanked Hayashi for the document, put it aside, and handed the Japanese a copy of the Sino-American agreement which he proposed as a basis for negotiation. The Japanese thanked him in return, promised that they would give it early consideration, and indicated that the audience was over.

Perry had, however, one further request. Two days before the conference, Private Robert Williams, a marine of the *Mississippi,* had died. Perry inquired whether a piece of ground could be procured in which the body could be buried. It was the same problem that had arisen at the time of Broughton's visit, but it took the commissioners by surprise. Nothing of the sort had been included in their instructions, yet the matter was obviously an emergency matter that required an immediate response. The Japanese retired to consider the request.

On their return, after a brief discussion, they reminded Perry that a temple had been set aside at Nagasaki for the burial of strangers and informed him that the body could be sent in a Japanese junk to Nagasaki. Perry refused the suggestion since, as he said, "undisturbed resting places for the dead were granted by all nations." He explained, privately, in a dispatch to his superiors, that he "was moreover anxious for special reasons to acquire an interest in this island to subserve some ulterior projects." His desire was to send boats to inter the body at Webster Island, a small island near the American anchorage.

Japan, fearing perhaps the establishment of an American settlement in their own harbor, finally consented to allow the burial to take place at Yokohama in a temple ground. "Thus," says Williams, "did the United States Marine, Williams, occupy his narrow bed within fifteen miles of Yedo, where Gongin-sama declared once that no Christian should ever come; yea, that even the God of the Christians should die, if he came. Thus are old things passing away in Japan." Japan provided a Buddhist priest to conduct a service and supplied a guard to watch over the grave.

Evidently the Japanese had little hope that the Americans would delay. Perry's refusal to postpone his visit out of respect for the memory of the dead Shogun warned them that the Americans were impatient. Perry was obviously relying on the power of his ships to force an entrance if peaceful admission were denied. When, therefore, he declined to leave Yedo Bay on the receipt of the new Shogun's answer, the Japanese commissioners knew that isolation was ended.

Opinion was again divided concerning the proper course to be pursued toward the determined foreigners, but now, with the threat of Perry's steam warships so close to Yedo, the fire-eaters were overruled. Japan was well aware that she had no defenses to resist such ships; she was equally sure that Perry was not the type of man to be worn down by protracted evasiveness. He had shown too much impatience and too ready willingness to lose his temper over trifles for Japan to risk his anger. Shioya Kozo's suggestion that Perry's fleet be captured by stretching "three lengths of large chain" across the channel found little support in the Shogun's Council.

Japan's recourse was to make the best possible agreements with a minimum of concession, and to drag out the negotiations for as long a time as possible. Thus the Japanese commissioners offered to allow Americans to use the port of Nagasaki on the same terms as the Dutch, holding out a vague hope that a second port might be opened within five years. Perry objected, because of the restrictions imposed on aliens at Nagasaki. When the Japanese declined to grant shipwrecked sailors full freedom of movement within the Empire, and when they planned to forbid Americans from communicating with any other foreigners in Japan, Perry wrathfully warned that such restraints would be offensive.

"I told them that I should expect, in the course of time, five ports to be opened to the American flag, but, at present, would be content with three." He demanded that trading rights should be available at Matsumai, Napa, and at either Uraga or Kagoshima within sixty days.

The Japanese protested vehemently, urging that Matsumai was in a distant possession, over which Japan had but limited control. Perry retorted that he must then sail at once for Matsumai to use force to compel its compliance. Japan compromised by substituting Hakodate as the northern port, and by agreeing to accept Shimoda, eighty miles from Yedo, as an open harbor. There was no question concerning the grant of trading privileges at Napa.

Williams was indignant at the demands of his Commodore:

While Perry is pleased that the Japanese government has granted all that Fillmore asked for, which as all the Cabinet at Washington expected to obtain, he says it is by no means all that *he* wants nor all the President intended and "will not satisfy his views." The latter last year asked for one port; now Perry wants five. That desired the Japanese to give assurances of good treatment; now Perry demands them to make a treaty, and threatens them in no obscure terms with a "larger force and more stringent terms and instructions" if they do not comply. . . . Perry cares no more for right, for consistency, for his country, than will advance his own aggrandizement and fame, and makes his ambition the test of all his conduct toward the Japanese.

As a final estimate of the Commodore's character, Williams declared that he was "as uneasy as a man with the toothache and seems happiest when stirring somebody up."

Williams made an important contribution to the making of the treaty. While the drafting was in progress, he noticed that an important clause seemed to have been overlooked. At his suggestion, therefore, Article 9 was inserted, granting to the United States any special privilege or advantage which might hereafter be given by Japan to any other nation. The most-favored-nation clause thereafter opened to the United States every port subsequently offered for the use of any foreign country, including the undesired city of Nagasaki.

Privileges were gained which even the most sanguine had not anticipated. Within a radius of ten American miles of the treaty ports Americans could move about freely, free from guards and without molestation so long as they comported themselves properly. The right to station a consul at Shimoda was another most important gain.

The crafty Japanese had, however, left a door open for repudiation of the treaty. By refusing to sign any copy of the agreement, save their own official Japanese version, they could consider themselves bound only by their own interpretation of their own somewhat cryptic writing. When Townsend Harris later arrived, as first American consular agent, he faced disputes arising out of the translation of the treaty text. It is, however, to be noted that the assurance of firm, lasting, and sincere friendship between the two nations, signed at Kanagawa on March 31, 1854, has bound them for more than eighty years.

Before the treaty was finally signed, Perry produced his presents. Most of them were highly utilitarian, but like the copies of the

Annals of Congress and the *Journal* of the New York Legislature, were astonishing to the recipients. A quarter-sized locomotive, complete with track, tender, and car, was a particular delight. "The Japanese are, I think, more pleased with this thing than with anything else." But the telegraph, with three miles of wire, was a close second. Two copper surfboats, a set of farming implements, a telescope, swords, muskets, and pistols were also popular. Casks of madeira, barrels of whisky, cases of champagnes and cordials, and a large collection of "assorted perfumery" rounded out the gifts, if one excepts the frequent mention of "ten cent boxes of fine tea." One unhappy councilor received a volume of Minnesota geology, and a lithograph of Washington, but the addition of ten gallons of whisky and nine bottles of assorted scents may have eased the sorrow. Another daimyo received a howitzer with ammunition.

The return gifts were somewhat more delicate than the American presents. Gold-lacquered tables, silver censors, and various other works of art were sent to the United States, together with 132 pieces of silk. In conformity with age-old Japanese custom, a dried fish, four dogs, three hundred chickens, and two hundred sacks of rice were added to the Imperial gifts.

In presenting the gifts, the Japanese took the opportunity to stage a demonstration of *sumo,* or Japanese wrestling, while the Americans countered with elaborate feasts and minstrel shows. The consumption of wine was enormous, and the good will thus generated caused vows of blood brotherhood to be freely exchanged. The diplomats might be squabbling over petty details of precedence, but the officers and common folk were extraordinarily happy.

The good will was to undergo a severe strain when Perry, having secured his treaty, resolved to celebrate by sailing to the forbidden Yedo. Against the protests of the Japanese, the *Powhatan* chugged onward toward the capital, ostensibly to disprove Hayashi's boast that foreigners would never be allowed to see the city. Moriyama and Kenziro Hirayama, the chief interpreters, warned against the trip. They said that Japanese laws were strict against such intrusion, that the result would bring civil war, that the bay was too shallow for the ship, that the Emperor would be angry, that, as Perry had professed friendly feelings, they wished him as a friend not to go, and that they would lose both honor and life. Then, to Perry's amazement, they calmed down and asked, since he was resolved to visit Yedo, that he take them as passengers aboard the *Powhatan.*

Perry was thunderstruck but agreed. Then, when he realized that the seemingly frivolous shift of his interpreters concealed a calm purpose of their committing harakiri upon the bridge of his ship if he persisted, Perry stopped the trip. His officers and crew, unaware of the reason for his change of heart, were, in their turn, amazed. They explained the failure to go up the bay as one of Perry's jests.

More trouble came when the officers and bluejackets were allowed to go ashore. The natives complained to Perry that an officer was trying to walk to Yedo. Chaplain Bittinger, he who had intruded on the Buddhist services at Napa, wandered beyond bounds with a bundle of tracts for distribution to the Japanese. Bittinger, having strayed as far as Kawasaki on the Yedo road, was, according to the Japanese, flourishing a sword to compel a boatman to ferry him across the river. The Japanese added slyly that they presumed he was waving the weapon "for amusement." They protested against his tracts, but Perry replied by complaints against the lascivious literature given to his men. Japan, said Williams, "is the most lewd of all nations."

Sailors were more carnal in their tastes. Two of the crew invaded a sake shop, pulled the spigot from a cask and, after drinking a basinful, let the rest flow over the floor. Sailors and shopkeeper alike were wounded in the scuffle that ensued. "Truly may it be said," wrote the horrified Williams, "that life in a man-of-war is too often like living on the outskirts of hell." On another occasion his complaint seemed more nearly accurate, for a local daimyo complained that sailors were gambling in the temples, climbing over walls to break into houses and stores, looting the shops and acting like madmen. Three officers who tramped twenty-five miles on a hunting expedition, only to bag one pheasant, a tail feather of another bird, and a fox that was dead before it was acquired by the Americans, went to sleep in a temple and were ordered away by the priests.

The real test of the treaty came in Hakodate and Napa. The Japanese commissioners, anxious to take the first inklings to their own provinces, asked for sixty days' delay before Perry appeared at Hakodate; Perry insisted on sailing there immediately. In consequence, the Hakodate official, Mogoro Kudo, faced by the sudden arrival of three foreign ships, acted precisely as his orders required him to act. Perry, indignant at Kudo's reluctance to honor the signed treaty, ordered a hundred bluejackets to be ready to attack the town. Fortunately he was calmed in time, but even so, it was necessary to warn the prefect not to have the American naval officers followed by spies and to request the citizens not to flee.

One matter of which, luckily, Perry remained all his life in ignorance, was much more serious. A fervid Japanese nationalist, fearful lest the coming of the foreigners would destroy the pure spirit of "Yamato Damashii," went to Uraga to murder the Commodore who, as he believed, had come to overthrow Japan.

Just as he neared the deck of the American man-of-war, one of the petty officers slipped. The American would have fallen overboard had the Commodore not caught him and helped him to his feet. The would-be assailant was so impressed by the fact that an officer of exalted rank would exert himself to save the live of a subordinate that he gave up the murderous attempt.

When all the treaty arrangements were finally completed, Perry departed. On June 28, 1854 the Japan Expedition weighed anchor, arriving at Napa, where a supplementary treaty was to be concluded, on July 1.

More trouble occurred here. The actual signing of the treaty proved comparatively easy but one of Perry's men, William Boardman, was murdered by an angry Luchu mob. Boardman, it appeared, had drunkenly broken into a house, and had attacked a woman. The Luchu populace stoned him and knocked him senseless into a pond where he drowned. Perry, knowing only that his man was dead, insisted on exacting vengeance.

There was ample excuse for Perry's seeming callousness in demanding that the avengers of the woman's honor should be punished. The local "superintendent of affairs," Shang Hiun-hiung, considered that the dignity of his district had been outraged by the assault and, in his formal report of the affair, had mentioned only that "a drunken sailor, in his incoherent stumbling and reeling, had fallen into the water and was drowned." Perry heard of the stoning and was misled into thinking that the Luchu natives had been guilty of an unwarranted attack. Rather than retreat from his position, however, he insisted that some punishment be inflicted for the mob's attack. Four deputy magistrates were dismissed, the mayor forced to serve without pay, the man who threw the first stone was banished for life and five others were banished for eight years.

Four days later a compact was completed with the Luchu government, granting to American seamen freedom to visit and to trade at any harbor. There was included an important clause:

Whenever persons from ships of the United States come ashore in Luchu, they shall be at liberty to ramble where they please, without hindrance, or having officials sent to follow them, or to spy what they do; but if they violently go into houses, or trifle with women, or force people to sell them things, or do other such like illegal acts, they shall be arrested by the local officers, but not maltreated, and shall be reported to the captain of the ship to which they belong, for punishment by him.

Seldom in any treaty have such rights of extra-territoriality been granted to the skippers of whalers and merchantmen. The need for specific mention of such offenses indicate that Perry's seamen had evidently been guilty of misconduct.

After completing arrangements for stone blocks to be brought from Hakodate and the Luchus for insertion in the Washington Monument, and for the purchase of a huge temple bell (which Perry thought might be hung at the top of the Monument but which has since been placed at the Naval Academy), the Americans sailed back to Hongkong in triumph. Japan and its Luchu dependency were open to foreign intercourse.

XXV

A CONSUL IN COVENTRY

MOST Americans give Perry the glory of opening Japan to Western intercourse; Japan would much prefer to credit the achievement to Townsend Harris, first American civilian to sign a treaty with the Shogun. Perry used no actual violence and was scrupulously correct in all his dealings, but he lost no opportunity for stressing his potential strength. The threat of bombardment was never absent during his visit. His successor, Harris, used milder methods, and wielded no military might.

Perry, moreover, paid but slight heed to Japanese desires; Harris was more conciliatory. By declining to observe the Japanese tabus, by refusing to accept the meeting place suggested by his hosts, by insisting on surveying the harbors, and by threatening to steam to Yedo, Perry advertised his scorn; Harris was more coöperative. The Japanese disliked the haughty Commodore and succumbed only under protest to his implied threat of force. Having signed his treaty, they preferred to forget both Perry and the concessions which he wrested from Japan; the Harris agreements which followed were, because concluded between equals, more carefully observed.

Even the *kami,* the gods of Japan, seemed hostile to the Perry pact. Within ten days after the Americans cleared from Shimoda, whither they had gone to inspect the newly granted harbor, the anger of the *kami* against the admission of aliens to Japan was made clearly evident to superstitious Japanese. On July 9, 1854, Japan's most sacred provinces, Yamato, home of the race, and Ise, beloved of the Sun Goddess, were devastated by earthquake. Since no major catastrophe had, within the memory of living men, struck at the Great Shrines wherein are preserved the Sacred Treasures of the

283

Sun Goddess, this calamity was of extraordinary import. The loss of five thousand houses and of three thousand lives was secondary in the consideration of loyal Japanese; more serious was the evident anger of the *kami* against Japan's weak-kneed truckling to the foreigners.

Popular misconceptions of the causes of the quake spread freely throughout the Empire. Perry never knew that to the masses of the people he was a harbinger of evil, a malignant visitor whose arrival spelled catastrophe. Had aliens been resident in Japan, a wholesale massacre, similar to that which cost the lives of hundreds of Koreans after the earthquake of 1923, would almost certainly have followed.

The Shogun's advisers, possessed of more scientific information than their superstitious fellow countrymen, tried to disregard the omen. Knowing far better than the ignorant yokels that no possible resistance could withstand the foreign might, and realizing that no true connection could be traced between the calamities and the conclusion of a treaty, the Yedo officials sought to modify the resentment. The anti-foreign feeling, it was understood, arose from fears of force and violence. By granting a hospitable reception to a peaceful ship, the Shogunate reasoned, the populace might be persuaded that the *kami* objected only to armed ships of alien powers and not to friendly merchantmen. The commoners could hold Perry's call responsible for the Ise earthquake and thus cherish the old superstitions; the Shogunate would gain the dual advantage of compliance with treaty provisions and of receiving necessary foreign merchandise.

The scheme was planned in theory; no Japanese official was aware that, by the adventitiousness of luck, an immediate opportunity was at hand for testing the idea.

Before the full effects of the earthquake had been made evident, and within fifteen days after Perry's departure from Shimoda, the clipper ship *Lady Pierce* from San Francisco, fitted out for the express purpose of being the first American ship to arrive after the opening of Japan, sailed into Yedo Bay.

Aboard the *Lady Pierce* was a shipwrecked Japanese, Diyonosuke, the sole survivor of fifteen men picked up off Hawaii after drifting helplessly for seven months in a disabled junk. His arrival at Uraga was the signal for a warm demonstration for himself and for Silas E. Burrows, owner of the ship.

"With pleasure we welcome you," said the Uraga mayor to Burrows,

and in doing so, can assure you that your ship, the *Lady Pierce,* is the first foreign vessel that has been received by us with pleasure. Commodore Perry brought with him too many large guns and fighting men to be pleasing to us; but you have come in your beautiful ship, which is superior to any we have before seen, to visit us, without any hostile weapons, and the Emperor has ordered that you shall have all the kindness and liberty extended to you that Commodore Perry received. . . .

But the Emperor is particularly desirous that you should extend the terms of the treaty made with Commodore Perry, wherever you may go, to prevent any more ships coming to Yedo Bay, as all must hereafter go to Shimoda or Hakodate. . . .

We understand what ships of war are; also what whaling ships and merchant ships are; but we never before heard, till you came here, of such a ship as yours—a private gentleman's pleasure ship—coming so far as you have, without any money-making business of trade, and only to see Japan, to become acquainted with us, and to bring home our shipwrecked people, the first that has returned to his country from American or foreign lands. . . . We hope we may meet you again and we hope you will come back to Japan. The Emperor has directed that two ships like yours shall be built.

The details mentioned in the address are not strictly accurate, to be sure, for the *Morrison* surely comes under the same category as the *Lady Pierce* and the presence at Uraga of Manjiro Nakahama, who may himself have drafted the address, was sufficient to disprove the statement that Diyonosuke was the first Japanese to return. But the spirit back of the speech is unmistakably friendly.

Such good luck as the timely arrival of the *Lady Pierce* at just the moment when the coming of a peaceful ship would exert the best psychologic effect, was not to last. Foreign warships were not far distant. On September 7, Admiral Sir James Stirling came to Nagasaki with three steamers and a frigate. He had the double mission of finding Poutiatine's Russian squadron and of procuring an agreement similar to that which Perry had exacted. Of the two purposes the latter was unquestionably the more important.

On his arrival, the Nagasaki port officials resorted to the old routine of throwing rings of guard boats about his ships, of ordering him to leave at once and of refusing him communication with the shore. Even had they been officially informed of the American agreement it is difficult to see what other action the Japanese authorities could take. Such practices were specifically required by Imperial edict; no superseding treaty had been signed with England. For Stirling, however, the situation was particularly galling, since the annual Dutch trading ship, a Netherlandish steamer, and two large Chinese junks were witnesses of his humiliation.

Stirling refused to accept the treatment, threatening unless the restrictions were removed to go to Yedo to protest. The Nagasaki officers, not knowing that the admiral would proceed to Yedo in any case, dragged on negotiations for a week, and then, on September 15, allowed Stirling to make a formal call upon the governor. The guard boats were withdrawn, under fear of force, the purchase of supplies was permitted (a freedom forbidden to the *Lady Pierce*), and British sailors were allowed to land upon an out-of-the-way island for exercise and drill. Four days later, after an exchange of presents, the squadron sailed. Nagasaki had comported itself admirably, in the Japanese view, by insisting on the old routine before yielding gracefully to foreign pressure.

Arriving at Yedo, as he had all the while intended, Stirling obtained on October 14 a treaty obtaining for Britain and her ally France the opening of Hakodate and Nagasaki for trade. Thus, under the most-favored-nations clause of Perry's treaty the United States also gained the right to enter Nagasaki. An absurd final clause stipulated that no changes could ever be made in the treaty's terms. Probably the Shogunate wished to stabilize the status quo, but for this, among other reasons, London repudiated the agreement and ordered it replaced by a more satisfactory treaty.

The British had missed Count Poutiatine but the Russian was not far distant. After Stirling's departure, the steam frigate *Diana* sailed into Shimoda Harbor. There was, to Japanese minds, an immediate but puzzling aftermath. Two days before Christmas 1854, a disastrous earthquake caused tremendous desolation along the entire coast of Japan, shaking down fifty thousand houses, killing seven thousand people, and almost completely wrecking the city of Osaka.

The *Diana,* anchored in Shimoda Bay, felt the full force of a tidal wave that accompanied the earthquake. According to a native chronicler, "The sea rose and fell sixty feet, five times over. The Russian frigate made forty-three revolutions within half an hour. The anchor held, but a gale wrecked the ship." A more conservative report declares that the tidal wave first receded, sweeping the entire bottom of the harbor bare and leaving no bottom but the rocks, and then rushed forward to engulf the town. The city of Shimoda was so destroyed that barely fourteen houses remained unharmed.

Amazingly, Poutiatine and his men escaped death, though the *Diana* sank while attempting to seek safety. Because no other explanation than the special guardianship of the *kami* could be imagined by the Japanese for the miraculous escape, Poutiatine, even without a warship, gained an agreement giving to Russia rights equal to those granted to England and America. The treaty was dated February 7, 1855.

During the last stages of the negotiations Commander Adams returned from Washington in the *Powhatan* bearing the ratified copy of Perry's compact. Almost a month was consumed in waiting for Japan to consent to proper ceremonies for exchanging ratifications, but two weeks after Poutiatine's treaty was finished, the exchange was completed. The log of the *Powhatan* contains a curious commentary on the celebration held in honor of the event. "Expended for entertainment of the Japanese commissioners 20 pounds of flour, 25 pounds of butter, 10 pounds of sugar, 1 bottle mustard." Evidently a cake was baked for the occasion, but the last item seems peculiar. The *Powhatan* passed on to China the next day, after "splicing the mainbrace in honor of the Birth Day of Washington" and giving the commissioners a case of whisky as a parting present.

Despite the treaties, neither official callers nor private skippers were invariably welcomed after Perry's time. The British warship *Barracouta* was compelled to fight her way through a Nagasaki bridge of boats in 1857. An American trading schooner, putting into Hakodate with a cargo of ship chandlery for the use of distressed whalers, was driven out of port. An American sloop, the *Vincennes,* charting the east coast, was attacked by armed men in Kagoshima Bay, and was threatened with violence at two different places on the important island of Oshima. At Napa, the Luchu islanders were reported by an American commander to be, "inveterately opposed to foreign intercourse, and seek to delay on every occasion by frivolous pretence, the assistance to ships which, by Commodore Perry's convention, they are bound to render." The Americans landed a hundred armed men to compel compliance.

In certain of these instances, to be sure, the alien ships were venturing into waters where no treaty provision authorized an entry, as at Kagoshima Bay and in the Oshima instances, but the incidents at Nagasaki, Hakodate, and Napa were clear violations of the treaty stipulations. Similar breaches of the treaty were seen at Shimoda when Townsend Harris, the American Consular Agent, arrived in August 1856.

Harris met ill luck at the very outset of his residence. Scarcely had he set up a flagpole for the display of the first American consular flag ever to be seen in Japan, before a typhoon wrecked the pole and destroyed his landing place. He could not easily secure a place to live. The Japanese insisted that, since the tidal wave of eighteen months before, no houses had been erected.

Indeed, the Japanese declared, Harris had no right to reside in Shimoda. When Harris displayed his copy of the treaty which plainly stated that the Americans could send an envoy, they replied that the Japanese version gave no such privilege. Even if it had, Japan asserted, both the United States and Japan had to agree on details, and thus far the Shogunate had granted no permission. They asked Harris to go away and, on his refusal, asked Commodore Armstrong to take him away. Armstrong of course refused, and then they requested him to carry a letter to Washington asking for Harris' removal. Again Armstrong declined, stating that all diplomatic correspondence must be sent through Harris himself. The Japanese urged Armstrong to write a private letter to Washington explaining that they did not desire Harris to remain. They also asked Harris to request his own dismissal.

Harris at last threatened to go to Yedo to complain. This threat caused the Japanese to consent that he might stay, but their attitude remained unfriendly. He met difficulty in securing servants, even those officially ordered to his house by the Shimoda headman begging to be excused from the assignment. Five women were at last sent to his house. They were chosen, the diary of the headman showed, because of their spying ability. And, as a commentary on the duties which they were expected to fulfil, the women were under orders to report to the magistrate "as soon as they became pregnant."

Okichi, a fifteen-year-old geisha, refused to serve in the Harris establishment. The headman insisted, and on her continued refusal, sentenced her to jail. Her lover was bribed to urge her to accept the duties. An elderly official gave her frequent lectures on "patriotic prostitutes in history." Okichi eventually consented, together with a still younger girl, described as the "plump and lovely daughter" of a local contractor. The churchly Harris knew nothing of these arrangements.

After the staff was recruited, Harris encountered difficulties in securing supplies. The townsfolk declined to sell provisions, except at exorbitant prices. On one occasion when Harris was suffering from an attack of his recurrent illness, Okichi bought milk at the price of $10 for two quarts! For five months, Harris repeatedly complained that his servants were refused the common courtesies, that his ordinary requests were unaccountably delayed in fulfilment, that he was ostracized, that his letters were opened, and that there was "a systematic campaign of obstruction and delay" against him.

From almost any other man, the accumulated charges might indicate an oppression psychosis, but Harris had no delusion of persecution. For each accusation he cited chapter and verse, and he carefully reminded his Japanese associates of their broken promises. Time and time again he proved them deceitful and mendacious. By May 1857 he was sufficiently exasperated to declare, "I do not think that any Japanese ever tells the truth if it can possibly be avoided."

Harris took, however, a firm stand from the start. When his Kakizaki house was finally provided, the Japanese announced that three rooms would be required for the use of Japanese officials "who are to be with me night and day 'to await my pleasure.' " Harris immediately replied that no Japanese were ever to enter his house without his express permission. He succeeded in freeing his private quarters from the officials, but every workman about the place, he discovered, was accompanied by a native guard for the prevention of communication. Harris constantly complained, but did not fully succeed in keeping out the "cloud of secretaries and spies" until half a year had passed.

Delay was especially noted in respect to Harris' request for a trip to Yedo to present his credentials to the government. On October 25, 1856, after having been in Japan for two months, Harris wrote to the ministry of foreign affairs announcing his desire to pay the customary diplomatic courtesy call. He received no reply until the following January and then only by word of mouth. He asked for written answers and was informed that the native law forbade replies in writing. Harris, having learned from Russian officers that no less than fifty letters had been written by the Japanese to the Tsar's officials within eighteen months, insisted on an explanation.

More time elapsed until, in July 1857, he was officially informed that Japan's law forbade any audience with the ruler. Harris again insisted, but not until September was he enabled to secure permission to make the call of courtesy. On November 30, 1857, after fifteen months on Japanese soil, he finally reached Yedo.

Only by good luck was he enabled to enter the capital in proper state. Harris preferred to ride horseback into the city and, to his amazement, was granted immediate permission to dismount from his palanquin. Thinking that there must be a reason for the consent, Harris made careful inquiries and found that only visitors of the highest rank could be carried into Yedo; all of inferior station were obliged by custom to ride horseback or to walk. He at once climbed back into the palanquin in order to preserve the dignity of a Presidential envoy.

Again, when his chief guide, Inouye, daimyo of Shinano, endeavored to assume the credit for allowing Harris to enter Yedo, the latter found it necessary to protest. Inouye "spoke of his anxious days and sleepless nights; that care and anxiety had taken away his appetite so that he had become lean in his person; and that his blood had frequently gushed from his nose from his great agitation; that he had done all this from his friendship for me, etc., etc." Harris shut off the flow of eloquence by reminding the daimyo that the United States insisted on its rights and that "it was no favor to me or to my country that they should listen to my advice, but that it was the Japanese who should feel grateful to the President for the friendship he had shown to Japan by the messages with which I was entrusted."

New efforts for isolation were tried at Yedo on the score that the city was unsafe and that "bad people might insult and maltreat me." Harris again protested his entire right of freedom and insisted that it was the Japanese duty to ensure his safety. He refused to be content with a horseback riding ground of thirty yards long by five yards wide, demanded the usual rights of ambassadors to free access to any portion of the nation, and warned that unless the Japanese scrupulously observed every provision of their treaty, the President of the United States would ask Congress to employ "stronger arguments" than mere persuasion. Japanese, said Harris, "have yielded nothing except from fear."

Harris came to Japan under instruction to secure a more complete commercial treaty than the clauses in the Perry agreement provided. His first efforts were to secure to the United States the benefit of concessions already made to Russia by Poutiatine's treaty of February 7, 1855, and to Holland by the Donker Curtius agreement of November 9, 1855. Slight difficulty should have been involved in this, for by the most-favored-nation clause all the benefits granted to aliens by those compacts accrued also to Americans.

Japan, however, resisted strenuously any attempt to extend the rights to the United States, denying at first that any treaty had been made with Hollanders. When Harris answered that he had himself seen the agreement with the Japanese seal affixed upon it, the Japanese commissioners themselves produced a copy of the very treaty whose existence they denied. They told him that it had been canceled but did not inform him that a substitute had been drawn and approved. Not until Harris read European newspapers seven months later was he aware of the second treaty, then twenty months old. It was yet another proof of what a British diplomat considered "the incorrigible tendency of the Japanese to withhold from foreigners, or disguise, the truth on all matters, great and small."

Harris was amazed to discover that aliens had been allowed for years to call the temporal ruler by a false title. The real name, he was informed, was not Shogun, or generalissimo, but Tycoon, or great ruler. He did not, however, know that neither title was synonymous with Emperor nor that the supreme power rested with the secluded dairi at Miako. To his shocked surprise, indeed, he learned that the correct title of the spiritual center was not Miako, or capital, as foreigners had always been allowed to think, but Kyoto.

To Harris, evidently, the Japanese were deliberately deceitful respecting the Mikado's power. "They spoke almost contemptuously of the Mikado, and roared with laughter when I quoted some remarks concerning the veneration in which he is held by the Japanese. They say he has neither money, political power, nor anything else that is valued in Japan. He is a mere cipher." A month later the commissioners suggested that an agreement then in process of completion ought first be presented to the Mikado for his assent but that "the Government had determined not to receive any objections" from him. The solemn ceremony of submission, they said, was but a form. Later they confessed that the Mikado's assent would be equivalent to "God has spoken."

Harris was, however, making progress in spite of the evasions, delays, and misrepresentations. On June 17, 1857, he concluded what has since been termed the Shimoda Convention whereby five important rights were granted to Americans. Nagasaki was opened; Americans were given the right of permanent residence, even for missionaries, at Shimoda and Hakodate, with permission to establish a vice-consulate at the latter port; the consul-general was permitted freedom of movement throughout Japan. Extra-territoriality, refused by Perry, was secured, and a better financial arrangement was perfected.

The last agreement was a matter of vital trade importance. By Perry's arrangements, a complicated rate of exchange had been installed whereby the Japanese accepted foreign coins at a ruinous discount. The American silver dollar, containing sufficient bullion to be worth 4,800 of the Japanese "cash," was given the purely artificial value of 1,600 "cash"; the gold dollar, when converted into Japanese currency, brought but 17¼ cents in exchange. Payments in gold thus became much worse for Americans than payments in silver. Up until the time of Perry's final departure the exchange had been more unfavorable to the Americans, for the Japanese had granted but 1,200 "cash" per dollar instead of the 1,600 later offered and the 4,800 which would have been a fair exchange.

Harris, rebellious at the inflated prices he was compelled to pay for the goods he bought, demanded that the Shimoda Convention include a more equitable exchange. He succeeded in having the dollar valued at 4,800 "cash," with a slight discount for re-coinage charges, so that prices of Japanese goods were reduced to approximately one-third the former costs.

A year after the Shimoda Convention, he won further diplomatic victories by his Treaty of Yedo, concluded July 29, 1858. This granted complete freedom of religion, allowed the United States to send a diplomatic agent to reside at Yedo with consuls at each open port, opened Yedo, Osaka, Hyogo (now Kobe), Niigata, and Kanagawa (now Yokohama), to American trade (though Shimoda was closed), and allowed the United States fleet to store supplies at Kanagawa, Hakodate, and Nagasaki.

The last provision was deemed of great value. Previously the United States, having no naval station in the Orient, was dependent upon the British for the use of Hongkong or upon the Portuguese for Macao. The danger of having American war supplies deposited in a possibly hostile port was one of the chief factors urging the United States to the acquisition of Port Lloyd or Napa. With the right to use the three Japanese harbors, it was thought, the need for annexation of the Bonins and the Luchus would be decidedly decreased.

The securing of the treaties was by no means plain sailing. Japan was violently opposed to making more concessions, and fought bitterly against the granting of more rights. Over and over again their commissioners warned that revolution would follow such radical provisions as the opening of Yedo, the grant of foreign residence at Kyoto, or the liberty of foreigners to move freely in Japan. Some concessions would be granted only if Harris agreed to keep them secret or if he would guarantee not to make use of the privileges. He was obliged to abandon the hope of securing Kyoto as a free city or of allowing even consuls to have complete liberty of movement. Only the consul-general and the minister would be privileged to journey as they pleased.

When the treaty was announced to the assembled daimyos, the immediate result was their recommendation to reject the agreement. Of the eighteen Great Daimyos of the realm, fourteen were opposed; of the three hundred lesser nobles, seventy percent were hostile. The Shogun, it was said, favored the ratification of the treaty, but it was intimated that the Mikado was opposed. The military men, the classicists, and the nationalists were almost unanimously against the treaty.

Japan delayed for months, therefore, in giving any indication of its final decision on the matter, and would have waited still longer had not Harris warned that an American fleet might be called upon to use cannon balls unless some answer was given. The treaty was reasonably complete on February 17, but was not signed until July.

One persuasive argument in securing Japan's compliance was, no doubt, the constant Townsend Harris insistence that England and France were about to threaten Japan with dire calamity. Harris pointed out that concessions granted voluntarily would be less extensive and would be more likely to preserve the national prestige than privileges extorted by force of foreign arms.

Japan was certain that the first threat would come from Britain. An English mission under Lord Elgin was known to be in China and, it was understood, was bound for Yedo. Only two weeks after Harris' first arrival, Admiral Sir Michael Seymour had forced his way with three ships into Nagasaki's inner harbor. Seymour had gone away without insisting on a complete commercial treaty, but Elgin, arriving with the *Furious* and *Retribution* in August 1858, was deemed more dangerous to peace. Japan signed the Harris treaty partly as a means for having a model agreement to present to the British. The Elgin treaty of Yedo, signed August 26, is almost parallel in its terms. It cancelled the unsatisfactory Stirling treaty, and gave Britain rights similar to those of the United States.

Each nation, as it arrived to discuss the making of a treaty, came with the desire to outshine its predecessor. The United States, first to come with Perry, had dazzled the Japanese with a model locomotive and telegraph outfit, and thereafter confined itself, as when Harris came to Yedo, to bringing dozens of bottles of liquors as its offerings. Poutiatine presented the Shogun with a small schooner, built in the Amur yards, and followed the gift by the giving of the fifty-two guns from the wrecked *Diana*. Donker Curtius outdid the Russian schooner by sending to Yedo a six-gun steam corvette, but Elgin arrived with a beautiful 318-ton steam yacht, the *Emperor,* for the Shogun's private use. It was in some ways an odd gift, for the Shogun was himself almost as secluded as the Mikado and would, in all probability, never have an opportunity to enjoy his present, but the Japanese officers and crew assigned to the ship—which they renamed *Dragon* in order to avoid any possible complication with the Mikado—proudly sailed the yacht about the harbor.

The die-hard conservatives, vehemently opposed to all these treaties, did all in their power to hinder good relations. Government orders were issued against the sale of books, and especially maps, to strangers. Attachés of the missions were menaced in the streets and though, as Harris pointedly remarked, official spies were in abundance, the offenders were never found. Plots to murder Harris were well known to the Shogunate and were disclosed to him by the government officers, but no records exist to show that the conspirators were punished.

The outlying regions of the Empire were, as might be expected, even less willing to accept the aliens than were the Yedo conservatives. Long years of Tokugawa discipline had drilled into the populace the idea that foreigners were to be scorned and humiliated. By the Harris treaty the Yedo authorities were required to acquaint all the people with the news that outsiders were to be given fair and courteous treatment, but the ingrained habits of two centuries were much too well established to be easily changed.

XXVI

JAPAN RESENTS THE OPENING

FOREIGNERS, absorbed in the study of their own political and commercial development, see in the Perry visits little more than picturesque incidents whereby the doors of a secluded Empire were thrown open for enlightened Westerners. The Perry calls receive a passing paragraph in occidental histories and then are more or less forgotten. The effect produced upon the West by Perry's success was comparatively unimportant.

To Japan, the Perry visits ended an epoch. The old feudal days, with their static social system carefully guarded by domestic espionage, were definitely closing. A Western ferment, with its revolutionary content of personal liberty, freedom of initiative, and criticism of established institutions, made change inevitable. The infiltration of European ideas, principles, and habits of thought brought social upheavals unwelcome to the ruling classes. No effort could be spared, by those who vested interests to preserve, or by those to whom precedent seemed sacred, to check these radical innovations. The clash of cultures, made certain by the coming of the foreigners, brought bloodshed and armed conflict.

Japan was arming for defense before the Perry Black Ships came. The coming of the Americans was certainly not unexpected, for the Dutch had long since warned the Shogun that a fleet was on its way. Perry's open preparations, together with his leisureliness in coming to the East, gave Japanese an ample time for finishing their preparations.

Two types of protection were considered. The *kami* were notified that Japan was in grave danger. The sacred and secluded Dairi, almost forgotten by the foreigners, was solemnly informed that his divine intervention was now needed. He responded by ordering that prayers for the destruction of the foreigners should be offered steadily at the seven leading shrines. If spiritual forces rallied to the protection of Japan, the mystics hoped, some supernatural assistance might safe-guard the Empire against pollution by the aliens.

For more practical resistance, the Shogun belatedly accepted the half-forgotten suggestions made long ago by Shozan Sakuma's eight-point program of reform. The ancient prohibitions against the build-ing of seagoing ships were now repealed, Holland was asked to furnish Japan with a modern man-of-war, the daimyos were invited to prepare a fleet, and efficient guns were ordered. A survey of the coast defenses disclosed that Hakodate, in the north, was guarded chiefly by ancient Portuguese cannon dating back to 1570.

Domestic difficulties, however, hampered this plan for more effi-cient military preparation. The Tokugawa Shoguns, long dictatorial *de facto* rulers of the Empire, had few friends and many bitter ene-mies. The great rival daimyos, more notably Satsuma, Choshu, Tosa, and Hizen, were restless to restore their ancient freedom. Satsuma in particular appreciated the importance of foreign intercourse as a means for obtaining modern guns, and hoped to import armament through the Luchus. These rival lords were well aware that decades of food riots had weakened the loyalty of Japanese toward the Yedo overlords, and that the Tokugawas retained power chiefly through censorship, espionage, and military force. A coalition of important daimyos, it was known, could cause serious embarrassment to the Shogunate.

Japan had, however, small intention of calling in the aid of foreign-ers. The nationalistic spirit was far too strong for aliens to be asked to intervene. The discontented daimyos preferred to rally around the cause of the secluded and neglected Dairi, for whom every Japanese professed unbounded reverence. The anti-Tokugawa groups, excited by the clamors of Shinto priests and of classic scholars, urged that the Dairi, or Mikado, reëmerge as a vital factor in Japan's affairs.

The plan implied a revolution, though not in the occidental sense of the word. The anti-Tokugawa daimyos, in thus demanding that the Mikado be "restored" to power, had no real intention that the Dairi should be a dynamic figure in the government. They hoped to replace the Tokugawa Shogunate by some new official group which should rule in the Mikado's name. Their aim was a transfer of power from the discredited and unpopular Tokugawa leaders into their own hands. Thus, they hoped, "Japan's polity might be renovated," the Emperor be "relieved of evil influences around the Throne," and Japan's "pure spirit would be restored." Such phrases as these, whispered after Perry's calls, presaged the downfall of the Tokugawas. Similar vague phrases, current in 1937, expressed the desire of still more ardent nationalists for a reactionary régime.

The Mito daimyos, whose headquarters were on the eastern coast just to the north of Yedo, nursed an ancient grievance. Their clan was one of the three great houses whose members were privileged, because of descent from Iyeyasu, to be considered as candidates for the Shogunate. But because no Mito man had ever been picked for that high office, the clan was angry. The long-continued slight to Mito prestige made the clansmen willing to "restore" the Mikado, even at the cost of total abolition of the Tokugawa Shogunate.

Indeed, the Mito clan was probably the group most intellectually active in the "restoration" movement. As early as 1715, the second Mito daimyo ordered a history of Japan to be compiled. This history, the famous *Nihonji,* so "cooked" the past records that the Emperor was regarded as the most puissant and most sacred power in the land. The *Nihonji* virtually described the Shoguns as usurpers ruling unjustly. Classic scholars, studying the history here set forth, were impressed by the contrast between the Emperor's supposed position in past eras and his seeming impotence in the later periods. The true spirit of Japan seemed to require that the Shoguns be restricted and that the Emperors resume their rule.

Mito, too, was blessed by a succession of able leaders. When other noble families degenerated into futile puppets of clever base-born councilors, Mito retained its eminence. Such men were not content to sit by placidly while Japan passed under the control of weaker, less noble, bureaucrats.

Yedo was well aware of Mito's restlessness. For years an elaborate spying system reported to the Shoguns Mito actions which seemed treasonable. Yedo dared not, because the Mito ancestry was quite as noble as that of the Shoguns, take a too aggressive action to repress the Mito malcontents. Cleverly the Shoguns sought to split the Mito party into rival factions, one upholding the Imperialist cause and championing the ancient liberties of Mito daimyos, the other, subsidized by Yedo, insisting that the clan pay homage to the Shogun. The party conflict long prevented the energetic Mito men from taking active part in national affairs.

By 1840, however, Mito was comparatively peaceful. The anti-
Yedo group, headed by Nariaki, assumed control. Nariaki, deaf and
anti-social, immune to the distractions of wealth and luxury, almost
fanatical in his adherence to the Mikado's cause, became the daimyo
of the province.

Around him gathered a group of firebrand youths. Hio Fujita, who
had wished to kill Captain Gibson's crew in 1824, was a chief lieutenant. Genjiro Mumeta, who sought to assassinate the *Diana* men,
Shoin Yoshida, Kowan Fujimori, and other violent Imperialists,
rallied to Nariaki's standards. This Mito group of hotheads formed
the so-called *Sonno-joi* movement to "reverence the Emperor and to
expel the foreigners."

Nariaki disliked foreigners, but he respected their war engines.
To cope efficiently with the expected invasions, he drilled his troops
in foreign fashion, supplied them with modern weapons procured
through the Dutch, and built a frigate according to plans discovered
in an old Dutch book.

The Shogun feared that Nariaki, like the Satsuma leaders, was
planning to open independent trading. To Yedo, the mustering and
drilling of an efficient army seemed the prelude for rebellion. When,
therefore, Nariaki melted the bells of Buddhist monasteries into material for casting cannon, he was promptly punished. A charge of
sacrilege was sufficiently grave to warrant prosecution even of a man
of Nariaki's lineage. For nine years, after 1844, Nariaki was held at
Yedo under "protective guardianship." His province was administered by the Shogun's *metsuke*.

Perry's arrival afforded Nariaki a new opportunity. Japan, startled
at the revelation of her helplessness, appealed to the disgraced daimyo
for assistance. Nariaki became, in 1853, commissioner for maritime
defense. He, and his *Sonno-joi* group, prepared for an Imperialist
"restoration," perhaps even for a *coup d'état*.

A prime mover in this nationalist movement of the Perry time was
Torajiro "Shoin" Yoshida, son of a Choshu vassal, who came to Yedo
in 1851. From his teacher, Teizo Miyabe, a loyal propagandist for the
Imperialist cause, Yoshida learned to rely on the Mikado as the authentic source of Japan's greatness. The Shoguns, Yoshida believed,
were vacillating weaklings who truckled to the foreigners. The succession of decrees permitting fair treatment to aliens landing in Japan
instead of enforcement of the new stern prohibitions of an earlier day,
the willingness to listen to Western envoys, the wasting of money on

cultural aims instead of on military defenses seemed to Yoshida to prove the cowardice of Tokugawa leaders. He himself realized that neither he nor any other protagonist of the Mikado was ready for direct action to overthrow the Shogun, but he considered that the time was nearly ripe. "His learning was not a preparation for another time, but what he studied today was to be put into action today," wrote his biographer. "It was as though a teacher of fencing should open a fencing hall in the midst of a battlefield."

Yoshida was opposed to foreigners. He believed that granting aliens the right to live on Japan's soil was a defilement of the Empire. But he was sufficiently practical to understand that the alien armaments were far too powerful for an unprotected Japan to resist. He wanted Yedo defended by modern forts and by better guns, but he was also certain that mere resistance was not enough. He clamored for Japan to undertake a campaign of conquest in Korea, Manchuria, South America, and India! "This will be be very difficult," he wrote, "as we are not strong enough yet. We must ally ourselves with our neighbor Russia."

But though Yoshida resented the arrival of Westerners in Japan, he realized that Japan must have a wider knowledge of the Western ways than could be given by the Dutch. He resolved to go abroad to learn the science, and especially the warfare, of the Occidentals. To further his desire to form friendship with Russia until such time as Japan might fall upon the unsuspecting Muscovites, he hurried down to Nagasaki to take passage on Count Poutiatine's warship. Arriving after the ship had cleared, he went back to Yokohama to await Perry's return.

All this, he was quite well aware, was strictly against the Shogun's edict. No Japanese was allowed to leave the country under penalty of death. Yoshida was ready to risk his life, hoping to escape to some Western land where he might learn enough to overthrow the Shogun's rule, and eventually to dislodge the alien intruder. He pledged his friends in secret that "he would not be like the masses who were content to be happy, and who were not concerned about the coming of the foreign warships. Even though Mount Fuji should crumble, and the rivers become dry, yet I will not break my pledge."

Five different attempts to steal aboard Perry's ships went awry. As a last resort, Yoshida and his friend Shigesuke Kaneko stole a fishing boat and planned to row directly to the ships. By slipping a letter into the hands of an American officer while the foreigner was strolling along the shore, Yoshida gave Perry notice of the time when the two conspirators planned to board the vessels.

At midnight, the two men rowed out to the warships. They came to one ship, which refused them admission. Yoshida was told to go direct to Perry's flagship. On the way, Yoshida's oarlock broke, so he tied the oars to the gunwales of his skiff, first by his undershirt, and when that tore, by his belt. At Perry's ship, the sentry warned them off, pushing the skiff away with a boat hook. The Japanese leaped for the ship's anchor chains and pulled themselves aboard, but Perry's officers, unwilling to endanger Japan's friendship by harboring fugitives, turned the two men over to the Shogun's officials. They were caged, as penalty for their attempt to break the law.

The nationalistic movement, seeking to "restore" the Mikado, was not seriously hampered by the loss of Yoshida. New leaders, headed by the Mito daimyo, took up the campaign for the overthrow of the Tokugawa Shogunate.

Nariaki was not, however, free from supervision, nor spared from slander. Shogun Iyeyoshi's death, almost immediately after Perry's first departure, seemed suspicious. The populace might think that this calamity was the *kami's* vengeance for the arrival of the alien ships, but the more sophisticated circle of officials, sceptical of divine intervention, believed that Iyeyoshi died as the result of Nariaki's plotting. Nariaki was accused, perhaps falsely, of poisoning the Shogun in order that Nariaki's own son, Yoshinobu Hitotsubashi, might become the Shogun.

Hitotsubashi was passed by, and Iyesada of Kii succeeded to the post. It was a thankless promotion, for the new ruler inherited the duty of signing an unpopular treaty allowing aliens to enter the Empire. Perry's powerful armada prevented any refusal. Iyesada was compelled to grant commercial rights, even though he knew that Japanese public opinion was violently opposed to granting such concessions.

Promptly the Imperialist faction, supporting "restoration" of the Mikado, accused Iyesada of treachery to Japan's traditions. The anti-Tokugawa group, headed by Choshu, Satsuma, Tosa, Hizen, and Uwajima, joined with Mito in demanding that Iyesada resign the Shogunate. The Mikado himself, the intensely anti-alien Komei, violated his seclusion to issue a public condemnation of Iyesada for "truckling to the Americans." Such an open accusation was virtually an excommunication of the Shogun; in some respects it was equivalent to declaring him an outlaw.

The situation was decidedly favorable to the Imperialist coalition. Like Iyesada, they realized that the Shogun had no other recourse than to sign the treaty; they were willing to have him assume all the responsibility for an act which could not be avoided. They were determined to ignore the provisions of the treaty on the ground that the Shogun's approval could not bind the Empire when the Mikado publicly opposed the deed. If, then, the foreigners punished Iyesada for failure to enforce the treaty, the Imperialist coalition would be only too well pleased. Any attack upon the Shogun would merely strengthen the position of the Mikado, Komei.

Iyesada's prime minister, Naosuke Ii, whose formal title was Gotairo, realized the seriousness of Iyesada's position. Ii learned through his secret agents of the Imperialist conspiracy to discredit the Shogun. Knowing that only bold action could save his master, Ii ordered Nariaki back into retirement and threatened to use force to destroy the Imperialistic clique.

In the midst of this confusion, in 1858, Iyesada, the unlucky Shogun, suddenly died, under circumstances strangely similar to those of Iyeyoshi's death. Again charges of poisoning were rife, though the Imperialists insisted that Iyesada died of *mikka korori,* the "three-days' cholera" that was sweeping Japan and, according to rumor, killed "many millions." Ii kept the news of Iyesada's death secret for a month, in order that he might perfect his plans for choosing a desirable successor. The Imperialists, when the news became public, accused Ii of arbitrary rule.

Hitotsubashi renewed his candidacy for the Shogunate. The coalition gained strength by the addition of Echizen to the Imperialistic group, but again Hitotsubashi was passed over, this time in favor of twelve-year-old Iyemochi of Kii. When the daimyos of Echizen, Tosa, and Uwajima protested at the choice, Gotairo Ii deposed them from their offices. Nariaki was ordered to commit harakiri. On his refusal, Ii sent an assassin to Nariaki's palace. Nariaki was murdered, after which the assassin committed harakiri.

The Gotairo took desperate chances. The Mito clan demanded vengeance; several of the strongest daimyos planned to destroy him; Komei was openly hostile. Realizing that his life was seriously threatened, Ii inaugurated a reign of terror against the Imperialists.

Nearly two thousand malcontents were rounded up in 1859; all communication was cut off between Komei and the Imperialistic daimyos. The measures were emergency devices to prevent the Imperialist plots from overthrowing Ii and the new Shogun.

Among the victims of this "calamity of Bogo" was Shoin Yoshida. Caged for attempting to flee the country on Perry's Black Ships, he had suffered twenty months' imprisonment. Kaneko, his associate, had died in jail; Shozan Sakuma, whose writings had inspired the attempt, had been kept in captivity for seven months because of the effect his books had produced upon the susceptible Yoshida.

Following the imprisonment, Yoshida was allowed to go home to Choshu provided that he agree to live in solitude for the remainder of his life. Yoshida construed the sentence to mean that he might live in his own house and that he could there conduct a private school. Ostensibly the little institution was for the teaching of military science, but, in practice, it was devoted almost entirely to promoting Imperialistic sentiment. From this school, never larger than one small room of about twelve feet square, were to come leaders high in Japan's future statecraft. Hirobumi Ito, later to draft Japan's constitution, Kiosuke Yamagata, famous field marshal, Bunda Inouye, financier and patriot, and other important statesmen, were among his pupils. The clan lord, Yoshichika Mori, daimyo of Choshu, was well aware that Yoshida's school was teaching the forbidden doctrine of restoration of the Mikado, but he was by no means averse to any movement that might undermine the Tokugawas.

But Mori had enemies within the clan; some of these gave secret information to the Shogunate that Yoshida was traitorous. Yoshida was again arrested. Probably the imprisonment was wholly justified, for he confessed proudly that he had intended to kill Nobukatsu Mabe, one of the high Shogunate officials as a protest against continued Tokugawa "usurpation." He probably also plotted to murder the Gotairo when Ii refused to obey the Mikado's commands to expel foreigners. "When I heard," he wrote, "that the samurai of Owari, Mito, and Echizen conceived a plan to kill Ii, I leaped up and danced three hundred times." But the official charges upon which Yoshida was sentenced to death, in 1859 at the age of thirty, do not list these offenses.

The words of the condemnation give five charges: "He tried to go to the United States. In spite of being kept in custody in his own house he sent advice to the government concerning coast defenses.

He opposed hereditary accession to office and favored the selection of men of ability by popular election. He planned to give his opinion concerning foreigners to the daimyo of Shimosa. These things were done while he was kept in custody, which shows great disrespect for high officials."

A monument to Yoshida, the Imperialist, was erected at Shimoda in 1916. The centenary of his birth was observed in 1930 by a eulogistic radio address.

Yoshida's death did not end Imperialist agitation; rather, it tightened the alliance between daimyos and super-patriots working in Komei's interests. Ii was accused of being "frightened by the empty threats of foreign barbarians." Probably the Gotairo was no more anxious for foreign intercourse than was his spiritual master at Miako, but Ii knew that the failure to sign treaties would cause bombardment of the seaboard towns. The landing of foreign troops was not unthinkable.

Under the circumstances, therefore, Ii resorted to the guile that weaker parties frequently employ. He sought to satisfy the aliens by treaties which need not necessarily be enforced. Thus Japan could gain time to fortify her coasts and to store up modern arms.

Foreign envoys were accordingly encouraged to believe that the Shogun possessed full power to make binding treaties. The old distinction, long ago made by Kaempfer, between the temporal Kubosama and the spiritual Dairi, served now a useful purpose for Japan. If the treaty proved not popular, it could be repudiated as not having been properly authorized, since the Mikado at Miako had not given his assent. So, it was hoped, young Iyemochi might escape the fate of his two predecessors, each of whom died mysteriously after signing treaties with Commodore Perry. Ii's reign of terror might thus save the lives of Iyemochi and of the Gotairo.

The grant of concessions, seemingly important but in reality trivial, was a second Ii plan. The aliens were at a disadvantage because they knew little of Japan's geography. It was amply evident that the foreigners would not be satisfied by admission to the prison-like Deshima, but the Gotairo hoped to spare Yedo from pollution by offering the Westerners a port of very slight importance. In the Townsend Harris treaty, the harbor of Shimoda was opened.

The Gotairo outwitted the foreigners. Shimoda was a poor harbor, far removed from Yedo, but at least it was accessible to foreign ships, though the port was none too safe in time of storm. But Kanagawa,

substituted by the Yedo treaties, had worse disadvantages. It lay at
the head of a large, deep bay, to be sure, but the Kanagawa shores
were a mile distant from the channel. Shoal waters, deep enough for
native junks but too shallow even for small-sized steamers, washed
the Kanagawa coast. This was the place which, by the strict interpretation of the treaties, was to be opened to alien commerce.

Across the bay lay a safe and commodious harbor at a tiny fishing
settlement called Yokohama. Here deep water extended so close to
the shore that *hatobas,* or landing places, could be provided for the
largest foreign ships. British and American merchants discovered
its advantages and asked permission to build warehouses and offices
there, rather than at the Kanagawa site. The Gotairo assented with
what might have seemed a suspicious alacrity; he even built granite
jetties into the sea to make the harbor more acceptable. The consuls,
it appeared, were to reside at Kanagawa; merchants would reside
and trade at Yokohama.

Only a short time elapsed before the foreigners learned the reason
for the Japanese alacrity in selling land at Yokohama. The site was
almost an island, bounded on three sides by the sea and by deep tidal
creeks, and on the fourth by an extensive swamp. Two exits were
provided on land, one by bridge across a creek, the other by a three-
mile viaduct across the swamp. Both exits were guarded by gates
and by guardhouses garrisoned by armed soldiers. Yokohama, it was
evident, was a second Deshima. The merchants, living in a limited
area, would be effectively barred in time of stress even from their
consuls, particularly as stringent regulations forbade natives from
ferrying the foreigners across the water.

Another difficulty sprang from the effort to forbid to foreigners
the use of the great Tokaido road. Ostensibly the reason was to prevent friction between the aliens and the crowds of natives who
thronged the highway, but in reality the motive was to cut off the
consuls from land communication with the isolated merchants at
the new Deshima. The Tokaido road ran through the heart of Kanagawa; if foreigners could be barred from its use, no other means of
travel would be easily available between the two settlements. The
other streets were not well suited for the use of wheeled vehicles,
and a mounted man would be obliged to ride through regions none
too thoroughly policed.

A third dissension came from the currency question. All the treaties
carefully provided for the exchange of foreign money into Japanese

coins at specified rates, but a loophole had been left of which Japan was quick to take advantage. Obliged to exchange two silver pieces for each Mexican dollar, Japan created a special coinage. Instead of its old silver piece a new coin worth but one-third of the old was provided. The letter of the treaties was scrupulously observed but the foreigners were cheated.

The effect was not, however, precisely as the Japanese had anticipated. In the hasty arrangement of their new coinage, they overlooked a proper relationship between their gold and silver coins. Foreigners soon discovered that by buying Japan's gold and shipping it to China to be sold at its true bullion value, a profit of upwards of one hundred and fifty percent could be made. Nearly all other trade came to a standstill while the foreigners trafficked in gold.

A new arrangement, almost equally bad, was substituted. Though bound by treaty to provide native currency in exchange for foreign coins, the Japanese insisted that the requirement applied only to the diplomatic corps and not to merchants. They agreed, therefore, to exchange monthly a stipulated amount for the legations. Business men were to buy their Japanese coin in the open market at a much less favorable rate. Thus the diplomats gained a financial interest in the new arrangement; the merchants insisted that consuls and ministers were in effect receiving a subsidy. Underling officials could, on nominally small salaries, "live well, keep a pony and drink champagne."

The split in the foreign community, cleverly if not purposely promoted by the currency arrangements, widened because of the type of foreigners who came to dwell in Yokohama. Young, restless, and ambitious, hoping to make money with great speed and to return to Europe, the business men were all too often devoid of any interest in either the social or political life of Japan. There were few white women and many Japanese distractions. Gossip and backbiting characterized Yokohama society; gambling, drinking, and quarreling provided ample fuel for stirring the emotions.

The diplomats were probably of higher caliber, but a few were unfortunate choices for their posts. Harris, pledged to Kanagawa, never set foot in Yokohama and refused to recognize the legality of foreign residence there. Sir Rutherford Alcock, peppery medical man who had for fifteen years been accustomed to dealing with the tractable Chinese, rubbed even his countrymen the wrong way. Because he once declared in a fit of temper that the Yokohama Englishman was the scum of Europe, both he and every other member of the British diplomatic staff were, for eight years, blackballed from the British Yokohama Club. The tiny Colonel Edward St. John Neale, Alcock's first assistant, was a sour and suspicious man who, in the words of his associates, "did not understand the circumstances into which he was thrown." Even Townsend Harris, himself an estimable gentleman, was little liked by Europeans because of the general impression that he had deliberately warned that the French and English would use force against Japan.

Truth compels the admission, too, that the Japanese with whom the foreigners associated were not always of the most attractive class. Native adventurers thronged to Yokohama to do business with the strangers. Recruited often from the lower social levels and unaccustomed to commercial ways, they took their contracts lightly, resorted to fraud, adulterated their raw silk with sand, or supplied tea far below the specifications of the sample. "The conviction that Japanese was a synonym for dishonest trader became so firmly seated in the minds of foreigners," wrote Sir Ernest Satow, "that it was impossible for any friendly feeling to exist."

XXVII

THE BLOODY YEARS

JAPAN was opened, against the express wish of the Mikado at Miako. Neither Komei, the Emperor, nor Gotairo Ii, prime minister for young Iyemochi, desired the aliens to enter. Nothing but the fear of force secured Japanese signatures to treaties which they would willingly have repudiated.

There was, if possible, even less enthusiasm among the commoners. Popular superstition firmly linked the foreigners to the coming of catastrophe. The diplomats and merchants were believed to be people of exceptionally low standards. For years after the opening of Japan to trade, the populace complained that the treaty ports "emitted a strong foreign odor that nauseates Japanese." The aliens were looked upon as hypocrites, as defrauders, as superstitious, corrupt, degraded folk whose "astonishing dissipation, and immoral, ignominious, unhuman, and brutal action merit the contempt of Japanese."

Nariaki's *sonno-joi* and the *kuge,* the Kyoto court officials, united in a resolve to drive out the aliens in order that "the Imperial heart shall find peace." Gotairo Ii, realizing that the foreigners were too strong to be pushed away by force, strove to mitigate the hostility and, through his secret agents, continued to arrest *sonno-joi* plotters whenever he could safely do so. But the opposition was too powerful for the Gotairo to crush.

Sir Rutherford Alcock was amazed at the intensity of opposition. Within a month after his arival, he was obliged to send a sharp protest to the Yedo officials.

No officer of the missions of either country, Great Britain or the United States, can walk out of the official residence without risk of rudeness, offense and violence of the most wanton and determined character. Day after day, these insults and outrages are offered; they increase in frequency and violence; no functionary interferes. Officers of the government are sometimes the assailants.

The protest required repeated renewal. For seven months after July 1859, when, Kanagawa was opened to foreign trade, the aliens walked in constant terror, never certain of their safety, and never assured that the Japanese authorities were making any real effort to protect them. Three Russians, landing from Count Muraviev-Amurski's frigate in August, were literally cut to pieces in a crowded market place. Russia secured a public apology and was given the promise that a memorial chapel should be built by the Japanese and kept forever guarded, but the murderers were never punished. Instead, the Kanagawa governor, who was presumably disgraced for allowing the outrage to occur, was later named by Japan as one of her chief envoys to St. Petersburg. Only the formal protest of the diplomatic corps prevented this typically oriental revenge upon the Russians.

The unprovoked murder of the three Russians was the first of a series of horrible massacres perpetrated by the two-sworded samurai retainers of the Imperialist daimyos. The Chinese servant of the French consul was attacked in broad daylight at the gates of the Consulate. "The cavities of both chest and abdomen were laid open by sword cuts." Long afterwards, a Japanese arrested for a less serious crime confessed that he had killed the Chinese in the belief that any person wearing "foreign clothes" was a European.

Undoubtedly the reactionaries planned to drive out the foreigners by systematic terrorism. During 1860, violence was unrestrained. Early in January, an Imperialist plot resulted in the simultaneous burning of the foreign settlement at Yokohama and of the Shogun's palace at Yedo. Rumors were widespread that the Japanese were arming for a massacre of foreigners. Townsend Harris learned that fifty ruffians planned to kill the Yokohama residents.

The first victim was, however, not a foreigner, but a British-naturalized Japanese. Dankichi, one of the sailors on the junk picked up by the *Auckland* in 1851, was serving as Alcock's translator. To Japanese such service has always seemed a form of treason. Kodaya had been sent into life imprisonment for teaching his language to the Russians; as late as 1936 all the Japanese attachés at the Russian Embassy at Tokyo were arrested for having translated vernacular newspaper items for the use of Russian diplomats. Dankichi was popularly regarded as a traitor to his country, first for having accepted British protection by his naturalization, and secondly for informing Alcock of the meaning of Japanese documents.

Quite possibly, Dankichi invited an attack. The ex-sailor, suddenly raised to a position of minor importance, was unduly elated. He swaggered about the vicinity of the Legation dressed in European clothes and, in lieu of the two samurai swords which his low caste denied him, stuck a huge pistol into his waistband. The Japanese constantly baited their ill-tempered fellow countryman, and Dankichi came into frequent collision with insolent retainers of the daimyos.

The native officials were very well aware that Dankichi was in danger. The Yedo commissioners of foreign affairs sent one of their number to Sir Rutherford suggesting that Dankichi be transferred out of Japan to some safer post. Alcock, insisting that Dankichi, as a naturalized Englishman, was entitled to reside at the Legation, refused to heed the warning. He thought that the danger was exaggerated, and that the Japanese were anxious to get rid of Dankichi because he was too efficient a translator. "He was undoubtedly obnoxious to the Government, as one capable of furnishing me with information not otherwise obtainable."

The blow fell in full daylight, while Dankichi was standing in the center of a group of women and children near the Legation flagstaff. "One or two men stole stealthily down to where he was, and a short sword was buried to the hilt in his body, transfixing him as he stood." The assailant was known to be one of two men, but though the police arrested both suspects, neither was punished. Alcock was convinced that the police had been intimidated into freeing the murderers.

To the astonishment of the Japanese, the murdered linguist was given a funeral equal in pomp to that which a daimyo might receive. The entire diplomatic corps attended and, at Alcock's insistence, over the Japanese protest, the Yedo commissioners of foreign affairs mourned publicly at the burial ceremonies of a low-caste former sailor. To many Japanese, the rites thus demanded by the British seemed a studied insult to the dignity of Japan's statesmen.

Six hours later, the anti-alien faction took its revenge. The French Legation was set afire, and an attendant was violently assaulted on the Legation grounds. The French, it was generally believed, were special victims because they were working in close association with

the British. When, soon thereafter, the French and British diverged
in their policies, the French were comparatively free from assault.
Holland, another British ally, also suffered. Within three weeks, two
Dutch sea captains were murdered on the main street of Yokohama.
Their heads and legs were almost amputated, and horrible gashes
were cut on both heads and torsos. One of the Dutchmen evidently
tried to defend himself by grasping the blade in his hand, for three
fingers were severed from one hand, while the right hand was cut
off at the wrist. It was found a hundred yards away.

These were obviously "political murders deliberately planned and
executed for political purposes." Alcock again protested, in the name
of the diplomatic corps, but his complaints won little notice. Japan
replied by sending policemen "who keep us in an odious quarantine
and prevent all free access to us. A cordon follows us to prevent all
educated and respectable Japanese from approaching near us."

The foreigners were not the only sufferers. The Imperialist clique
was determined to punish the Gotairo for opening the Empire in
violation of the Mikado's expressed desire. Ii knew that his life was
forfeit, but he hoped that his opponents would recognize the situation
and realize that he could not have acted differently. His plan of
offering the alien tricky concessions, Ii hoped, might win support
even from his enemies.

The Mito, Satsuma, Choshu, Tosa, Hizen, and Owari coalition was
not appeased. On a wet, bleak, half-snowy, half-rainy morning in
March 1860, when Ii was on his way to the Shogun's palace, his small
escort was caught between two great retinues. His guards were hampered by their heavy, straw raincoats, and when twenty armed men
suddenly attacked the Gotairo, no effective resistance could be offered. The Gotairo was cut to pieces.

Twenty-two men of Ii's retinue were killed in the attack. In *Kinsei
Sakurada Kibun,* the Imperialist version of the affair, a note of
jubilation is stressed throughout. "Just as the terrible scene had
closed," the account relates, "the snowstorm cleared away and the
sky showed bright and radiant like a spring morning. The blood-
bespattered snow looked as if a shower of cherry blossoms had fallen."
The omens, evidently, predicted a glorious future for Japan now that
the oppressor was no more.

One of the assailants ran off "with a gory trophy in his hand." It
was supposed to be the head of the Gotairo, hacked off on the spot.
"But strangest of all these startling incidents, it is further related

that two heads were missing, and that which was seen in the fugitive's hand was only a lure to the pursuing party, while the real trophy had been secreted on the person of another, and was thus carried off, though the decoy paid the penalty of his life."

Ii's head was carried to the Mito daimyo, "who spat upon it with maledictions." Then it was taken to Kyoto, to be exposed at the public execution place. Over it was fastened a placard, "This is the head of a traitor who has violated the most sacred law of Japan, that which forbids the admission of foreigners into the country."

During the eighty years that have elapsed since the tragic murder of the Gotairo, Japan has used the popular reaction toward Naosuke Ii as an index of the national feeling toward the foreigners. The Ii supporters have, by and large, included those who favored foreign theories; the antagonists of Ii have been the super-patriots who hold that Japan stands above and beyond all alien peoples.

Few but the members of his old Hikone clan now profess a veneration for the baffled statesman who signed treaties with the outer world because he could not help himself. When, in 1893, Saburo Shimada, one of the pioneer parliamentarians, prepared a defense of Ii, vindicating the Gotairo from the charge of treason, a wave of protest engulfed the Empire. Scholars of the Mito clan, aided by the leading journalist of the day, made open charges that Shimada had been bribed to clear the Gotairo's name. A manuscript, embodying the "truth," as seen through Mito eyes, was prepared and was used to extort money from the Ii family, under the blackmailing threat that unless the Ii descendants bought the papers at huge cost, the Ii name would be forever blackened. Although the facts were generally known, no real effort seems to have been put forth by the Satsuma-Choshu clan government of the day to punish the extortionists.

Again, in 1909, when the Hikone clan erected as a memorial to Ii, the finest portrait bronze statue ever cast to that date in Japan, the Satsuma, Choshu, and Mito groups protested vehemently. Unluckily for the Imperialist factions, the government in power was headed by Count Okuma, an ancient opponent of the so-called Sat-Cho coalition. In a blistering speech, Okuma castigated the Ii murderers, but in the following year, on the fiftieth anniversary of the attack, a solemn religious ceremony was held in honor of the assassins' memory.

By 1920, public sentiment was so strongly anti-Ii that a play, *The Death of Ii,* had to be withdrawn from production at Tokyo because of the bitter opposition of the Mito groups. The police, it was ascertained, refused to offer protection to any actors in the play because the drama was assumed to be a warm defense of Ii's actions. In 1935, the great twenty-two-foot statue was thrown down by a reactionary mob. The anti-alienists were in complete control of Japan's policies.

For eight months after the Ii murder, comparative quiet reigned. Outwardly, the restless samurai were accepting the presence of the foreigners; but, at constant conferences between the Imperialists and the Tokugawa faction, plans for united action were being drawn. The death of Ii was sufficient proof for the Shogunate that the isolationists were in almost complete control.

Prussia, however, pressed for a treaty similar to those secured by her European and American rivals. Much against their will, because the Germans threatened force, Iyemochi's advisers were compelled to consent. C. J. Heusken, a Hollander employed by Harris as interpreter, acted as the Prussians' interpreter in the deliberations.

Soon after the conclusion of the treaty, in January 1861, Heusken, riding home at night from the Prussian Legation, was suddenly waylaid by half a dozen swordsmen. His native guard, the *yakunin,* who accompanied him bearing lanterns marked with the Shogun's insignia as a safe-conduct, fled. Heusken had only a hunting whip for his protection. He was cut down from his horse, was mercilessly slashed, and was left to die in a ditch. Almost simultaneously, the foreign affairs commissioner who had concluded the treaty committed harakiri to show his shame at having granted foreigners the right to reside in the Empire.

No punishments seem to have been visited on the assassins who killed Heusken, the Dutch sea captains, the Russians, or the French servant; no real investigations were made into the arson at the Legations. The foreign envoys, realizing that the Yedo government was either unwilling or unable to guarantee the safety of foreigners, announced their intention of leaving Yedo—which was precisely what the reactionaries desired—and of retiring to Yokohama. There, they declared, the aliens would be under the protection of foreign warships and could be guarded by bluejackets and marines landed from the fleet. Harris alone refused to leave the Shogun's capital. He sent a letter of protest at the Heusken murder, but did not threaten to bring troops. Four weeks after the departure of the allied envoys, the Shogun sent a formal invitation for the diplomats to return. The fear of armed intervention was a determining factor. In order to forestall the landing of large military forces, the Shogunate made a show of welcoming the aliens. Yedo was gaily decorated at the time of the reëntry; each of the ministers was welcomed by a twenty-one-gun salute.

During his stay at Yokohama, Sir Rutherford Alcock arranged for a trip through Japan to visit all the open ports. The Shogunate was aghast at his intention, considering his visit to the interior a violation of Japan's privacy; it tried in every possible way to dissuade him from the trip. The ease of water transportation was stressed, and the difficulties of land travel were vividly described. The Yedo officials warned the British that banditry was common in the interior, and that they, as guardians of an envoy's safety, were unwilling to expose him to danger. They told of the recurrent famines, of the hardships that the British must face, and of the reluctance of ignorant peasants to meet Westerners. Each of the warnings served only to strengthen Alcock's belief that extra-territoriality was justified, and that Britain must continue to exert strong military control over the regions where Englishmen were permitted to reside.

Insisting that both the Harris and the Elgin treaties gave diplomats the right to travel where they pleased, Alcock refused to modify his plans. One of his objectives was the climbing of Fujiyama. Because this feat was ordinarily possible only during July and August, the Shogunate delayed the expedition so long that Alcock suspected the Shogunate waited until an early snowfall made the mountain inaccessible.

In all probability, this overland trip first convinced Sir Rutherford that the foreigners were supporting the wrong political faction. Curious because the Yedo authorities argued so earnestly against his going to Kyoto, and because of the elaborate precautions taken against his associating with any Japanese other than the officials assigned by Yedo, Alcock began an exhaustive study of Japan's government. He and his assistant, Sir Ernest Mason Satow, had learned to converse fluently in colloquial Japanese; Satow, in addition, could read the characters. Both men discovered that the real ruler was not the Shogun, but the Mikado. They determined that future British treaties should be made with Kyoto, not with Yedo, and that the Mikado should be asked to ratify the treaties already signed. The British thereafter so reworded their documents that the Shogun no longer seemed accepted as an equal to the British Queen; the documents referred to him as equal in rank to the Prime Minister.

Alcock returned to Yedo in July 1861, and found the city buzzing with anger against the aggressions of British and Russian naval forces. Russia had tried to take the island of Tsushima, in the Korea Straits, as a naval base; England had occupied the fine, deep harbor of Port Hamilton, off the southernmost tip of Korea. The daimyo of Tsushima, whose sphere of influence included both places, was indignant. His retainers had come to Yedo to demand revenge.

Evidently the original plan was to waylay Alcock somewhere en route in the interior, but the retainers failed to intercept the British minister. At midnight of his first day at the Legation, he was awakened by a rush of *ronin,* the strong-arm samurai desperadoes. The 150 *yakunin,* provided by the Shogun as a Legation guard, fled in terror. The five Englishmen of the Legation staff were left to fight off the attackers. Secretary of Legation Lawrence Olyphant (whose *Account of Lord Elgin's Mission* had first awakened Satow's interest in Japan) was dangerously wounded; eighteen ronin were injured. Three of the attackers committed harakiri because their assault had failed.

A document, signed by fourteen names, was left behind when the assailers finally withdrew. It indicated that the attack was part of a definite anti-alien conspiracy:

I, though I am a person of low standing, have not patience to stand by, and see the sacred Empire defiled by the foreigner. This time I have undertaken in my heart to carry out my master's will. Though being altogether humble myself, I cannot make the light of my country to shine in foreign lands, yet with a little faith, and a warrior's power, I hope, though I am a person of low degree, to bestow upon my country a great benefit. If this thing, from time to time, may cause the foreigner to retire, and partly tranquillize the minds of the Mikado and the government, I shall take to myself the highest praise. Regardless of my own life, I am determined to take action.

Governor Ando, at Alcock's insistence, tried to trace the ronin. His zeal resulted in no prosecutions, but a menacing placard was posted on his door, warning him to stop his investigations. Some weeks later he was attacked by twelve armed men who resented his "championing the foreign cause."

A British warship was sent to Tsushima to register a protest with the daimyo. Blandly the daimyo denied all knowledge of the incident.

He even professed complete ignorance that Russians had ever visited the island, though they had been occupying a convenient harbor for almost half a year. The British gained no satisfaction, and realizing that the English presence at Port Hamilton put them in a somewhat equivocal position, the Englishmen returned to Yedo. Sir Rutherford Alcock, announcing that Great Britain "evinced a profound sympathy for Japan," agreed with the Russians for a mutual withdrawal from the captured harbors.

Japan, in appreciation of the peaceful settlement of the naval station affair, promised to provide more efficient protection for the foreigners. With truly oriental humor, the Shogunate suggested that Alcock command all Englishmen not to use the Japanese highways. Thus, it was pointed out, the Britishers would be safeguarded against ronin who might otherwise cause them injury. When Alcock refused to have his countrymen penned in small settlements, the Japanese locked the Yokohama gates, forcing the British into an isolation similar to that of Deshima. Alcock demanded that the gates be opened, under threat of sending marines to batter down the barriers. Japan quickly explained that the gates had been closed under a misunderstanding.

Seemingly propitious circumstances marked the opening of 1862. No violence had been employed against foreigners for several months; Alcock, whom the Japanese believed too truculent, was home in Great Britain on a leave of absence; the first Japanese envoys sent to England and America reported that they had received warm welcomes. In May, the Shogun approved a plan for opening a Yedo University for the study of foreign languages, science, and history. Townsend Harris, forced out of office by the political shifts in the United States, left Japan, feeling that he had seen the secluded Empire safely introduced into the community of peaceful nations.

Japan regretted his departure, but did not feel the need of putting up a monument to his memory until 1927, long after Roland S. Morris, American Ambassador during the World War, had renewed Japanese interest in the first diplomat to treat Japan as an equal. Even to this day, the Harris memorial at Shimoda, where he lived as consul, is less grand than that erected in honor of his serving maid, Okichi. The girl's monument, incidentally, is smaller than that erected by the Butchers' Guild in memory of the cow killed to provide Harris with beef during one of his illnesses. The animal is mistakenly regarded as the first of its kind to be slaughtered for food in Japan. Since 1934 an annual festival has been held in April in honor of the cow, the local hot springs, and the Perry Black Ships.

The calm of 1862 was rudely shattered. On the anniversary of the ronin attack upon Sir Rutherford Alcock, a daring samurai made a single-handed attack upon the British Legation. By giving the proper password, he made his way safely through the grounds to the sleeping quarters of gingery Colonel St. John Neale, the chargé d'affaires. The Japanese guard of five hundred soldiers, supplied by a pro-Satsuma daimyo, fled without putting up resistance. Two Englishmen, caught unawares, were murdered. Then a sentry, stationed outside Neale's bedroom, gave a sharp challenge. The invader, Gumpei Ito, ran away to his own house, where he committed harakiri.

Again the British protested to the Shogun. No formal answer was received, for, although the Yedo authorities feared armed intervention, they dared not go on public record as caring for the safety of the foreigners. Such a written document would prove to the ronin and the other fervid super-patriots that the Shogunate was acting in the foreign interest. The restless Imperialists were already sufficiently dangerous without giving them excuse for further action. Yedo preferred to let such matters rest with verbal answers that might satisfy the foreigners without committing itself too publicly.

A more brutal incident followed in September. Three Englishmen escorted a lady, the sister-in-law of one of their number, on a horseback ride along the Tokaido, within the treaty limits. Two of the gentlemen, Woodthorpe Clarke and William Marshall, were Yokohama merchants; the third, Charles Lennox Richardson, was a Shanghailander on his way to retirement in England.

Seven miles from Yokohama, the party met a Satsuma retinue. Scores of two-sworded warriors, accompanied by a hundred men, marched in single file on either side of the highway. The foreigners, well aware that Japanese propriety required travelers to give the right of way to any high official, were in a quandary. They could not easily draw over to the side of the road because the daimyo's train occupied the entire Tokaido. In attempting to guide their horses entirely off the road to vacant ground which would not be traversed by the procession, they committed a double fault. They seemed, for a moment, to be about to block the passage of the marching men; more unforgivably, they rode to a small hillock above the level of the road.

For a commoner, and particularly for a foreigner, and most of all for an alien woman, to stand upon an eminence looking down upon a Japanese noble constituted a grievous breach of etiquette. Altitude, even to this day, takes an important place in native courtesy codes. Although Japanese and foreign versions of the so-called Richardson incident differ on almost every other point, both are agreed that Satsuma boiled with indignation.

Angered samurai, convinced that their chief, Saburo Shimadzu, had been insulted, fell upon the British horsemen. Richardson was killed; the other two men were badly wounded; Mrs. Borrodaile, her face, hands, and clothing spattered with blood, galloped to safety at Yokohama.

Little question was voiced at the time concerning the Satsuma iniquity. Thirteen years later, Edward H. House, an American newspaperman working as publicity agent for the Japanese, defended Shimadzu's deed. The riders, House declared, had broken the law of the land by not dismounting and kneeling by the roadside, heads bowed in humility, until the Satsuma retinue had passed. The Satsuma men, insulted by the want of proper deference, acted in accordance with Japanese custom. This curious defense, it was learned long after, was inspired by the American minister, Robert H. Pruyn, who followed Townsend Harris and who, by virtue of an anti-British bias, wrote a report to Washington which "made as little use of the facts as possible." Still later a Japanese publicist, Inazo Ota Nitobe, further embroidered on the facts by imagining that Richardson had shouted, "I know how to deal with these dogs." There seems to be no basis whatever for the Nitobe accusations.

Certainly the contemporary Yokohama residents felt that the Satsuma samurai had acted with ruthless savagery. The hot bloods demanded that a volunteer force go forth to capture Saburo Shimadzu so that suitable punishment could be inflicted. Neale, the British chargé, forbade the attempt. He feared that the capture of Shimadzu would not only bring on war between England and Satsuma, but might easily precipitate a Japanese civil war between the Imperialists, defending Satsuma, and the Shogun who would thus seem a British tool.

From a long-range aspect, Neale's advice was undoubtedly wise, but to the fiery young Britishers of the settlement, it seemed a craven's opinion. When, on the day after the outrage, the British consul issued a formal request to all British subjects asking them to avoid using the Tokaido "until the Japanese Government have completed the measures of precaution upon which they are at present engaged," the hostility of the settlement toward their own officials was intensified. The native Japanese, it was soon evident, construed the British actions as evidence of the inferiority of the foreigners. A proper retort, the Japanese believed, to the murderous actions of Shimadzu's men would have been an immediate military attack.

Neale referred the matter to his superiors in London, and new difficulties arose during the delay. Believing that, by the issue of two further warnings against using the Tokaido, the Englishmen were properly subdued, the Japanese undertook to expel the British diplomat.

After the attack upon the British Legation, the foreign envoys had demanded a safe site upon which legations might be built. The conditions laid down were that the locations should be accessible by both land and sea and that they should be capable of easy fortification. The hill of Goten-yama in Yedo seemed to the foreigners an admirable situation. It was an elevation raised perhaps a hundred feet above the surrounding plain, it completely commanded the Shinagawa forts which lay below, and it dominated the Tokaido. A few riflemen could easily control all possible approaches.

From Iyeyasu's time, Goten-yama had been set aside for public recreation. Popular opposition to the granting of the site to foreigners became intense; the Mikado issued orders that the hill should not be alienated; ronin announced that they would forcibly prevent the use of Goten-yama by the foreigners. The British and the French, none the less, insisted that their safety required the hill, and that the attacks upon individuals and legations were sufficient proof that the Japanese were either unwilling or unable to protect the foreigners. The British insistence was particularly strong after the Japanese government announced, in January 1863, that ronin had gone to Yokohama to kill all the foreign diplomatic chiefs. Both British and French pressed forward the work of finishing the Yedo offices on the safe Goten-yama hill; the Hollanders and the Americans hurried to start operations.

On February 1, when the British Legation was virtually finished, fire destroyed the Goten-yama buildings. Flames burst out in several places simultaneously. During the conflagration, explosions of gunpowder frequently occurred. The British were positive that the fire was the work of Choshu incendiaries. "No sooner was it evident that the flames and combustibles had done their work effectively than a salute was fired from a Japanese man-of-war at the Shinagawa anchorage."

Neale protested to the government and was promised a military guard. But when the guard arrived it was discovered that the care of the British was entrusted to the same Satsuma troops who had killed Richardson. Neale objected, but the Shogun replied that he could do nothing more until he had paid a formal call upon the Mikado at Kyoto. Neale believed that the Kyoto trip was merely an excuse to delay action.

On April 6 Neale, after receiving London's orders, demanded reparation for the Richardson murder and for the attacks on the Legation. He pointed out the British tolerance and remarked on the fact that though British citizens far outnumbered any other foreigners in Japan, "no noticeable instance of violence against Japanese has been complained of regarding one of them." His instructions from London, he declared, compelled him to make "the following explicit and peremptory demands: first, an ample and formal apology for the offense of permitting a murderous attack on British subjects passing on a road open by Treaty to them. Secondly, the payment of 100,000 pounds as a penalty on Japan for this offense." Twenty days were allowed for Japan's consent or rejection. If Japan failed to answer satisfactorily, the British fleet would act.

By a supplement to the ultimatum, Neale also asked for the arrest of the chief perpetrators of the Richardson murder, their trial in the presence of a British naval delegation, and their execution for murder. He demanded £25,000 additional indemnity from Satsuma.

The ultimatum expired without any action being taken by the Japanese. They asked for, and received, an extension of time on the plea that the personal attention of the Shogun should be given to the British demands. On May 16, nearly four weeks after the expiration of the ultimatum, the Shogun's Council announced that his return to Yedo was indefinitely postponed and that the British would be required to wait for their answer for at least three months and perhaps for a thousand days. It was very evident that the Shogun intended to do nothing about the British demands.

Meanwhile the American minister, Robert H. Pruyn, was living quietly at his Yedo temple. On May 24, he too suffered from the general anti-foreign persecution. The American Legation was burned to the ground, General Pruyn losing personal effects valued at $10,000. A week later, as he sat at dinner in temporary quarters, an officer rushed in to warn him that he must depart at once, as his life was in danger. Pruyn left forthwith for Yokohama. Exactly the same tactics were used to secure the removal of the American consul from Kanagawa to the new Deshima at Yokohama.

On the same day, May 31, that Pruyn moved to Yokohama, an official communication to all consuls announced that ronin were so numerous that Yokohama was in danger. Additional Japanese guards were posted about the settlement; a strong military force guarded the *hatoba*. The foreigners were completely cut off from all communication by either land or sea. Rumors multiplied that the Mikado had issued orders that all aliens were to be expelled from the country by June 25.

Neale continued his negotiations until he was convinced that "the Japanese Ministers have flagrantly, unequivocally and designedly broken their faith." On June 24 he put the matter into the hands of the British fleet. The results were almost instantaneous. The money, "in the form of 440,000 good Mexican dollars," was delivered to his door at seven o'clock the following morning.

THE GUNBOATS FORCE PEACE

IF Iyemochi hoped that, by paying the debt really owed by Satsuma, the peril of British bombardment would be ended, he was disappointed. Later in the same morning, June 25, 1863, Komei, the Mikado, forwarded an order which the Shogun could not ignore. Iyemochi was commanded to tell the foreigners that all ports must be closed and all aliens evacuated from the Empire.

The diplomats were enraged. Colonel Neale, as dean of the corps, was instructed to deliver an indignant protest. "The indiscreet communication," Neale told the Shogun, "is unparalleled in the history of all nations, civilized or uncivilized. It is, in fact, a declaration of war against the whole of the treaty powers. If the consequences are not at once arrested, Japan will receive the severest and most merited chastisement."

Probably because Iyemochi considered that his duty was fulfilled by the mere delivery of the Mikado's edict, no further immediate action on the expulsion was taken at Yedo. Eight days after the peremptory demand for the dismissal of the foreigners, the Council formally apologized for the Richardson murder. So far as Yedo was concerned, the incident was closed. The Shogunate had satisfied all the British demands, although in extremely dilatory fashion. Nothing had been done to punish Satsuma.

Though the aliens at Yedo and at Yokohama were not molested, the more remote daimyos attempted to enforce the Mikado's expulsion edict. Mori of Choshu, commanding the Straits of Shimonoseki, between Kyushu and the main island, fired upon an American steamer. Two Choshu warships, flying the Japanese war ensign, joined with the shore batteries to attack the little merchant vessel

Pembroke. The ship escaped, suffering only slight damages, but the American minister, General Pruyn, was outraged. Because of his desire to give America a favored place in Japanese opinion, he, like Townsend Harris, had patiently endured treatment which had called forth angry protests from the British. Pruyn had even arranged to purchase two modern warships for the Japanese from American builders; his enemies declared that he received a commission on the deal.

Japan's official explanation was that she had a right to close the waterway, and that the *Pembroke* refused to heed the blank cartridges fired as warnings. The master of the *Pembroke* retorted that no such warning shots were fired, but that signal guns, set off along the shore, had been used to start the attack. In any case, Pruyn pointed out, the proper procedure, in the event that Japan desired to close the straits, was not to fire upon innocent merchant ships, but to give ample notice through the consulates of the intention to close traffic. No such notice was ever given to the alien consuls.

Pruyn sent the warship *Wyoming* to exact retribution. On its arrival at Shimonoseki, the *Wyoming* was itself fired upon by the two Japanese steamers and by six shore batteries. No previous warning was given, nor had the *Wyoming* any opportunity for announcing the purpose of her visit. In an engagement which lasted seventy minutes, the *Wyoming* exploded the boilers of one ship, sank the second, and silenced the batteries. In return the American ship received eleven shots in her hull, and about thirty through her rigging. The *Wyoming* then returned to Yokohama.

Other foreign ships also suffered. A French mailship, lying at anchor in the straits, was fired upon by the batteries. Two days later a Dutch vessel, carrying the consul-general, was attacked, receiving twenty-one projectiles in the hull, and losing four dead. Both ships escaped, and reported their experiences to their diplomatic representatives.

Holland had then no warships in nearby waters, but France, with a frigate and a gunboat close at hand, undertook a punitive expedition. Since all reports agreed that only the forts on the north side of the straits, those controlled by Daimyo Daizen Mori of Choshu, had been guilty of offense, and since the Shogunate professed complete ignorance of the attacks, the French resolved on vengeance. The ships bombarded and silenced the forts, landed a small force of 250 men to rout a Choshu army of two thousand infantry, and after the barracks were burned, the expeditionary force departed.

The consequences were quite different from those anticipated by the French. Choshu, realizing that its military forces were inefficient, undertook a complete reorganization of its army. Daimyo Mori, profiting by the overwhelming defeat of his forces, resolved to build a military force stronger than that of any other provincial leader. For years following the French attack, Choshu clansmen were the most skilled warriors of the Empire. After the Mikado's "restoration" in 1868, the Imperial armies were long regarded as under the especial care of Choshu officers.

Satsuma, similarly, took over the navy leadership. When, after long and fruitless dickering with the Shogun, the British suspected that no real punishment would be inflicted upon Saburo Shimadzu for the Richardson affair, seven English warships were sent to Kagoshima. The Satsuma officials gave the naval officers a discourteous reception and refused to accept the British ultimatum for punishment of the plotters. Such matters, they said, should be discussed with the Shogun, for he had made the treaty admitting aliens to Japan.

Satsuma, like Iyemochi, temporized. Regret was expressed that the murderers could not be found, but, said the Satsuma officials, no indemnity could possibly be paid until after the culprits had been arrested. Shoji Ichiji, the chief Satsuma spokesman, then suddenly evidenced a desire to spend a great amount of time aboard the British flagship. The English officers were flattered, not knowing that Ichiji's intention was to make a sudden onslaught upon them to kill the principal naval leaders. He later regretted that the British were so well guarded that the attack was not possible.

England waited a reasonable time, and then, realizing that Satsuma had no real intention of complying with the British demands, took drastic action. Three Satsuma steamers, for which a quarter of a million dollars had been paid, were confiscated. The shore batteries fired upon the British fleet, and the British replied by silencing the batteries. Then the captured ships were burned, the city of Kagoshima was destroyed, and scores of Japanese were killed. The British loss was thirteen killed and fifty wounded. When a typhoon began to blow, the British squadron withdrew to safer anchorages. Satsuma claimed that the withdrawal was a naval victory for Japan.

Three months later, Satsuma officials visited Yokohama to pay the indemnity and to make the requisite apologies for the Richardson attack. Later it was learned that the indemnity money had been borrowed from the Shogun and that it never was repaid. The murderers of Richardson were never identified.

Satsuma thereafter concentrated its attention on building an efficient naval force to prevent a repetition of the Kagoshima affair. Just as Choshu long controlled the Japanese army, Satsuma naval officers dominated the Imperial navy.

Japan now realized that foreigners could not be dislodged by military force. Her next attempt was by passive resistance. Alien merchants found new hindrances in their business relationships. Silk became scarce, for Iyemochi in 1863 ordered the destruction of three-quarters of the silk crop. Ostensibly the edict was to maintain high prices, but the foreigners were sure that the real intention was to force them out of business. Eighteen large foreign firms were compelled to close their doors.

Even with the silk restrictions in force, the foreigners might have continued business had they been able to secure sufficient coolies for the 'longshore work, or if the supply of coastwise shipping had been sufficient. Since these were Japanese government monopolies, the foreigners could do nothing other than to register protests with the Shogunate. The alien merchants also complained that the Japanese discriminated against Yokohama by neglecting to install proper drainage, good paving, or efficient lighting in the native sections of the city. Similar complaints concerning communities inhabited by foreigners have since been common, especially after the great 1923 earthquake when the foreign business section of Yokohama was among the last portions of the devastated area to be restored.

Young Iyemochi was in a serious predicament. The foreign powers were holding him responsible for the maintaining of good order and for the full observance of all treaty obligations. At Kyoto the Mikado, Komei, was insisting on immediate expulsion of the foreigners. The Shogun knowing that the foreigners were too strong, did not dare transmit the Mikado's orders in their full severity. Nor, with the great daimyos of Mito, Choshu, Satsuma, Tosa, and Hizen arrayed upon the Mikado's side, did he dare defy the spiritual chief. He tried by secret encouragements to conciliate both sides and succeeded, as might have been expected, in antagonizing everybody.

The silk orders were a case in point. Kyoto and Osaka were pla-
carded with notices warning Japanese against sending silk, tea, or
cotton to the Yokohama factors, and insisting that merchants who
owed money to Yokohama traders must not pay the bills. "If you
disregard this," said the notices, "you, your children and all your
relations will be crushed." The placards were signed "The executors
of justice."

Iyemochi was well aware that such notices could not be posted
without some type of official sanction from the court at Kyoto, but
he dared not admit the knowledge to the angry foreigners. By
promising to remedy the difficulty, he merely brought down upon
himself the further accusation that he was leagued with foreigners
to betray Japan. The accusation was considered proved when, in
September 1863, Iyemochi, under French pressure, agreed to withdraw the June order requiring all foreigners to leave the Empire.

The renewed hostility to foreigners became evident on October
15, when the horribly mutilated body of Sub-lieutenant Camus, a
French officer, was found lying in a bridle path about a mile from
Yokohama. Twenty wounds, most of them serious enough to be
fatal, had been inflicted. The right arm was completely severed from
the trunk and was found ten paces from the body. The left arm was
hanging by a piece of skin, the right side was open to the heart, the
vertebral column was completely severed, and the throat was cut.
The murderer was never identified.

Nine days later, Pruyn and the Dutch envoy were summoned to
attend a special session of the Shogun's Council. They were informed
that the proclamation closing the ports was withdrawn—an untrue
statement—but that "if trade continues to be carried on at Yokohama,
a revolution will ensue. The trade must be transferred to Nagasaki
and Hakodate." The ministers were asked to surrender their rights
of settlement at Yokohama. The request was of course denied.

The Shogunate was trying, in a painless way, to carry out the
Mikado's expulsion order. Komei was becoming restless at the continued presence of the aliens. He ordered Iyemochi to come to Kyoto
to receive "the sword symbolic of authority to expel the barbarians."
The seventeen-year-old Shogun was conveniently taken sick and in
his stead sent Hitotsubashi, recently released from jail and made
guardian of the Shogun and Vice Shogun. Hitotsubashi could not
refuse the commission. He went to meet Komei at the war god

Hachiman's shrine. There he "was extremely embarrassed, and, pretending illness, descended from the shrine." The attendant samurai scornfully commented, "Bah, this sluggard is unfit for his duty."

Part of the pressure on both Iyemochi and Hitotsubashi was relieved when Mori of Choshu overreached himself. Long violently anti-alien, like Komei, and anxious to ruin his Tokugawa rival by "restoring the Mikado," Choshu's agents at Kyoto rashly announced that the Mikado would take the field in person to expel the barbarians. They were exiled from the capital, stripped of their titles, and disgraced. Mori, in desperation, tried to capture Komei (realizing that whoever controls the Mikado and the Imperial insignia controls Japan), but he was beaten back by Iyemochi's troops. The disgrace of Mori aided the growing reconciliation between Mikado and Shogun. Japan was reunited. The Shogun could take stern action against the foreigners without fear that the discontented daimyos would take the opportunity for civil war.

Just at this juncture, the special mission sent to Paris to apologize for the Camus murder returned with the draft of French demands. France required an indemnity of $140,000 and insisted that within three months the Shimonoseki straits should be opened to free passage. The French fleet was to be allowed to police the passage.

The British believed that Napoleon III gave certain secret instructions to his commissioners. France, it was known, was anxious to set up a colony in the Orient. Napoleon therefore offered, according to the British Legation officials, to aid the Shogun financially against the Emperor in return for exclusive territorial concessions. In such event, the British were prepared to make peace with Satsuma and to join the Mikado in a campaign against the Tokugawa forces. The Shogun, however, refused to take advantage of the French offers.

Komei, Iyemochi, and Mori unanimously rejected the suggestions. The Japanese commissioners who had brought the treaty draft were sent to jail for having considered such ideas. Mori made his peace with his two superiors and again blocked the free passage of the straits. France, in spite of the rejection of the treaty, invited the other nations holding most-favored-nation rights to join an expedition to reopen the Shimonoseki waterway. Seventeen ships, bearing 4,600 men and more than two hundred guns, were sent by France, Great Britain, Holland, and the United States. The American contribution was a small one-gun ship, chartered for the purpose, and manned by only 258 men.

The expedition arrived off Shimonoseki in September 1864. Two young Choshu samurai, former pupils of Yoshida—Hirobumi Ito, who later framed the Japanese Constitution, and Bunda Inouye, later an eminent statesman—were sent down by the British. Alcock did not know that these two men, former pupils of Yoshida, were the incendiaries who had set fire to the British Legation! Because they asserted that Mori favored the foreigners, the expedition landed them near Mori's retreat at Yamaguchi with instructions to intercede with their daimyo. Mori refused to listen to their suggestions, asserting, according to the messengers, that he was acting under orders of both the Emperor and the Shogun. He proposed that the bombardment be delayed for three months until he should have time to go to Kyoto for consultation with Komei. It was a curious suggestion from one who had lately been forbidden ever to set foot in the capital again, and indicates the extent to which he had been rehabilitated into favor.

The Allies refused to wait. Believing that Mori was acting independently, they sought to crush him by force. In the attack, sixty Choshu guns were captured, the armies were routed, and peace was restored on the Allies' own terms.

An indemnity of $3,000,000 was at first demanded, but the foreign powers offered to remit a third of this if Shimonoseki were immediately opened to trade, or if Hyogo (the present Kobe) and Osaka were opened before the 1868 date already agreed upon. Much to Mori's indignation, Iyemochi refused the offer. Mori believed, like so many other daimyos whose ports were distant from the opened harbors, that the Shogun was attempting to monopolize foreign commodities. The Choshu daimyo planned another break with Iyemochi, considering the employment of foreign soldiers of fortune such as had helped the Taipings in China. General Henry Andrea Burgevine, former language professor at Chapel Hill and one of "Chinese" Gordon's assistants, was, it was believed, ready to assist Mori. Arms were being illegally imported for the building of a more powerful military force.

The British worried greatly over the possibility that Choshu might form a combination with the other discontented daimyos. Through Von Siebold, now a British agent, they sounded out the leaders of Iyo, Hizen, and Chikuzen provinces. All seemed anxious for foreign trade, and all resented the restrictions that gave foreign munitions only to the Shogun's favorites. Von Seibold cautiously proposed that ports be independently opened, with the trading rights monopolized by the daimyos.

Discovering the strong anti-Shogun opposition, and realizing that the Kyushu daimyos in particular were unwilling to open Hyogo and Osaka before their own ports had an opportunity to profit by the foreign trade, the British persisted in their plan of backing the Mikado as against the Shogun. A pamphlet written by Ernest Satow urged the confederation of the daimyos under the Mikado's leadership and advised the reduction of the Tokugawas to a subordinate rôle. The document was translated by Satow into Japanese and was widely read in Japan as *Eikoku Sakuron,* or *British Policy.*

After the Shimonoseki bombardment was completely finished, Alcock received orders from London, dated long before the attack, forbidding British participation in armed intervention. He hastened to London to explain the situation, and, on proving that he had acted in ignorance of the instructions, was forgiven for the seeming insubordination. He was, however, promoted to be British Minister to China, a transfer which led Japanese to think that he was being disciplined for his behavior.

Though the rebellious daimyos now enjoyed a measure of British support, they did not abandon their anti-alien policy. Partly this antagonism was due to desire to embroil the Shogun in international strife, more probably it was a sincere manifestation of provincial bigotry. There was, despite the years of foreign intercourse through Deshima, much misunderstanding of foreign ways. Shinsaku Takasugi, a loyal Choshu samurai, believed that by organizing a force of four hundred volunteers, in the *Kiheitai,* or Strategic Detachment, he could defend the Choshu coast against the foreigners. Another samurai, Hattori, was so naïf that he set out for Nagasaki to buy a steamer without having the slightest idea of what a steamer really was. The killing of a few foreigners would, it was believed, terrify all the others into leaving.

In November 1864, two British officers, Major Baldwin and Lieutenant Bird, were waylaid while riding on the Kamakura road. Baldwin was slashed from shoulder to hip, with his spine completely cut in two; Bird was badly cut, but crawled off to temporary safety. A rescue party supposedly sent to help him chopped his arms and legs to bits, and almost completely severed his head from his trunk.

Robert Lindau, the Swiss consul, who headed an investigating group, reported that "not the slightest fault could be laid to the men to mitigate the atrocity of the crime. The only reason for the deaths must have been that the men were not Japanese." Further investigation disclosed an elaborate plot to kill all foreigners.

At the insistence of the foreign community, the Japanese police produced two men, not the murderers, who confessed to extorting money from a farmer for the financing of the plot. They were decapitated. Later the actual killer, Seiji Shimadzu, confessed his guilt. At his execution he chanted a poem of his own composition. It read:

> I do not regret being taken and put to death,
> For to kill barbarians is the true spirit of a Japanese.

These men, the first to be punished in all the long list of ronin who murdered foreigners, were further disgraced by having their heads exposed for three days. Outrages against aliens thereafter ceased for many months, although they have never completely ended.

The sudden and unexplained death of young Iyemochi, in August 1866, followed soon after by that of the Mikado, the anti-alien Komei, cleared the way for peaceful settlement of both the civil war and of the anti-foreign troubles. The usual canards were not absent; Hitotsubashi was alleged to have murdered the Shogun; Komei was represented as a victim of the Western blight. The Mikado died of smallpox, a disease common enough in Japan at that time, but one which had never before attacked the sacred person. His death by a plebeian disease was proof enough, to the superstitious super-patriots, that the gods had withdrawn divinity from Komei because he had tolerated foreign entry.

Hitotsubashi at last gained the coveted Shogunate, taking the name Keiki, but he did not hold the office long. The southern allies, who once had supported his father Nariaki, turned against the only Mito man ever to become the Shogun. Within four days after his accession, Keiki received an urgent message from Tosa asking for his resignation. Satsuma, Choshu, and others made it clear that they were hostile to a continuance of the Yedo rule. Satsuma urged the new Mikado to take the field against the foreigners. On November 20, 1867, Keiki resigned and though, a few months later, he was maneuvered into starting a military move for the defeat of the Imperialists, the new Mikado, now called Meiji, won the day. The sole rule of the Mikado was restored.

Anti-foreignism was not, however, wholly at an end. Men of Bizen province, led by Ise Ikeda and Tatewaki Heiki, swaggered through the streets of newly opened Hyogo on February 4, 1868. An American sailor chanced to cross a street some distance in advance of the Bizen retinue. He was attacked and wounded. Two English Legation attachés who refused to bow sufficiently low, and two French marines were also injured. Foreigners were targets for Bizen shots. Four days later, Tosa warriors slashed three fingers from an American marine and gave a sailor severe sword cuts in the face. The French and British Legations were robbed of all their furnishings. Four thousand suspected native Christians were exiled from the Nagasaki district for professing "a pernicious doctrine." On March 8, a band of Tosa men attacked twelve French sailors who were giving bread to children, and slashed eleven of them to death.

The envoys of the foreign nations, then at Kyoto arranging for the final recognition of their treaty rights, not only insisted that the Mikado punish the criminals who attacked and murdered the aliens, but demanded that he issue a formal proclamation, backed by the force of his supreme sanctity, peremptorily forbidding any further attacks upon the foreigners.

Zenzaburo Taki, commander of the Bizen troops who gave the order to fire upon the foreigners at Hyogo, was compelled to commit harakiri; eleven Tosa men were decapitated and an indemnity of $150,000 was paid to the families of the French victims. A Japanese who tried to attack the new British minister, Sir Harry Smythe Parkes, was executed.

Then, in April 1868, the Mikado, Meiji, issued a formal proclamation declaring that all attacks upon foreigners were "infamous and detestable, that samurai guilty of such attacks would be henceforth degraded, their swords taken from them, and their dishonored names erased forever from the rolls. Then they should be beheaded by the common executioner and their heads exposed for three days."

For the first time since the official closing of Japan in 1637, aliens were placed under the full protection of the law. It is important to note, however, that the party which came to power by the so-called Meiji Restoration of 1868, that which destroyed the Shogunate and exalted the formerly secluded Mikado, was the party which had for years violently opposed the entry of the aliens. Though the Mikado formally commanded the fair treatment of the foreigners, the officials selected to secure justice were drawn almost entirely from the Satsuma, Choshu, and Tosa factions who had long caused difficulties.

For a generation after the Meiji Restoration the three anti-alien clans controlled Japan. Despite the official orders of the sacred Mikado, the foreigners underwent abuse, injustice, and attack. They have not even yet received a whole-hearted welcome from Japan.

Indeed, the tendency in recent years seems to indicate that the tolerance reluctantly shown to foreigners is again approaching an end. There is, of course, no danger that the arson, murder, and ronin violence of past years will return. Japan has settled down to a calm acceptance of the fact that foreigners must be admitted to the land. But, increasingly, a popular spirit of hostility is apparent. Laws are passed to limit the activities in which aliens may engage; legislation restricts the foreigners to comparatively subordinate positions in such activities as law, education, social work, and, as might be anticipated, in those special fields which have a direct bearing on national defence. Anti-alienism may at times flare out into direct bodily assaults upon unpopular or untactful foreigners but the Japanese are not today a violent people. Their words are fiery and their attitudes are threatening but their actions are more indirect. The anti-alienism of modern times is furthered by the laws rather than by bloodshed. Meiji's admonitions assure the foreigner a personal safety though they do not guarantee him either livelihood or lasting welcome.

XXIX

THE PAST EXPLAINS THE PRESENT

JAPAN has never liked the foreigner. The machines and manufactures, the war munitions, and the markets which the aliens offered have been fully utilized, but every effort has been made to keep the foreigners from corrupting the pure spirit of the Empire with unwanted and disapproved ideas. By the silent force of social ostracism, by pressure of official propaganda, and when necessary by the vigor of the sword, the Japanese have kept the foreigner subordinate. The tendency is not now likely to suffer a reverse.

Diplomats and business men today note the same method of dissimulation of which Carletti spoke three centuries ago; social and economic investigators in the land realize that Kaempfer's "enforced reticence" still holds true. Though the foreigner is not now isolated in a well-guarded Deshima or in a Yokohama from which but one carefully inspected outlet leads, the alien is cut off from contact with the vast majority of Japanese. Japan boasts, and with good reason, that she knows far more about the outer world than foreigners know about Japan, but the cause is not alone the cryptic language or the widely varying social customs. Japan makes every effort to keep the nations isolated.

For decades it has been most perilous for any Japanese to champion the foreign cause. The deaths of two Shoguns soon after they had signed the Perry treaties, albeit against their wills, the murder of the Gotairo Ii who conducted business dealings with the strangers, the assassination of the early Japanese who favored following the western fashions, still serve as warnings to a modern politician who defends a foreign point of view. A few Western-minded liberals, it is true, are permitted to make speeches for propaganda, outside the limits of Japan. Their documents show Japan as a progressive democratic land. Within Japan the liberals of whom the West hears such glowing tributes exert but trifling power.

The roll of men murdered for advocating new ideas is an impressive roster of Japan's progressive leaders. Premiers and cabinet officials have been daggered, business leaders have been shot, statesmen have been assassinated for daring to betray Japan by even such comparatively mild activities as the signing of the London Naval Treaty. Employes of the Soviet Embassy were arrested in 1936 for espionage; diplomats have been deprived of the customary courtesy and arrested on wild charges of vice, treason, and fraud. Business men know that the open door in any land controlled by Japan's puppets is a mockery. The treatment today is a direct continuation of the Legation burning of the early days, of the stoning of the embassies at the time the Constitution was proclaimed, and of the attempt upon the lives of Russia's Tsarevitch and China's special envoy in 1895. Even Colonel Lindbergh was officially denounced as a spy in open session of the Diet.

Japan's best friends have long been aware of the narrow provincialism of the native outlook. "The more Japan has assimilated European excellences," wrote Japan's best propagandist, Captain Frank Brinkley, "the more critical she has become of Europe. The latent conservatism of the people, their inordinate vanity, the indiscreet rapidity with which they have absorbed the science of the West, the consciousness of national strength have turned the heads of Japanese." Brinkley was writing to try to stem the rising tide of opposition to what was then called "the foreign intoxication."

As in the past, the missionaries are still the special butt of abuse. Japan has never tired of terming them "second-rate incompetents who are not brave enough to go to Africa or the South Seas." Buddhist leaders long thought that Christian missionaries were financing members of the Diet in order to have Christianity declared Japan's official faith. The violence of such attacks has diminished of late years because strict regulations have deprived the foreign missionary boards of control over their own institutions, but anti-missionary accusations are still frequent.

Trained in a social code unlike that of any Western land, reared under circumstances widely variant from our own, Japan's psychology is wholly strange to Occidentals. A nation that kills its Cabinet in order, as the murderers aver, "to secure the peace," that blandly insists that militarism is dead at the very moment that militarism flourishes as never before, that breaks its promises, and that attempts, as it did in 1936, to restore a medieval feudalism, is difficult to understand.

Partly the confusion springs perhaps from the belief that words used in Japan have precisely the same connotation that they would have in the United States. Japan is democratic, but in Japan democracy is "the Imperial House reigning in perfect harmony with the welfare of the people." Japan reveres the memory of Washington and has done so since long before Commodore Perry came to Japan's shores, but the Washington she reverences is not the man we know, but a samurai of Old Japan. Japan has a Parliament which cannot run the nation, a premier who does not need majority support, an Emperor who keeps as aloof from all mundane activities as did the Dairi of the past, and an Elder Statesman who enters the arena only in emergencies. Westerners who read the news about Japan construe the terms as they would be construed in Washington or London, not as Tokyo interprets them. Japan is, so far as any modern people can be, a nation apart.

Two hundred years of enforced isolation bred a special character into the people of Japan. From 1637 until long after Perry's Black Ships came in 1853, Japan was living under rigid martial law. Spy systems spread like a secret web to every corner of the Empire. No one dared utter an unconventionality lest swift vengeance descend. The executioner and the guardian of Japan's birdcage prison cells, too small in size to allow an adult to stand erect or to recline, were extraordinarily alert. Rigid rules of caste prescribed minutely the rights and privileges of each unit of the population and laid down the duties to be paid to all superiors.

Barely two generations have gone by since these restrictions were imposed in all their severities, and the effects still linger in the minds of Japanese. The special qualities which slaves and oppressed classes always evolve to outwit their masters still survive among the descendants of the underprivileged peoples. A servile eagerness to please, a tendency to mold the facts into more pleasant form, a sullen resentment, a flight into the mystic, all these are found in contemporary Japan and all are products of the Tokugawa times when martial law prevailed. Even though the nation has been revolutionized as far as politics and economics are concerned, the mental state reflects past feudalism.

Regimented to the last imaginable degree, disciplined to absolute obedience, trained not to indulge in independent thought, Japan suddenly, in the years after Perry, was thrust into the mêlée of modernism. Not all the bonds were immediately loosed, for many still fetter the land today, but enough laxity was allowed, after the downfall of the Shogunate in 1868, for Japanese to run riot with new ideas. And Japan behaved precisely as the lads let loose from school behave.

Madly the Japanese plunged into the indiscriminate acceptance of each and every new idea. Fads of dress, of action, of ideas, of every phase of life, were taken over en masse from the West. What Europe or America was preferring had to Japan the stamp of authenticity. That curiosity which is so marked a trait of Japanese had unrestrained opportunity.

Quickly, to be sure, the foreign fever burned itself away. Like the Athenians of old, the Japanese are constant only in their search for novelty. When Western ideas lost their freshness, Japan turned back into her own history to dredge out from the past new inspirations for the future.

It is in this era that the Japanese are living now. Intense nationalism grips the people; alien ideas are at a grievous discount. Democracy, rule by Parliament, slow and orderly evolution of events, are scorned by the great masses. Japan has never had these boons, nor has she, as a nation, ever really wished them. Her history has been composed of long periods of static social situations briefly interrupted by violent upheaval.

Left to herself, as Japan would probably prefer to be, she would today return to static modes. Therein lies the tragedy for, once caught in modern industrialism and once enmeshed in international affairs, Japan is swept along by forces far beyond her own control. Desperately her rulers try to stem the tide by passing regulations that to Westerners seem childish and absurd.

Thus, police in Kobe arrested a hundred girls for smoking publicly, jailed 150 men on the strange charge of "pretending to be students." Foreign styles of dancing are tabu in certain centers, while other cities limit dancing to the upper floors of buildings (where passersby cannot peep in) and order dance halls to close at ten o'clock. Students are forbidden to attend the public dances unless they first have patronized the shop which rents civilian suits to students. Under no circumstances must a taxi dancer converse with her partner, nor must she meet any man within a radius of two blocks from her dance hall. "Spiritual martial law," in the words of Tokyo authorities, has been declared upon the corrupting Western forces.

Undoubtedly the "café civilization" which once took Japan by storm was only a passing phase, but it was symptomatic of a sweeping psychological phase. The famous *modan gaaru,* or modern girl, with ghastly heavy powder down to the mid-neck mark where the dark oriental skin was visible, eyebrows angled at the fashionable "fifteen minutes past seven" angle, and costly foreign clothes, presented a grave problem to the police censors. For the *modan gaaru* might be honest, and she might be thoroughly sincere, but there was always a decided possibility that she was scabbing on the licensed ladies of the restricted districts. And her companion, the *mobo* might be an authentic "Marx boy" full of fashionably radical ideas, or he might be a mobster masquerading as a student.

The deference toward teachers, toward employers, and toward parents was being swiftly undermined by new ideas. The old traditions of feudal loyalty, of industrial paternalism, of obedience to wisdom and to elders, were being shipwrecked. The responsibility for the evils that beset Japan was to be found in new ideas imported from the West.

Japan, therefore, has turned violently anti-alien, though she is now invariably scrupulously courteous to her foreign visitors. A new Puritanism has come over the nation's guardians, marked by a vigorous campaign against laxities and luxuries, against Westernisms and against liberal ideas.

Less than most other modern nations does Japan possess an uninfluenced public opinion. Although she is a land wherein the average per capita consumption of newspapers, journals of opinion, and news magazines is extraordinarily high, she is none the less a land in which censorship and direct propaganda have been extraordinarily developed. The mass mind is unquestionably molded to an incredible degree. While newspapers have a well-publicized freedom of opposition and are notorious for their consistent criticism of the administration, it is well to note that almost never is the government hammered for its aggression but always for its presumed timidity in dealing with the outer world. Statesmen are condemned for their corruption, but rarely does the editor dare to attack the Army or the Navy policies, and under no thinkable circumstances would he be less than reverential toward the Throne.

Japan's mind is molded, therefore, always in the interests of aggressive nationalism. The press preys upon the gullibility of the public, printing the most amazing rumors as truth, casting aspersion upon the characters and private lives of both Japanese and eminent resident aliens, accusing foreign lands of the most despicable aggressions, and warning Japanese of the dangers of trusting programs not completely in accord with Japanese tradition. Libel laws exist to check these evils, but because of the obstacles thrown in the use of those laws, a tradition springs into existence of refusing to take action for the grossest, and at times most obscene, public reference to private individuals.

For excitable people such as the Japanese, such propaganda is exceedingly dangerous. Naturally the Japanese tend toward extremism in their views and in their deeds. Lacking a developed humor of the Anglo-Saxon type (Japan's humor is of the lampooning, hyperbolic type that chuckles over discomfitures and incongruities), it is easy to inflame a susceptible folk with anger against those who seem to have threatened the sacred institutions of Japan. When, therefore, a perfervid orator fires verbal hot shot at Imperial advisers who have, as he says, sacrificed the welfare of Japan for private gain, a mob spirit is easily aroused.

Super-patriotic hotheads, indeed, may win a measure of approval for their violence if they have prepared the way, as Tokyo's 1936 assassins did prepare the way, by appeal to patriotism, by declaration that the deed is in the interest of the sacred Emperor, and by playing on the sentimentalism of a people easily moved to tears. Japan admires the political eccentric with a flair for the dramatic. Especially will she forgive the man who by his own self-destruction immediately proves that there was no private selfish motive for the drastic deed. Hero worship has been raised to a high place by long centuries of military despotism.

Never has patriotism needed a fillip in Japan, for the Empire and its divine ruler have been ever dear to Japanese. Worship of the sovereign as a living embodiment of Japan's private goddess, Amaterasu the Mighty, is the sacred duty of every subject. Obedience to his commands, even though never actually expressed in words, is every Japanese individual's constant care. Toward him are focused two strong streams of religious awe, the veneration of one's ancestors, since he is the father of the nation, and the devotion to the sacred soul of Japan itself. Knowing that the Emperor is the embodiment of every virtue and that the welfare of the world depends upon the satisfaction of his desires, Japan is filled with an intense, an overwhelming, pride of nationality inconceivable to Westerners. The Emperor is infallible and cannot err, nor can the nation do a wrongful act, nor can any of the Emperor's servants commit crimes when acting as he wills them to act.

With such certainties as these to guide their thoughts and deeds, Japan need not concern herself unduly with abstract metaphysical ideas of justice. Any act, whether at home or abroad, done in the interest of the Emperor, has an ethical excuse. As an intensely practical people, reverencing the idealistic, but not necessarily seeking idealistic justification for a necessary deed, the Japanese forgive the criminal who works in a cause which he believes helpful to his Emperor.

Centuries of formalism have taught them that the essential needs of social intercourse can be expressed in one brief phrase, "calm and imperturbably polite." If, in addition, Japanese can be artistic, clean and kind, frank and faithful, filial and loyal, they have proved themselves perfect subjects of a sacred ruler. Some foreigners, like St. Francis Xavier, will understand and say, as Xavier declared, "This nation is the delight of my soul." Others will not understand and that, as every Japanese well knows, is simply because the foreigner is baseborn and not of Japan's godlike blood.

APPENDIX

LIST OF ILLEGAL ARRIVALS IN JAPAN

SHOGUNS	SHIPS ARRIVED	VISITORS	PORT OF CALL	DATE
Ashikaga Line:				
Yoshimasu 1449–1471	Wrecked junk	Zeimoto de Moto Peixotto	Tanegashima,	October 1543
Yoshihisa 1472–1489				
Yoshitane 1490–1493				
Yoshizumi 1494–1507				
Yoshitane (restored) 1508–1520				
Yoshiharu 1521–1545				
Yoshiteru 1546–1573				
Nobunaga 1573–1582				
Hideyoshi 1583–1598 (Taiko or Great Kubo-sama)				
Tokugawa Line:				
Iyeyasu 1603–1616				
Hidetada 1616–1622				
Iyemitsu 1623–1651	Portuguese galleon wrecked off Kyushu			1640
	Kastrikoom	de Vries	Mutsu	1643

LIST OF ILLEGAL ARRIVALS IN JAPAN (continued)

SHOGUNS	SHIPS ARRIVED	VISITORS	PORT OF CALL	DATE
Iyemitsu (continued)	Breskens	Schaep	Mutsu	1643
	Portuguese mission calls at Nagasaki	Frisius	Yedo	1644
	Batavia mission			1645
Iyetsuna 1651–1680	Return	Delboe	Nagasaki	July 1673
Tsunayoshi 1681–1709	British ship	Fryke	Nagasaki	1683
Iyenobu 1709–1712	Spanish ship	Sidotti	Kyushu	1709
	Russian ship	Kosirewski	Kuriles	August 1711
	"	"	"	1712
Iyetsugu 1713–1716	"	"	"	1713
Yoshimune 1717–1744	Nadezhda, St. Gabriel, Archangel Michael	Luzhin-Yevreinov	"	1720
	Nadezhda	Spanberg	"	June 1738
	St. Gabriel	Spanberg	Mito	June 1739
	St. John	Walton	Kochi	June 1739
		Spanberg	Komaishi	May 1742
Iyeshige 1745–1760	Russian ship	Beniowski	Takashima	June 1771
Iyeharu 1760–1786	French ship	de la Perouse	Hokkaido	1797
Iyenori 1786–1837	Lady Washington	Kendrick	Wakayama	May 1791
	Grace	Douglas	"	
	Argonaut	Colnett	Hirado-Fukuoka	August 1791
	Russian ship	Laxman	Hokkaido	1792
	Providence	Broughton	Hokkaido	1795, 1797
	Eliza	Stewart	Nagasaki	1797, 1798, 1799
	Franklin	Devereaux	Nagasaki	July 1799
	Emperor of Japan	Stewart	Nagasaki	1800
	Margaret	Derby	Nagasaki	July 1801
	Nagasaki-maru	Stewart	Nagasaki	1803
	Frederick	Torey	Nagasaki	1803
	Nadezhda	Rezanov-Krusenstern	Nagasaki	October 1804

LIST OF ILLEGAL ARRIVALS IN JAPAN (*continued*)

SHOGUNS	SHIPS ARRIVED	VISITORS	PORT OF CALL	DATE
Iyenori (*continued*)	Russian cutters	Chvostov-Davidov	Kuriles	1806–1807
	Eclipse	O'Kean	Nagasaki	June 1807
	Phaeton	Pellew	Nagasaki	October 1808
	Diana	Golovnin	Hokkaido	1811–1813
	Charlotte-Mary	Waardenaar	Nagasaki	1813, 1814
	Alceste-Lyra	Murray-Hall	Napa	October 1816
	The Brothers	Gordon	Yedo Bay	June 1818
	Unknown	—	Mito	1823
	British whaler	Gibson	Otsu	June 1824
	Blossom	Beechey	Napa-Bonins	1827
	Cyprus	Convict crew	Kyushu	1830
	Morrison	King-Williams	Yedo-Kagoshima	1837
Iyeyoshi 1838–1853	Lady Rowena		Hokkaido	1842?
	Cleopatra	Cecille	Napa	1844
	Manhattan	Cooper	Yedo Bay	April 1845
	Samarang	Belcher	Nagasaki	April 1845
	Lawrence	Baker-Howe	Kuriles	May 1846
	Columbus-Vincennes	Biddle	Yedo Bay	July 1846
	Cleopatra	Cecille	Nagasaki	July 1846
	Catherine	—	Kuriles	1847
	Lagoda	—	Hokkaido	June 1848
	Pocahontas	—	Kuriles	1848
	Whaleboat	MacDonald	Hokkaido-Nagasaki	July 1848–April 1849
	Preble	Glynn	Nagasaki	April 1849
	Mariner	Matheson	Yedo Bay	June 1849
	Edmond	Lovitt	Hokkaido	1850
Iyesada 1853–1858	Black Ships	Perry	Yedo Bay	July 1853
	Diana	Poutiatine	Nagasaki	August 1853
	Black Ships	Perry	Yedo Bay	February 1854
Iyemochi 1858–1866				
Keiki 1866–1867				
(Hitotsubashi)				

BIBLIOGRAPHY

Adams, Will, "Letters," in *Pilgrimes,* edited by Samuel Purchas, Glasgow, 1905

"Ahaole" (Mrs. D. B. Bates), *Sandwich Island Notes,* New York, 1854

Alcock, Sir Rutherford, *Three Years in the Capital of the Tycoon,* London, 1863

Allen, J. F., "The First Voyage to Japan," Essex Institute, *Historical Collections,* vol. 2, No. 4 (1860)

Anesaki, Masaharu, and Tahamuro, Kozohiko, "Foreigners in Japan," *Proceedings,* Imperial Academy, Tokyo, 1928

Aston, W. G., "His Majesty's Ship 'Phaeton' at Nagasaki," *Transactions,* Asiatic Society of Japan, vol. 7, Part 4 (1879)

———, "The Russian Descents Upon Saghalien and Itorup," *Transactions,* Asiatic Society of Japan, vol. 1 (1873)

Barrows, Edward M., *The Great Commodore,* Indianapolis, 1935

Bates, Mrs. D. B., see "Ahaole"

Beechey, Sir Frederick William, *Voyage to the Pacific,* London, 1831

Belcher, Sir Edward, *Voyage of the 'Samarang,'* London, 1848

Beniowski, Moriz August, Graf von, *Memoirs and Travels,* London, 1898

Bouhours, Father Dominick, *Life of St. Francis Xavier,* Dublin, 1812

Boxer, C. R., "Anglo-Dutch Rivalry in Japan," *Transactions,* Asiatic Society of Japan, 2nd Series, vol. 7 (1930)

———, *Jan Compagnie in Japan,* The Hague, 1936

———, "Notes on Military Influence in Japan," *Transactions,* Asiatic Society of Japan, 2nd Series, vol. 8 (December 1931)

———, *Portuguese Embassy to Japan,* London, 1928

Brooks, Charles Walcott, "Japanese Wrecks," *Transactions,* California Academy of Science, 1875

Broughton, William Robert, *Voyage of Discovery to the North Pacific Ocean,* London (1804)

Bullard, S., "Life of Noburu Watanabe," *Transactions,* Asiatic Society of Japan, vol. 32, Part 1 (1904)

Bulloch, John Malcolm, "The Adventures of Capt. Peter Gordon," *Banffshire Reporter*, October 10, 1910

——, "Capt. Peter Gordon," *Banffshire Journal*, April 5, 1932

——, "Capt. Peter Gordon," *Scottish Notes and Queries*, July 1916

——, "Peter Gordon, the Explorer," *Aberdeen Weekly Journal*, July 5, 1912

——, *The Gay Gordons*, London, 1908

——, "The Identity of a Hero," *Aberdeen Free Press*, August 30, 1910

Burney, James, *Chronological History of Voyages and Discoveries in the South Seas*, London, 1813

Campbell, Archibald, *Voyage Around the World*, New York, 1817

Campbell, W., *Formosa Under the Dutch*, London, 1904

Carey, Rev. Frank, "The Morrison Venture," *Japan Weekly Chronicle*, April 8, 1937

Carletti, Francesco, "The Carletti Discourse," *Transactions*, Asiatic Society of Japan, 2nd Series, vol. 9 (1932)

Caron, François, "Account of Japan," in Pinkerton, John, *Collection of Voyages*, vol. 7, London, 1808

Cholmondeley, L. B., *History of the Bonin Islands*, London, 1915

Clement, E. W., "Mito Samurai and British Sailors," *Transactions*, Asiatic Society of Japan, vol. 33, Part 1 (1905)

——, "The Dutch in Early Japan," *Japan Weekly Mail*, January 10, 1891

——, "The Last of the Shoguns," *Japan Weekly Mail*, March 1, 1902

——, "The Tokugawa Princes of Mito," *Transactions*, Asiatic Society of Japan, vol. 18, Part 1 (1889)

Coleman, Horace E., "Iichiro Tokutomi's Life of Yoshida," *Transactions*, Asiatic Society of Japan, vol. 45, No. 1 (Sept. 1917)

Colnett, James, *Voyage to the South Pacific*, London, 1798

Cooper, Mercator, "Entering a Forbidden Port," *Southampton Magazine*, vol. 1, No. 1 (1912)

Crewdson, Wilson, "The Dawn of Western Influence in Japan," *Proceedings*, Japan Society of London, vol. 6, Part 2 (1903)

Davidson, J. W., *The Island of Formosa*, Yokohama, 1903

Davis, George, *Origin of the Japan Expedition*, Baltimore, 1860

Delano, Capt. Amasa, *Narrative of Voyages and Travels*, Boston, 1817

Dening, Walter, *Life of Toyotomi Hideyoshi*, Yokohama, 1904

de Parra, Andres, *A Short Account of the Great and Rigorous Martyrdoms*, Madrid, 1624. (Translated in *Japan Weekly Chronicle*, February 17 and 24, 1927)

Dixon, Capt. George, *Voyage Around the World*, London, 1789

Doeff, Hendrik, *Recollections of Japan*, London, 1836

Eden, Richard, and Willis, Richard, *History of Travayle,* London, 1577

Ellis, George E., "The First American Embassy to Japan," *Proceedings,* Massachusetts Historical Society, vol. 2 (1885–86)

Enomoto, Viscount Buyo, "The Kuriles and Kamchatka," *Japan Weekly Mail,* May–June 1882

Fillmore, Millard, "How Japan Was Opened," *American Historical Review,* vol. 3 (1874)

Fischer, J. F. van Overmeer, *Bijdrage tot de Kennis van het Japansche Rijk,* Amsterdam, 1833

Foster, John W., *American Diplomacy in the Orient,* Boston, 1903

Golder, Frank A., *Russian Expansion in the Pacific,* Cleveland, 1914

Golovnin, Vasili M., *Memoirs of a Captivity in Japan,* London, 1824

Greene, D. C., "Correspondence Between William II of Holland and the Shogun of Japan," *Transactions,* Asiatic Society of Japan, vol. 34, Part 4 (1907)

Gubbins, John H., "Introduction of Christianity into China and Japan," *Transactions,* Asiatic Society of Japan, vol. 6 (1877)

Hakluyt, Richard, *Collection of Voyages,* London, 1811

Hall, Capt. Basil, *Voyage of Discovery to the West Coast of Korea and the Great Loo-Choo Island,* Philadelphia, 1818

Harris, Townsend, *Complete Journal,* Garden City, 1930

Hawkes, Francis L., *Narrative of the Expedition of an American Squadron to Japan,* Washington, 1855. (Senate Executive Document No. 79, 33d Congress, 2nd Session)

Hildreth, Richard, *Japan As It Was and Is,* New York, 1855

House, Edward H., *Shimonoseki* and *Kagoshima,* Tokyo, 1875

Howay, Frederic W., "Early Relations Between Hawaii and the Northwest Coast," *Proceedings,* Capt. Cook Sesquicentennial, Honolulu, 1928

——, "John Kendrick and His Sons," *Quarterly,* Oregon Historical Society, vol. 23, No. 4 (December 1922)

——, "The Barrell Letters," *Quarterly,* Washington Historical Society, vol. 12, No. 4 (October 1921)

James, J. M., "Modern Japanese Adventurers," *Transactions,* Asiatic Society of Japan, vol. 7 (1879)

Kaempfer, Engelbrecht, *History of Japan,* London, 1727

King, C. W., "The Dutch Intercourse with Japan," *Chinese Repository,* vol. 6, No. 12 (April 1838)

King, C. W., "Portuguese and Spanish Intercourse with Japan," *Chinese Repository,* vol. 6, No. 10 (February 1838)

——, *Voyages of the 'Morrison' and 'Himmaleh,'* New York, 1839

Knapp, H. S., "Naval Officers in Diplomacy," *Proceedings,* Naval Institute, September 1927

Krashennikov, Stepan Petrovich, *History of Kamchatka and the Kurilski Islands,* Gloucester (England), 1764

Krusenstern, A. J., *Voyage Around the World,* London, 1813

Kubalski, Nikolai Ambrozy, *Voyages dans l'Ocean Pacifique,* Tours, 1863

Kuiper, J. Feenstra, "Notes on the Foreign Relations of Japan in the Early Napoleonic Period," *Transactions,* Asiatic Society of Japan, 2nd Series, vol. 1 (1924)

Kuykendall, Ralph, "James Colnett and the 'Princess Royal,' " *Quarterly,* Oregon Historical Society, vol. 25 (1924)

Lewis, William S., see MacDonald, Ranald

Lisiansky, Urey, *Voyage Around the World,* London, 1814

Lloyd, Rev. Arthur, "Historical Development of Shushi Philosophy," *Transactions,* Asiatic Society of Japan, vol. 34, Part 4 (1907)

Luce, S. B., "Personal Experiences in Japan," *Japan Weekly Mail,* March 14, 1903

MacDonald, Ranald, *Autobiography,* edited by William S. Lewis and Naojiro Murakami, Spokane, 1923

Maclay, Edwin S., *History of the United States Navy,* New York, 1898

MacLeod, J., *Voyage in His Majesty's Ship "Alceste,"* London, 1817

Manning, William Ray, "The Nootka Sound Controversy," *Report,* American Historical Society, 1904

Matsumoto, Sogo, "Shozan Sakuma," *Aoyami Hyoron,* Tokyo, February 1897

Matsuura, Toh, *Nagasaki Kokon Shuron,* Nagasaki, 1811. Reprinted in *Transactions,* Asiatic Society of Japan, vol. 9, Part 2 (1881)

McClellan, Edwin North, *History of the United States Marine Corps,* 1st Edition, MS.

Meylan, G. F., *Japan,* Amsterdam, 1830

Mueller, Gerhard Friedrich, *Voyages from Asia to America,* London, 1764

Murakami, Naojiro, see MacDonald, Ranald

Muramatsu, Shinsei, "Diary of Kinoyao Inouye," *Bungei-shunju,* Tokyo, 1929

Murdoch, James, *History of Japan,* New York and London, 1925–27

Nagaoka, H., *Histoire des Relations du Japon avec l'Europe,* Paris, 1905

Nieuhoff, John, "Embassy of Peter de Goyer," in Pinkerton, vol. 7

Nitobe, Inazo Ota, "American-Japanese Intercourse Prior to Perry," *Report,* American Historical Society, 1913
———, *Intercourse Between the United States and Japan,* Baltimore, 1891

Oka, Goro, "The Bonin Islands," *Kyoiku Koku,* No. 255, Tokyo, 1902
Olyphant, Lawrence, *Narrative of the Earl of Elgin's Mission,* London, 1860

Palafox, Juan de, *Histoire de la Conquet de la Chine,* Paris, 1670
Palmer, Aaron Haight, *Documents and Facts Illustrating the Origin of the Mission to Japan,* Washington, 1857
———, "Letter to John M. Clayton," *National Intelligencer,* September 6, 1849
Paske-Smith, Montague, *History of the English House at Hirado,* Kobe, 1927
———, *Japanese Traditions of Christianity,* Kobe, 1930
———, *Western Barbarians in Japan and Formosa in Tokugawa Days,* Kobe, 1930
Pinkerton, John, *Collection of Voyages and Travels,* London, 1808
Pinto, Fernan Mendez, *Peregrinations in the East,* London, 1891
Pratt, Peter, *History of Japan,* London, 1822

Raffles, Sir Stamford, *History of Java,* London, 1830
Ramsden, William, "Diary of the 'Return,'" in Pinkerton, vol. 7
Reiss, Ludwig, "History of the English Factory at Hirado," *Transactions,* Asiatic Society of Japan, vol. 26, Part 1 (1898)
Rennie, D. F., *British Arms in North China and Japan,* London, 1864
Ritter, Pastor H., *History of Protestant Missions in Japan,* Tokyo, 1898
Roberts, Edmund, *Embassy to the Eastern Courts,* New York, 1837
Robertson, Russell, "The Bonin Islands," *Transactions,* Asiatic Society of Japan, vol. 4 (1877)

Sadler, A. L., *Iyeyasu Tokugawa,* London, 1937
Sansom, G. B., *Japan, A Short Cultural History,* New York, 1931
Satoh, Henry, *Agitated Japan,* Tokyo, 1905
———, *Lord Hotta, Pioneer Diplomat of Japan,* Tokyo, 1908
Satow, Sir Ernest, *A Diplomat in Japan,* London, 1921
———, "Intercourse Between Japan and Siam in the 17th Century," *Transactions,* Asiatic Society of Japan, vol. 13 (1884)
———, *Kinsei Shiriaku,* Yokohama, 1873
———, "The Church at Yamaguchi," *Transactions,* Asiatic Society of Japan, vol. 7 (1878)
Shimada, Saburo, *Kaikoku Shaimatsu,* Tokyo, 1901

Sidotti, Pere G. B., "Capture and Captivity," *Transactions,* Asiatic Society of Japan, vol. 9, Part 3 (1881)

Spalding, J. W., *Japan and Around the World,* London, 1855

Starbuck, Alexander, *The American Whaling Industry,* Waltham, 1878

Staunton, George, *Authentic Account of an Embassy to China,* London, 1797

Steichen, E., *The Christian Daimyos in Japan,* Tokyo, 1903

Stewart, C. W., "Early American Visitors to Japan," *Proceedings,* Naval Institute, vol. 31 (1905)

Tahamuro, Kozohiko, see Anesaki, Masaharu

Tanabe, Taichi, *Bakumatsu Gaiko-dan,* Tokyo, 1898

Tanaka, Suichiro, *Toyo Kinseishi,* Tokyo, 1900

Thompson, E. Maude, *Diary of Richard Cocks,* London, 1883

Thunberg, C. P., *Travels in Europe and Asia,* London, 1795

Treat, Payson, J., *The Far East,* New York, 1928

Tronson, J. M., *Voyage to Japan in H.M.S. "Barracouta,"* London, 1856

Volpius, Rutgerus, *Epistolae Japonicae,* Louvain, 1569

von Langsdorff, G. H., *Voyages and Travels,* London, 1817

von Siebold, Dr. P. F., *Nippon,* London, 1841

Walker, Robert J., *Annual Report of the Secretary of the Treasury,* Washington, 1848

Walter, James, "Will Adams," *Japan Weekly Mail,* April 15, 1905

Wildes, Harry Emerson, *Japan in Crisis,* New York, 1934

——, *Social Currents in Japan,* Chicago, 1927

Wilkes, Charles, *Narrative of the U.S. Exploring Expedition,* Philadelphia, 1844

Williams, S. Wells, "Journal of the Perry Expedition," *Transactions,* Asiatic Society of Japan, vol. 37, Part 2 (1910)

——, Miscellaneous Notes on Japan in *Chinese Repository,* vol. 3, No. 4 (August 1834); vol. 7, No. 4 (August 1838), and vol. 7, No. 11 (March 1839)

——, "A Voyage to the Luchus and Japan," *Chinese Repository,* vol. 6, No. 5 (September 1837), and vol. 6, No. 8 (December 1837)

Willis, Richard, see Eden, Richard

Winslow, C. F., "Mercator Cooper's Visit to Japan," *Seaman's Friend,* Oahu, February 2, 1846

Wooley, W. A., "Historical Notes on Nagasaki," *Transactions,* Asiatic Society of Japan, vol. 9, Part 2 (1881)

Yamada, Kiichi, *History of the Bonins,* Tokyo, 1916

Yamagata, Shozo, "Political Relations of Japan and Holland in the Tokugawa Era," *Japan Weekly Mail,* April 9, 1892

"The Dutch in Japan," *Japan Weekly Chronicle,* September–October 1913

"The First Dutchmen in Korea," *Korea Magazine,* March 1917

"The First Voyage to Japan" (Reply to J. F. Allen), *Historical Collections,* Essex Institute, vol. 2, No. 6 (1860)

The *Lagoda* Incident:

   Singapore Free Press, January 6, 1848; *Chinese Repository,* vol. 18, No. 6 (June 1849), *Nantucket Inquirer,* February 2, 1849; *Providence Journal,* September 13, 1848

"Present Relations with Japan," *Senate Executive Document,* No. 59, 32nd Congress, 1st Session (1852)

   House Executive Document, No. 138, 28th Congress, 2nd Session (1845)

   Senate Executive Document, No. 34, 33d Congress, 2nd Session (1854)

Secret Documents of the Shogunate, Tokyo, 1937

   "Anti-Foreignism," *Japan Herald,* July 12, July 19, September 16, 1862; "Sensation Diplomacy in Japan," *Blackwood's,* vol. 93, April 1863; "Political Tragedies in Japan," *Blackwood's,* vol. 91, April 1862

The Shipwrecked Japanese:

   Chinese Repository, vol. 10, No. 2 (February 1841); vol. 11, No. 7 (July 1842); vol. 20, No. 2 (February 1851)

   Fairhaven (Massachusetts) *Star,* July 5, 1918; *Seaman's Friend,* Honolulu, October 1884; *National Intelligencer,* November 10 and 11, 1851

France in the Luchus, *Japan Weekly Chronicle,* December 6, 1906

Murder of Ii:

   Kinsei Sakurada Kibun, Tokyo, 1877

   Shunnan Shiden, Tokyo, 1878

Persecution of the Christians:

   Jesuit Letters, reprinted in *Japan Weekly Chronicle,* July 5, 1906, and October 4, 1906

   Nihon ni okeru, Kirusutokyo shoha, kakuha seiritsu shoshi, Tokyo, 1912

INDEX